CONSUMER LAW AND PRACTICE

AUSTRALIA
The Law Book Company Ltd.
Sydney : Melbourne : Brisbane

CANADA AND U.S.A.
The Carswell Company Ltd.
Agincourt, Ontario

INDIA
N.M. Tripathi Private Ltd.
Bombay
and
Eastern Law House Private Ltd.
Calcutta
M.P.P. House
Bangalore

ISRAEL
Steimatzky's Agency Ltd.
Jerusalem : Tel Aviv : Haifa

MALAYSIA : SINGAPORE : BRUNEI
Malayan Law Journal (Pte.) Ltd.
Singapore

NEW ZEALAND
Sweet & Maxwell (N.Z.) Ltd.
Auckland

PAKISTAN
Pakistan Law House
Karachi

CONSUMER LAW AND PRACTICE

By

ROBERT LOWE, LL.B.
*Solicitor, Member of the Board of Management and Director of
Continuing Education, the
College of Law*

and

GEOFFREY F. WOODROFFE, M.A.(Cantab.)
*Solicitor, Senior Lecturer in Law, Brunel University Formerly a
Member of the Board of Management of the College of Law*

LONDON
SWEET AND MAXWELL LIMITED
1980

Published in 1980 by
Sweet and Maxwell Ltd.
11, New Fetter Lane, London
and printed in Great Britain by
Page Bros. (Norwich) Ltd.

Reprinted 1983

ISBN hardback 0 421 23630 2
paperback 0 421 23640 X

PREFACE

There are many ways of writing a book on consumer protection. One can trace the historical development; one can analyse the economic and social effects; one can deal with the subject from a comparative point of view. In this book we have decided to concentrate on practical problems and remedies. The book is written primarily for law students and for those who are called upon to advise on consumer problems, whether legal or para-legal practitioners. We hope that it will also be useful to persons in industry and their legal advisers as an indication of the growing battery of controls—civil, criminal and administrative—which the law now imposes on business activity. With this aim in mind we have tried to adopt a very practical approach.

A further problem for writers on this subject is that of selection. The term "consumer protection" has no precise definition and it could quite properly be given an immensely wide meaning. Thus every citizen of this country is a consumer, or potential consumer, of welfare benefits, public utilities, health services, educational services and so on. Then again it can be argued that the term "consumer protection" should include the law relating to the supply of housing. Another relevant area is the law of competition which has an underlying consumer protection philosophy. Finally, we have had Government regulation of business activity and in particular we have had price control. In view of our basic approach outlined above we have decided not to deal in any detail with these wide areas. Indeed, we shall concentrate on the types of problem most likely to arise where an individual consumer orders goods or services from a supplier who then proceeds to render defective performance or no performance at all.

Our remedies-based approach has influenced the structure of this book. Part I is entitled "The Consumer and the Civil Law" and deals with such matters as defective performance of contracts to supply goods or services, product liability, the remedies available to the consumer, attempts to exclude them and finally the all-important question of how the remedies can be enforced. Special attention is given to the methods of extra-legal enforcement provided by the growing number of voluntary Codes of Practice. Part II of the book is entitled "The Consumer and the Criminal Law";

special consideration is given to the Trade Description Act 1968 and there is also a chapter dealing with compensation orders. Part III of the book describes the most significant development of consumer protection—administrative control under the Fair Trading Act 1973. Part IV contains nine chapters dealing with "Consumer Protection in Credit Transactions." The book ends with a chapter entitled "The EEC Dimension."

This is a new venture and we would welcome suggestions for improvement. In the meantime we would like to thank the many people who took the trouble to read parts of the typescript and to answer our questions. Special thanks are due to a number of individuals at the Office of Fair Trading, Department of Trade, National Consumer Council, Society of Motor Manufacturers and Traders, Motor Traders Association and the Manchester Arbitration Scheme. The views which they expressed are necessarily personal ones but nevertheless we have found them of great value. We would also like to thank Bill Thomas (solicitor), Valerie Chiswell (consumer adviser), Malcolm Leder (Senior Lecturer at Middlesex Polytechnic), and Peter Chiswell, Peter Hawkins, Tony King, and Chris Whitehouse (all at the College of Law). All of them made very helpful suggestions and assisted in the tiresome task of proof reading.

At the time of going to press there is a Bill before Parliament entitled the Sale of Goods Bill. This is a pure consolidation measure which does not make any changes in the law. The future of the London Small Claims Court, which is discussed in Chapter 9, is still in the balance; we understand that a grant of £5,000 will enable it to survive.

We have tried to state the law as at October 1, 1979.

Robert Lowe
Geoffrey Woodroffe

CONTENTS

TABLE OF CASES

xi

TABLE OF STATUTES

CHAPTER 1

INTRODUCTION

"The bottle started to leak as I was putting it into my bag"
"The central heating isn't working"
"The holiday was ruined"
"The car has been off the road for a month"
"The underpants had too much sulphite"
"There were worms in the pork chops"

This book is concerned with complaints which the consumer may
have against a supplier of goods or services and with the remedies
available to him. It is a vast subject and, as indicated in the preface[1]
it is necessary to curtail it.

In the words of the Molony Committee on Consumer Protection
(1961) "the consumer, unlike some classes with claims on public
bounty, is everybody all the time." In the present book, however,
the word "consumer" will be used to describe a customer who
buys for personal use and not for business purposes.

A number of learned writers, e.g., Borrie and Diamond in their
excellent book *The Consumer, Society and the Law* have traced
the history of the subject and have shown that, although the subject
is comparatively new, its roots are old. Thus the law has imposed
duties on persons exercising certain callings for many centuries
(e.g. innkeepers and carriers). Nevertheless, the explosion of
interest in consumer matters is very much a creature of the second
half of the twentieth century. We can see this simply by looking
at the dates of some of the principal reforming statutes:

Hire Purchase Acts 1954 and 1964
Misrepresentation Act 1967
Trade Descriptions Act 1968
Unsolicited Goods and Services Act 1971
Fair Trading Act 1973
Supply of Goods (Implied Terms) Act 1973

[1] *Ante*, p. v.

1

Consumer Credit Act 1974
Unfair Contract Terms Act 1977
Consumer Safety Act 1978

What is the reason for this tremendous upsurge of activity? The answer is twofold—a combination of new business methods and changing social attitudes. The key factors on business methods are to be found in the complexity of the goods themselves and in the changing forms of advertising and distribution. To quote again from the Molony Report, (p. 31):

> "[The last half century] has seen a growing tendency for manufacturers . . . to appeal directly to the public by forceful national advertising and other promotional methods . . . a further influence during the same period has been the development of a mass market for extremely complex mechanical and electrical goods . . . Their performance cannot in some cases be accurately established by a short trial; shortcomings of design are not apparent to the inexpert eye; inherent faults may only come to light when the article breaks down after a period of use."

In other words, the need for what is called consumer protection has become far greater because the consumer is no longer in a position to rely on his own judgment when buying a complex article.

The second motivating force is the general move from individualism to collectivism. The twentieth century has seen not only consumer protection but also the Rent Acts protecting tenants, the large volume of legislation protecting employees and, of course, the welfare state. The extent to which some of these measures hamper business activity is of course a matter of keen political debate.

The international dimension

A modern textbook[2] has demonstrated that the judiciary of the United States has been a long way ahead of this country in recognising and dealing with consumer problems. In particular, the American courts have increased the manufacturer's liability in two respects (1) by moving from negligence liability to strict liability

---

[2] Miller and Lovell, *Product Liability*, esp. pp. 58 and 186.

and (2) by breaking the shackles of the privity of contract rule. In this country it seems unlikely that the courts will follow the American lead and any changes will have to be brought about by legislation.

The subject of consumer protection is also very much alive in the EEC and other Western countries. Both the Council of Europe and the EEC have made proposals on product liability and draft directives have been issued in fields such as advertising and consumer credit. A section on EEC matters appears at the end of this book. (Chapter 24, *post* p. 302.)

Consumer protection agencies

There are a very large number of bodies concerned with consumer protection matters and they can be divided into Government Departments, Government-sponsored bodies, local authorities and voluntary bodies.

(a) *Government Departments*

As a result of the 1979 general election the Department of Prices and Consumer Affairs was absorbed into the Department of Trade; that Department now has a Minister of State for Consumer Affairs. Among its principal duties are the making of Orders under Part II of the Fair Trading Act 1973[3] and the Consumer Safety Act 1978. It also makes regulations under the Consumer Credit Act 1974. In addition the Home Office has responsibilities in certain areas, including firearms and explosives and the Ministry of Agriculture Fisheries and Food has a number of duties under the Food and Drugs Act 1955.

Closely linked with the Department of Trade is the Office of Fair Trading which was set up as a result of the Fair Trading Act 1973. The extensive powers and duties of the Director General will be discussed later in this book. The bulk of the provisions in the Act are concerned with restrictive practices, monopolies and mergers but the Director General of Fair Trading is also given very extensive powers in relation to consumer protection matters. His duties include:

---

[3] *Post,* p. 216 *et seq.*

  (i) keeping under review the commercial supply of goods and
     services to consumers in the United Kingdom.
  (ii) making recommendations to the Department of Trade—
     either if asked to do so or on his own initiative.
  (iii) taking action against individual traders who have persisted
     in a course of conduct which is unfair to consumers[4].
  (iv) providing information to the public.
  (v) encouraging trade associations to prepare codes of practice
     for their members.[5]

In other words he is a statutory watchdog who can take action if
undesirable trade practices come to his notice. He has also been
given very extensive powers to supervise and control the consumer
credit industry under the Consumer Credit Act 1974. His principal
weapon of control lies in the operation of the licensing system;
every trader who carries on a consumer credit business needs a
licence[6] and the Director General is responsible for the grant,
renewal, suspension and revocation of licences. He is also responsible, along with trading standards inspectors, for the enforcement
of the Act by criminal proceedings. The Consumer Credit Act is
examined in Part IV of this book

(b) *Government-sponsored bodies*

    The Consumer Council, set up as a result of the Molony Com-
mittee recommendations, was abolished by the Conservative Government in 1971, but a new body—named the National Consumer
Council—was set up by the Labour Government in 1974 and is
financed by a Government grant. It has no executive power and
does not deal with individual complaints. Its principal functions
are to act as a pressure group to represent the consumer interest
in negotiations with Government and other bodies. It gives an
immensely wide meaning to the term "consumer"; thus it has
recently published papers dealing with security of tenure for tenants
and with the powers of the police. A recent article has contrasted
the relatively generous help given to the National Consumer Council with the very inadequate funds made available for legal aid[6a].

---

[4] Part III of the Fair Trading Act 1973, *post* p. 230.
[5] *Post*, p. 121.
[6] *Post*, p. 255.
[6a] [1978] Law Society Gazette 822.

The Department of Trade also makes a grant to the British Standards Institute. This voluntary body has been in existence for more than seventy five years, and one of its functions is to lay down uniform specifications for certain products. If a product contains a B.S.I. "kite mark" this means that it has been tested by B.S.I. Regular spot checks will follow and the mark will be withdrawn if these prove unsatisfactory.

(c) *Local authorities*

The county councils and the London boroughs make two major contributions to consumer protection. First they employ trading standards inspectors (their former name was weights and measures inspectors) who have extensive responsibilities in the enforcement of the Trade Descriptions Act 1968, the Consumer Credit Act 1974 and Part II of the Fair Trading Act 1973. In all these cases they must give the Director General of Fair Trading notice of an intended prosecution[7] and they will also keep him informed of undesirable trade practices which come to their notice.

The second major field of local authority involvement lies in the field of consumer advice. Centres have been set up in many parts of the country under the Local Government Act 1972 and there are now more than 100 of them. They give pre-shopping advice and they also give advice on complaints. Sometimes they take up individual complaints with the object of achieving a satisfactory settlement but they do not normally assist in litigation if a settlement proves impossible.

(d) *Voluntary bodies*

The Consumers Association is widely known for its comparative testing of goods and services. The results are published in "Which" and certain other journals, (e.g. "Motoring Which," "Money Which") and are clearly of great value to prospective consumers. The Association is also very active in promoting legislation dealing with consumer affairs. Thus it played a large part in seeing the Unfair Contract Terms Act 1977 on to the statute book.

There are also a number of consumer groups at local level; their main function is to carry our research into the quality of local services and to publish the results of these surveys to their members.

---

[7] See, *e.g.* s. 130 of the Fair Trading Act 1973.

There is a central co-ordinating body known as the Federation of Consumer Groups and it is believed that total membership of the groups is in the region of 11,000

Finally we should mention trade associations (for example the Motor Trades Association or the Association of British Travel Agents. These are in no sense consumer protection agencies but many of them operate voluntary conciliation and arbitration procedures. A consumer with a complaint may well find that an approach to the relevant trade association may produce a more satisfactory outcome than embarking on the hazards of litigation. The codes of practice operated by a number of trade associations are examined in Chapter 9 of this book (*post*, p. 121).

PART I: THE CONSUMER AND THE CIVIL LAW

The civil law assists the consumer by imposing certain obligations on manufacturers and suppliers of goods and services and by restricting attempts to exclude or cut down these obligations or the remedies available on breach.

It must be said at once that the law relating to many of these obligations is in a very uncertain state. Two particularly thorny questions are (1) when are goods unmerchantable and (2) when does the buyer lose his right of rejection by "accepting" the goods? There is also the question of "reasonableness" under s. 3 of the Unfair Contract Terms Act where, for example, a builder seeks to avoid liability for delay or non-performance. Finally we have contracts of hire, work and materials and exchange where the terms implied by law are still uncertain.[8] When one thinks of the many millions of consumer contracts concluded each day this absence of authority may seem surprising. A charitable view would be that traders, for reasons of commercial goodwill, settle all genuine complaints without litigation. A more realistic view is that consumers are deterred from bringing proceedings by a variety of factors including ignorance, lethargy and cost.

In Chapters 2–5 we shall consider some basic duties of a supplier to pass title, to deliver the goods contracted for, to deliver goods of the right quality and fitness and to deliver them at the right time. We shall also consider in Chapter 6 the manufacturer's liability under the law as it now stands and we will indicate how the law might move in the light of the Pearson Report, the Law Commission Report and the proposals emanating from Brussels and Strasbourg. In Chapter 7 we shall examine the remedies available to the consumer and to members of his family. This will be followed in Chapter 8 by an examination of exemption clauses. Finally in Chapter 9 we shall examine the various ways in which the consumer can seek redress for his complaint. This will include (1) trade arbitration (2) small claims courts (3) arbitration in the county court.

[8] See Law Commission Second Report on Exemption Clauses (Law Com. No. 69, pp. 7–8). Proposals for reform which will clarify the matter are contained in Law Commission Report No. 95.

CHAPTER 2

"THEY SAY IT ISN'T MINE"

(1) A owns a diamond ring. B steals it and sells it to C who sells it to D. The police have now traced the ring and have seized it from D's home.

(2) E takes his car to F, a car dealer, and says "Find me a buyer but don't sell for less than £1000." F sells to G for £600 and disappears.

(3) H, a finance house, supply a car to I on hire-purchase. Before completing his payments I sells the car to J, a motor dealer, who lets the car out to K on a fresh hire-purchase agreement. H now claim from K the unpaid balance due on the original agreement.

In unravelling this type of problem three closely connected principles must be distinguished:

1. Does any buyer acquire title to the goods?

2. What are the rights as between each buyer and his seller? This question will usually only be relevant in advising a buyer who has not acquired title.

3. What are the rights of a buyer who has spent money on improving the goods?

In this Chapter it is proposed to deal separately with these three questions.

1. DOES THE BUYER GET TITLE?

Where goods are sold by a non-owner the law is faced with a clear policy choice. Lord Denning M.R. has described it[1]:

> "In the development of our law two principles have striven for mastery. The first is for the protection of property; no one can give a better title than he himself possesses.[2] The second is for the protection of commercial transactions;

---

[1] *Bishopsgate Motor Finance Corpn. Ltd.* v. *Transport Brakes Ltd.* [1949] I.K.B. 322, 336–337.

[2] This is commonly referred to as the "nemo dat" rule, *i.e. nemo dat quod non habet.*

8

the person who takes in good faith and for value without notice should get a good title.

Faced with this choice the law has developed in a piecemeal and haphazard way with a basic rule protecting property and a number of exceptions protecting commercial transactions. The Crowther Committee on Consumer Credit described the rules as "arbitrary and capricious" and pointed out that their application depended, "not on principles of equity or justice but on fine technicalities which have little rhyme and less reason."[3]

The nemo dat rule

With this warning we can examine the relevant provisions. The cornerstone is to be found in section 21(1) of the Sale of Goods Act 1893. It reads:

> "Subject to the provisions of this Act where goods are sold by a person who is not the owner thereof, and who does not sell them under the authority or with the consent of the owner, the buyer acquires no better title to the goods than the seller had, unless the owner of the goods is by his conduct precluded from denying the seller's authority to sell."

If we revert to our three examples, the effect of section 21(1) is that the goods will still belong to A, E and H unless someone along the line acquired title under one of the exceptions to the basic rule. We must now consider the scope and extent of these exceptions.

Does an exception apply?

Let us first list the principal exceptions:

- (i) Sale under order of court.
- (ii) Sale under a common law or statutory power.
- (iii) Sale with the owner's consent.
- (iv) Sale where the owner is precluded from denying the seller's right to sell ("estoppel").
- (v) Disposition by a mercantile agent.
- (vi) Sale in market overt.
- (vii) Sale under a voidable title.
- (viii) Disposition by a seller in possession.
- (ix) Disposition by a buyer in possession.
- (x) Disposition of a motor vehicle under Part III of the Hire-Purchase Act 1964.

[3] Report, p. 178.

It is now proposed to examine some of the more important of these exceptions. Nearly all of the examples chosen relate to motor cars; this is clearly the area where the consumer is most likely to buy goods which turn out to have been stolen. There is substantial overlap between these provisions and it is often advisable to plead more than one.

(i) *Is the owner estopped?*

Section 21 itself displaces the basic *nemo dat* rule where the owner, by his conduct, is precluded from denying the seller's right to sell. The courts have construed this provision in a fairly narrow way. In the words of Lord Wilberforce:

"English law has generally taken the robust line that the man who owns property is not under a general duty to safeguard it and that he may sue for its recovery any person into whose hands it has come."[4]

In *Central Newbury Car Auctions Ltd* v. *Unity Finance Ltd,*[5]

a distinguished looking swindler wished to acquire a car from Central Newbury Car Auctions on hire-purchase terms and he intimated that he was prepared to leave his own car in part exchange. He filled up an application form for a hire-purchase agreement. If the deal went through the dealer would sell to a finance company who would let the car to him on hire-purchase. Central Newbury allowed him to take the new car and its registration book away. Within a very short time it was discovered that (i) he had given a false name, address and employer (ii) the car which he had left in part exchange did not belong to him and (iii) he had sold the new car to Unity Finance. Central Newbury sued Unity Finance for the return of the car.

It was the classic situation; which of two innocent parties should suffer for the fraud of a third? Many people would agree with Lord Denning that the loss should fall on Central Newbury in view of their carelessness in parting with the car. Nevertheless this was a minority view; the majority in the Court of Appeal applied what Lord Wilberforce has described as the "robust" view.[6] All that Central Newbury had done was to hand over physical possession; that was not conduct which precluded them from setting up their ownership; the car was still theirs. The only right of Unity Finance would be an action against the swindler under section 12

[4] *Moorgate Mercantile Co.* v. *Twitchings* [1976] 3 W.L.R. 66, 70.
[5] [1957] 1 Q.B. 371.
[6] See above.

of the Sale of Goods Act[7] and this would almost certainly be worthless.

In the more recent case of *Moorgate Mercantile Co.* v. *Twitchings*[8]:

> Finance Companies set up a company called HPI and ninety-eight per cent. of all Finance Companies belonged to it. The object was to register subsisting hire-purchase agreements—some four and a half million—and to pass on information to motor dealers who were associated members. Any dealer who was considering buying a car could contact HPI to find out whether a hire-purchase agreement relating to that car was registered. Several thousand enquiries were made each day. The M. Finance Co. entered into a hire-purchase agreement, but for some unexplained reason they failed to register it with HPI. The hirer offered to sell the car to T, a dealer. T. contacted HPI and was told that nothing had been registered. He then bought the car from the hirer. M. Finance Co claimed that the car was still theirs. The House of Lords, by a majority, upheld this claim.

The case was fought on two grounds—estoppel and negligence. As to estoppel the question was twofold: (i) were HPI the agents of the finance companies? (ii) did their answers amount to a representation that no finance company had an interest in the car? By a majority of four to one (Lord Salmon dissenting) the House of Lords gave a negative answer to both of these questions. The other argument was negligence—the M. Finance Company owed a legal duty of care to dealers and were in breach of that duty. This argument was accepted by the Court of Appeal and by Lords Salmon and Wilberforce but the majority of the House of Lords rejected it. One of the main reasons which influenced the majority was the fact that (i) membership of HPI was voluntary and (ii) there was no duty to register agreements. Neither of these arguments appears totally convincing but they indicate that the owner of goods will seldom lose his ownership by reason of carelessness, even though this causes serious loss to an innocent buyer. We shall see later that HPI can also be used by a prospective private buyer[9].

The only type of case where the owner may be estopped is where he makes a positive representation that the seller owns the goods[10] or where he signs a document which clearly conveys that impression.[11]

---

[7] *Post,* pp. 22–23.
[8] [1977] A.C. 890.
[9] *Post,* p. 22.
[10] See *Henderson* v. *Williams* [1895] Q.B. 521.
[11] See *Eastern Distributors* v. *Goldring* [1957] 2 Q.B. 600.

(ii) Was there a disposition by a mercantile agent?

We have seen that the mere delivery of possession does not preclude the owner from setting up his ownership. There is, however, one statutory exception. The basic effect of section 2 of the Factors Act 1889 is that if the owner transfers possession to a "mercantile agent" this may amount to a representation that the agent has authority to sell. If the agent then sells in the ordinary course of business the owner may lose his ownership even though the agent went beyond his instructions.

The Act of 1889 starts by defining a mercantile agent. By section 1:

> "a mercantile agent is a mercantile agent having in the customary course of his business as such agent authority to sell goods, or to consign goods for the purpose of sale or to buy goods or to raise money on the security of goods."

Then comes the key provision. By section 2(1):

> "where a mercantile agent is, with the consent of the owner in the possession of goods . . . any sale, pledge or other disposition of the goods made by him when acting in the ordinary course of business of a mercantile agent is as valid as if he were expressly authorised by the owner of the goods to make the same; provided that the person taking under the disposition acts in good faith and has not at the time of the disposition notice that the person making the disposition has not authority to make the same."

This section could apply to the second example at the beginning of this chapter.[12] If the agent receives instructions not to sell for less than £1,000, or if he is merely instructed to take offers, the buyer will usually not be aware of these restrictions and will get a good title under section 2 even though the agent exceeded his authority.

The sale by the agent must be in the ordinary course of business and the buyer must have no notice of the restrictions on the agent's authority. In practice these points are unlikely to give rise to difficulty. There are, however, two other points which could defeat the buyer's claim. Thus:

(a) The section will only apply if the agent was in possession *in his capacity of mercantile agent*. It would not apply if, for example, a garage who happened to be a mercantile agent received a car for servicing or repair and then sold it.[13]

(b) The agent must have received possession of the goods with the owner's consent. The mere fact that consent was obtained by fraud[14] or that consent has ended[15] does not affect the buyer unless he knows of this—an obviously sensible rule. On the other hand, the owner may decide to keep the registration document and/or the ignition key. What happens if he accidentally leaves them with the dealer or in the car? In *Pearson* v. *Rose and Young*[16]

> The owner of a car instructed a dealer to obtain offers. He never intended to hand over the registration book but by mistake he left it in the dealer's showroom. The dealer sold the car with its registration book to a buyer. The Court of Appeal held that (i) in the case of a second hand car the word 'goods' included the registration book and the consent of the owner must extend to the registration book as well as to the car itself (ii) there had been no consent to the handing over of the book (iii) the dealer must therefore be treated as if he had sold the car without the book (iv) such a sale would not be in the ordinary course of business (v) consequently the buyer got no title under section 2.[17]

(iii) *Was the sale in market overt?*

This is probably the most ancient of all the *nemo dat* exceptions, dating back to the sixteenth century. It is riddled with technical rules and anomalies and has little to do with the realities of modern commercial life. The rule is set out in section 22 of the Sale of Goods Act 1893 as follows:

> Where goods are sold in market overt, according to the usage of the market, the buyer acquires a good title to the goods, provided he buys them in good faith and without notice of any defect or want of title on the part of the seller.

This section could be relevant to the first of the examples at the beginning of this chapter.[18] In one sense it is wider than any other

[13] See, *e.g. Belvoir Finance Co. Ltd.* v. *Harold G. Cole & Co. Ltd.* [1969] I.W.L.R. 1877.
[14] *Folkes* v. *King* [1923] 1.K.B. 282; but perhaps the position would be different if the owner was under a fundamental mistake as to the agent's identity. See *Benjamin on Sale of Goods*, p. 232.
[15] Act of 1889, s. 2(2).
[16] [1951] I.K.B. 275.
[17] See also *Stadium Finance Ltd.* v. *Robbins* [1962] 2 Q.B. 664 C.A. (book accidentally left in car; key not handed over at all; buyer from agent not protected.)
[18] *ante*, p. 8.

of the *nemo dat* exceptions. In the two which we have already considered and in the four which we still have to consider[19] there has been some contractual relationship between the owner and the seller. Market overt is the only exception where such a relationship may be entirely absent. A sale by a thief may pass title.

To find out whether the consumer (or one of his predecessors in title) got a market overt title a number of questions have to be asked. Title will only pass if the answer to all the questions is "yes."

(a) Did the sale take place in market overt? A market overt is a market or fair established by charter or custom; there is a very ancient custom that every shop in the City of London is market overt.

(b) Were the goods of a kind normally dealt with in the market?

(c) Did the sale take place "according to the usage of the market?" Thus the section would not apply to a private sale at a market where goods were normally sold only by auction.

(d) Was the sale public and open in the public part of the market or shop? It is necessary that the goods themselves should be displayed there and not only a sample. It must also be shown that the sale is *by* the shopkeeper not *to* him.[20]

(e) Was the sale between sunrise and sunset? In a recent case this point was crucial and the buyer lost because the sale to him took place before sunrise.[21]

(f) Did the buyer take in good faith and without notice of any defect in the seller's title?

(g) Did the sale take place in England? There is no market overt in Wales (Laws in Wales Act 1542), nor does it apply in Scotland

These points can now be illustrated by considering two of the very few market overt cases to reach the courts.

In *Bishopsgate Finance Co. Ltd.* v. *Transport Brakes Ltd.*[22]:

> X had a car on hire-purchase with no right to sell. He took it to Maidstone market, unsuccessfully tried to sell it by auction

[19] *Post*, pp. 16–22.
[20] *Ardath Tobacco Ltd.* v. *Ocker* (1931) 47 T.L.R. 177.
[21] See p. 15.
[22] [1949] 1 K.B. 322.

and eventually sold it privately there. The finance company who had let it to X claimed it from the buyer. The claim failed.

The Court of Appeal found that Maidstone market had been running since 1747 and they had little difficulty in finding that it was market overt. It was also proved that cars were regularly sold there both by auction and privately. Hence the sale in this case was "according to the usage of the market" and the buyer acquired title.

In a more recent case involving a candelabra a claim of market overt title failed. In *Reid* v. *Metropolitan Police Commissioner*[23] the facts were vividly described by the Master of the Rolls:

> "The centre-piece of this story is a pair of candelabra, made of well-cut glass, each supporting two candles with sparkling pear-drops all about . . . In December 1969 this lovely pair of candelabra stood on the table of Mr. Reid . . . He and his wife went away for the weekend. During their absence thieves broke in and ransacked the house. They took many things. In their haul they stole the pair of Adam candelabra. The next we hear of them is two months later. This time it is at the New Caledonian Market in Southwark. That market is open every Friday from seven in the morning onwards, but dealers go there before that time so as to get the best bargains. It is the early bird that catches the worm. On Friday, February 13, 1970 Norman Cocks, an art dealer, the defendant went early to the market. It was still only half-light. The sun had not risen. He saw a man putting up a stall . . . On the stall there was a cardboard box . . . Wrapped up in a newspaper there were the main parts of a pair of candelabra . . . He did not ask the man where he got them from. No one ever asks questions of that kind in the market. . . Mr. Cocks said 'I'll give you £200.' The man agreed."

Some time later, when Mr. Cocks was negotiating a re-sale, Mr. Reid appeared and claimed that the candelabra was the one which had been stolen from his house. The police took it away and the ownership was fought out between Reid and Cocks. The Court of Appeal held that as Cocks had bought before sunrise, he acquired no market overt title. Consequently the candelabra still belonged to Reid.

In both of these cases the buyers were commercial buyers. It will be appreciated that if either of them had resold the goods to a consumer then (i) in the *Bishopsgate* case the first buyer's market overt title would have passed to the buyer and (ii) in the *Reid* case the buyer would acquire no title unless the sale *to him* was in

[23] [1973] Q.B. 551.

market overt or unless one of the other *nemo dat* exceptions applied. The market overt rules apply equally to private and business buyers.

(iv) *Did the seller have a voidable title?*

Where a contract is voidable (*e.g.* for misrepresentation) it is a valid contract until the innocent party takes steps to set it aside, *i.e.* rescinds the contract. The remedy of rescission is an equitable one and in certain cases it will not be possible to rescind. One such case is concerned with third party rights—once a third party has acquired rights under the voidable contract it will be too late to rescind it. This principle now appears in section 23 of the 1893 Act as follows:

> When the seller of goods has a voidable title thereto, but his title has not been avoided at the time of the sale, the buyer acquires a good title to the goods, provided that he buys them in good faith and without notice of the seller's defect of title.

In virtually all the reported cases under this section the goods were obtained as a result of a fraudulent misrepresentation. The position of the ultimate buyer depends on a highly technical rule— was the title of the fraudulent buyer *voidable* for misrepresentation or *void* for mistake? In the well-known case of *Ingram* v. *Little*[24];

> Three ladies agreed to sell a car to a man who called himself "Hutchinson." They were reluctant to take a cheque from him but he gave them the initials and address of a real Hutchinson. After checking in the telephone directory they let him take the car away in return for a cheque. He sold the car to a buyer; the cheque was dishonoured. The Court of Appeal held that (i) the offer to sell was made to Hutchinson and could not be accepted by anyone else; (ii) consequently the contract with the rogue was void; (iii) consequently section 23 did not apply and the buyer acquired no title.

The Law Reform Committee recommended that the fraudulent person should always be treated as having a *voidable* title, so that the ultimate buyer would be protected. No such legislation has been enacted but the courts have, in effect, achieved this result. In the more recent case of *Lewis* v. *Averay*[25] the facts were somewhat similar to those in *Ingram* v. *Little* but the decision went the other way. In that case,

[24] [1961] 1 Q.B. 31.
[25] [1972] 1 Q.B. 198.

A rogue calling himself Green—a well known television actor—induced the owner of a car to sell it to him in return for a cheque. He re-sold the car to a buyer. The cheque was dishonoured.

The Court of Appeal held that the rogue had a voidable title, with the result that section 23 protected the buyer. They treated *Ingram* v. *Little* as a case turning on very special facts and they laid down the broad principle that where the parties were face to face the seller would normally be treated as intending to deal with the actual person in front of him. If this intention was brought about by fraud or by a trick this would make the transaction voidable but not void.

Section 23 does not apply if the owner has avoided the contract *before* the resale takes place. In general the innocent party must give notice of rescission and this can raise a practical problem, since not all fraudulent buyers supply their sellers with an address. In *Car and Universal Finance Co.* v. *Caldwell*[26] the Court of Appeal held that avoidance was possible in this type of case without notifying the fraudulent buyer. In that case the seller reported the matter to police and the A.A. as soon as the cheque was dishonoured and he asked them to trace the car. It was held that his conduct did amount to an avoidance of the contract. The practical effect of this case has however been largely undermined by the later case of *Newtons of Wembley Ltd.* v. *Williams* which is considered later in this chapter.[27]

(v) *Did the seller remain in possession after a previous sale?*

We have seen that the owner of goods may lose his ownership if he transfers possession to a mercantile agent who disposes of them in the ordinary course of business.[28] We now meet two further cases where ownership and possession are split. The first concerns a sale where the buyer becomes the owner but the seller retains possession. Let us assume that X, an antique dealer, agrees to sell to Y an antique vase. Y agrees to collect it on the following day. By mistake the dealer sells the same vase to Z who pays for it and takes it away. On these facts the first sale may have passed the ownership to Y[29] but the second sale, coupled with delivery, may

---

[26] [1965] 1 Q.B. 525.
[27] *Post,* p. 19.
[28] *Ante,* p. 12.
[29] Section 18, rule 1, *post,* p. 60.

have passed the ownership to Z. The authority for this is section 25(1) of the Sale of Goods Act 1893 which reads as follows:

> Where a person having sold goods continues or is in possession of the goods . . . the delivery or transfer by that person or by a mercantile agent acting for him of the goods . . . under a sale, pledge or other disposition thereof to any person receiving the same in good faith and without notice of the previous sale shall have the same effect as if the person making the delivery or transfer were expressly authorised by the owner of the goods to make the same.

Thus in advising Z one would start by claiming that X was still the owner at the time of the sale to him. If this is not so (see above) Z may acquire title under section 25, provided that the sale to him was coupled with delivery. After earlier doubts it now seems clear that the nature of X's possession is immaterial—he may be in possession as seller, or as repairer, or as warehouseman or in any other capacity.

As already stated[30] these rules are highly technical. Consider the following problem:

> X sells a car to Y as a result of a fraudulent misrepresentation made by Y. Y pays by cheque. Y sells to Z and retains possession. When Y's cheque is dishonoured X comes to Y's premises. X allows Y to take the car back in return for a promise by X not to enforce the cheque.

The sale from Y to Z gave Z a title under section 23.[31] After that sale Y became a "seller in possession." The return of the car to X amounts to a delivery under a "sale, pledge *or other disposition*" within section 25(1). Consequently title is re-transferred to X.[32]

(vi) *Was the sale by a buyer in possession?*

Section 25(2) is the exact converse of section 25(1). It is again concerned with a split between ownership and possession but this time it is the seller who retains ownership and the buyer who obtains possession. There is, in fact, a very substantial overlap with section 23. Let us assume that A buys a car from B and pays by cheque. The contract provides that no property shall pass to A until the cheque is cleared. A obtains possession of the car with

[30] *Ante*, p. 9.
[31] *Ante*, p. 16.
[32] See *Worcester Works Finance Ltd.* v. *Cooden Engineering Co. Ltd.* [1972] 1 Q.B. 210, C.A.

B's consent, and sells and delivers the car to C. A's cheque is dishonoured. Although C bought from a non-owner he may acquire title under section 25(2). The section reads as follows:

> "Where a person having bought or agreed to buy goods obtains, with the consent of the seller possession of the goods . . . the delivery or transfer by that person, or by a mercantile agent acting for him, of the goods . . . under any sale, pledge or other disposition thereof to any person receiving the same in good faith and without notice of any lien or other right of the original seller in respect of the goods, shall have the same effect as if the person making the delivery or transfer were a mercantile agent in possession of the goods . . . with the consent of the owner."

This subsection has been before the courts on a number of occasions and the following points emerge.

(a) The section only applies where a person has bought or agreed to buy goods. It does not apply where, for example, the goods have been let out on hire-purchase.[33]

(b) The first buyer must obtain possession with the *consent* of the seller; this includes consent obtained by fraud.[34]

(c) The section can apply even where the first buyer has obtained a voidable title. It has been held that a disposition by such a buyer is protected (subject to d below) even *after* the title has been avoided.

(d) What are the meaning of the obscure words "shall have the same effect as if the person making the delivery or transfer were a mercantile agent in possession . . . with the consent of the owner?" In *Newtons of Wembley Ltd.* v. *Williams*[35] the Court of Appeal reached the astonishing conclusion that the disposition by the first buyer must be in the ordinary course of business of a mercantile agent—even though that buyer is not such an agent! In that case:

A agreed to buy a Sunbeam Rapier car from Newtons of Wembley. The contract provided that no property should pass to the buyer until his cheque was cleared. When the cheque was dishonoured Newtons took steps to trace the car and recover it. A then sold it to B in an open-air market in Warren Street. B resold it to Williams. A pleaded guilty to obtaining the car by false pretences and Newtons of Wembley sued Williams for the return of the car. The claim was unsuccessful.

[33] *Helby* v. *Matthews* [1895] A.C. 471.
[34] *Du Jardin* v. *Beadman Bros.* [1952] 2 Q.B. 712
[35] [1965] 1 Q.B. 560.

The Court of Appeal held that A was a buyer in possession; even though he was not a mercantile agent the sale to B was in the ordinary course of business of a mercantile agent; B took in good faith; accordingly B acquired a good title which he could pass on to Williams.

It will be appreciated that the first transferee from the original buyer must take "in good faith". This condition was satisfied in this case but not in the earlier case of *Car and Universal Finance Co. Ltd.* v. *Caldwell.*[36] The effect of the *Newton* decision is to make section 23[37] largely superfluous, since there will not be many cases in practice which are covered by that section and not by section 25(2).

(vii) *Was there a disposition of a motor vehicle held on hire-purchase or conditional sale?*

The final rule which may protect the consumer was introduced by Part III of the Hire-Purchase Act 1964. It now appears, with verbal amendments, in Schedule 4 to the Consumer Credit Act 1974 but the original wording is used in this chapter. The provision was introduced after an earlier proposal had been rejected, for administrative reasons, by the finance companies. This would have provided for the retention of the registration books by the companies and the issue of cards to the hirers. One of the real problems in this area of law is that many people ignore the warning in the registration book that the person in whose name the car is registered is not necessarily the owner.

Part III applies if the following conditions are satisfied:
- (a) A motor vehicle is let out on hire-purchase or agreed to be sold under a conditional sale agreement; and
- (b) the hirer or buyer disposes of it before the property has passed to him.

The Act then makes a distinction between:

- (a) a disposition to a *private purchaser* and
- (b) a disposition to a *trade or finance purchaser*.

In the former case the purchaser may get a good title. In the words of section 27 of the 1964 Act (as originally drafted):

[36] *Ante*, p. 17.
[37] *Ante*, p. 16.

Where the disposition is to a private purchaser and he is a purchaser of the motor vehicle in good faith and without notice of the hire-purchase or conditional sale agreement that disposition shall have effect as if the title of the owner or seller had been vested in the hirer or buyer immediately before that disposition.

Two points can be made here. First, the private purchaser must have no actual notice of a subsisting hire-purchase or conditional sale agreement. Secondly, the "title of the owner" means the title of the person who was described as the owner in the hire-purchase agreement.

Suppose that X, a thief, sells a car to Y not in market overt. Y lets it on hire-purchase to Z and Z sells it to A. Even if A takes in good faith he will only get the title which was vested in Y. Since Y had no title the section does not protect A.

If we now assume that the hirer or buyer disposes of the vehicle to a trade or finance purchaser, that purchaser has no Part III protection (presumably because he will be able to use the HPI facilities[38]) but if further dispositions take place the Act protects the first private purchaser if he takes in good faith and without notice. It, therefore, becomes crucial to find out whether the original transferee was a trade or finance purchaser. A trade purchaser is defined as a person who at the time of the disposition carries on a business of buying motor vehicles for resale, while a finance purchaser is one who provides finance by buying motor vehicles and letting them out under hire-purchase or conditional sale agreements. Any other purchaser is a private purchaser. The following points can be important:

(i) "Private purchaser" is much wider than "private person"; thus many large public companies will enjoy the "private purchaser" protection of the Act.
(ii) If the purchaser is a trade or finance purchaser he will not have Part III protection even if he buys for his private use.
(iii) The term "disposition" can include a fresh hire-purchase agreement. Thus in the third example at the beginning of this chapter[39] the ultimate hirer will be entitled to remain in possession under Part III even though he finds out about the original agreement before completing his payments.

[38] *Ante*, p. 11.
[39] p. 8.

Two final points can be made. First, there are bound to be serious practical problems in proving that the vehicle was transferred by the hirer or buyer to a private purchaser. The purchaser's job is made somewhat easier by a series of rebuttable presumptions which are to be found in section 28 of the 1964 Act. Secondly, one must always bear in mind that prevention is better than cure. A member of the public who is considering buying a car can always check with HPI.[40] HPI make their information available to the AA, RAC and Citizens Advice Bureaux.

Hire-purchase generally

X lets out goods to Y on hire-purchase and it then transpires that X is not the owner of the goods. A number of the provisions discussed in this chapter refer to a "disposition" and this is clearly wide enough to cover a hire-purchase agreement. Thus Y could, in appropriate cases, claim the protection of section 2 of the Factors Act,[40a] sections 25(1) or (2) of the Sale of Goods Act[40b] or Part III of the Hire-Purchase Act (supra). He would also be protected if X had a voidable title, since it will be too late for the original owner to rescind the agreement once third party rights have been acquired.[40c]

2. BUYER'S RIGHTS AGAINST SELLER

We have dealt at some length with the *nemo dat* rules because it is likely that the real battle in practice is likely to be fought between the original owner and the buyer. We must now consider the position as between buyer and seller. The general principle is clear enough; under a contract of sale the transfer of ownership from seller to buyer is a fundamental term around which the whole contract revolves. Section 12(1)[41] spells out the seller's basic obligation:

> "In every contract of sale, other than one to which subsection (2) of this section applies there is—

[40] *Ante*, p. 11.
[40a] *Ante*, p. 12.
[40b] *Ante*, pp. 17–19.
[40c] *Ante*, p. 16.
[41] As amended by the Supply of Goods (Implied Terms) Act 1973.

(a) an implied condition on the part of the seller that in the case of a sale, he has a right to sell the goods, and in the case of an agreement to sell he will have a right to sell when the property is to pass; and

(b) an implied warranty that the goods are free and will remain free until the time when the property is to pass from any charge or incumbrance not disclosed or known to the buyer before the contract is made and that the buyer will enjoy quiet possession of the goods except so far as it may be disturbed by the owner or other person entitled to the benefit of any charge or incumbrance so disclosed or known.''

The condition in section 12(1)(*a*) has been before the courts on a number of occasions and the following points emerge from the cases:

(1) if the goods are delivered in such a form that any sale can be stopped by an injunction there is no "right to sell."

(2) if the seller is in breach of this essential condition the buyer can recover the price even though he has used the goods for a considerable time.[41a] The basis of his claim is a "total failure of consideration." If he asks for the return of the price his right will crystallise and will not be affected by anything done *after* this to cure the defect. If the principle of "total failure" is applied literally it would enable a buyer of stolen wine to have the best of both worlds—consume the wine and get his money back on discovering the theft!

(3) If the buyer has incurred other expenses e.g. the cost of necessary repairs, these can also be claimed from the seller.[42]

An unsettled question is the precise relationship between section 12 and the *nemo dat* exceptions considered earlier in this chapter. If the seller had no title he would technically have no *right* to sell, even though the effect of the sale would be to pass title to the buyer. Nevertheless, it is inconceivable that a court would allow a claim based on "total failure of consideration" if the buyer got exactly what he paid for, *i.e.* the property in the goods. If, however, he was put to trouble and expense in proving his title he might well have a claim.

Can section 12(1) be excluded?

There may be cases where the seller of goods is uncertain as to whether or not he has a right to sell and he may wish the buyer

[41a] *Rowland* v. *Divall* [1923] 2 K.B. 500.
[42] *Mason* v. *Burningham* [1949] 2 K.B. 545.

to bear this risk. Section 12(2) allows the seller to give a more limited undertaking:

> In a contract of sale, in the case of which there appears from the contract or is to be inferred from the circumstances of the contract an intention that the seller should transfer only such title as he or a third person may have, there is
> (a) an implied warranty that all charges and encumbrances known to the seller and not to the buyer have been disclosed to the buyer before the contract is made; and
> (b) an implied warranty that neither
>> (i) the seller; nor
>> (ii) in a case where the parties to the contract intend that the seller should transfer only such title as a third person may have, that person; nor
>> (iii) anyone claiming through or under the seller or that third person otherwise than under a charge or encumbrance disclosed or known to the buyer before the contract is made;
> will disturb the buyer's quiet possession of the goods.

Subject to this, section 12 cannot be excluded.

Hire-purchase

The terms as to right to sell, quiet possession and freedom from encumbrances implied into hire-purchase agreements are similar to those implied in sale of goods[43] and only one point calls for brief mention. Under section 8(1) the condition of "right to sell" is a condition that the owner will have a right to sell when the property is to pass (this usually occurs when the hirer has completed his payments). It seems, however, that the hirer may be in an even stronger position under a term implied at common law, *i.e.* that the owner has the right to sell at time of delivery to the hirer.[44] A breach of the condition gives the hirer the right to recover all his payments with no set-off for user (*Warman* v. *Southern Counties Finance Corporation*).[45]

3. IMPROVEMENTS AND REPAIRS

S sells goods to B who spends £200 on repairs and improvements. It then transpires that the goods belong to C who claims them, or

---

[43] See s. 8 of the Supply of Goods (Implied Terms) Act 1973.
[44] *Karflex Ltd.* v. *Poole* [1933] 2 K.B. 251.
[45] [1949] 2 K.B. 576, C.A.

their value, from B. It has been well established for many years that, in assessing damages for conversion, credit must be given for improvements made by the defendant.[46] In *Greenwood* v. *Bennett*[47] this principle was applied in interpleader proceedings between the owner and the improver. This seems fair enough but one point is unclear; if the owner seizes the goods from the improver, does the improver have a cause of action to recover the cost of the improvements from the owner? No English authority supports such a claim, although Lord Denning M.R. suggested (*obiter*) that such a claim would be allowed on the basis of unjust enrichment (for further discussion and criticism see (1973) 36 M.L.R. 89).

The principle of *Greenwood* v. *Bennett* now appears in statutory form in section 6(1) of the Torts (Interference with Goods) Act 1977.

It reads:

> If in proceedings for wrongful interference against a person (the "improver") who has improved the goods, it is shown that the improver acted in the mistaken but honest belief that he had a good title to them, an allowance shall be made for the extent to which, at the time as at which the goods fall to be valued in assessing damages, the value of the goods is attributable to the improvement.

The section goes on to give a similar right to a subsequent buyer who acted in good faith.[48] If the buyer then sues his seller under section 12[49] the seller can claim a similar reduction provided that he acted in good faith.[50]

> O owns a car which is stolen by T who sells it to A. It is worth £200 but A increases its value to £900. He then sells it to B for £900. O claims the car from B.

If we can assume that O has been the owner at all material times, the court may well order O to pay B the sum of £700 (the improvement figure reflected in the price paid by B to A) as a condition of getting the car back. In the result, B is out of pocket to the tune of £200. If he then sues A for the return of the £900 it seems only right that his claim should be limited to £200 and

---

[46] *Munro* v. *Willmott* [1949] 1 K.B. 295 C.A.
[47] [1973] 1 Q.B. 195.
[48] s. 6(2).
[49] *Ante,* pp. 22–23.
[50] s. 6(3).

(assuming that A acted in good faith) section 6(3) allows such a reduction.

Two final points may be made. It will be seen that the section uses the words "if in proceedings . . . against a person." In other words it does not create a new cause of action. If the owner seizes the goods from the improver, there is nothing in the Act to give the improver a claim against the owner.[51] Secondly the right to claim compensation for improvements will only be relevant where the improver or his successor in title is liable to the owner and it will not be relevant where the improver or his successor in title has himself become the owner under one of the *nemo dat* exceptions discussed at the beginning of this chapter.

---

[51] He may of course have a claim against the seller—see *Mason* v. *Burningham* note 42 *supra*.

CHAPTER 3

"IT'S A GOOD LITTLE BUS"

(1) During negotiations for the sale of a car the dealer says to the consumer "it's a good little bus—I'd stake my life on it." The consumer then takes the car on hire-purchase from a finance company. The steering is defective and the consumer is injured.

(2) The vendor of a site of a petrol filling station tells the prospective purchaser that it would have a throughput of 200,000 gallons per year. This is far too high and the purchaser suffers severe financial loss.

(3) A prospective hirer of barges asks the owner how much they could carry and the owner replies "1,600 tonnes." The hirer makes the contract but the statement is wrong and the hirer refuses to pay the hire charges.

The supplier of goods is likely to make extravagant claims about them during negotiations. What are the remedies of the consumer if, as in the three cases cited, the statement turns out to be wrong? The position depends on how the statement is classified. There are at least five possibilities:

    (a) the statement may be nothing more than "trader's puff." In this case the consumer has no remedy.

    (b) the statement may be an actionable misrepresentation; in this case the consumer may have (i) a right to rescind the contract unless it is too late to do so; (ii) a right to damages at common law if the supplier was fraudulent; (iii) a right to damages under section 2(1) of the Misrepresentation Act 1967 unless the supplier can prove that he had reasonable grounds for believing the statement to be true.

    (c) it may be a negligent misstatement giving rise to an action for damages in tort. This branch of the law of negligence is based on the House of Lords decision in *Hedley Byrne & Co. Ltd.* v. *Heller & Partners Ltd.*[1] but the law has been

---

[1] [1964] A.C. 465.

developing very slowly and the precise scope of liability has still to be determined.

(d) it may be a contractual term. In this case the consumer can claim damages; whether he can also treat the contract as discharged depends upon the importance of the term and upon the seriousness and the consequences of the breach.

(e) it may form part of the description of the goods (this overlaps with (d) above). If this is so a breach will be a breach of condition and the consumer can choose between (i) treating the contract as repudiated and (ii) affirming the contract and claiming damages.[2] Until recently the term "description" has been given a very wide meaning but it seems that the pendulum is now swinging the other way.[3]

It remains to add that the supplier may be in breach of the Trade Descriptions Act 1968[4] and a criminal conviction could lead to an award of compensation under the Powers of Criminal Courts Act 1973.[5] These matters are examined in Part II of this book.

1. MERE PUFF

The praising of goods by a prospective supplier is a universal fact of commercial life and the lifeblood of the advertising industry. The following phrases are typical:

"the most popular bike in Britain"
"clean, healthy and alive"
"super value for money"
"the bathroom bargains of the year."

This is typical sales patter; it is not intended to give rise to legal liability and it does not do so. The difficulty is to know where to draw the line between (a) mere puff (b) a representation or contractual term. In the above examples the statements were vague and unspecified; as soon as the supplier makes an inaccurate specific statement, for example, as to measurements or ingredients, the consumer should have little difficulty in proving an actionable misrepresentation or breach of a contractual term. In an early case

[2] Sale of Goods Act 1893, ss 11, 13.
[3] See *post*, p. 38.
[4] *Post*, p. 155.
[5] *Post*, p. 204.

a seller of port who described it as "superior old port" was held liable as the maker of a contractual promise. More recently in *Andrews* v. *Hopkinson*,[6] the facts of which appear in example 1,[7] the dealer who described the car as a "good little bus" was liable for breach of a collateral contract (and also in tort under the rule in *Donoghue* v. *Stevenson*).[8]

2. MISREPRESENTATION

A misrepresentation can broadly be described as a half-way house between mere puff and a contractual term. The essence of a misrepresentation is that it is a statement made *before* the making of the contract which *induces* the other party to enter into the contract. There can, of course, be an overlap between a misrepresentation and a contractual term; a dealer may represent a car as being a 1977 model and this may later be incorporated into the contract. Subject to this, a mere pre-contractual inducement is less potent than a term of the contract itself.

Until the nineteen sixties it was often vital for the injured party to prove that the statement was something more than a misrepresentation; the reason was that the only remedy for misrepresentation was the equitable remedy of rescission, with no right to damages unless there was fraud. If it was too late to rescind the innocent party might find himself with no remedy at all. This is what happened in *Oscar Chess Ltd.* v. *Williams*[9] where the following facts arose:

> A consumer who was buying a car was asked by the dealer to state the age of the car which he was giving in part-exchange. He said that is was a 1948 model, as appeared from the registration book. In fact it was a 1939 model and the dealer suffered loss in that the part-exchange allowance was too high. He sued the buyer for damages.

The Court of Appeal held that the statement made by Mr. Williams was a mere representation and not a contractual warranty. Accordingly, as the law then stood, no damages could be awarded. In the words of Lord Denning M.R.:

[6] [1957] 1 Q.B. 229.
[7] *Ante* p. 27.
[8] [1932] A.C. 562.
[9] [1957] 1 W.L.R. 370.

"If, however, the seller, when he states a fact, makes it clear that he has no knowledge of his own but has got his information elsewhere and is merely passing it on it is not so easy to infer a warranty."

On these particular facts the result of this case might well be same today even after the changes made by section 2 of the Misrepresentation Act 1967 and even after *Hedley Byrne* v. *Heller*.[10]

If the parties are on an equal bargaining footing the courts may again be reluctant to find a contractual promise. Thus in *Howard Marine and Dredging Co. Ltd.* v. *Ogden & Sons (Excavation) Ltd.*[11] the facts of which appear in example 3 at the beginning of this chapter[12] the statement about the barge capacity was held to be non-contractual; in this case, however, the hirers recovered damages under section 2(1) of the Misrepresentation Act.[13]

If, however, we turn to the normal dealer-consumer situation a statement made by the dealer will frequently be classified as a contractual promise because of the dealer's special knowledge. In *Dick Bentley* v. *Harold Smith Ltd.*:[14]

A dealer told a prospective buyer that the engine of a second-hand car had done 20,000 miles. It was later discovered that the engine had done 100,000 miles. The buyer claimed damages.

The Court of Appeal gave judgment for the buyer. Here was a statement about a matter within the special knowledge of the seller. It was a contractual warranty and the seller was liable for breach of it.

In this type of case, therefore, the plaintiff should allege in the alternative (i) a contractual term (ii) a misrepresentation and (iii) a negligent statement.[15] The advantage of (i) is that the consumer will be entitled to damages for *any* breach of the term, even though the maker had reasonable grounds for believing the statement to be true.

---

[10] *Post,* pp. 32–33.
[11] [1978] 2 W.L.R. 515.
[12] *Ante* p. 27.
[13] *Post,* p. 79.
[14] [1965] 1 W.L.R. 623.
[15] *Post,* p. 31.

The various remedies available for misrepresentation will be further considered[16] but before leaving misrepresentation three further points can be made:

(a) It may be necessary to distinguish a representation of *fact* from a mere statement of *opinion*—a problem which can cause particular difficulty on a sale of a painting which is attributed to an old master.

(b) Whether a person relies on the statement is a question of fact. The maker of a statement cannot avoid liability simply by saying "the accuracy of this statement is not guaranteed and the buyer should make his own enquiries." If, in such a case, the buyer *does* rely on the statement he will have the usual remedies for misrepresentation if the statement is incorrect.

(c) The action for damages for misrepresentation is only available where the statement was made by the other party to the contract. Thus it would not be available if, for example, a consumer bought from a retailer in reliance on a statement made by the manufacturer. There may, however, be a claim against the manufacturer if a collateral contract can be established or if he is liable in negligence under the *Hedley Bryne* rule, which is discussed below.

3. Liability in Tort for Careless Statements

The history of the law of tort is one of gradual and cautious development. Although the industrial revolution started in the eighteenth century it was not until 1932 that the modern law of negligence was born. Until then it was widely accepted that where A negligently performed a contract with B and therefore caused loss to C, A was not liable to C. It was not until *Donoghue* v. *Stevenson*[17] that the House of Lords, by a bare majority, came down in favour of a more realistic approach. In that case the House decided that in certain circumstances the manufacturer of a product owed a duty of care to the ultimate consumer. The case is also a landmark because Lord Atkin laid down his famous "neighbour" test as the basis of liability in negligence. He said:

[16] *Post*, p. 77.
[17] [1932] A.C. 562.

"The liability for negligence . . . is no doubt placed upon a general public sentiment of moral wrongdoing for which the offender must pay. But acts or omissions which any moral code would censure cannot in a practical world be treated so as to give a right to every person injured by them to demand relief. In this way rules of law arise which limit the range of complainants and the extent of their remedy. The rule that you are to love your neighbour becomes in law—you must not injure your neighbour; and the lawyers' question; who is my neighbour? receives a restricted reply. You must take reasonable care to avoid acts or omissions which you can reasonably forsee would be likely to injure your neighbour. Who, then, in law, is my neighbour? The answer seems to be—persons who are so closely and directly affected by my act that I ought reasonably to have them in contemplation as being so affected when I am directing my mind to the acts or omissions which are called in question."

Despite *Donoghue* v. *Stevenson* there were still important areas of non-liability. In particular the courts were very reluctant to hold that a careless statement causing economic loss gave rise to legal liability; the plaintiff could not succeed merely by proving that he was a "neighbour" of the defendant within Lord Atkin's test. The reason for this refusal to apply *Donoghue* v. *Stevenson* to statements was their potentially lethal effect. A distinguished American judge referred to the "three indeterminates"—a careless statement might make the maker liable "in an indeterminate amount for an indeterminate time to an indeterminate class."[18] The refusal of the law to provide a remedy was not without its critics. In *Candler* v. *Crane, Christmas*[19] Lord Denning adopted a statement from an earlier case that:

"A country whose administration of justice did not afford redress in a case of the present description would not be in a state of civilization."

It was not until 1964 that the House of Lords altered the law. The case of *Hedley Byrne & Co. Ltd.* v. *Heller and Partners Ltd.*[20]

---

[18] Cardozo J. in *Ultramores Corporation* v. *Touche* (1931) 255 N.Y. Rep. 170, cited in *Candler* v. *Crane Christmas, infra.*
[19] [1951] K.B. 164.
[20] [1964] A.C. 465.

shows a cautious approach and it is difficult to extract one really clear-cut principle from the five speeches. In one sense all the pronouncements in the *Hedley Byrne* case were *obiter* because the actual decision was that the defendants were absolved from liability because of a disclaimer. The facts were as follows:

> The plaintiffs were advertising agents. They placed orders on behalf of E. Ltd. with various newspapers and television. They were personally liable to the sellers of the advertising space and they were anxious to make sure that E. Ltd. were financially sound. The plaintiffs' bankers got in touch with the defendants who were the bankers of E. Ltd. The defendants gave favourable references "without responsibility." The plaintiffs thereupon made the contracts. The references turned out to be unjustified and the plaintiffs lost £17,000 on the contracts. They sued the defendants on the references. The House of Lords gave judgment for the defendants.

Lord Reid pointed out that a duty of care existed if there was a "special relationship"; he considered that this could be proved

> "where it is plain that the party seeking information or advice was trusting the other to exercise such a degree of care as the circumstances required, where it was reasonable for him to do that, and where the other gave the information or advice when he knew or ought to know that the enquirer was relying on him."

It is clear from a careful reading of the speeches that the key factor is an assumption of responsibility. In the words of Lord Morris:

> "My Lords, it seems to me that if A assumes a responsibility to B to tender him deliberate advice, there could be a liability if the advice is negligently given."

The case was decided in favour of the bank because (a) the disclaimer made it clear that no responsibility was being assumed and (b) even without such disclaimer it could well be argued that the only duty expected in this type of case was a duty to be honest.

In all the decided cases since 1964 the defendants supplied information in answer to an enquiry; in some of these cases they were held liable. It has also been held by a majority of the Privy Council that the *Hedley Byrne* principle only applies where the maker of the statement is in the business of giving advice or (perhaps) if he has a financial interest in the transaction.[21] This narrow view has twice been rejected by the Court of Appeal.[22]

---

[21] *Mutual Life and Citizens Assurance Co. Ltd.* v. *Evatt* [1971] A.C. 793.
[22] *Esso Petroleum Ltd.* v. *Mardon* [1976] 2 Q.B. 801; *Howard Marine & Dredging Co. Ltd.* v. *Ogden & Son Ltd.* [1978] Q.B. 574.

What is the relevance of all this to consumer transactions? If
the statement is made by the supplier it may be useful to plead
Hedley Byrne as an alternative to other forms of liability. It is
unlikely, however, to add a great deal to consumers' chances of
success, as the facts will usually disclose a *Bentley* v. *Smith* contractual term[23] or an actionable misrepresentation under section
2(1) of the Misrepresentation Act 1967[24] as well as a *Hedley Byrne*
duty situation. Apart from the inherent uncertainty of establishing
such a duty situation, the plaintiff is on stronger ground under the
Misrepresentation Act because under that Act the burden is on
the defendant to prove that he had reasonable grounds for believing
the statement to be true. There is, however, a possibility that a
Hedley Byrne claim could be pursued where the consumer has
relied on a statement made by the manufacturer (for example in
sales literature or in a leaflet giving instructions for use). There is
no doubt, however, that this would represent a major extension
of the *Hedley Byrne* rule.

4. CONTRACTUAL TERMS

We have already seen that a statement made during negotiations
may sometimes be classified as a contractual term.[25] When will this
occur? The leading case is *Heilbut, Symons & Co.* v. *Buckleton*[26]
where Lord Moulton said:

> "An affirmation at the time of the sale is a warranty, provided it appears on
> evidence to be so intended."

The key word here is the word "intended" and the courts apply
an objective test; they do not look into the minds of the parties
but at their conduct. In the words of Lord Denning M.R.:

> "If an intelligent bystander would reasonably infer that a warranty was
> intended, that will suffice."[26a]

To avoid confusion it must be stressed that the word warranty has
at least two meanings. In the above examples it is used in its
normal sense to mean "a term" or "a contractual promise." There

[23] *Ante,* p. 30.
[24] *Ante,* p. 27 and *post*, p. 79.
[25] *Ante,* p. 28.
[26] [1913] A.C. 30.
[26a] *Dick Bentley* v. *Harold Smith* [1965] 1 W.L.R. 623, 627.

is, however, a second meaning which is used in the Sale of Goods Act 1893. By section 62:

> warranty . . . means an agreement with reference to goods which are the subject of a contract of sale, but collateral to the main purpose of the contract, the breach of which gives rise to a claim to damages, but not to a right to reject the goods and treat the contract as repudiated.

In other words it means a minor term.

If an express statement is classified as a contractual term we have seen that the innocent party can claim damages. Can he also treat the contract as repudiated and reject the goods? The answer is that he may be able to do so, provided that he has been substantially deprived of what he bargained for. Under the Sale of Goods Act 1893 terms are classified as conditions or warranties but it has recently been held by the Court of Appeal that this rigid classification is not exhaustive.[27] The court held that there were intermediate stipulations where the right to reject depended on the consequences of the breach. This decision helps to bring the law of sale of goods more into line with the rest of the law of contract and with the reasonable expectations of the parties.

5. DESCRIPTION

The final possibility is that the statement formed part of the description of the goods. By section 13 of the Sale of Goods Act 1893:

> "(1) Where there is a contract for the sale of goods by description, there is an implied condition that the goods shall correspond with the description; and if the sale be by sample, as well as by description, it is not sufficient that the bulk of the goods corresponds with the sample if the goods do not also correspond with the description.
> (2) A sale of goods shall not be prevented from being a sale by description by reason only that, being exposed for sale or hire, they are selected by the buyer."

The section is largely self-explanatory. Thus if a handbag is described as "leather" there will be a breach of section 13 if it is plastic; if a car is described as a 1976 model there is a breach of section 13 if it is a 1966 model; if the seller agrees to sell "woollen

[27] *Cehave N.V.* v. *Bremer Handelgesellschaft G.m.b.H.* [1976] Q.B. 44.

underpants" he will be in breach if the material is cotton or rayon or linen. In this type of case the section adds nothing to the general law. It is a central obligation of the seller to supply the goods contracted for and he is guilty of non-performance if he fails to do so.
We now have to consider two problems, namely:

    (1) What is a sale by description?
    (2) What stipulations form part of the contract description?

What is a sale by description?

The courts have given a very wide meaning to this term—in the words of the Law Commission "It [is] to all intents and purposes comprehensive." The following examples show how wide it is.

    (a) Sales of purely generic goods, *e.g.* "50 rolls of hand-blocked wallpaper."
    (b) Sales of specific goods which the buyer has not seen where he is relying on the description ("my 1978 wooden skis, ideal for Alpine downhill skiing").
    (c) Sales of specific goods which the buyer has seen if they are sold as goods answering a description ("Canadian salmon").
    (d) Goods selected by the buyer at a self-service store or supermarket. This is the effect of section 13(2) which was added by the Supply of Goods (Implied Terms) Act 1973. Thus if a tin on a supermarket shelf is labelled "Scotch salmon" and it contains Canadian salmon there will be a breach of section 13—so also if a label wrongly states the ingredients or quantity.

The principle that goods can describe themselves was laid down by the courts several years before the passing of the 1973 Act. In *Beale* v. *Taylor*[28]

> The plaintiff saw an advertisement "Herald convertible white 1961." He went to see it and saw a "1200" disc on the rear of the car. He agreed to buy it for £190 in the belief that he was buying a 1961 Triumph Herald model. Unfortunately, he was only half right; the front part consisted of an earlier model which had been welded on to the rear end of a 1961 Herald 1200. He claimed damages from the seller, but the county court judge dismissed the claim. The Court of Appeal allowed his appeal.

The court held that the combined effect of the advertisement and the disc was that the seller was offering to sell a 1961 Herald.

[28] [1967] 1 W.L.R. 1193.

This was, therefore, a sale by description and the seller was in breach of section 13. Damages were agreed at £125 (the price less the scrap value to the buyer).

It is not clear from the judgments whether the buyer would have succeeded on the strength of the disc alone. It is clear, however, that if a seller says to the buyer "I am offering to sell this to you— I am making no representations and you must exercise your own judgment" there would not be a sale by description. It was presumably on this ground that the county court judge had given judgment for the seller.

What statements form part of the description?

Until recently the courts have given an extremely wide meaning to the term "description." The term has been held to include such matters as the quantity, the measurements, the manner of packing and even the date of shipment. The practical result of this can be very serious from the seller's point of view and unduly favourable to the buyer. We have seen that if the goods do not comply with their description there is a breach of "condition"; this means that the buyer can reject the goods, even though he has suffered no loss. In the leading case of *Arcos Ltd.* v. *Ronaasen*;[29]

> Sellers sold a quantity of wooden staves to the buyers. The thickness was given as half an inch. When the goods were delivered the arbitrator found that (i) only 5 per cent were half an inch thick; (ii) a large proportion were between half an inch and five-sixteenths of an inch; (iii) some were between half an inch and five-eighths of an inch; (iv) a very small proportion were more than five-eighths of an inch; (v) the staves were fit for the buyer's purpose and commercially within, and merchantable under, the contract specification. Despite the finding in (v) the buyer claimed that he was entitled to reject them. The High Court, the Court of Appeal and the House of Lords upheld the buyer's claim.

The judgments in the House of Lords are brief but they emphasize the need for strict compliance. In the words of Lord Buckmaster:[30]

> "If the article they have purchased is not in fact the article that has been delivered, they are entitled to reject it, even though it is the commercial equivalent of that which they have bought."

Lord Atkin, in a well-known passage, commented that:

[29] [1933] A.C. 470.
[30] *ibid.* at p. 475.

"If the written contract specifies conditions of weight, measurement and the like, these conditions must be complied with. A ton does not mean about a ton, or a yard about a yard. Still less, when you descend to minute measurements does ½ inch mean about ½ inch. If the seller wants a margin he must and in my experience does stipulate for it."

He did, however, go on to add that:

"No doubt there may be microscopic deviations which businessmen, and therefore lawyers will ignore."

Another well-known illustration of the doctrine of strict compliance is *Re Moore & Co. and Landauer & Co.*[31] which, like the previous case, reached the courts via an arbitrator.

Sellers agreed to sell tinned fruit in boxes containing 30 tins. When delivered some contained only 24 tins. The arbitrator found that there was no difference in the market value of the goods whether they were packed in 24 tins or 30 tins in a case. The Court of Appeal upheld a claim by the buyer that he was entitled to reject the entire consignment.

Such a construction may well be out of line with the reasonable expectations of the parties as commercial men. It may be that Lord Wilberforce had this in mind in a recent House of Lords case when he commented that:

"Some of these cases . . . I find to be excessively technical and due for fresh examination in this House. Even if a strict and technical view must be taken as regards the description of unascertained future goods (*e.g.* commodities) as to which each detail of the description may be assumed to be vital, it may be, and in my opinion is, right to treat other contracts of sale of goods in a similar manner to other contracts generally so as to ask whether a particular item in a description constitutes a substantial ingredient of the "identity" of the thing sold, and only if it does to treat it as a condition."[32]

Special meaning

If words have acquired a special trade meaning there will be no breach of section 13 if they answer that meaning. Thus in the case of *Grenfell* v. *E. B. Meyrowitz Ltd.*[33] it was proved that the words "safety glass" had acquired a special meaning and that this was known to the buyer. It was held that the sellers were not in breach of section 13 when they supplied "safety glass" goggles which corresponded to the special trade meaning.

[31] [1921] 2 K.B. 519.
[32] *Reardon Smith* v. *Hansen-Tangen* [1976] 1 W.L.R. 989, 998.
[33] [1936] 2 All E.R. 1313.

Relationship between description and fitness

A final question which can be important for the consumer relates to the distinction between description and fitness for purpose. If goods are unfit for the buyer's particular purpose can he allege that there is a breach of section 13 or must he rely on the condition of fitness for purpose under section 14 (which is considered in Chapter 4)? This is yet another problem where the law is uncertain; the practical importance lies in the sphere of private sales.

> Suppose that the seller of a house agrees to sell to the buyer his furniture, lawnmower and television set. Both the lawnmower and the television set break down almost immediately and the cocktail cabinet collapses shortly afterwards.

As the law stands at the moment it is very unlikely that the buyer would have a remedy against the seller. Section 14 only applies to a sale "in the course of a business." There is nothing to suggest that any of the goods have been misdescribed. One point which is clear is that unfitness for one particular use does not amount to a breach of section 13. Thus "herring-meal" is still "herring-meal" even if it has defects making it lethal when fed to mink.[34] If, however, the goods have only one use (*e.g.* "touring skis") it might be arguable that fitness for purpose forms an intrinsic part of the description. Perhaps the courts might adapt the words spoken by Birkett L. J. in another context that "a car which will not go is not a car at all."[35]

6. HIRE PURCHASE

Where goods are let out on hire-purchase the condition as to description is identical to that for sale of goods.[36]

---

[34] *Christopher Hill* v. *Ashington Piggeries* [1972] A.C. 441.
[35] *Karsales (Harrow) Ltd.* v. *Wallis* [1956] 1 W.L.R. 936, 942.
[36] Supply of Goods (Implied Terms) Act 1973, s. 9.

CHAPTER 4

"IT DOESN'T WORK"

(1) A buys a dishwasher. It fails to work. The seller calls on numerous occasions to try to put it right. It invariably breaks down again after a few days.

(2) B orders central heating which is installed by X. The radiators leak and damage the carpet.

(3) C takes his suit to the cleaners. It comes back in a ruined condition.

(4) D buys a pair of new patent leather shoes for a party. The soles come away from the uppers almost immediately and D is unable to wear them.

(5) E takes his car to a garage for repair. The garage puts in faulty brake linings and E is injured when the brakes fail.

By far the most common consumer complaint is that the goods or services were not up to the expected standard. How does the law protect the consumer? There are three sets of provisions which may give him rights against the supplier:

   (a) Section 14 of the Sale of Goods Act 1893 (as amended) is vitally important if the contract was a contract of sale.

   (b) Section 10 of the Supply of Goods (Implied Terms) Act 1973 contains virtually identical provisions relating to hire-purchase agreements.

   (c) If the contract is a contract of hire, repair, exchange or work and materials the precise scope of the terms are uncertain but they are probably similar to those which are implied in sale and hire-purchase (see *post*, pp. 54–56).

1. CLASSIFICATION

It may therefore be necessary, as a preliminary matter, to classify the contract. The hire-purchase agreement should create no problems—it is essentially a bailment of goods coupled with an option

40

to purchase them.[1] When we turn to sale and work and materials we have to look at the substance of the contract—is the consumer paying for the finished product or for the skill of the contractor? Consider the following examples:

- (a) A agrees to paint a portrait for B. This is a contract for work and materials.[2]
- (b) C agrees to manufacture a ship's propellor in accordance with a specification supplied by D. This is sale of goods.[3]
- (c) E agrees to make up an expensive fur coat for F and to supply the fur. This is sale of goods.[4]
- (d) G, a dentist, agrees to make a set of false teeth for H. Unfortunately they do not fit properly. Is this a contract of sale of goods or for work and materials? The Court of Appeal found it unnecessary to decide the point because a condition of fitness for purpose would be implied in either case.[5]
- (e) I and J go into a restaurant and order food. It seems that the restaurant makes a contract of sale of goods with both I and J so that either of them will have a claim in contract if, for example, he or she is served with bad food and becomes ill.[6]
- (f) K has work done by a plumber, decorator or garage. In the course of this materials are supplied. The contract is one for work and materials and the terms are governed by the common law.[7]

2. SALE OF GOODS

(1) The general position

If the contract is for the sale of goods the obligations of the seller are governed by s. 14 of the Sale of Goods Act 1893 which is one of the most important provisions of the Act.[8] Unfortunately, the

---

[1] See, e.g. s. 189 of the Consumer Credit Act 1974.
[2] *Robinson* v. *Graves* [1935] 1 K.B. 579.
[3] *Cammell Laird & Co. Ltd.* v. *Manganeze Bronze and Brass Co. Ltd.* [1934] A.C. 402.
[4] *Marcel (Furriers)* v. *Tapper* [1953] 1 W.L.R. 49.
[5] *Samuels* v. *Davis* [1943] K.B. 526.
[6] *Lockett* v. *A. M. Charles Ltd.* [1938] 4 All E.R. 170.
[7] *Stewart* v. *Reavells Garage* [1952] 2 Q.B. 545.
[8] See Law Commission Report No. 24, p. 9.

Act was drafted before the consumer explosion of the present century and the language of the Act (*e.g.* "merchantable quality") is more appropriate to a contract between two businessmen than to a contract between a businessman and a consumer. This point will come out even more strongly when we examine the question of remedies.[9] We shall see that the two remedies which the consumer most wants—a right to have the defective goods repaired or replaced by the seller—are not provided for by the Act. Section 14 was amended by the Supply of Goods (Implied Terms) Act 1973 which gave effect to a number of recommendations made by the Law Commission. In this chapter the sections are reproduced in their amended form.

(2) **Let the buyer beware**

In the light of what has been said above, the early law developed on the basis that it was for the parties to make their own bargain— it was up to the buyer to decide whether the goods were merchantable and fit before he agreed to buy them. This principle (*"caveat emptor"* or "let the buyer beware") has been severely eroded but is not entirely extinct. By section 14(1):

> Except as provided by this section . . . there is no implied condition or warranty as to the quality or fitness for any particular purpose of goods supplied under a contract of sale.

We shall see that the Act protects the consumer if the seller sells in the course of a business. If, however, the seller is a private seller the principle of *caveat emptor* may still apply.

> Suppose that A, a private individual, sell his hedgecutter to B. It is in poor condition and breaks down after a few days. In the absence of any express promise or representation B has no claim against A.

The distinction then is between a sale "in the course of a business" and a sale which is not in the course of a business. There is one hybrid situation; what about a dealer who sells in the course of a business as agent for a private seller? Section 14(5) makes it clear that the seller must endeavour to bring this fact to the buyer's notice. It provides that:

> [The conditions of quality and fitness] apply to a sale by a person who in the course of business is acting as agent for another as they apply to a sale by a

---

[9] *Post*, p. 83.

principal in the course of a business except where that other is not selling in the course of a business and either the buyer knows that fact or reasonable steps are taken to bring it to the notice of the buyer before the contract is made.

Presumably the seller should instruct the dealer to inform prospective buyers of his private status; the dealer might then have to indemnify the seller against liability arising through failure to perform this duty.

Section 14(5) is concerned with the case where a private seller appears to be selling in the course of a business. What about the converse case—trade sellers masquerading as private sellers. An enquiry under Part II of the Fair Trading Act 1973 disclosed that some motor traders were guilty of this practice—they advertised their cars for sale in newspapers and gave only their private addresses. Such practices are now a criminal offence (Business Advertisements (Disclosure) Order 1977 *post*, p. 225).

(3) **Privity of contract**

The conditions of merchantable quality and fitness are implied *as between seller and buyer*. If, for example, a lady buys an unmerchantable washing machine and gives it to her daughter as a present the daughter has no claim against the supplier if it breaks down. The mother would have a claim but she might find it difficult to prove damage flowing from the breach (although she might have a claim if she paid for the cost of repairs).[10] The question of "who made the contract?" has already been touched on in connection with meals in a restaurant[11] and questions of agency must also be borne in mind in this connection. A woman who does the shopping may do so as agent for her husband or cohabitee, so that *he* would have a claim in contract if the goods turn out to be defective. There is no agency case (so far) the other way round. Thus if a man buys typhoid-infected milk which he gives to his wife it was held in *Frost* v. *Aylesbury Dairy Co.*[12] that the husband alone has a claim in contract. In modern social conditions it might well be possible for the courts to hold that the husband was buying for himself and as agent for his wife. An argument on these lines

---

[10] But see *Jackson* v. *Horizon Holidays* [1975] 1 W.L.R. 1468, *post*, p. 206, for a novel approach to damages.
[11] *Ante,* p. 41.
[12] [1905] 1 K.B. 608.

should certainly be tried in appropriate cases; if it was accepted it could loosen the shackles of the privity rule.

(4) Strict liability

The practical importance of the point just mentioned lies in the concept of strict liability. Section 14(2) says "are of merchantable quality." It is clear from the case of *Frost* v. *Aylesbury Dairy Co.* (*supra*) that the absence of negligence is no defence. If, however, the privity rules bar a claim in contract an injured plaintiff will have to bring proceedings in tort and this will usually mean having to prove negligence—by no means an easy task.[13]

(5) Merchantable quality

The implied condition of merchantable quality should be of great importance to the consumer. Unfortunately, it is beset with difficulties. In its amended form section 14(2) reads as follows:

> Where the seller sells goods in the course of a business, there is an implied condition that the goods supplied under the contract are of merchantable quality, except that there is no such condition—
> (a) as regards defects specifically drawn to the buyer's attention before the contract is made; or
> (b) if the buyer examines the goods before the contract is made, as regards defects which that examination ought to reveal.

In advising a consumer a number of points must be considered. In particular:

    (a) Was the sale in the course of a business?
    (b) What is the meaning of "goods supplied"?
    (c) Are the goods unmerchantable?
    (d) Do either of the exceptions apply?

    (a) **Are the goods supplied "in the course of a business?"** In the vast majority of cases this should present no problems. A consumer buying from a shop, warehouse or mail order firm will have no difficulty in clearing this hurdle. The mere fact that the seller is handling a particular product for the first time is immaterial, and it is not necessary that he should be a dealer in that particular class of goods. The example given by the Law Commission was a coal merchant selling off one of his lorries; presumably a sale of a cash register by a shopkeeper or surplus office furniture by a

---

[13] *Post*, p. 70 *et seq.*

solicitor would fall within the same category. There can, of course, be borderline cases. What about goods sold at a charity or tennis club bazaar or jumble sale? It could be argued that such a "one-off" activity was not a business sale. Again, if a dentist or an accountant sells his private car, the mere fact that he sometimes used it for business would not, it is believed, make it a sale "in the course of a business." The Act itself merely provides that the term "trade" includes a profession and the activities of a local authority, government department or statutory undertaker. The concept of "business" is also central to the Unfair Contract Terms 1977[14] and to the Consumer Credit Act 1974[15] and both of these Acts merely give a limited definition similar to the one referred to above.

(b) **What is the meaning of "goods supplied?"** The courts have given a sensible answer to this question by giving the words their normal meaning. Thus the condition of merchantable quality can apply not only to the *contents* of a bottle or tin but also to the bottle or tin itself, even if it has to be returned—it is still "supplied" under the contract.[16] Similarly, if the goods actually supplied contain a foreign body (for example, a worm, a snail, a piece of glass or a detonator) the totality of the goods actually supplied may be unmerchantable.[17]

(c) **When are goods unmerchantable?** This is the gut question and in practice it is often extremely hard to answer. The 1893 Act contained no definition and the dicta in a number of cases were not always easy to reconcile. Eventually in 1973 a statutory definition was inserted but this has yet to be fully worked out. In advising the consumer three particular problems stand out, namely:

(i) What standard is required for second-hand goods?
(ii) If a new article is delivered with minor defects does that make it unmerchantable?
(iii) For how long must the goods remain merchantable?

In practice the seller may be willing to deal with the matter for reasons of commercial goodwill but if he refuses to do so the buyer may face an uphill task—and a potentially expensive one. No

[14] *Post,* p. 105.
[15] *Post,* pp. 245 and 255.
[16] *Geddling* v. *Marsh* [1920] 1 K.B. 668.
[17] See the well-known case of *Wilson* v. *Rickett Cockerell & Co. Ltd.* [1958] 1 Q.B. 598 where a detonator was mistakenly included in a bag of coalite.

doubt this helps to explain the popularity of manufacturers' guarantees.

Section 62(1A) of the 1893 Act, as amended, provides that

> Goods of any kind are of merchantable quality . . . if they are as fit for the purpose or purposes for which goods of that kind are commonly bought as it is reasonable to expect having regard to any descriptions applied to them, the price (if relevant) and all the other relevant circumstances.

It is clear from this definition that if the goods are unfit for their only proper use they will not be merchantable. If a thermos flask breaks when it is filled, if a jigsaw piece is missing, if a wallpaper cannot be stuck to the wall, the seller is liable. In the words of Lord Ellenborough in an early case[18]

> "The purchaser cannot be expected to buy the goods to lay them on the dunghill."

Again in the well-known "sulphite in the pants" case of *Grant* v. *Australian Knitting Mills Ltd.*[19] Lord Wright commented that

> "it [merchantable quality] does mean that the article sold, if only meant for one particular use, is fit for that use"[20]

Four other points arising from the statutory definition call for comment. In the first place the definition appears to be a functional one, but presumably the aesthetic aspect will also be taken into account. A dishwasher is delivered with chipped enamel; it cleans the dishes perfectly well; is it "unmerchantable?" A car is delivered with a damaged front wing and bumper; a pair of leather shoes look shoddy even though they are perfectly wearable. It is felt that in all such cases the buyer should be entitled to return the goods or to claim damages for any loss caused. Secondly, the definition uses the word "are." This confirms the ruling in *Jackson* v. *Rotax Motor Co. Ltd.*[21] that if goods are unmerchantable the mere fact that they can be made merchantable by a simple process is immaterial. Thirdly, the reference to price supports what Lord Reid said in *Brown & Son Ltd* v. *Craiks*[22], namely that if a particular description covers different qualities of goods, a buyer who pays a price appropriate to a *superior* quality can reasonably

---

[18] *Gardiner* v. *Gray* (1815) 4 Camp 144.
[19] [1936] A.C. 85.
[20] *Ibid* at p. 100.
[21] [1910] 2 K.B. 937.
[22] [1910] 1 W.L.R. 752.

expect to receive that quality, and can regard the goods as unmerchantable if he receives an inferior quality. Fourthly, what about goods bought at a "sale" at reduced prices? It can be strongly argued that this does not affect the seller's obligation. The reduction of price is a commercial decision to dispose of surplus stock and should not be allowed to justify the supply of inferior products.

Second hand goods. There have been three fairly recent cases dealing with "merchantability" of second-hand cars. The first was *Bartlett* v. *Sidney Marcus*[23] where the following facts arose:

> The plaintiff bought a second-hand Jaguar car for £950. It was pointed out that the clutch was in need of repair, but the defect was believed to be a small one. After driving for 300 miles the plaintiff took the car to a garage who found that the defect was more serious than the plaintiff had expected. The cost of repairs came to £84 and the plaintiff claimed this amount from the seller.

The county court judge gave judgment for the buyer but the Court of Appeal allowed the seller's appeal. On the question of merchantability Lord Denning M.R. pointed out that:

> "on the sale of a second-hand car, it is merchantable if it is in usable condition, even if not perfect. . . .A buyer should realise that when he buys a second-hand car defects may appear sooner or later and, in the absence of an express warranty, he has no redress."

In *Crowther* v. *Shannon Motor Co.*[24] which was also concerned with a second-hand Jaguar, the buyer was more successful.

> The car was eight years old; the engine had done 82,165 miles; the buyer paid a price of £390. He drove the car for another 2,300 miles in three weeks. Then the engine expired. The evidence showed that (a) this engine was in a "clapped out" state when the car was sold to the buyer; (b) the buyer of a Jaguar car could reasonably expect the engine to do 100,000 miles. On these facts the Court of Appeal held that the seller was liable.

In the third case the buyer scored a somewhat Pyrrhic victory. The case was *Lee* v. *York Coach and Marine*[25] and the facts were as follows:

> Mrs Lee bought a second-hand Morris 1100 for £355. Almost immediately it developed defects and it was off the road for a considerable time while the sellers sought unsuccessfully to remedy the defects. After seven weeks her

[23] [1965] 1 W.L.R. 1013.
[24] [1975] 1 W.L.R. 30.
[25] [1977] Road Traffic Report 35.

solicitors wrote to the sellers saying "we must ask you please to remedy all these defects without delay or to refund £355 to Mrs Lee." The sellers then offered to do some further work on the car; a Department of Environment examiner found very serious defects, and two weeks later a further letter was written by the solicitors. "Mrs Lee would have been justified in rescinding the contract on that basis—that is on the basis that the car was unroadworthy— in our opinion she may still be entitled to do so." Four months later the buyer brought an action claiming the return of the price. The evidence showed (inter alia) that the brakes were so poor that they could not have survived an attempt to test them.

The Court of Appeal held that the car, being unsafe to be driven, was clearly unmerchantable. They also held, however, that neither of the solicitors' letters amounted to a rejection of the car. By the time that the buyer finally sought to reject (the start of the proceedings) it was too late to reject.[26] Accordingly, she was only entitled to damages and the figure of £100 was not disputed. Presumably Mrs Lee would have seen very little of the £100 since the court made no order for costs in the Court of Appeal.

New goods with minor defects. The definition uses the words "as fit . . . as it is reasonable to expect." How do these words apply to a new car with teething troubles?

A learned writer has commented on the surprising lack of authority on this problem.[27] In view of the publicity given to defects in new cars it is astonishing that there is so little clear authority on the "merchantability" of a new car with "teething troubles."

If the defect is a very serious one (e.g. a broken back axle) it will almost certainly make the car unmerchantable[28] and a similar result is likely where there are numerous defects which combine to make the car unroadworthy and unsafe.[29] The really difficult question relates to defects which are not in themselves very serious and which do not make the car unroadworthy. What happens if the car has starting trouble or if the heater fails to function, or if the brakes squeal, or if there is a slight oil leak. Two views are possible:

(i) The buyer is entitled to expect that a new car is more than merely roadworthy but comes up to the standard of comfort, finish,

[26] See *post,* p. 85.
[27] See M. Whincup in [1975] 38 M.L.R. 660.
[28] See *Charterhouse Credit* v. *Tolley* [1963] 2 Q.B. 683.
[29] See *Yeoman Credit Ltd.* v. *Apps* [1962] 2 Q.B. 508; *Farnworth Finance Facilities* v. *Attryde* [1970] 1 W.L.R. 1053.

performance and troublefree motoring which a buyer paying that price could reasonably expect.

(ii) Every buyer must be taken to know that new cars have "teething troubles." In other words all that he can reasonably expect is a car which functions as well (or as badly) as any car of that model usually does, together with a "guarantee" covering defects arising soon after purchase.

Both views have their difficulties. On the one hand it could be unreasonable if the buyer was held entitled to return the car (which may have depreciated heavily) and to demand the return of his price for very minor breaches.[30] On the other hand a decision that the car was "merchantable" would mean that the buyer would have no remedy at all even though the car was off the road for a considerable time with resulting expense and inconvenience. What the buyer really wants is to have the defects put right, to be compensated for inconvenience, and to reject or claim a price reduction if the defects persist. In one unreported case[31] there were *dicta* to the effect that minor defects, while no doubt very irritating, were not grounds for rejecting the car. The case however was decided in favour of the buyer on another point and so the question of minor defects is still an open one.

It may well be that the attitude of the courts would depend on the remedy sought. If the buyer sought rejection and return of price for very minor defects the courts might be reluctant to allow this.[32] On the other hand the courts might well be much more favourably inclined to uphold a claim for damages, either by holding that the car was unmerchantable (having regard to such matters as the price) or by implying some lesser term. It is true that section 14(1) precludes any additional implied condition or warranty as to quality or fitness, but we have seen that the classification of condition—warranty is not exhaustive.[33] Thus, there is nothing to prevent the courts from finding that the facts of the

[30] See the Scottish case of *Millars of Falkirk Ltd.* v. *Turpie* [1977] Journal of Business Law 165 and *Leaves* v *Washam Stringer (Clifton)* "The Daily Telegraph" 19 October, 1979.

[31] *Spencer* v *Claude Rye (Vehicles) Ltd.* The Guardian, December 19, 1972, cited in Mr. Whincup's article, *supra*. See also an article by Mr. Robin Young in *The Times*, July 11, 1978.

[32] See the unusual commercial case of *Cehave* v. *Bremer* [1976] Q.B. 44.

[33] *Cehave* v. *Bremer, ante*, p. 35.

case gave rise to an express or implied "intermediate stipulation" giving rise to a claim for damages or, if the consequences of breach were very serious, a right to reject. Such a development would be in line with the judicial willingness to imply terms in other areas of law (*e.g.* contracts of employment) and it would bring the contract more into line with the reasonable expectations of the parties. The whole matter is at present under investigation by the Law Commission.

Merchantability—acts to be done before use. If both parties contemplate that some act will be done to the goods before use they must be merchantable *after* this has been done but not necessarily before. Thus in *Heil* v. *Hedges*[34] the buyer of pork chops failed to cook them properly and became ill as the result of the chops becoming infected by worms. Had she cooked them properly the infection would not have occurred. Her claim for damages failed. On the other hand in the underpants case[35] the pants were sold for immediate use. Therefore the fact that the sulphite might have been removed by washing was held to be irrelevant.

Merchantability—for how long? It is clear from commercial cases involving the sale of rabbits and potatoes that if defects appear soon after purchase this may show that the goods were unmerchantable at the time of the contract.[36] What does that mean in the consumer context? A vacuum cleaner breaks down after one month, a freezer after two months, a carpet starts to wear away after three months and an expensive camera breaks down after six months. The consumer *may* be able to show that the goods were not merchantable right at the beginning but it will not be easy. If the seller wishes to resist a claim he will point out that all sorts of things could have caused the breakdown and that it is up to the buyer to produce evidence linking the breakdown to the condition of the goods when he bought them. The buyer will argue, "I used the goods in the normal way—a freezer should not break down after only two months." This argument *should* be successful[37] but

---

[34] [1951] 1 T.L.R. 512.
[35] *Grant* v *Australian Knitting Mills* [1936] A.C. 85.
[36] See *Beer* v. *Walker* (1877) 46 L.J.Q.B. 677; *Mash & Murrell* v. *Joseph I. Emmanuel Ltd.* [1961] 1 All E.R. 485.

the seller may well fight the claim—especially if the buyer is asking for his money back.

(d) "**Do either of the exceptions apply?** The first exception applies where defects are specifically drawn to the buyer's attention before the contract is made. This could apply if, for example a defective clutch or a dent or scratch or other defect was pointed out to the buyer—perhaps with an abatement in price. There could of course be room for argument—the buyer might say "the seller told me that the clutch was rather worn but I had no idea I would have to spend £150 on it a week after buying the car."

The second exception relates to examination where the buyer has examined the goods *before* the making of the contract. The condition does not apply as regards defects which that examination ought to reveal. Two points can be made with regard to this exception. First, it only applies to a buyer who has *actually* examined the goods—not to a buyer who has declined an opportunity to do so. Secondly, what is the meaning of "defects which that examination ought to reveal?" This wording, which formed part of the 1973 redraft, differs slightly from the original wording "defects which such examination ought to have revealed." In either case the words appear to refer solely to the examination actually made. If, for example, the buyer of a handbag only examines the outside, he will still be able to complain if on arriving home he finds that the inside has numerous defects including a broken zip (but he could not claim for an external defect which he should have seen, *e.g.* a broken handle). There is a Court of Appeal case which appears to confirm this view.[38] However, in *Thornett & Fehr* v. *Beer & Sons*[39] Bray J. at first instance appeared to treat the words "such examination" as if they read "a reasonable examination." He held that (a) the buyers had examined the goods; (b) an examination would "in the ordinary way" have revealed the defect; (c) accordingly, the condition was not implied.

It is possible that this decision is wrong on the wording of the Act and it appears to be inconsistent with the *Bristol Tramways* case (which was not cited). It can also be argued that if the case

[37] See Law Commission Report No. 95, pp. 32–3.
[38] *Bristol Tramways* v. *Fiat Motors* [1910] 2 K.B. 831.
[39] [1919] 1 K.B. 486.

was wrong on the original wording of the Act, it may well be even more incorrect on the amended wording. Thus, the courts may well refuse to follow it.

(6) Fitness

Section 14 of the Sale of Goods Act implies a condition of reasonable fitness as well as the condition of merchantable quality which has just been considered. In its amended form section 14(3) reads as follows

> Where the seller sells goods in the course of a business and the buyer, expressly or by implication, makes known to the seller . . . any particular purpose for which the goods are being bought, there is an implied condition that the goods supplied under the contract are reasonably fit for that purpose, whether or not that is a purpose for which such goods are commonly supplied, except where the circumstances show that the buyer does not rely, or that it is unreasonable for him to rely on the skill or judgment of the seller.

What is the relationship between the two conditions? It can be argued that in the case of "single purpose" goods section 14(3) is completely unnecessary because the concept of "fitness" is built into the definition of merchantable quality.[40] Thus, if a catapult or a drill breaks when it is first used, or if a hot water bottle bursts, it is neither "merchantable" nor "fit." In the previous discussion on new and second-hand cars no distinction has been drawn between the two conditions because the test to be applied is basically the same. It should also be mentioned that a number of rules are common to both subsections. Thus (a) in both cases liability is strict,[41] (b) in both cases the seller is only liable if he supplied the goods in the course of a "business", (c) both conditions apply to all goods "supplied" under the contract, (d) in both cases the condition only applies as between seller and buyer and (e) in both cases the seller may be relieved from liability if the buyer failed to do something to the goods before use.[41a]

What then is the need for section 14(3)? The key is to be found in the words "any particular purpose . . . whether or not that is a purpose for which such goods are commonly supplied."

> Suppose that a law student goes to a bookseller and says "I want to buy some books which are suitable for the solicitors examinations". The seller supplies books which are only suitable for the Bar or University examinations.

[40] *Ante*, p. 46.
[41] *Ante*, p. 44.
[41a] See, *ante*, p. 50.

On these facts the seller would clearly be liable under section 14(3); there might well be no breach of section 14(2).

The sub-section applies where the purpose is made known ρxpressly or by implication. In the case of single purpose goods such as weedkiller, a bun or a hot water bottle, the buyer does not have to go through the ritual of spelling out his purpose—this will be implied.[42] In this type of case the courts would not give much weight to a clause in a standard form contract (even if signed by the buyer) stating that "the buyer has not made known the purpose for which the goods are required." This type of clause was used in the hire-purchase case of *Lowe* v. *Lombank*[43] a case involving a car with numerous defects. The Court of Appeal found no difficulty in holding that the supplier (the finance company) was liable under the implied condition of fitness. The purpose was obvious and the clause was inconsistent with the facts. If, however, the purpose is a special one (for example a textbook suitable for a particular course) then the seller will be liable only if that purpose was *expressly* made known. In *Griffiths* v. *Peter Conway Ltd.*[44]

> a lady bought a Harris tweed coat. She had an abnormally sensitive skin and contracted dermatitis from wearing the coat. The evidence showed that the coat would not have caused problems apart from this one special fact. It was held that as this fact had not been disclosed to the seller he was not liable.

The condition of fitness is not implied if the seller can prove that the buyer did not rely on the seller's skill or judgment. Thus, suppose that John, an amateur jeweller, goes to a general hardware store and asks for glue suitable for jewellery-making. The seller might say "I have no idea whether this brand is suitable—you must decide for yourself and not rely on me." In such a case he might escape liability under section 14(3) (and perhaps also under section 14(2) since the circumstances surrounding the purchase would be one of the "circumstances" in section 62(1A)). The buyer's reliance on the seller's skill or judgment may well be partial. If the goods turn out to be unfit for the buyer's particular purpose the seller will be liable unless he can prove that the defect fell outside the area of reliance.[45-46]

---

[42] See *Priest* v. *Last* [1903] 2 K.B. 148—the well-known case of a bursting hot water bottle.
[43] [1960] 1 W.L.R. 196.
[44] [1939] 1 All E.R. 685.
[45-46] *Christopher Hill Ltd.* v. *Ashington Piggeries Ltd.* [1971] 2 A.C. 441.

3. HIRE-PURCHASE

The implied terms as to fitness and quality are virtually the same
as in sale of goods.[47] The only difference arises from the fact that
the consumer will usually conduct the negotiations with a dealer
who then sells the goods to a finance company. It is the finance
company which makes the "hire purchase agreement" but for the
purpose of the implied condition of fitness[48] it is sufficient if the
consumer makes his purpose known to the "person by whom
antecedent negotiations are conducted," *i.e.* the dealer.[49]

4. WORK AND MATERIALS

We have seen earlier in this chapter that certain contracts may be
classified as contracts for "work and materials" rather than "sale
of goods." Contracts to repair a house or car, or to insulate a loft,
or to clean a suit are obvious examples. In the words of Stable J
in a case where a hairdresser applied a hairdye to the head of a
customer:

> [It] is really half the rendering of services and, in a sense, half the supply of
> goods.[50]

The law applies different standards to the two halves of the contractual obligation. On the first half (*i.e.* the provision of work)
there is an implied duty to take reasonable care; on the second
half (*i.e.* the provision of materials) there is strict liability. Thus
we have already seen that in *Samuels* v. *Davis*[51] the defendant was
liable when the denture which he had made did not fit the mouth
of the plaintiff's wife. The Court of Appeal found it unnecessary
to decide whether it was sale of goods or work and materials. The
important point is that the dentist was liable even though the
county court judge had found that he was not negligent. The court

---

[47] See Supply of Goods (Implied Terms) Act 1973, s. 10 as redrafted in Schedule
4 to the Consumer Credit Act 1974.
[48] s. 10(3).
[49] See *post*, chap. 21.
[50] *Watson* v. *Buckley Osborne & Co.* [1940] 1 All E.R. 174, 179.
[51] [1943] K.B. 526 *ante* p. 41.

approved the reasoning in the earlier Divisional Court case of *GH Myers & Co* v. *Brent Cross Service Co.*[52] In that case:

> The plaintiff asked the defendants to "knock-in" the engine of his car and to renew any parts which required replacement. In the course of the work the defendants bought six connecting rods and fitted them. Owing to a latent defect one of the rods broke and damage of nearly £70 was caused. When the plaintiff claimed damages the defendant argued that he was not liable because the defect could not have been discovered by the exercise of reasonable care and skill. The defence was rejected.

The Divisional Court made it clear that if the consumer relied on the repairers' skill and judgment then liability was strict. In the words of du Parcq J:

> I think that the true view is that a person contracting to do work and supply materials warrants that the materials which he uses will be of good quality and reasonably fit for the purpose for which he is using them, unless the circumstances of the contract are such as to exclude any such warranty. There may be circumstances which would clearly exclude it. A man goes to a repairer and says "repair my car; get the parts from the makers and fit them." In such a case it is made plain that the person ordering the repairs is not relying upon any warranty, except that the parts used will be parts ordered and obtained from the makers. On the other hand if he says "do the work—fit any necessary parts" he is in no way limiting the person doing the repair work, and the person doing the repair work is in my view liable if there is any defect in the materials supplied, even if it was one which reasonable care would not have discovered.

Thus, for example, the repairer will be liable where the defect was due to the faulty work of a sub-contractor—unless this was a person selected by the customer.[53]

5. HIRE

The precise scope of the implied fitness of goods supplied under a contract of hire is uncertain. In all the reported cases the owner was acting in the course of a business, but no case expressly refers to this point as an essential ingredient of liability. Then there is the question—how strict is the term relating to fitness? Is the absence of negligence a defence? An examination of the cases

[52] [1934] 1 K.B. 46.
[53] *Stewart* v. *Reavell's Garage* [1952] 2 Q.B. 545.

reveals some conflicting dicta,[54] but there appears to be no actual
decision where a plaintiff has failed because the defect was a latent
one. There is much to be said for the Law Commission's view that
the fitness obligation undertaken by suppliers should be identical
in sale of goods, hire-purchase, hire, work and materials and other
contracts (for example, exchange). Only the first two have been
assimilated by legislation but a recent law Commission Report
entitled "Implied Terms in Contracts for the Supply of Goods"
contains a draft bill which sets out in statutory form the obligations
of suppliers of goods under contracts of hire and contracts analogous to sale.[55]

[54] See Law Commission Working Paper No. 71, pp. 27–36 where all the cases are
reviewed.
[55] Law Com. No. 95.

CHAPTER 5

"DO I HAVE TO PAY?"

IF the supplier is guilty of a misrepresentation or a serious breach
of contract the consumer may be able to rescind the contract or
treat it as repudiated. In either case this will relieve him of his
obligation to pay the price. Some examples of this were examined
in Chapters 2–4 and the matter will be considered again in Chapter
7. This chapter is concerned with a group of four unrelated but
important topics on which the consumer may seek legal advice.
The topics are:
  1. Delivery of unordered goods
  2. Loss or damage after contract but before delivery.
  3. Late performance.
  4. A dispute about the price.

1. I NEVER ORDERED THESE GOODS

An aggressive salesman may try to boost his sales by delivering
goods which the customer has never ordered, followed by an
invoice demanding payment. He clearly hopes that the consumer
will be induced, by a combination of ignorance, lethargy and fear,
to pay the price. Some years ago there was a considerable outcry
at these and similar practices, and there was a growing demand
for legislation to curtail them. Eventually a Bill was introduced
into Parliament and this passed into law as the Unsolicited Goods
and Services Act 1971.

Before considering this Act it may be useful to dispose of one
problem which has arisen under the general law: is the consumer
legally liable if the goods are lost or damaged while they are in his
possession? Under the tort of negligence the plaintiff must prove
that the defendant owed him a legal duty of care.[1] A person
receiving unordered goods is known as an "involuntary bailee"
and he does not owe a duty of care. Therefore he will generally

---

[1] *Bourhill* v. *Young* [1943] A.C. 92.

not be liable for accidental loss or damage.[2] On the other hand he may be liable for the tort of conversion if he deliberately destroys the goods or converts them to his own use. Where is the line to be drawn? Thus, if a tradesman delivers an unordered ten volume encyclopaedia the consumer might well be liable if he puts them outside his house and allows them to disintegrate. A learned writer has suggested that the consumer might be entitled to destroy the goods in an emergency.[3]

The Act of 1971

The sanctions provided by this Act are both civil and criminal. The civil sanction is that, as between himself and the sender, the recipient can:

> use, deal with or dispose of [the goods] as if they were an unconditional gift to him, and any right of the sender to the goods shall be extinguished.[4]

The recipient will have these rights if the following conditions are satisfied:

(1) the goods were sent to him without any prior request made by him or on his behalf[5];

(2) they were delivered or sent to him with a view to his acquiring them;

(3) he had no reasonable cause to believe that they were sent with a view to their being acquired for the purposes of a trade or business;

(4) the consumer has neither agreed to acquire the goods nor agreed to return them;

(5)(a) during the period of six months beginning with the date of receipt the sender did not take possession and the recipient did not unreasonably refuse to permit him to do so; or

(b) the recipient served a notice in writing on the sender, stating that the goods were unsolicited and giving the address where they could be collected, and during a period of thirty days from the giving of the notice the sender did not take possession and the recipient did not unreasonably refuse to permit him to do so.

Thus if the recipient serves a notice on April 2 saying, "I never ordered these goods—take them away" and if the sender ignores the notice the goods will become the property of the recipient on May 3.

The criminal sanction is provided in section 2 which is confined to persons acting in the course of a trade or business. The section

---

[2] See *Howard* v. *Harris* (1884) C & E 253.
[3] Winfield and Jolowitz on Tort (10th ed.), p. 415.
[4] s. 1(1).
[5] See s. 6 of the 1971 Act.

deals with a trader who makes a demand for payment for goods where (a) the goods are unsolicited goods and (b) he has no reasonable cause to believe that there is a right to payment. An offence is also committed where a person, in such a case, (i) asserts a right to payment, or (ii) threatens to bring legal proceedings or (iii) places, or threatens to place, the name of any person on a defaulters' list or (iv) invokes, or threatens to invoke, any other collection procedure.

2. WHEN I OPENED THE BOX THE PLATES WERE BROKEN

We have already seen that where goods are supplied in the course of a business, they must be of merchantable quality. What happens if they were clearly merchantable at the time of the contract but are accidentally damaged or destroyed at a later date? The basic rules in the Sale of Goods Act 1893 are straightforward but their application in practice is far from easy.

The basic rule as to risk

Section 20 of the Act provides as follows:

> Unless otherwise agreed, the goods remain at the seller's risk until the property therein is transferred to the buyer, but when the property therein is transferred to the buyer, the goods are at the buyer's risk whether delivery has been made or not.

So the key question for the consumer is—had the property passed to him when the loss or damage occurred? If the answer is yes then (unless otherwise agreed) the risk will also have passed to him and he must bear the loss; this means that, for example, he will remain liable to pay the contract price. Most consumers would be very surprised to learn that the property (*i.e.* ownership) had passed to them before delivery, but in many cases this will in fact be so.

When does property pass?

The rules as to the passing of property are to be found in sections 16–18 of the Act. The essential distinction is between specific and unascertained goods and it will be convenient to deal with these matters first.

(a) **Specific goods.** These are defined by section 62 as goods identified and agreed upon at the time of the contract. The obvious example is goods selected by the buyer in a shop, showroom or store.

(b) **Unascertained goods.** This term is not defined in the Act but it is clear that the terms "specific" and "unascertained" are mutually exclusive. Thus, goods are "unascertained" if they are purely generic, as where a buyer gives an order of "10 tons of coal." Goods are also unascertained if they form part of a larger consignment which is specified in the contract, as where a buyer agrees to buy "ten bottles of wine from the case in the seller's warehouse."

Passing of property—specific goods

The basic rule of section 17 is that property passes when the parties intend it to pass. There is nothing in the Sale of Goods Act to prevent an agreement that "no property in the goods shall pass until the buyer has paid the price." Such a clause, or an extension of it,[6] is sometimes inserted into commercial contracts and this can give rise to many legal, financial and accounting problems.[7]

Then again if the price is payable by instalments there may be a clause that ownership shall remain with the seller until the final instalment has been paid. Such an agreement is known as a "conditional sale agreement."[8] Apart from these cases, it is unusual to have a passing of property clause in a consumer sale agreement and we must therefore examine the first four rules of section 18. These rules govern the passing of property in specific goods where no contrary intention appears. The courts have held that a "contrary intention" will only oust the statutory rules if present at the time of the contract.[9] The four rules can be summarised as follows:

(i) In the usual case of an unconditional contract for the sale of specific goods in a deliverable state, the property passes to the buyer when the contract is made (**rule 1**). Thus, if he goes to a store, selects a suite of furniture, and agrees to have it delivered

---

[6] *e.g.* "the property in the goods shall remain in the seller until all sums due from the buyer to the seller under this or any other contract shall have been paid.".
[7] The leading case is *Aluminium Industrie Vaasen BV* v. *Romalpa Aluminium Ltd.* [1976] 1 W.L.R. 676.
[8] *Post,* p. 241.
[9] *Dennant* v. *Skinner* [1948] K.B. 164.

in a week's time, the property and risk will pass to the buyer as soon as the contract has been made. If, therefore, the contents of the showroom are destroyed by fire, or damaged by vandals, at any time after the contract the buyer must bear the loss and must pay the agreed price for the lost or damaged goods. In other words, the insurable risk was on him as from the making of the contract. It has, however, been suggested that the courts will be very ready to infer an intention (ousting the statutory rule) that property is not to pass until delivery or payment.[10] A well-advised consumer of a domestic appliance should try to insert a clause that the risk shall not pass to the buyer until the goods have been installed in his home; in the case of a car he should try to agree that the risk should remain with the seller until delivery.

(ii) If a contract for the sale of specific goods requires the seller to do something to put the goods into a deliverable state, the effect of **rule 2** is that no property passes to the buyer until the seller has done this and the buyer has notice thereof. If we turn to section 62 we will find that goods are in a deliverable state when they are in such a state that the buyer would under the contract be bound to take them. Thus if the seller agreed to enlarge a watchstrap or ring, or to instal a heater in a car, the risk would remain on the seller until the buyer has received notice that this work has been done.

It will be observed that the Act uses the clear and positive words "the buyer has notice thereof." Thus, if the seller sends off a letter saying that the work has been done this would not, of itself, pass the property and risk.

(iii) In the rather less common case where the seller has to do some act to ascertain the price (for example, weighing or measuring the goods) the effect of **rule 3** is that property does not pass to the buyer until the seller has done this and the buyer has notice thereof.

(iv) If the buyer agrees to take goods on approval or on sale or return (for example, some bottles of beer for a party) the effect of **rule 4** is that the property will pass to the buyer (a) if he intimates acceptance or otherwise adopts the transaction, or (b) if he retains the goods beyond the stipulated time, or, if no time has been stipulated, beyond a reasonable time, without intimating rejection.

[10] *Per* Diplock L.J. in *R. V. Ward Ltd.* v. *Bignall* [1967] 1 Q.B. 534, 545.

An extreme example of the risk rules can be seen from the early case of *Elphick* v. *Barnes*[11] where a horse, which was delivered on sale or return, died during the approval period without the buyer's fault. It was held that the buyer was not bound to pay the price.

It should be added that all these rules as to risk pre-suppose that the loss or damage was purely accidental. This principle is underlined by the two provisos to section 20 which read as follows:

> Provided that where delivery has been delayed through the fault of either buyer or seller the goods are at the risk of the party in fault as regards any loss which might not have occurred but for such fault.
>
> Provided also that nothing in this section shall affect the duties and liabilities of either seller or buyer as a bailee of the goods for the other party.

A bailment would arise if, for example, the seller of goods agreed to store them for the buyer. If the goods were lost or damaged the onus would be on the seller (as bailee) to disprove negligence.[12]

Passing of property—unascertained goods

If a buyer agrees to buy "ten rolls of wallpaper" or "twenty square metres of carpet," this would be a contract for the sale of unascertained goods. Bearing in mind the basic rule that risk passes with property[13] we must start with section 16 which provides that:

> Where there is a contract for the sale of unascertained goods no property in the goods is transferred to the buyer unless and until the goods are ascertained.

Thus, if in the above example, the manufacturer of carpet sends a large roll to the seller, no property can pass to the buyer until a piece measuring twenty square metres has been cut and set aside for the buyer's contract.

We can now turn to section 18, rule 5, which applies where no contrary intention appears. It reads as follows:

> (1) Where there is a contract for the sale of unascertained or future goods by description, and goods of that description and in a deliverable state are unconditionally appropriated to the contract, either by the seller with the assent of the buyer, or by the buyer with the assent of the seller, the property in the goods thereupon passes to the buyer. Such assent may be express or implied and may be given either before or after the appropriation is made.
>
> (2) Where, in pursuance of the contract, the seller delivers the goods to the buyer or to a carrier or other bailee . . . for the purpose of transmission to

[11] (1880) 5 CPD 321.
[12] See, *e.g. Houghland* v. *Low (Luxury Coaches) Ltd.* [1962] 1 Q.B. 694.
[13] *Ante*, p. 59.

the buyer, and does not reserve the right of disposal, he is deemed to have unconditionally appropriated the goods to the contract.

Two points call for comment. First, rule 5(2) refers to delivery of "the goods" to the carrier. Thus, if the seller merely delivers a larger consignment (of which the buyer's goods form an unascertained part) section 16[14] will apply. The result is that the property and risk remain with the seller; if therefore they are lost or damaged before becoming ascertained the buyer can reject them.[15] Secondly, there is the question of consent. If the buyer orders goods by post, does he automatically consent in advance to the seller's appropriation? If this is so then the risk will be on the buyer before he ever sees the goods—a clearly unreasonable result since he will usually not be in a position to insure them. Even here, however, the buyer is not entirely without a remedy. He might, for example, be able to prove that the seller has failed to make a reasonable contract of carriage.[16] In such a case the buyer can refuse delivery or he can claim damages from the seller—even if the loss or damage was not causally connected with the seller's default. Secondly, the buyer may have rights under section 14(2)[17] if the condition of the goods at the time of delivery suggests that they were not merchantable at the time of the contract.[18]

The question of when property and risk pass where a consumer orders goods from a mail order house has never been expressly decided. In one case a commercial buyer ordered goods from a Swiss seller and it was held by the House of Lords that property passed to the buyer as soon as the goods were posted by the seller.[19] This case, if applied to the consumer mail order purchase, would produce a result which is out of line with the reasonable expectation of most consumers[20] and, as already stated, it can be most unfair to the consumer.[21] The *Badische Anilin* case was not a risk case at all and it turned on a point of patent law. The courts

---

[14] *Ante*, p. 62.
[15] *Healy* v. *Howlett* [1917] 1 K.B. 337.
[16] s. 32(2).
[17] *Ante*, p. 50.
[18] See, *e.g.* the pre-Act case of *Beer* v. *Walker* (1877) 46 L.J.Q.B. 677—rabbits go putrid on the Brighton train—condition of merchantable quality broken.
[19] See *Badische Anilin und Soda Fabrik* v. *Basle Chemical Works* [1898] A.C. 200.
[20] See *Which?*, May 1978, p. 316.
[21] *Supra*.

could always side-step this decision by finding an implied "contrary
intention" which would oust section 18 altogether.

Effect of risk rules

The Act, the cases and the textbooks are remarkably silent on
the precise operation of the risk rules in the case of damage. A
distinction can be drawn between (a) total destruction, and
(b) damage.

(a) **Total destruction** If the goods are totally destroyed either
physically or commercially, they can be said to "perish." In advising
the consumer in a case where the goods have perished after the
making of the contract we must again distinguish between specific
and unascertained goods.

    (i) If specific goods perish, without the fault of either party,
after contract but before the risk has passed to the buyer,
the contract is avoided.[22] Thus, if in the example cited
above,[23] the jeweller's entire stock is destroyed by an accidental fire before he has given notice that the enlarged ring
is ready, the provisions of section 7 will apply. Further, the
perishing of specific goods is not a case to which the Law
Reform (Frustrated Contract) Act 1943 applies. Accordingly, since the contract is avoided by section 7, the buyer
will not have to pay the price; if he has paid it or some of
it, he can recover it because the consideration has failed; he
cannot claim damages for non-delivery; the unfortunate
seller cannot sue for the price, nor can he claim any payment
for work done by him on the goods before the fire broke
out.

    (ii) When we turn to unascertained goods we must draw yet
another distinction. In the case of purely generic goods (*e.g.*
"twenty square metres of Wilton carpet") no question of
perishing can arise. If the goods which the seller intends to
supply cease to be available the seller must find the goods
from another source or pay damages for non-delivery unless
he has covered himself by an effective exemption clause.[24]
If, however, the source of the goods is specified in the
contract (*e.g.* "ten bottles of wine from the crate in my

---

[22] s. 7.
[23] *Ante*, p. 61.
[24] *Post*, p. 95.

warehouse") the destruction of the source after contract but before the risk has passed to the buyer will frustrate the contract. The position of the parties is similar to that under section 7[25] except that the Act of 1943 will regulate the rights of the parties so that adjustments for expenses incurred, and benefits received, are possible.

(b) **Damage.** What happens if goods are accidentally damaged while they are still at the seller's risk? This problem could arise if, *e.g.*, the furniture ordered by the buyer is damaged when the delivery van is involved in a road accident for which the seller is not responsible. Presumably the buyer can refuse to accept the damaged goods and then bring an action for non-delivery. The precise nature and the precise legal basis of the buyer's rights does not appear to have been analysed in any reported case; perhaps it is based on an implied undertaking by the seller that the quality of the goods delivered will correspond precisely with the quality of the goods when the buyer agreed to take them.[26]

3. LATE PERFORMANCE

Late performance, whether by sellers, electricians, builders, plumbers, carriers or holiday operators, is a frequent source of complaint by consumers. The legal principles governing this topic can be summarised as follows:

(1) If the contract specifies a date for performance a supplier who fails to perform by that date will be liable for damages for breach of contract (unless this liability has been effectively excluded[27] or unless the contract is frustrated). This claim for damages can be pleaded by way of set-off or counter-claim in an action by the supplier for the price.[28]

(2) If the contract does not specify a date for performance the supplier must perform within a "reasonable" time. The question of reasonableness is a question of fact; even a long delay will not necessarily amount to a breach of contract if it was due to circum-

---

[25] *Ante.*

[26] For a somewhat similar principle in a slightly different context see *Financings Ltd.* v. *Stimson* [1962] 1 W.L.R. 1184 C.A.—damage to car between hirer's initial inspection and delivery under contract.

[27] See, Chap. 8 *post*, p. 95.

[28] For the assessment of damages, see *post*, p. 90.

stances beyond the supplier's control. In one case a car owner took his car to a garage for repair following an accident. A normally competent repairer would have taken five weeks; the garage gave priority to other work and took eight weeks. It was held by the Court of Appeal that they had failed to carry out the work within a reasonable time and were therefore liable in damages.[29]

(3) Can the consumer go further and claim to be discharged from the contract altogether? This depends on whether time is "of the essence" *i.e.* a vital term or, in sale of goods language, a condition. The following statement in Halsbury's Laws of England has recently received judicial approval:

> Time will not be considered to be of the essence unless (1) the parties expressly stipulate that conditions as to time must be strictly complied with, or (2) the nature of the subject-matter of the contract or the surrounding circumstances show that time should be considered to be of the essence.[30]

It is probably true to say that under a contract to supply goods or services to a consumer a failure to observe the agreed performance date is not of itself a repudiation of the contract. There can, of course, be difficult cases; what about an operator who agrees to provide his client with a fifteen-day holiday in Majorca starting on August 1, but is prevented from carrying out that obligation by reason of industrial action for which he is not responsible? It could be argued that if he is unable to transport his clients on August 1, he will have broken an essential term of the contract which enables the clients to treat the contract as discharged; alternatively, it might be argued that the contract has been frustrated.[30a]

(4) If a reasonable time has elapsed, or if the breach of an essential time clause has been waived, the consumer can serve a notice fixing a time for performance. The time limit in this notice must itself be a reasonable one, but subject to this the consumer can treat the contract as discharged if the supplier fails to perform by the date specified in the notice.[31]

Thus the consumer should always make it clear, in appropriate cases, that the date for performance is vital.

---

[29] *Charnock* v. *Liverpool Corporation and Another* [1968] 1 W.L.R. 1498.

[30] Halsbury's Laws (4th ed.) para. 481, approved by Lord Salmon in *Universal Scientific Holdings Ltd.* v. *Burnley Council* [1977] 2 W.L.R. 806 H.L.

[30a] In practice the contract will usually deal with the matter under the Code of Practice discussed in Chap. 9, *post*, p. 138.

[31] *Charles Rickards Ltd.* v. *Oppenheim* [1950] 1 K.B. 616 CA.

4. THE PRICE SEEMS RATHER HIGH

In the case of sale of goods it is fairly rare to find an agreement without a price; indeed the absence of a price may indicate that the parties are still negotiating and that consequently there is no contract at all.[32] Section 8 of the 1893 Act, which is more appropriate to a commercial contract, provides that the price can be fixed by the contract itself, or in manner thereby agreed, or by usage. It then goes on to provide that if the price is not fixed in this way the buyer must pay a reasonable price.

In the case of services, it is rather more common to call in a repairer, or to take a suit to the cleaners, or a car for a service without agreeing a price in advance. In such a case the supplier is entitled to be paid a "reasonable price." This, of course, is much easier said than done. If a consumer feels that the price is too high the onus will be on him to find expert evidence to substantiate his claim, and he will also be put to great practical inconvenience if the supplier has the goods in his possession and refuses to release them until he has been paid. The consumer should also be very careful to limit his potential liability. Instead of saying "the car is starting badly—put it right" he should say "tell me if the work is going to cost more than £50."

Incidentally, what about an "estimate?" If an estimate amounts to an offer which is accepted the estimate will become the contract price.[33] This, however, is rather unusual and the general rule is that the estimate is not legally binding; if however the estimate is a long way short of the final bill, the court might take the estimate into account in fixing a "reasonable price."

Can a supplier of services claim an additional amount if additional work is required? This again depends on what the parties have agreed. If, for example, a builder is employed to convert a loft the onus will be on him to ensure that the work will comply with the local bye-laws and building regulations. If it turns out that the local authority require extra work to be done (for example, fireproofing) he will generally be unable to recover any additional payment for this extra work from the owner—he should have checked on the point before fixing his price.

---

[32] *May and Butcher* v. *R.* [1934] 2 K.B. 17.
[33] *Crowshaw* v. *Pritchard* (1899) 16 T.L.R. 45.

CHAPTER 6

"I SUPPOSE THAT THE MANUFACTURER WILL PUT IT RIGHT"

THE present state of English product liability law is widely misunderstood. Millions of people are induced to buy goods by extensive and expensive advertising and promotion conducted by the manufacturer. They believe, reasonably enough, that the manufacturer will be responsible if things go wrong—if, for example, the chairs fall to pieces or the curtains shrink. In many cases this is not so—the prime responsibility for merchantable quality and fitness is on the seller.[1] It must also be said that a number of retailers do nothing to dispel this basic misunderstanding. If the defective article is brought back to them they may say to the consumer "yes, it's faulty but you must send it back to the manufacturer under guarantee." Perhaps in due course (after reading this book!) more consumers will reply "under the Sale of Goods Act it is your responsibility." The liability of the manufacturer, as the law now stands, is twofold:

(1) he may be liable under his own "guarantee."

(2) he may be liable in negligence if the goods are not merely "unmerchantable" but "defective" and cause personal injury or damage to property.

These two areas of liability will now be examined. The whole question of product liability is an area of law which has been much discussed in the past few years (in the United Kingdom the motivating force was the thalidomide tragedy). Recommendations for reform have been made by the Law Commissions for England and Scotland, the Pearson Commission, the Council of Europe and the EEC. It should perhaps be emphasised that none of the proposals affect the basic rule outlined above—unmerchantability is a matter for the seller rather than the manufacturer. The main thrust of reform is confined to "defective" goods; the central proposal is that liability should cease to be based on negligence and should be strict.

[1] See, *ante*, Chap. 4.

68

1. Manufacturers' Guarantees

A guarantee is familiar to millions of consumers and it has become an integral part of the purchase of durable goods. The manufacturer usually agrees to replace defective parts within a specified time (for example, 12 months). The attraction of this for the consumer may be cut down by further clauses requiring the consumer to pay the cost of carriage and sometimes even the cost of labour. Subject to this, a guarantee can have very real commercial advantages for both parties. For the manufacturer it helps to promote his product and the card which the customer signs and returns may be valuable for the purposes of market research. For the customer, the guarantee may be a valuable way of sidestepping the hazards of litigation, especially as the remedy which he *really* wants—repair or replacement—is not available against the retailer.[2]

There have been very few cases on guarantees and their precise legal status is uncertain. As a matter of strict legal analysis the problem is one of offer, acceptance and consideration. Is there a contract if the consumer is unaware that the guarantee exists when he buys the goods? What is the consideration to support the manufacturer's promise? In practical terms, it is highly unlikely that these matters will ever be litigated; it is difficult to imagine a manufacturer giving a guarantee and then refusing to honour it. The legal points might one day be taken by a liquidator of the guarantee-giving manufacturer. If the points ever did come to court it is likely that the courts would uphold the guarantee as a collateral contract, the consideration being the customer's purchase of the goods from the retailer. The onus will be on the buyer to prove that he knew of the guarantee when he bought the goods; in practice it should not be too difficult for him to prove this, especially as the guarantee often forms part of the advertising and promotional material

The legal liability of the manufacturer can also be established in another way. The consumer is sometimes asked to complete and return a card containing market research questions, *e.g.* "how did you learn of this product?" or "what persuaded you to buy it?" or "did you compare this unit with other models?" The act of the

[2] *Post,* p. 83.

consumer in completing and returning the card may itself be consideration to support the manufacturer's promise.

The value of the guarantee to the consumer depends on its terms. The most generous ones provide that:

> If owing to a defect in workmanship or material your appliance breaks down within 6 (or 12) months of purchase we will repair or replace it free of charge.

We have seen, however, that the consumer may sometimes be required to pay the cost of transporting the goods; occasionally he even has to pay the cost of labour which can render the guarantee virtually useless. There is also the possibility that the manufacturer may say "there is nothing wrong with this appliance—you have mishandled it." (A similar argument is sometimes advanced by a seller when a buyer complains that the goods are unmerchantable). In such a case the consumer might have to negotiate for an independent examination of the goods, with the manufacturer paying the whole or part of the cost. The provisions of the various Codes of Practice (*e.g.* for electrical goods) should also be borne in mind.

2. LIABILITY FOR NEGLIGENCE

Formerly some guarantees contained clauses excluding the manufacturer's liability in negligence, but such clauses are now void in many cases.[2a] Apart from guarantees a manufacturer is not liable to the ultimate consumer merely because the goods turn out to be of poor quality. This is so even though the quality of the goods as delivered falls a long way short of the quality as advertised. The authors are not aware of any attempt to argue that an advertisement, with its representations as to quality, is itself actionable as a collateral contract on the same basis as a guarantee. Such an argument would clearly involve an extension of the existing law as laid down in the leading case of *Carlill* v. *Carbolic Ball Co. Ltd.*[3] but in the present judicial climate it is by no means impossible.

If, however, the goods are not merely unmerchantable but defective and actually cause damage to person or property other

---

[2a] *Post*, p. 114.
[3] [1893] 1 Q.B. 256. Consider also *Shanklin Pier Ltd.* v. *Detel Products Ltd.* [1951] 2 K.B. 854.

considerations will arise. The starting point must be the "narrow rule" in *Donoghue* v. *Stevenson*.[4] The principle of law was stated by Lord Atkin in the following well-known passage:

> A manufacturer of products, which he sells in such a form as to show that he intends them to reach the ultimate consumer in the form in which they left him with no reasonable possibility of intermediate examination, and with the knowledge that the absence of reasonable care in the preparation or putting up of the products will result in an injury to the consumer's life or property, owes a duty to the consumer to take reasonable care."

Lord Atkin added that this was a self-evident proposition which no-one who was not a lawyer would for one moment doubt.

The duty outlined above is merely one particular type of "duty situation" in the context of the general law of negligence. The cases decided since 1932 show a gradual extension of liability. Thus:

(1) There is no limit to the type of goods covered by the rule. Examples include hair-dye, underpants, cars, lifts and even a tombstone.

(2) Liability has been extended beyond manufacturers to cover, for example, repairers and assemblers. In one case even a car dealer was held liable.[5]

(3) The word "consumer" is not confined to the ultimate buyer; it means anyone likely to be injured by the lack of reasonable care. Perhaps the best illustration is provided by *Stennett* v. *Hancock and Peters*[6] where part of the wheel of a lorry came off and struck a pedestrian on the pavement. She recovered damages from the second defendant who had negligently repaired the wheel shortly before the accident.

(4) The "possibility of an intermediate examination" will only defeat the claim if there was a real likelihood of the type of examination which would (or should) reveal the defect. Thus in *Evans* v. *Triplex Safety Glass Co.*[7] the buyer of a Vauxhall car was injured when the windscreen shattered. His action against the manufacturers of the windscreen failed for various reasons; one reason was the likelihood of an intermediate examination by Vauxhall before it was fitted into the car; another reason was a failure

[4] [1932] A.C. 562.
[5] *Andrews* v. *Hopkinson* [1957] 1 Q.B. 229
[6] [1939] 2 All E.R. 568.
[7] [1936] 1 All E.R. 283.

D

to prove that the windscreen was defective when it left the manufacturer. This case can be contrasted with the sale of goods case of *Wren* v. *Holt*[8] where beer containing arsenic was sold by a publican to a customer. The case was fought on section 14(2) of the Sale of Goods Act[9] and the publican was liable even though the customer had examined the beer before drinking it; the defect was not discoverable by any normal examination. Presumably the same reasoning would have applied if the buyer had sued the brewer, *i.e.* the manufacturer would have been liable if negligence could have been proved.

Proof of negligence and causation

As the law stands at present the task facing the injured consumer is not an easy one. He must prove (a) that the product was defective when it left the manufacturer (b) that this was due to negligence and (c) that this was the cause of his injury. Items (a) and (c) will continue to pose major problems even if a system of strict liability is introduced. If the article is completely destroyed in the accident the plaintiff's task may well be insuperable unless the court is prepared to make a generous use of circumstantial evidence.

Was the product defective?

In many cases this should present no problem; a bun containing a stone, a loaf of bread containing a cigarette butt, a car with faulty brakes—these are obvious examples. There may, however, be other cases which are less obvious. Thus in *Evans* v. *Triplex Safety Glass Co*, the facts of which have already been given[10] the plaintiff failed to prove that the windscreen was defective when it left the manufacturer.

The question of when goods are "defective" has never been authoritatively decided by the English courts. The Law Commission in the Report on Liability for Defective Products, use the term to mean "unsafe."[11] It must be appreciated, however, that this is a relative concept; after all, as Miller and Lovell point out,

[8] [1903] 1 K.B. 610.
[9] *Ante,* p. 44.
[10] *Ante,* p. 71.
[11] Cmnd. 6831, para 47.

"it is difficult to think of a product which is totally incapable of causing harm when it is misused."[12]

In the examples previously given (for example, arsenic in the beer) the defective beer was out of line with the general run of goods produced by the manufacturers. Alternatively, it may be possible to argue that there is a fault in manufacture or design affecting all goods of a particular type. The cost of such a finding could be potentially astronomic for the manufacturer and for intermediate suppliers; they could be faced with a very large number of claims when the decision became known, or they might have to call in all the defective goods for repair. In view of this the courts (both here and in the United States) have been cautious to base a negligence finding on this ground. There have however been cases in which the injured party has been successful.[13]

Has the manufacturer been negligent?

This question and the previous one are closely linked. Thus in *Vacwell Engineering Co. Ltd.* v. *B.D.H. Chemicals Ltd.*[14] the defendants, who manufactured a chemical, were liable in negligence for failing to appreciate, and to warn prospective users, that contact with water could lead to an explosion. Similarly, in *Wright* v. *Dunlop Rubber Co. Ltd. and ICI,*[15] the Court of Appeal held that ICI were liable in negligence for continuing to market a product with knowledge that it constituted a serious health hazard. Finally in *Fisher* v. *Harrods Ltd.,*[16] Mrs Fisher recovered damages from Harrods when they sold an untested bottle of cleaning fluid to her husband. She suffered personal injury when it came into contact with her eyes.

The duty owed by the manufacturer is not an absolute one—it is merely a duty to take reasonable care. This is particularly relevant where a manufacturer of (say) a car buys brake linings or sparking plugs which prove to be defective and cause injury to the ultimate consumer. A case from another branch of the law of negligence (employer's liability) is highly relevant here. In *Davie* v. *New*

---

[12] Miller and Lovell, *Product Liability*, p. 187.
[13] *Ibid*, pp. 208–228.
[14] [1971] 1 Q.B. 88.
[15] [1972] Knights Industrial Reports 255.
[16] [1966] Lloyds L.R. 500.

Merton Board Mills[17] an employer supplied his employee with a tool which he (the employer) had bought from a reputable supplier. The tool had a latent defect which the employer had no means of discovering. The employee was injured when the tool broke and he sued the employer for damages for negligence. The House of Lords dismissed the claim on the ground that the employer had not been negligent. In the employment field the principle underlying this case has been reversed by statute[18] but in the product liability field the principle still stands. If the manufacturer has an adequate inspection system and an adequate system for checking faults this may well be sufficient.

As already stated, the onus of proving negligence is on the injured party and it can be immensely difficult, especially in the case of a highly complex piece of equipment or a chemical or drug. Evidence of previous accidents caused by the same product is highly relevant and should be sought. Sometimes the facts themselves point to negligence; if a consumer loses a tooth through eating a bun containing a stone this suggests that the manufacturer has been negligent and, under the doctrine of *res ipsa loquitur*, the manufacturer will have to adduce evidence from which the inference of negligence can be rebutted *Moore* v. *R. Fox & Son.*[19] He may say "the defect was in a component and I myself took all reasonable care" or even "I have no idea how the acid got into the lemonade bottle but I had a foolproof system of inspection." (This latter argument was successfully raised in *Daniels* v. *White Ltd. and Tarbard*[20] but this decision has been criticized and is unlikely to be followed.[21]

When studying all the vast number of reported cases on negligence (perhaps far too many are reported) one point must never be forgotten; whether a defendant has performed his duty of care is a pure question of fact and a decision on this point is not a binding precedent for any future case.[22]

---

[17] [1959] A.C. 604.
[18] Employers' Liability (Defective Equipment) Act 1969.
[19] [1956] 1 Q.B. 896.
[20] [1938] 4 All E.R. 258.
[21] For a recent case where the court refused to follow the *Daniels* decision see *Hill* v. *James Crowe* (Cases) *Ltd* [1978] 1 All E.R. 812.
[22] *Qualcast (Wolverhampton) Ltd* v. *Haynes* [1959] A.C. 743 HL.

Did the defendant's negligence cause the plaintiff's injury?

The injured plaintiff must be able to prove a causal link between the defect, the negligence and his injury. This again can be a difficult matter in practice and the result of the case may turn on the inferences which the court is willing to draw from the facts. In the leading case of *Grant* v. *Australian Knitting Mills*[22a] where the plaintiff, a doctor, contracted dermatitis, the Privy Council accepted his argument that it was caused by an excess of sulphite in underpants manufactured by the defendants. The court reached this decision even though the evidence showed that more than 4 million of these pants had been sold without complaint. On the other hand, the plaintiff will fail if the injury would have occurred in any event. Thus, to borrow again from employment law, an employer is generally not liable for failing to provide safety equipment if he can show that the employee would not have worn it.[23] Similarly, a manufacturer of a car will not be liable for faulty brakes if the plaintiff was driving so fast the accident would have occurred even if the brakes had been in perfect working order.

For what damage can the plaintiff recover?

Two points are clear. First, the plaintiff can recover damages where the defective product causes personal injury or damage to other property (as where furniture is damaged by a boiler explosion or where a defective deep freeze causes food to go bad). Secondly, the plaintiff cannot recover damages for pure economic loss. Thus a restaurant owner cannot sue the manufacturer of a defective oven for loss of profit as a result of not being able to serve hot meals.[24] The one unsettled point is whether "damage to property" includes damage to the defective chattel itself. The Law Commission Working Paper No. 64 para 20 stated that:

> Although the law on the point cannot be stated with absolute certainty it seems probable that in England and Wales an action will not lie in tort in respect of a defective product unless the defect is likely to cause injury to the person or damage to *other* property.

Although there is no actual decision where damages have been recovered for damage to the product itself, it may be that such

---

[22a] *Ante* p. 46.
[23] *Qualcast (Wolverhampton) Ltd.* v. *Haynes* [1959] A.C. 743; *McWilliams* v. *Arrol* [1962] 1 W.L.R. 295 HL.
[24] *SCM (United Kingdom) Ltd.* v. *Whittal* [1971] 1 Q.B. 137.

a claim will be allowed where in the words of the Law Commission, "the defect is likely to cause injury." The Law Commission Working Paper referred to above was published in 1975; since then the House of Lords and the Court of Appeal have held builders liable in negligence even though the only damage was to the house itself.[25] In both these cases the court held where the defect was likely to affect the safety and health of the occupiers it was something more than mere economic loss and it was something for which the builders were liable. On this reasoning if the buyer of a car can prove that the defective brakes were caused by the manufacturer's negligence he should be able to sue the manufacturer for the cost of repair (*i.e.* the cost of averting a potential danger).[26]

Proposals for reform

As already stated The Law Commission, The Royal Commission, the EEC and the Council of Europe have all proposed a system of strict liability to replace the present negligence system. The Law Commission, however, would limit this change to cases involving death or personal injury.

---

[25] *Anns* v. *Merton LBC* [1978] A.C. 728; *Batty* v. *Metropolitan Property Realisations Ltd,* [1978] Q.B. 554.
[26] The general question of economic loss is discussed in an article in Law Society's Gazette [1978] 1297.

CHAPTER 7

WHAT ARE MY REMEDIES?

IN the previous five Chapters we have considered some of the
supplier's basic obligations. We now come to the subject of remedies which, as stated in the preface, is what this book is all about;
it is also the area in which the consumer is most likely to seek
legal advice. In practice three questions are likely to arise, namely
(a) what are the consumer's remedies (b) can they be excluded,
and (c) how can they be enforced? These topics are considered in
this chapter and the two following ones.

One preliminary point can be made. This Chapter and the next
one are concerned with questions of strict law. In Chapter 9 we
shall see that in many cases consumers may be able to sidestep the
worry, uncertainty and expense of litigation as a result of voluntary
codes of practice drawn up by a number of trade associations with
the encouragement of the Office of Fair Trading. We shall also
see that a complaint to a trading standards inspector can lead to
a prosecution in certain cases and that this, in turn, can lead to a
compensation order.[1]

This chapter is divided into three parts, namely:
1. Remedies for misrepresentation
2. Remedies for breach of contract
3. Remedies in tort.

1. REMEDIES FOR MISREPRESENTATION

The remedies for misrepresentation can be summarised as follows:
  (1) Fraudulent misrepresentation;
    (a) damages in tort for deceit;
    (b) rescission.
  (2) Negligent misrepresentation;
    (a) damages under section 2(1) of the Misrepresentation Act
       1967;

---

[1] *Post,* p. 155 & p. 203.

(b) rescission (or damages in lieu under section 2(2) of the 1967 Act).

(3) "Innocent" misrepresentation (*i.e.* neither fraudulent nor negligent);

rescission (or damages in lieu under section 2(2) of the 1967 Act).

These matters will now be considered.

(1) Fraudulent misrepresentation

A person commits the tort of deceit (or fraud) if he makes a false statement of fact knowingly, or without belief in its truth, or recklessly (*i.e.* careless whether true or false) with the intention that it should be acted upon by the plaintiff who does act on it and thereby suffers damage.[2] In practice, fraud is notoriously hard to prove. If, however, the consumer can prove that, for example, the dealer deliberately misrepresented the age or mileage of a car then, as we have seen, he may have the remedies of damages and/or rescission.[2a] If he rescinds the contract he can claim to be put back into his pre-contractual position, so that, for example, he can recover any part of the price which he has paid. The action for damages can be considered (a) if the innocent party does not wish to rescind or (b) if it is too late to rescind[3] or (c) if he has suffered damage over and above the price.

What, then, is the measure of damages for fraudulent misrepresentation? Basically the rules are designed to provide compensation for all loss flowing directly from the fraud, whether reasonably foreseeable or not. Thus, in a sale of goods or land the starting point is the difference (if any) between the price paid by the consumer and the true value of the goods or land.[4] Money spent on repair and improvement before discovering the fraud can also be recovered[5] but not, it seems, damages for loss of bargain. Damages for personal injury or damage to property can also be recovered.[6]

---

[2] See the leading case of *Derry* v. *Peek* (1889), 14 App. Cas. 337 HL.
[2a] *Ante*, p. 77.
[3] See *post*, p. 79.
[4] *Doyle* v. *Olby (Ironmongers) Ltd.* [1969] 2 Q.B. 158—a case of the sale of business.
[5] *Ibid.*
[6] *Langridge* v. *Levy* (1838) 4 M & W 337—exploding gun.

Negligent misrepresentation

Until the passing of the Misrepresentation Act 1967 the court had no general power to award damages for a non-fraudulent misrepresentation—hence the importance of proving that there had been a breach of a contractual term.[7] A Law Reform Committee recommended a change in the law and accordingly section 2(1) of the 1967 Act was passed to give a statutory right to damages in certain cases. It reads:

> Where a person has entered into a contract after a misrepresentation has been made to him by another party thereto and as a result thereof he has suffered loss then if the person making the representation would be liable to damages in respect thereof had the representation been made fraudulently, that person shall be so liable notwithstanding that the misrepresentation was not made fraudulently, unless he proves that he had reasonable grounds to believe and did believe up to the time that the contract was made that the facts represented were true.

It now seems clear from the recent case of *Howard Marine & Dredging Co. Ltd.* v. *A. Ogden & Son (Excavation) Ltd.*[8] that a section 2(1) claim is a claim in tort, although the measure of damages are not necessarily as severe as in deceit. We have seen that the object of damages in tort is to put the innocent party in the same position *as if the contract had never been made.* This can be contrasted with a different rule in contract where the damages are designed to put the innocent party in the same position *as if the contract had been performed.* Thus damages for loss of bargain are appropriate to contract but not to tort; the case of *Watts* v. *Spence*[9] where damages for loss of bargain were awarded under section 2(1) of the 1967 Act, may well be wrongly decided.

Rescission

We can now turn to the equitable remedy of rescission. This has already been mentioned[10] and it only remains to consider the cases where it is not available. There are four well-established bars to rescission and these can be summarised as follows:

    (a) where the parties can no longer be restored to their previous position. Thus the right of rescission would disappear if

[7] *Ante,* p. 29.
[8] [1978] Q.B. 574.
[9] [1976] Ch. 165.
[10] *Ante,* p. 78.

goods were destroyed before the buyer had elected to
rescind;

(b) where third party rights have been acquired. Perhaps the
clearest example is where B, by misrepresentation, persuades
S to sell the goods to B and then resells the goods to C[11];

(c) where the innocent party has affirmed the contract with
knowledge of the misrepresentation[12];

(d) where the innocent party has been guilty of unreasonable
delay. In the well-known case of *Leaf* v. *International Galleries*,[13] the buyer of a painting which was described as by
J. Constable, sought to rescind for misrepresentation five
years after the making of the contract on discovering that
it was the work of another artist. The Court of Appeal held
that it was far too late to rescind. In the words of Jenkins
L.J.

> "If he is allowed to wait five, ten or twenty years and then re-open the
> bargain, there can be no finality at all."

If the buyer had claimed damages under section 13 of the
Sale of Goods Act[14] the claim would presumably have been
unanswerable.

Statutory restriction on rescission

If none of these four bars apply, the general rule is that the
innocent party can rescind the contract. The exercise of this remedy
can have far-reaching results.

> Suppose that P buys a house from V for £20,000. V made a misrepresentation
> relating to the drains; the defect will cost £200 to put right. V has spent the
> whole of the £20,000 in buying another house.

If P were to rescind V would have to find £20,000 (and might
well be rendered homeless) because of a statement which caused
damage of £200. It was clearly with this kind of case in mind that
section 2(2) of the Misrepresentation Act was enacted. It provides
that:

[11] See s. 23 of the Sale of Goods Act 1893, *ante,* p. 16.
[12] *Long* v. *Lloyd* [1958] 2 All E.R. 402.
[13] [1950] 2 K.B. 86.
[14] *Ante,* p. 35.

where a person has entered into a contract after a misrepresentation has been made to him otherwise than fraudulently, and he would be entitled, by reason of the misrepresentation, to rescind the contract, then, if it is claimed in any proceedings arising out of the contract, that the contract ought to be or has been rescinded, the court or arbitrator may declare the contract subsisting and award damages in lieu of rescission, if of opinion that it would be equitable to do so, having regard to the nature of the misrepresentation and the loss that would be caused by it if the contract was upheld, as well as to the loss that rescission would cause to the other party.

Thus, in the above example, the court might refuse rescission and award P damages of £200.

This power to award discretionary damages only applies where a person "would be entitled . . . to rescind the contract." It would seem that the operative time is the time of the hearing. If by that date the right to rescind has already been lost[14a] the innocent party would not be "entitled" to rescind, and accordingly the right to discretionary damages would also be lost.

"Innocent" misrepresentation

If the misrepresentation is neither fraudulent nor negligent the only possible remedy is rescission. This is subject to the usual equitable bars[14b] and the court's discretionary powers under section 2(2) to award damages in lieu of rescission.

Exclusion clauses

A clause excluding liability for misrepresentation or cutting down the consumer's remedies for misrepresentation is only valid if it satisfies the test of "reasonableness."[15]

Misrepresentation and breach of contract

It is clear from section 1 of the Misrepresentation Act that the innocent party will have remedies for misrepresentation even thought the representation has become a term of contract. The precise relationship between the two sets of remedies has yet to be worked out but presumably they are complementary. There is also an interesting problem relating to exemption clauses; if a contract contains a wide exemption clause covering breaches of

[14a] *Ante*, p. 79.
[14b] Ante, p. 79.
[15] *Post,* p. 115.

contract, can the innocent party sidestep the clause by bringing a claim based on misrepresentation? The answer appears to be yes.

2. REMEDIES FOR BREACH OF CONTRACT

This topic will be considered under four main headings, namely:
(1) can I make him perform the contract?
(2) can I have the goods repaired or replaced?
(3) can I get my money back?
(4) can I get compensation?

(1) **Can I make him perform the contract?**

Let us suppose that a consumer has ordered goods from a supplier, or work from a builder, and the supplier or builder has failed to turn up to do it. We have already seen[16] that the consumer may be able to serve a notice making time of the essence; if the supplier or builder then fails to perform by the stipulated date the consumer may be able to treat the contract as discharged. Let us suppose, however, that the consumer does not want to do this—what he wants is to compel the supplier or builder to perform the contract. In practical terms this may be more trouble than it is worth—the consumer may be better advised to obtain the goods or work elsewhere and claim compensation from the defaulting party.[17] If, however, the consumer insists on performance can the law help him? Historically the courts of common law only granted the remedy of damages, but the courts of equity supplemented this by granting decrees of specific performance in cases where damages would not be an adequate remedy. In the case of sale of goods the power to award specific performance is now enacted in section 52 of the Sale of Goods Act 1893 as follows:

> In any action for breach of contract to deliver specific or ascertained goods the court may, if it thinks fit, on the application of the plaintiff . . . direct that the contract shall be performed specifically, without giving the defendant the option or retaining the goods on payment of damages . . .

Two points must be stressed. In the first place the goods must be specific or ascertained. We have already seen that goods are specific if they are identified and agreed upon at the time of the contract.[18] Although the term "ascertained" is not defined in the

[16] *Ante*, p. 66.
[17] *Post*, p. 90.
[18] s. 62, *ante*, p. 60.

Act it probably refers to goods which are identified *after* the making of the contract. Thus if a consumer merely orders "a deep freeze" or a "heated trolley" and the seller, who is out of stock, fails to obtain one the remedy of specific performance would not be available.[19] Secondly, the remedy of specific performance is, and has always been, a discretionary remedy and a court will not grant it if damages would be an adequate remedy. In the vast majority of consumer contracts the buyer can get similar goods elsewhere and any loss can be compensated by an award of damages. Accordingly, specific performance would not be granted. It follows that the scope of the remedy, in practical terms, is extremely limited.

In the case of a contract for services (*e.g.* building, cleaning or repairing) the remedy is even less appropriate[19a] and it is difficult to think of any case in which it will be granted.

(2) Can I have the goods repaired or replaced?

In considering this problem there is a vast difference between law and practice. If, for example, a car, television set or a lawn-mower prove to be defective, the consumer will usually take it to the seller and ask for it to be repaired or replaced. In practice the seller (or the manufacturer in guarantee cases) will endeavour to repair it. Alternatively, the seller may take the goods back and give the consumer a replacement or a credit note; in the case of a car, however, it is very rare for the car to be taken back. All this is a matter of business practice; *there is no legal right to have the goods repaired or replaced.*

What happens if the buyer's expensive dishwasher breaks down and the seller tells him "we can't replace the defective part because this particular model has been discontinued?" A recent Law Commission report confirms that the retailer is under no legal duty to keep a stock of spare parts and servicing facilities; the report does not recommend that the retailer should be placed under seal of duty.[20] However, such an obligation is being gradually adapted on a voluntary basis (see the Electrical Code of Practice).[20a]

---

[19] See *Re Wait* [1927], Ch 606.
[19a] The courts will not grant specific performance if this requires constant supervision of the defendant's work (see *e.g. Ryan* v. *Mutual Tontine Westminster Chambers Assn.* [1893] 1 Ch. 116).
[20] Law Com. Rep. No. 95 pp. 36–41.
[20a] *Post,* p. 138.

(3) Can I get my money back?

If a consumer makes a contract for the purchase of goods or services he is under a basic obligation to pay the contract price. Thus, if he has booked a holiday at a seaside hotel he cannot simply cancel his booking. If he does so then, as a matter of strict law, the hotel can forfeit his deposit and can even sue him for damages if they have suffered additional loss by reason of his cancellation.

There may, however, be cases where the consumer is relieved of his basic duty to pay the price; in these cases he can recover the price (or a deposit) if he has already paid it. This will be so in at least three cases:

(a) Where the contract is rescinded for misrepresentation[21].

(b) Where specific goods perish before the risk has passed to the buyer.[22]

(c) Where the contract is discharged as a result of the supplier's breach.

Discharge by breach

Where the supplier breaks a vital term of the contract, or commits a breach which deprives the consumer of the whole of the benefit of the contract, the consumer can treat the contract as discharged.[23] Alternatively, he can affirm the contract and claim damages. In the case of sale of goods the position outlined above is expressly preserved by section 11(1)(a). Thus, where the seller breaks a condition, the buyer, unless he waives the breach, has the following option:

(i) he can treat the contract as repudiated, reject the goods, refuse to pay the price and claim damages for any additional loss or

(ii) he can affirm the contract, treat the breach as a breach of warranty, keep the goods and claim damages.

---

[21] *Ante*, p. 79.
[22] *Ante*, p. 64.
[23] See per Diplock L. J. in *Hong Kong Fir Shipping Co. Ltd.* v. *Kawasaki* [1962] 2 Q.B. 26.

In the former case he can also recover any part of the price which he has paid, either as part of a claim for damages or in quasi-contract, *i.e.* total failure of consideration.[24]

Loss of right to reject

There is, however, an important case where the above option is not available and where the consumer is compelled, unless otherwise agreed, to take course (ii) above. Section 11(1)(c) provides that:

> Where a contract of sale is not severable and the buyer has accepted the goods or part thereof . . . the breach of any condition to be fulfilled by the seller can only be treated as a breach of warranty, and not as a ground for rejecting the goods and treating the contract as repudiated, unless there be a term of the contract, express or implied, to that effect.

When is a contract severable?

The opening words of the subsection refer to a contract which is "severable." Thus, if a consumer made a contract with a supplier for the delivery of a 12-part encyclopaedia, one part to be delivered each month and to be separately paid for, this would be a severable contract. The result would be that the acceptance of one instalment would not prevent the buyer from rejecting a later one on the grounds that, for example, a number of pages were blank. A further question then arises; does a breach with regard to one or more instalments amount to a repudiation of the entire contract or is it merely a severable breach? In other words, can a buyer who rejects instalment number two be compelled to accept the remaining 10 instalments? There is no clear cut answer to this question; by section 31(2):

> it is a question in each case depending on the terms of the contract and the circumstances of the case.

In this example the buyer might well be able to refuse further instalments if, for example, the set as a whole is useless without the missing part. This raises a further unsettled point; if a seller tenders a defective instalment which is lawfully rejected, can he put the matter right by delivering a non-defective instalment? On principle, the answer ought to be yes—provided that he is not in breach of an essential time clause.

---

[24] See s. 54.

What is acceptance?

In the overwhelming majority of consumer sales the contract will be non-severable and the buyer will lose the right to reject when he accepts the goods or any part thereof. As already stated[24a] this is one of the two most difficult areas of this branch of the law—the other being the definition of "merchantable quality." The statutory provisions are contained in sections 34 and 35 of the 1893 Act. Section 34 reads as follows:

> (1) Where goods are delivered to the buyer which he has not previously examined he is not deemed to have accepted them unless and until he has had a reasonable opportunity of examining them for the purpose of ascertaining whether they are in conformity with the contract.
> (2) Unless otherwise agreed, when the seller tenders delivery of the goods to the buyer, he is bound, on request, to afford the buyer a reasonable opportunity of examining the goods for the purpose of ascertaining whether they are in conformity with the contract.

This section is clearly of considerable importance to consumers. It would apply, for example, to a purchase by mail order; it would also apply to a purchase of a cooker or washing machine where the consumer had merely examined a demonstration model. In practice, the goods themselves are usually delivered in a large closed box and the consumer is required to sign a form stating that the contents are satisfactory. Some consumers take the precaution of adding the words "contents unexamined" above their signature, but even if this is not done it is felt that a court would look at the realities of the situation and would hold that the signature would not, of itself, prevent rejection of the cooker or washing machine if it was not of merchantable quality.

Let us now turn to section 35.[25] It reads as follows:

> The buyer is deemed to have accepted the goods when he intimates to the seller that he has accepted them or (except where section 34 otherwise provides) when the goods have been delivered to him and he does any act in relation to the goods which is inconsistent with the ownership of the seller, or when after the lapse of a reasonable time, he retains the goods without intimating to the seller that he has rejected them.

Thus section 35 specifies three types of "acceptance."

(i) **Intimation of acceptance.** There has been no reported case on this topic; it is felt that there must be conduct on the part of

[24a] *Ante*, p. 7.
[25] as amended by s. 4 of the Misrepresentation Act 1967.

the buyer which makes it clear to the seller that the goods have been accepted. One example might be a letter asking the seller to carry out modifications. On the other hand, a form signed by the consumer stating "I accept these goods" would probably not be conclusive.

(ii) **Act after delivery inconsistent with the seller's ownership.** The leading cases are concerned with commercial contracts under which a delivery to a sub-buyer has destroyed the right to reject.[26] The underlying principle appears to be an inability to restore the goods to the seller. Thus, if a consumer receives a large consignment of wood and starts sawing it up in order to build a shed the act of cutting it up might destroy his right to reject if he then discovers that, for example, the wood does not answer the contract description. Another grey area concerns negligent damage. What happens if the buyer of a defective suit stains it with ink when he wears it for the first time? If the stain is indelible it could affect his right of rejection, since it would prevent him from returning the goods in their original form. It must, however, be remembered that the words in brackets, which were added by the 1967 Act, could affect the position. Under the amended wording an act done by the buyer before he has had a reasonable opportunity for examination will not necessarily destroy the right to reject; it is possible that some of the earlier cases[26] might now be decided differently.

(iii) **Retention beyond a reasonable time.** This, in the consumer context, is the really difficult one, and once again there is very little case law. The question of what is a reasonable time must depend, to some extent, on the nature of the goods—the period may be far shorter for pork chops than for furniture. There are, however, two really difficult points. First, what about an article which breaks down, while in normal use, after six months? If it can be shown that it was unmerchantable at the time of the contract, can the buyer still reject it? There is no clear authority on the point but the "reasonable time" should run from the date when the consumer knew or ought to have known of the defect (this is in line with the bars to rescission for misrepresentation—see *Leaf* v.

---

[26] See, *e.g. Ruben* v. *Faire Bros.* [1949] 1 K.B. 254 as an illustration of this point.

International Galleries[27] and *Long* v. *Lloyd*.)[28] If this reasoning is adopted then, in the example given above, rejection should still be available.

The second point concerns the effect of complaints. Let us suppose that an expensive camera fails to work. The consumer will usually ask the supplier (or manufacturer) to repair it. What happens if the defect persists after (say) 10 attempts to repair it? Alternatively, what happens if a large number of different defects manifest themselves in the first year or so after purchase? The buyer is certainly entitled to wait for a certain time to see if the defects can be put right. Thus in *Lee* v. *York Coach and Marine Ltd*.[29] the critical factor which destroyed the right to reject was the delay of six months after the final repair. Nevertheless, if the defect does persist for more than a few months there must come a time when the buyer must make up his mind—"do I want to keep the goods or not?" A book published by the Consumers Association entitled "How to Sue in the County Court" takes the reader through a case involving a defective washing machine. The book assumes, without discussion, that rejection is still available after seven months of complaints and attempts at repair. Although the point is not covered by authority is is highly unlikely that a registrar or county court judge would allow rejection in such a case. Accordingly, the buyer should make it clear at the outset that he will reject the goods if the defects are not rectified.

Absence of title. If the supplier of goods has no right to sell, the consumer can recover the price on the basis of total failure of consideration. His right to do this is not lost by "acceptance" as Atkin LJ pointed out in *Rowland* v. *Divall*.[30] He will, however, lose his right to get his money back if the defect is put right before he purports to reject.[31] This is reasonable enough—it would obviously be wrong to allow a claim based on "total failure of consideration" if the buyer has received substantially what he paid for, *i.e.* the property in the goods.

Hire-purchase. There is nothing in the Consumer Credit Act 1974 nor in the Supply of Goods (Implied Terms) Act 1973 regu-

---

[27] [1950] 2 K.B. 86.
[28] [1958] 2 All E.R. 402.
[29] *Ante*, p. 47.
[30] [1923] 2 K.B. 500 and see, *ante*, p. 23.
[31] *Butterworth* v. *Kingsway Motors* [1954] 1 W.L.R. 1286.

lating the remedies of the hirer. The cases at common law show a fairly broad approach. In *Farnworth Finance Facilities* v. *Attryde*[32];

> Mr. Attryde took a new motor cycle on hire-purchase terms on July 11, 1964. There were a very large number of defects and finally on November 23 he purported to reject it and claimed the return of all his payments.

Counsel for the defendants argued that by driving the motor cycle for 4,000 miles Mr. Attryde had affirmed the contract so as to lose his right to reject. The Court of Appeal rejected this argument. In the words of Lord Denning M.R.[33]:

> Affirmation is a matter of election. A man only affirms a contract when he knows of the defects and by his conduct elects to go on with the contract despite them. In this case Mr. Attryde complained from the beginning of the defects and sent the machine back for them to be remedied. He did not elect to accept it unless they were remedied. But the defects were never satisfactorily remedied. When the rear chain broke it was the last straw.

As already stated there is nothing in hire-purchase law comparable to section 35 of the Sale of Goods Act and it may well be therefore that the right to reject is more readily available than in a sale.

Can the buyer reject part? What happens if some of the goods are merchantable while others are not? We have seen that under a non-severable contract the buyer has a straight choice—to keep all the goods or to reject them; by accepting part his right to reject is lost.[34] This rule is however modified by section 30 which gives the buyer additional rights in three cases. The effect of section 30 can be summarised as follows:

    (a) If the seller supplies too many goods the buyer can (i) reject all the goods or (ii) reject the surplus or (iii) keep all the goods and pay for them at the contract rate.

    (b) If the seller tenders too little the buyer can (i) reject the goods or (ii) keep them and pay at the contract rate.

    (c) If the seller tenders the contract goods mixed with goods of a different description the buyer can (i) reject all the goods of (ii) reject the goods not answering the description. There is no statutory right to keep the latter goods, but the courts

[32] [1970] 1 W.L.R. 1053.
[33] p. 1059.
[34] s. 11(1)(c), *ante*, p. 85.

might treat the delivery as an offer to sell them. If the buyer
accepted this offer he might be liable to pay a reasonable
price.[35] Alternatively if the buyer does not initially accept
the offer he might be able to take advantage of section 1 of
the Unsolicited Goods and Services Act 1971 which was
considered in Chapter 5.[36]

Practical considerations.

There will, in many cases, be practical barriers to repudiation
in cases where the price has already been paid. Section 36 of the
Act of 1893 provides that the buyer can send the seller a notice
of rejection; if the property and risk have passed to the buyer the
effect of the notice is to re-transfer them to the seller. In practice,
however, the seller is likely to dispute the buyer's right to reject
and this can mean that the buyer will have neither his money nor
the use of the goods until his right to reject has been upheld by
a court and until the judgment for the return of the price has been
satisfied.

(4) **Can I get compensation?**

The consumer is always entitled to damages if the other party
has broken a term of the contract, express or implied. When we
turn to the difficult question of quantifying the claim we must
consider two closely related problems, namely (a) for what items
of loss is the defendant liable? and (b) on what principles should
the compensation be assessed?

For what loss is the defendant liable?

The general principles governing remoteness of damage were
laid down more than 100 years ago in *Hadley* v. *Baxendale*[37] and
more recently by the House of Lords in *Koufos* v. *Czarnikow
Ltd.*[38] The defendant is clearly liable for damages arising naturally
from the breach. He is also liable for other damage which can
fairly and reasonably have been within the contemplation of both
parties, at the time they made the contract, as the probable result
of the breach of it. It has recently been held that where the general
type of damage was within the contemplation of the parties the

[35] s. 8.
[36] *Ante*, p. 58.
[37] (1854) 9 Exch. 341, 354.
[38] [1969] 1 A.C. 350.

defendant is liable even though the precise extent of the damage, or the precise form of the damage, was outside his contemplation.[39]

Mitigation

Another basic rule is that of mitigation—the injured party must take reasonable steps to mitigate his loss. Thus, to take an obvious example, a buyer of a defective product could not sue the seller for the cost of having it repaired by a third party if the supplier had previously offered to repair it free of charge.

General principles of compensation

If the damage is not too remote under the rules set out above the general principle is that damages should, so far as possible, place the injured party in the same position as if the contract had been performed.

Some particular cases

In the case of sale of goods the buyer may have an action for damages against the seller (a) if the seller fails to deliver or (b) if the seller breaks a condition or a warranty. In all these cases the general principles laid down in *Hadley* v. *Baxendale*[40] appear in statutory form; thus section 51(2) which deals with non-delivery provides that:

> The measure of damages is the estimated loss directly and naturally resulting, in the ordinary course of events, from the seller's breach of contract.

As an example of this section 51(3) provides that:

> Where there is an available market for the goods in question the measure of damages is prima facie . . . the difference between the contract price and the market or current price of the goods at the time or times when they ought to have been delivered, or if no time was fixed, then at the time of refusal to deliver.

Let us suppose that John agrees to buy a new Ford Escort car from a dealer for £3000. The contract provides that the car must be delivered by May 1 but the dealer fails to deliver. By that date the price of Ford Escorts has increased by £300. If John has to pay

[39] *Parsons (Livestock) Ltd.* v. *Uttley Ingham & Co.* [1978] Q.B. 791—sale and construction of hopper for feeding nuts to pigs—ventilator left unopened—nuts became mouldy—pigs died—supplier of hopper liable.
[40] *Supra.*

an extra £300 to buy one from another dealer this sum will prima facie be his damages under section 51(3).

The so-called second limb of *Hadley* v. *Baxendale*, damage within the reasonable contemplation of the parties, is preserved by section 54 which reads:

> Nothing in this Act shall affect the right of the buyer or the seller to recover interest or special damages in any case where by law interest or special damages may be recoverable. . . .

Thus, if, as a result of the non-delivery of the car, John loses a valuable business contract, that would be "special damages" and the defaulting dealer will only be liable for it if it was brought to his attention before the agreement was made.

Damages for breach of warranty

In this situation damages arising naturally are covered by section 53(2) while "contemplated" damages are covered by section 54.[41] Where the warranty relates to quality the damages are prima facie the difference between the value of the defective goods and their value if they had answered the warranty.[42] It is clear, however, that damages are not necessarily confined to that amount. Thus, for example, damages for personal injury or death can be recovered on a sale of a defective toy.[43] Then, if a defective car is "off the road" for repair the buyer will be able to recover from the seller not only the cost of repair (if any) but also the cost of hiring a substitute car during this period. The magazine "Which?" recently cited a case where a buyer of a leaking caravan spent large sums of money on petrol on numerous journeys to have it repaired. He also planned to have a caravan holiday but was compelled to move into a guest house when the defects reappeared. He successfully recovered both the cost of the petrol and the boarding house expenses in county court proceedings.

If the seller is in breach of the condition of "right to sell"[44] the damage recoverable by the buyer can include not merely the price paid but also the cost of necessary repairs.[45]

---

[41] *Supra.*
[42] s. 53(3) and see *Lee* v. *York (Coach and Marine Ltd., ante,* p. 47.
[43] *Godley* v. *Perry* [1960] 1 W.L.R. 9.
[44] *Ante*, p. 23.
[45] *Mason* v. *Burningham* [1949] 2 K.B. 545.

Mental distress

Can the buyer claim damages for mental distress if the car of his dreams turns out to be a mangled mass of iron? This is an area of the law where the courts are proceeding slowly. So far damages for mental distress have been recovered in holiday contracts[46], contracts of employment where the employee was demoted[47] and in proceedings for negligence against a solicitor who had failed to obtain a non-molestation injunction on behalf of a client.[48] It could well be that such damages could one day be awarded in a sale of goods case,[48a] but in view of the enormously wide scope of such claims the courts are likely to approach such claims with consideration caution.

Hire-purchase

The principles set out above are equally relevant to hire-purchase transactions. Thus in *Yeoman Credit Ltd.* v. *Apps*[49] the hirer of a car which took one and a half hours to do three or four miles successfully sued for damages. The damages were assessed at the difference between what the car should have been worth and what it was actually worth; on that basis the hirer recovered all his payments, less a very small allowance for use.

Holiday contracts

If the customer finds, on arrival at his resort, that his room has been double booked, or that the hotel does not exist, he can claim the cost of having to stay at an equivalent hotel plus (as already stated) damages for mental distress.

Cleaners

If a cleaner ruins or loses a blanket, a carpet or a suit, the damages will be based on the cost of acquiring a replacement, but this will be subject to a discount for age and use.

---

[46] *Jarvis* v. *Swans Tours* [1973] 1 Q.B. 233.
[47] *Cox* v. *Phillips Industries* [1976] 1 W.L.R. 638.
[48] *Heywood* v. *Wellers* [1976] Q.B. 446.
[48a] In *Jackson* v. *Chrysler Acceptances* (1978) 12 Current Law, para 46 a consumer told the dealer that he wanted a car for a holiday. The car was defective. The county court judge awarded (*inter alia*) £75 for a spoilt holiday. Although the award was varied on appeal there was no suggestion that such damages could not be recovered.
[49] [1962] 2 Q.B. 508.

Builders

If a builder, decorator or plumber does a job badly, the damages would include not only the money paid to another firm to have it put right but also damages for the resulting inconvenience.[50] If the work is done extremely badly the consumer may be entitled to refuse to pay anything at all.[50a]

3. REMEDIES IN TORT

Perhaps the most likely case of a tort claim would be where the consumer has a claim for negligence against the manufacturer. In personal injury cases the damages would include loss of actual and future earnings, medical expenses, pain and suffering and loss of amenities. For further details readers are referred to the standard textbooks on tort and to McGregor on Damages.

In a case where the same facts give rise to liability in both contract and tort the rules as to damages are being brought very close together.[51]

---

[50] See *e.g. Batty* v. *Metropolitan Realisations* [1978] Q.B. 554.
[50a] See *e.g. Bolton* v. *Mahadeva* [1972] 1 W.L.R. 1009.
[51] *Parsons & Co. (Livestock) Ltd.* v. *Uttley Ingham & Co. (ante,* p. 91.)

CHAPTER 8

"THEY SAY THAT I HAVE SIGNED AWAY MY RIGHTS"

EXEMPTION clauses have been widely used in standard form contracts in the past 40 or 50 years and have come in for severe criticism from the courts and other bodies. The courts have developed certain techniques to control the legal effect of these clauses. Unfortunately the control exercised by the courts has been unsatisfactory because, with the exception of Lord Denning M.R., they have felt themselves unable to break out of the straightjacket of freedom of contract. Accordingly, the use of exemption clauses has been increasingly controlled by statute and the overwhelming majority of these clauses are now controlled by the Unfair Contract Terms Act 1977.

Examples

The first four examples are taken from Law Commission Working Paper No 39, pp. 74–88.

(1) The shipowner shall be exempt from all liability in respect of any detention, delay, overcarriage, loss, expenses, damage, sickness or injury of whatever kind, whenever and wherever occurring and however and by whomsoever caused of or to any passenger or of or to any person or child travelling with him or her or in his or her care or of or to any baggage, property, goods, effects, articles, matters or things belonging to or carried by, with or for any passenger or any such person or child.

(2) [The ferry company] shall not be liable for the death or any injury, damage, loss, delay or accident . . . wheresoever, whensoever and howsoever caused and whether by negligence or their servants or agents or by unseaworthiness of the vessel.

(3) The contractors shall not under any circumstances be liable for any loss or damage caused by or resulting from or in connection with fire, howsoever caused.

(4) The Post Office shall not be liable to the subscriber for or on account of or in respect of any loss or damage suffered by reason of any failure to provide, or delay in providing, under this

95

agreement, telecommunications service, any equipment or apparatus or any service ancillary thereto.

(5) All cars parked at owner's risk.

(6) In the case of loss or damage the liability of the company is limited to the value of the garment.

(7) All claims within seven days.

Justification

In deciding on the price of his product a supplier is bound to consider the question of loss apportionment. He can also cut down very substantially on administration overheads by having standard form contracts (thus avoiding the need to negotiate each contract separately) and by avoiding litigation. A survey carried out by Mr. David Yates in *Exclusion Clauses in Contracts*, pp. 1–29 contains the following passage at p. 14:

> By far the most common reason advanced for the incorporation of exclusion clauses into contracts was the desire to avoid court proceeding should something go wrong . . . distrust of the lawyer's ability to understand the businessman's problems was very marked.

Criticism

When due allowance has been made for the points set out above there is no doubt that exemption clauses are open to abuse. The following passage is taken from the Law Commission's Second Report on Exemption Clauses, on which the Unfair Contract Terms Act was based

> We are in no doubt that in many cases they operate against the public interest and that the prevailing judicial attitude of suspicion, or indeed of hostility, to such clauses is well founded. All too often they are introduced in ways which result in the party affected by them remaining ignorant of their presence or import until it is too late. That party, even if he knows of the exemption clause, will often be unable to appreciate what he may lose by accepting it. In any case he may not have sufficient bargaining strength to refuse to accept it. The result is that the risk of carelessness or of failure to achieve satisfactory standards of performance is thrown on to the party who is not responsible for it or who is unable to guard against it. Moreover, by excluding liability for such carelessness or failure the economic pressures to maintain high standards of performance are reduced.[1]

[1] Law Com. No. 69, para 11.

Scheme of this chapter

It is proposed to start by examining the attitude of the courts to exemption clauses and then to consider the statutory controls imposed by the Unfair Contract Terms Act. The broad scope of the Act has made the former topic far less important and accordingly it will be examined fairly briefly. A brief reference to other legislation will be made at the end of this Chapter.

1. JUDICIAL CONTROL OF EXEMPTION CLAUSES

The reasons for judicial hostility to exemption clauses have already been mentioned; ignorance, non-negotiation and inequality of bargaining power. Perhaps the first of these points is the strongest. After all, the law of contract is, or should be, about agreement. If the consumer were asked "do you know that you have signed away your right to complain if the cleaners lose the carpet?" or "do you know that you will receive no compensation at all if the carriers damage your furniture?" it is unlikely that his reply could be printed in this book; at all events it is likely to include the word "no." When he made the contract he would reasonably have expected that the work would be done with reasonable care, and that he would receive compensation if this was not so. His expectations may have been increased by a glowing advertisement in a newspaper or magazine or on television. Accordingly exemption clauses, which are often inconsistent with his reasonable expectations, are closely scrutinised by the courts.

The courts have to decide two basic problems, namely:

(1) was the clause duly incorporated into the contract, and

(2) does it, on its true construction, cover the event which has occurred?

(1) Incorporation

The general contractual principles relating to incorporation have been well established for a considerable time. Thus:

(a) If the contractual document is signed this operates as an incorporation of all the terms which appear on that document or which are referred to in it.[2] The signer will not be bound, however, if:

[2] The leading case is *L'Estrange* v. *Graucob* [1934] 2 K.B. 394.

    (i) he signed the document without negligence and it turns out to be a document of a fundamentally different kind from the document which he thought that he was signing[3]; or

    (ii) if the other party has misrepresented the effect of the clause.[4]

(b) If the consumer has not signed a contractual document a clause will only be incorporated if reasonable steps were taken before contract to bring it to his notice. The following cases illustrate how this principle is applied in practice.

    (i) In the case of *Thompson* v. *LMS Railway*[5] a lady bought a railway excursion ticket containing the words "For conditions see back." The back of the ticket referred to conditions in the railway timetables which were available for purchase. Had Mrs Thompson obtained and read it (by which time she would certainly have missed her train) she would have seen an exclusion clause excluding liability for negligence. The Court of Appeal held that the exemption clause had been incorporated into the contract.

    (ii) The case of *Chapelton* v. *Barry UDC*[6] concerned an exclusion clause on a deckchair receipt. It was held that there was no incorporation; this was not the type of document on which the consumer could reasonably expect to find conditions and therefore the company had not taken sufficient steps to bring the clause to the consumer's attention.

    (iii) In *Olley* v. *Marlborough Court Hotel*[7] a consumer booked a hotel room. After he had done so he saw an exemption notice in the bedroom. It was held that there was no incorporation since the clause had been introduced too late. The position might have been different if the notice was prominently displayed at the reception

---

[3] *Saunders* v. *Anglia Building Society* [1971] A.C. 1039, in which the House of Lords emphasised that this so-called *"non est factum"* defence must be confined within narrow limits.

[4] *Curtis* v. *Chemical Cleaning and Dyeing Co.* [1951] 1 K.B. 805 C.A.

[5] [1930] 1 K.B. 41.

[6] [1940] 1 K.B. 532.

[7] [1949] 1 K.B. 532.

desk or if the customer had stayed at the hotel on previous occasions. In the latter case the notice might have been incorporated on the basis of a previous course of dealing. Nevertheless, this principle, which can readily be implied in commercial contracts, is very rarely applied in consumer contracts.[8]

(iv) *Thornton* v. *Shoe Lane Parking Co. Ltd.*[9] is perhaps the best modern example of how the basic rules of "contract" are being adapted, in a realistic way, to standard form consumer transactions.

Mr. Thornton, a trumpeter of the highest quality, went to park his car at a new multistorey car park—he had not been there before. On arriving opposite the ticket machine a ticket popped out, the light turned from red to green and Mr. Thornton went through and parked his car. The ticket referred to conditions displayed on the premises. These conditions (*inter alia*) excluded liability for personal injuries caused by negligence. There was an accident caused partly by the defendant's negligence and Mr. Thornton was injured.

The Court of Appeal held that the defendants had not taken reasonable steps to bring this particular clause to the notice of Mr. Thornton. In the words of Lord Denning M.R. at p. 170.

"It is so wide and destructive of rights that the court should not hold any man bound by it unless it is drawn to his attention in the most explicit way . . . In order to give sufficient notice, it would need to be printed in red ink with a red hand pointing to it—or something equally startling."

Megaw L.J. gave an equally vivid example when he said at p. 173:

"It does not take much imagination to picture the indignation of the defendants if their potential customers . . . were one after the other to get out of their cars leaving the cars blocking the entrance to the garages in order to search for, find and peruse the notices! Yet unless the defendants genuinely intended that potential customers should do just that it would be fiction, if not farce, to treat those customers as persons who have been given a fair opportunity, before the contracts are made, of discovering the conditions by which they are to be bound."

Lord Denning M.R. went so far as to hold that the contract was complete when the customer dropped his money into the machine, with the result that the conditions on the ticket would be introduced

[8] See, *e.g. McCutcheon* v. *David MacBrayne Ltd.* [1964] 1 W.L.R. 125 HL.
[9] [1971] 2 Q.B. 163.

too late.[10] The trouble with this approach is that in many cases the customer does *not* put money into the slot—he merely collects a ticket and pays later. Nevertheless both Lord Denning M.R. and Sir Gordon Willmer were influenced by the finality of a contract made with a machine. To quote again from Lord Denning:

> The customer pays his money and gets a ticket. He cannot refuse it. He cannot get his money back. He may protest to the machine, even swear at it. But it will remain unmoved. He is committed beyond recall.

These interesting problems may never be decided because it may be unnecessary to do so. If the facts of *Thornton* were to recur, a clause excluding liability for death or personal injury resulting from negligence would in any event be void[11] and accordingly the question of incorporation would have no practical importance. The point might, however, remain relevant if the customer suffered damage to his property. In that case the exemption clause would be valid if reasonable[12] and accordingly the customer might well raise the argument of "no incorporation" as his first line of attack.

(2) Does the clause cover the event which has occurred?

Even if the clause has been duly incorporated into the contract it is not automatically effective. The courts have evolved a number of techniques to counter their effect.

(a) *Privity*

After earlier doubts the House of Lords have held that an exemption clause in a contract between A and B could not protect C, even if C was an employee or contractor employed by B to perform the contract.[13] It seems however that this can be outflanked by having a clause whereby a party contracts, as agent for his employees etc, that they shall have the benefit of the clause. As a matter of strict legal analysis this can create a new contract between the employees and the other party and the performance of the main contract will provide the consideration for it.[14]

---

[10] cf. *Olley* v. *Marlborough Court Hotel ante*, p. 98.
[11] Unfair Contract Terms Act 1977, s. 2(1) *post*, p. 109.
[12] *Ibid.* s. 2(2).
[13] *Scruttons* v. *Midland Silicones Ltd.* [1962] A.C. 446.
[14] *New Zealand Shipping Co. Ltd.* v. *Satterthwaite & Co. Ltd.* [1975] A.C. 154 PC.

(b) *Strict construction and the contra proferentem rule*

A party seeking the protection of an exemption clause must show that the wording is clear enough to cover the alleged breach. This is well illustrated by three cases involving sale of goods.

In *Wallis Son and Wells* v. *Pratt and Haynes*[15] a commercial contract for the sale of seed excluded "all warranties." The seller supplied seed of a different description and the buyer claimed damages. The House of Lords held that the seller had broken a *condition* and that a clause referring only to *warranties* did not protect him. The mere fact that the buyer, in ignorance of the breach, had "accepted" the goods, and was therefore compelled to treat the breach as a breach of warranty[16] was immaterial.

In *Andrews Bros (Bournemouth) Ltd* v. *Singer & Co. Ltd.*[17] the seller sold of a "new Singer car" with a clause excluding "implied conditions and warranties." The seller supplied a car which was not new. The Court of Appeal held that he had broken an *express* condition and accordingly a clause which merely referred to *implied* conditions did not protect him. The same result could have been reached on the basis that the seller was guilty of breach of a fundamental term, or entire non-performance.

In *Nichol* v. *Godts*[18] the sellers agreed to supply rape oil "warranted only equal to sample." Sellers supplied a mixture of rape oil and hemp oil. It was held that the exclusion clause did not protect them from their overriding duty to supply rape oil (this is another example of the doctrine of entire non-performance mentioned above).

The rule of strict construction leads on naturally to the so-called "contra proferentem" rule which provides that an ambiguity must be construed against the party who wishes to rely on the clause. Thus if a plaintiff has two distinct claims against the defendent (one in contract and one in tort for negligence) an exemption clause may well be construed so as to cover only the former and not the latter.[19] Even words like "the company will not be liable for damage caused by fire" may merely operate as a warning that

[15] [1911] A.C. 394.
[16] *Ante*, p. 85.
[17] [1934] 1 K.B. 17.
[18] (1854) 10 Exch. 191.
[19] See, *e.g. White* v. *John Warwick* [1953] 1 W.L.R. 1285.

the company will only be liable if negligent.[20] It follows that very clear words are required to cover liability for negligence, for example, "howsoever caused" or "whether or not due to negligence."

(c) *Inconsistent oral promise*

An exemption clause will be overridden by an oral promise which is inconsistent with it. Thus in *Mendelssohn* v. *Normand*[21] a suitcase was stolen from a car which the plaintiff had parked at the defendant's car park. An employee of the defendants promised the plaintiff that he would lock the car, but he failed to do so. The Court of Appeal held that a clause excluding "loss or damage howsoever caused" was ineffective.

(d) *Deviation cases*

The case of *Mendelssohn* v. *Normand* (supra) was also decided on another ground. Even if an exemption clause is very widely drawn it will only give protection while the party seeking to rely on it is carrying out the contract in its essential respects.

(e) *Fundamental breach*

The twin doctrines of "fundamental breach" and "breach of fundamental term" have been widely used in recent years as a weapon to protect the consumer against unreasonable exemption clauses. The two terms are often used interchangeably but there is a difference between them. A "fundamental term" has been described by Lord Devlin as "something narrower than a condition—something which underlies the whole contract so that if it is not complied with the performance becomes totally different from that which the contract contemplates."[22] A seller who supplies peas instead of beans or a cleaner who wrongly sub-contracts the work is guilty of entire non-performance, and hence a breach of a fundamental term. A fundamental breach, on the other hand, is a serious breach of contract often with disastrous consequences for the innocent party. Thus, although the term was not used, the deviation by the employee in *Mendelssohn* v. *Normand* (supra)

---

[20] *Hollier* v. *Rambler Motors (AMC) Ltd.* [1972] 2 Q.B. 71.
[21] [1970] 1 Q.B. 177. See also *J. Evans & Sons (Portsmouth) Ltd.* v. *Andrea Merzario Ltd.* [1976] 2 All E.R. 930 C.A.
[22] *Smeaton Hanscomb & Co. Ltd.* v. *Setty (Sassoon) Sons & Co.* [1953] 1 W.L.R. 1468.

could be classified as a fundamental breach. So also was the conduct of a cloakroom attendant in allowing an unauthorised person to open the plaintiff's suitcase and to take items from it.[23] So too was the delivery of an unsafe motor cycle in *Farnworth Finance Co. Ltd.* v. *Attryde*.[24]

There is only one practical difference between a fundamental breach and the breach of a fundamental term. In the former case there is some form of contractual performance and accordingly the innocent party has the option to treat the contract as repudiated or to affirm it. In the latter case, however, the contract ends automatically and a buyer of peas who accepts a tender of beans is, in effect, making an entirely new contract.[25]

What is the relevance of all this to exemption clauses? We have already seen[26] that very clear wording is required to exclude liability for negligence. This applies, *a fortiori*, to fundamental breach. The policy of the courts is to look at the contract *apart from the exemption clause* to find out what the contract is all about. They will then be ready to strike down an exemption clause if it is repugnant to the main purpose of the contract.[27] Alternatively, they may hold that the parties could not have intended the clause to be read literally, if the effect of this would be to deprive the agreement of all contractual effect. Borrie and Diamond, in the latest edition of *The Consumer, Society and The Law*, give the example of a contract to sell a new Singer car followed by a clause excluding "all express conditions." Then follows this memorable passage.[28]

"The effect of the exemption clause then, if it is to be taken literally, is to wipe out the express promise itself. Thus nothing is left of the contract; the ultimate in exemption clauses is reached and the whole transaction is itself excluded."

Not surprisingly, the courts invariably decide that, as a matter of construction, this could not have been intended and they will

[23] *Alexander* v. *Railway Executive* [1951] 2 K.B. 882.
[24] *Ante*, p. 89.
[25] See the very valuable discussion by Yates, Exclusion Clauses in Contracts, Chap. 6.
[26] *Ante*, p. 102.
[27] See, *e.g. Sze Hai Tong Bank Ltd.* v. *Rambler Cycle Co.* [1959] A.C. 576.
[28] (3rd. ed.), p. 44.

E

find ways of construing the exemption clause in such a way as to leave the "core" of the contract intact.

Until 1967 there appeared to be a rule of law that an exemption clause could never cover a fundamental breach but in that year the House of Lords held in *Suisse Atlantique* v. *NV Rotterdamsche Kolen Centrale*[29] that there was no such rule; it was in each case a question of construction. It was not long however, before the Court of Appeal returned to the attack. On the particular facts of the *Suisse Atlantique* case the innocent party had elected to affirm the contract. This was seized upon by the Court of Appeal in the much-criticised case of *Harbutts (Plasticine) Ltd.* v. *Wayne Tank & Pump Co. Ltd.*[30] The court there held that if the innocent party affirms the contract the question of whether a fundamental breach is covered by the clause is a question of construction. If, however, the innocent party elects to treat the contract as repudiated, or is compelled to do so because all further performance has become impossible, *the whole contract is at an end and the exemption clause ceases to be operative.* As already stated, this proposition has been criticised[31] and it does seem wrong on both principle and authority. The courts can usually outflank the exemption clause on the less controversial ground that, as a matter of construction the breach was not covered by the clause. If, however, the clause does cover the breach, then on principle it should be applied (incidentally it is interesting to speculate on the effect of a clause which expressly takes away the right to treat the contract as discharged). The *Harbutt* rule has been modified in certain cases by section 9 of the Unfair Contract Terms Act 1977.[32]

(f) *Burden of proof*

The previous discussion of fundamental breach leads on to a final point concerning bailments. A bailee (for example, garage, warehouseman, cleaner or carrier) owes a legal duty of care and the onus is on him to disprove negligence if the goods are lost or damaged. Alternatively, if he is covered by an exemption clause which refers to negligence he can escape liability by proving that he *was* negligent and that his negligence was covered by the clause.

[29] [1967] 1 A.C. 361.
[30] [1971] 1 Q.B. 447.
[31] See, *e.g.* Law Commission Second Report on Exemption Clauses, para. 43.
[32] *Post*, p.119.

This defence in now subject to the reasonableness test under sections 2 and 3 of the Unfair Contract Terms Act 1977. If, however, the goods are lost and he cannot offer any explanation at all then the courts will infer that the loss *might* have been caused by a fundamental breach. In the light of the principles of construction set out above he will be liable.[33]

2. UNFAIR CONTRACT TERMS ACT 1977

The Act received the Royal Assent of October 26, 1977 and came into force on February 1, 1978. It is largely based on the Law Commission's Second Report on Exemption Clauses, but it differs from the Law Commission's Draft Bill in several material respects.

Transitional matters

By section 31 the Act does not apply to contracts made before February 1, 1978; subject to this it applies to liability (for example, in tort) for any loss or damage suffered on or after that date. Thus the common law rules described earlier in this chapter will remain relevant for a considerable time. Two problems arise:

(a) Does the Act apply to a contract made before February 1, 1978, and renewed after that date? In the absence of authority it is felt that the renewal might well be treated as a new contract to which the Act will apply.

(b) If the same set of facts give rise to liability in contract and tort can an injured party claim the protection of the Act by suing in tort where the contract was made before February 1, 1978, but the injury occurred on or after that date? On principle, the answer ought to be no, having regard to the wide wording of section 31 and the general presumption against a statute being retrospective. The matter, however, is not free from doubt.

Scope of the Act

The Act operates in five overlapping areas, namely:

(a) negligence;

(b) contractual obligations;

---

[33] *Levison* v. *Patent Steam Carpet Cleaning Co. Ltd.* [1977] 3 W.L.R. 90.

(c) terms implied in contracts for sale of goods, hire-purchase and certain analogous contracts;
(d) guarantees and indemnities;
(e) misrepresentation.

Before considering these areas it is necessary to mention some preliminary points.

Preliminary matters

(1) The Act does not create new duties—it merely controls clauses which cut down a duty which would otherwise exist or which exclude or modify the remedies available on breach of that duty.

> Let us suppose that Richard parks his car in a car park and keeps the key. There is a large notice at the entrance "The company is not liable for any loss or damage to vehicle or contents, whether or not due to negligence of the company or its servants or agents." When Richard comes back to collect his car it cannot be found.

The notice set out above would be controlled by section 2 of the Act[34] and it would be subject to the reasonableness test. This, however, is likely to be completely irrelevant; the company can avoid liability on the more basic ground that the transaction was a mere licence and not a bailment and therefore they owed Richard no duty of care. That was the position before the Act[35] and, as already stated, the Act does not create new duties.

(2) The name of the Act is misleading—it is both too narrow and too wide. It is too narrow because it only refers to "contract"; the Act also applies to negligence both at common law and under the Occupiers' Liability Act 1957. It is too wide because it does not control all "unfair terms"; it merely controls exemption clauses and notices.

(3) With very minor ex-ceptions the key provisions of the Act (sections 2–7) only apply to "business liability." By section 1(3) this means:

> liability for breach of obligations or duties arising—
> (a) from things done or to be done by a person in the course of a business (whether his own business or another's): or
> (b) from the occupation of premises used for business purposes of the occupier.

---

[34] See *post*, p. 109.
[35] *Ashby* v. *Tolhurst* [1937] 2 K.B. 242.

When we turn to section 14 we find that the term "business" includes a profession and the activities of any government department or local or public authority.

The term "business" crops up at various points in this book. Thus we have already come across it in connection with (a) sale of goods—implied conditions of quality and fitness,[35a] and (b) unsolicited goods and services.[36] We shall meet it again later in this chapter when considering the phrase "deals as consumer."[37] It is also critical for certain provisions of the Consumer Credit Act, for example, non-commercial agreements[38] and the licensing provisions.[39] There are bound to be borderline cases. Is a landlord carrying on a "business" when he lets a block of flats? Is a charity "bazaar" a business? The tax cases show that the key factors include the frequency of the transaction, the manner of operation and the profit motive. It is felt that, on these criteria, a charity bazaar would not be a business, whereas a landlord might well be carrying on a business—especially if he provided services for the tenants.

Reverting now to section 2(3) the question arises as to whether the Act would apply to the premises of a professional man who worked from his home. The answer is "yes", because the Act does not require the premises to be used *exclusively* for business purposes. The point is rather academic since the home is unlikely to be plastered with exclusion notices.

(4) Sections 2–4 do not apply to certain contracts listed in Schedule 1. For the consumer the two most important are (a) contracts of insurance and (b) any contract so far as it relates to the creation, transfer or termination of an interest in land. The words "so far as" are important. If, for example, a landlord of a block of flats remains the occupier of the common staircase a notice stating that "visitors enter these premises at their own risk" would be controlled: thus if the landlord negligently allows the staircase to fall into disrepair he would be liable in damages to an injured visitor under the Occupiers' Liability Act 1957, section 2(2) and the exemption notice would be void by the Act of 1977, section 2 (1). (*post*, p. 109).

[35a] *Ante*, p. 44.
[36] *Ante*, p. 58.
[37] *Post*, p. 110.
[38] *Post*, p. 246.
[39] *Post*, pp. 255–256.

(5) The Act repeatedly refers to a clause which "excludes or restricts liability." This clearly covers a clause that "no liability is accepted for any loss or damage howsoever caused" or "liability shall be limited to the cost of replacing the appliance and all liability for consequential loss is excluded." Then when we turn to section 13(1) we find that:

> "To the extent that this Part of this Act prevents the exclusion or restriction of any liability it also prevents
>> (a) making the liability or its enforcement subject to restrictive or onerous conditions;
>> (b) excluding or restricting any right or remedy in respect of the liability, or subjecting a person to any prejudice in consequence of his pursuing any such right or remedy;
>> (c) excluding or restricting rules of evidence or procedure."

Thus the following would be caught:

(a) "all claims within seven days"
(b) "before starting proceedings the customer must pay £1,000 into a joint bank account
(c) "no rejection"
(d) "if you sue us we will see that you get no further supplies"
(e) "the report by our engineer shall be conclusive"

Section 13(1) then concludes with these words:

> "and (to that extent) sections 2 and 5 to 7 also prevent excluding or restricting liability by reference to terms and notices which exclude or restrict the relevant obligation or duty."

What does this mean? How can the Act control a clause which prevents a duty from arising? What is "the relevant obligation or duty"? The probable answer is to adopt the approach of Lord Denning M.R. in *Karsales (Harrow) Ltd.* v. *Wallis*[40] and look at the contract or activity apart from the clause. If, for example it is a contract giving rise to a condition of reasonable fitness or a duty of reasonable care the Act would control a clause or notice providing that "no condition of fitness is implied herein" or "the occupier shall be under no duty of care."

Two final points can be made on this topic. First, an agreement in writing to submit present or future disputes to arbitration is *not*

---

[40] [1956] 1 W.L.R. 936.

a clause "excluding or restricting liability."[41] Secondly, it is thought
that the Act would not apply to a genuine "liquidated damages"
clause, nor to a genuine settlement out of court ("I accept this
sum [or credit note] in full and final settlement of all claims").

(6) With one exception, the common law rules as to incorporation, privity and construction mentioned earlier in this chapter
remain unaffected, although, as already stated[42] they will become
of far less practical importance. A court is unlikely to embark on
a long investigation on "incorporation" if the clause is void anyway.
The one exception is fundamental breach and this is considered
later.[43]

The five areas affected by the Act

(a) *Negligence*

Section 1(1) defines negligence as the breach;

(a) of any obligation, arising from the express or implied terms
of a contract, to take reasonable care or exercise reasonable
skill in the performance of the contract;

(b) of any common law duty to take reasonable care or exercise
reasonable skill (but not any stricter duty);

(c) of the common duty of care imposed by the Occupiers'
Liability Act 1957. . .

We can now consider section 2—one of the most important
sections of the Act. It reads as follows:

(1) A person cannot by reference to any contract term or to a notice given to
persons generally or to particular persons exclude or restrict his liability for
death or personal injury resulting from negligence.

(2) In the case of other loss or damage, a person cannot so exclude or restrict
his liability except in so far as the term or notice satisfies the requirement of
reasonableness.

(3) Where a contract term or notice purports to exclude or restrict liability for
negligence a person's agreement to or awareness of it is not of itself to be
taken as voluntary acceptance of any risk.

The scope of section 2 is wide. Examples include architects,
builders, cleaners, dancehalls, cinemas, garages, decorators, restaurants and holiday tour operators. In all these cases—and there

---

[41] s. 13(2).
[42] *Ante,* p. 97.
[43] *Post,* p. 119.

are many more—an exemption clause or notice will be totally void in cases of death or personal injury. If the negligence results in damage to property or economic loss the clause or notice will only be effective if it satisfies the reasonableness test.[44]

(b) *Contractual obligations*

The other really far-reaching provision in the Act—and one bristling with problems—is section 3. It reads as follows:

> (1) This section applies as between contracting parties where one of them deals as consumer or on the other's written standard terms of business.
> (2) As against that party, the other cannot by reference to any contract term—
>> (a) when himself in breach of contract, exclude or restrict any liability of his in respect of the breach; or
>> (b) claim to be entitled:
>>> (i) to render a contractual performance substantially different from that which was reasonably expected of him, or
>>> (ii) in respect of the whole or any part of his contractual obligations, to render no performance at all,
> except in so far as (in the cases mentioned above in this subsection) the contract term satisfies the requirement of reasonableness.

This section is based on the recommendation of The Law Commission in their Second Report on Exemption Clauses[45] and is discussed on pages 52–62 of that Report. It applies to a contract between a businessman and a person dealing as consumer; it also applies to a contract between two businessmen where it is made on the standard written terms of business of one of them. Thus in the consumer situation there is no distinction between a standard form contract and a negotiated contract. The term "deals as consumer" is defined in section 12 as follows:

> (1) a party to a contract "deals as consumer" in relation to another party if—
>> (a) he neither makes the contract in the course of a business nor holds himself out as doing so; and
>> (b) the other party does make the contract in the course of a business; and
>> (c) in the case of a contract governed by the law of sale of goods or hire-purchase or [any other contract under which ownership or possession of goods pass] the goods passing under or in pursuance of the contract are of a type ordinarily supplied for private use or consumption.

---

[44] s. 11, *post,* p. 116.
[45] Law Com. No. 69.

(2) But on a sale by auction or competitive tender the buyer is not in any circumstances to be regarded as dealing as consumer.

(3) Subject to this, it is for those claiming that a party does not deal as consumer to prove that he does not.

If a solicitor ordered a carpet or car for his private use, and if the order was given on business notepaper, the solicitor would "hold himself out" as buying in the course of a business and he would *not* be dealing as consumer. Conversely, it seems that a holding company which has no business can "deal as consumer" for the purposes of the Act.[46] Presumably, the same result might be reached if the company merely made the contract for the benefit of the controlling shareholder. Section 12(1)(c) could give rise to problems in the case of "do-it-yourself" materials. Are wiring, cement and builders' tools "goods . . . of a type ordinarily supplied for private use or consumption?" If sales outside the trade are extremely rare, the answer would be no.

Let us assume, however, that the client does deal as consumer. In that case section 3 applies the reasonableness test in three cases. The first case is where the trader is in breach of contract and the clause excludes or restricts his liability (for example, liability limited to £100). The second case is where the trader relies on a clause giving him the right to render a contractual performance substantially different from that which was reasonably expected of him. This would apply to a condition on a theatre ticket whereby "the management reserve the right to alter the performance of any member of the cast." In the case of holidays the section would apply to a clause like the one in *Anglo-Continental Holidays Ltd.* v. *Typaldos Lines (London) Ltd.*[47] "Steamers, Sailing Dates, Rates and Itineraries are subject to change without notice." The final case covered by section 3 is where a contractual term gives the trader the right to offer no performance at all. It would seem that this provision is wide enough to cover the so-called "force majeure" clause which is very common in practice. It may provide that "the seller shall not be liable for non-delivery if delay is caused by strikes, lockouts or other acts beyond the seller's control." Even a clause giving the right of cancellation might be caught by this provision.[48] One final comment may be made: if a trader tenders

[46] *Rasbora Ltd.* v. *J. C. L. Marine Ltd.* [1977] 1 Lloyd's Rep. 645, *per* Lawson J.
[47] [1967] 2 Lloyd's Rep. 61.
[48] See Law Commission Report No. 69 *op cit.* p. 119.

a performance substantially different from that "reasonably expected of him" can the clause which allows him to do so ever be reasonable?" The question of reasonableness is considered later[49] but it might be reasonable if it formed part of an arms-length business contract between two traders where the trader attacking the clause had exactly the same provision in his own standard terms.

(c) *Implied terms*

Sale of goods. In Chapters 2, 3 and 4 we examined the terms implied by sections 12–15 of the Sale of Goods Act 1893, as amended by the Supply of Goods (Implied Terms) Act 1973. Under the 1893 Act the parties had complete freedom to exclude these obligations, because section 55, as originally drawn, provided that "where any right, duty or liability would arise under a contract of sale by operation of law it can be modified or varied by express agreement or by the course of dealing between the parties or by usage if the usage be such as to bind both parties to the contract." This provision was radically altered by the Supply of Goods (Implied Terms) Act 1973 and the controls introduced by that Act are substantially re-enacted by section 6 of the Unfair Contract Terms Act. There are three basic rules:

  (i) The condition and warranties in section 12 (right to sell) can *never* be excluded.
 (ii) Where the buyer deals as consumer (*ante*, p. 110) the conditions under sections 13 (description) and 14 (quality and fitness) can never be excluded.
(iii) Where the buyer does not deal as consumer a clause excluding the obligations referred to in (ii) above will only be valid if it satisfies the test of reasonableness.

Despite section 6 a limited amount of "contracting out" is permitted by the sections themselves. Thus it will be recalled that under section 12 the seller can agree to transfer only such title as he himself has, while section 14(2) allows the seller to avoid liability for merchantable quality by drawing the buyer's attention to the defects before the contract is made.

[49] *Post*, p. 116.

Hire-purchase. The terms implied into a hire-purchase agreement are virtually identical to those set out above[50] and section 6 of the 1977 Act controls them in exactly the same way as it does for sale of goods.

Private sales. As an exception to the general rule section 6 also applies where the seller is *not* acting in the course of a business.[51] This is unlikely to be of great practical importance because private sales are unlikely to contain exemption clauses and because, in relation to quality and fitness, there will be nothing to exclude.[52] Thus the significance of this provision is limited to attempts to exclude liability under section 13.

Other contracts. As already stated section 6 is basically a reenactment of the previous law. Section 7, however, breaks new ground. Until the passing of the 1977 Act there was a sharp distinction between sale of goods and hire-purchase on the one hand and similar contracts on the other. In the former case, the terms as to title, fitness etc were implied by statute and their exclusion was closely controlled. In the latter case the terms as to title, fitness etc were implied by common law; their exact scope was uncertain and they could be freely excluded. Section 7 of the 1977 Act does not tell us what the terms are, although it is likely that they are similar in many respects to those in sale of goods and hire-purchase contracts[53] What section 7 does do, however, is to control attempts to exclude them. The section applies where the possession or ownership of goods passes under or in pursuance of a contract not governed by the law of sale of goods and hire-purchase. With one exception, the rules are similar to those summarised under section 6. The exception is that the terms (if any) as to title are subject to the reasonableness test and not to an outright ban.[54]

If a consumer has a complaint relating to a "work and materials" contract (*e.g.* repairs to a car) it may be necessary to find out what was wrong. If the materials themselves were defective there may be strict liability and an exemption clause would be void under

[50] *Ante,* pp. 24, 39 and 54 and *post,* p. 284.
[51] See s. 6(4).
[52] *Ante,* p. 44.
[53] See Law Commission Second Report on Exemption Clauses, p. 7 and their Report on Implied Terms (Law. Com. 95).
[54] See s. 7(4).

section 7. If, however, the complaint relates to the work itself the
supplier will only be liable if negligent and a clause excluding this
liability will be subject to the "reasonableness" test under section
2(2) (or totally void if the negligence causes personal injury or
death).

(d) *Guarantees and Indemnities*

(i) **Indemnities.** Perhaps one of the most unreasonable clauses
imaginable was formerly used by a ferry company. It said in effect
"if we (the company) incur liability to a third party in carrying
your car, you (the consumer) must indemnify us—even if the
liability was entirely due to our negligence." Not surprisingly such
clauses are now controlled—perhaps the only surprising thing is
that they are not subject to an outright ban. Section 4(1) provides
that:

> A person dealing as consumer cannot by reference to any contract term be
> made to indemnify another person (whether a party to the contract or not)
> in respect of liability that may be incurred by the other for negligence or
> breach of contract, except in so far as the contract term satisfies the requirement
> of reasonableness.

The section is expressed to apply not only where the liability is
to a third party but also where the liability is to the consumer
himself. This could give rise to a conflict between section 4 and
other provisions of the Act. To take an extreme case let us suppose
that goods are supplied subject to the following condition: "the
buyer agrees that if the goods are unmerchantable the buyer will
indemnify the seller against any damages and costs payable under
any judgment obtained by the buyer against the seller." This would
be an attempt to exclude the non-excludable condition of merchantable quality[55] and would be totally void under section 6 (read
with the definition of exemption clause in section 13). It would be
extraordinary if the clause were saved by section 4.

(ii) **Guarantees.** As already stated[56] it was common practice for
a manufacturer's guarantee to exclude negligence liability. The
result was that the consumer, who thought that he was gaining
valuable rights, was in effect giving up valuable rights in return for
something which might well be far less valuable. Lord Denning

[55] *Ante*, p. 112.
[56] *Ante*, p. 70.

M.R. severely criticised such clauses in *Adams* v. *Richardson*[57]. In ringing tones he declared that "If he wished to excuse himself from liability he should say so plainly. Instead of heading it boldly 'GUARANTEE' he should head it 'NON-GUARANTEE'; for that is what it is."

Fortunately, this type of problem should now be a thing of the past because section 5 of the 1977 Act nullifies a large number of such clauses. By section 5(1):

> "In the case of goods of a type ordinarily supplied for private use or consumption, where loss or damage—
> (a) arises from the goods proving defective while in consumer use; and
> (b) results from the negligence of a person concerned in the manufacture or distribution of the goods;
> liability for the loss or damage cannot be excluded or restricted by reference to any contract term or notice contained in or operating by reference to a guarantee of the goods."

It will be appreciated that this provision neatly sidesteps the question of whether a guarantee is a contract; even if it is not a contract the purported exclusion notice will be ineffective to exclude liability for negligence.

Two further points should be noted. First, goods are "in consumer use" when a person is using them, or has them in his possession for use, otherwise than exclusively for the purpose of a business.[58] Thus if the buyer of a car and his wife are injured while the car is being used on a combined business-and-pleasure journey section 5 would control a clause in the guarantee excluding liability for the manufacturer's negligence. Presumably, if the negligence resulted in damage to property the "outright ban" in section 5 would override the section 2 "reasonableness" test. Secondly, the section does not apply as between the parties to a contract under or in pursuance of which possession or ownership of the goods passed.[59] In such cases the consumer would have the benefit of section 2 in relation to negligence and sections 6 and 7 in relation to the implied terms.

(e) *Misrepresentation*

Exemption clauses relating to misrepresentation have been controlled since the passing of section 3 of the Misrepresentation Act

[57] [1969] 1 W.L.R. 1647.
[58] s. 5(2) (*a*).
[59] s. 5(3).

1967. Section 3 is redrafted by section 8 of the Unfair Contract
Terms Act so that it now reads as follows:

> If a contract contains a term which would exclude or restrict—
>> (a) any liability to which a party to a contract may be subject by reason of
>> any misrepresentation made by him before the contract was made; or
>> (b) any remedy available to another party to the contract by reason of such
>> a misrepresentation,
> the term shall be of no effect except in so far as it satisfies the requirement
> of reasonableness as stated in section 11(1) of the Unfair Contract Terms Act
> 1977; and it is for those claiming that the term satisfies that requirement to
> show that it does.

The first point to notice here is that the law is to be found in
section 3 of the Misrepresentation Act 1967 (as amended) and not
in the Unfair Contract Terms Act. It follows that the section
applies to all contracts (including those excluded from the Unfair
Contract Terms Act) and it is not confined to "business liability."

What type of clauses are caught by section 3? Some cases are
obvious: "The purchaser shall have no right to rescind this agreement" or "All liability for misrepresentation is excluded." On the
other hand a clause stating that "no employee of the company has
any authority to make representations on the company's behalf"
might be effective.[59a] Finally, the contract might state that
"although every care has been taken the vendors do not warrant
the accuracy of these particulars and the purchaser shall not rely
on them." If such a clause were upheld it would severely limit the
scope of section 3. It seems that if the other party does rely on the
incorrect particulars there will be a misrepresentation and the
clause will be treated as an exemption clause to which section 3
applies.[60]

The reasonableness test

Sections 2, 3, 4, 6, 7 and 8 all refer to the reasonableness test.
The concept is not a new one; it has applied to misrepresentation
since 1967 and it has applied to the implied terms in sale of goods
and hire-purchase since 1973. Section 11 draws a distinction
between contractual clauses and non-contractual notices. In the
case of contract the person claiming that the term is reasonable
must prove that:

[59a] See *Overbrooke Estates Ltd.* v. *Glencombe Properties Ltd.* [1974] 1 W.L.R.
1335.
[60] *Cremdean Properties Ltd* v. *Nash* (1977) 244 E.G. 547, C.A.

the term shall have been a fair and reasonable one to be included having regard to the circumstances which were, or which ought reasonably to have been, known to or in the contemplation of the parties when the contract was made.[61]

Thus the critical date is the date of the contract. For example, a limitation of damages clause which was reasonable at the date of the contract will be upheld even though by the time of the hearing it has become hopelessly inadequate by reason of inflation or by reason of the plaintiff's loss being far greater than expected.

If we turn now to non-contractual notices the party relying on the notice must prove that:

it should be fair and reasonable to allow reliance on it, having regard to all the circumstances obtaining when the liability arose or (but for the notice) would have arisen.[62]

Guidelines. In any case involving the reasonableness test the court has a wide discretion and must consider all the relevant circumstances; presumably if the matter comes to court the defendant should be advised to plead the facts on which he relies to support his claim of reasonableness. Schedule 2 contains a non-exhaustive list of guidelines but these only apply under sections 6 and 7. They are virtually identical to the guidelines which previously appeared in the Supply of Goods (Implied Terms) Act 1973, and can be summarised as follows:

(a) The bargaining strength of the parties (including the alternatives (if any) available to the customer).

(b) Any inducement given to the customer.

(c) Whether the customer had an opportunity of entering into a similar contract with other persons without the disputed clause

(d) Whether the customer knew, or ought to have known, of the existence of the term.

(e) Where the term excludes or restricts liability if some condition is not complied with, whether it was reasonable at the time of the contract to expect that compliance would be practicable.

(f) Whether the goods were manufactured, processed or adapted to the special order of the customer.

---

[61] s. 11(1).
[62] s. 11(3).

In other cases no specific guidelines are laid down but it is felt that the first three of the above matters—bargaining power, knowledge and choice—are likely to be critical in most cases. The size of print would also be relevant, and a clause is unlikely to be upheld if it is out of line with a Code of Practice adopted by the trader's Trade Association.[63] The continued use of immensely wide exemption clauses could influence the court in a case involving the reasonableness test. It may be that a clause that "the seller can cancel this agreement in the event of strikes etc" should now be redrafted so as to give a mutual right to rescind. It is also possible, although unlikely, that the contract will specify the factors on which the trader relies in support of his claim of reasonableness. Perhaps we may see the emergence of a dual price contract, £X with full responsibility or £Y without it. We may also see "split clauses"—different clauses dealing with consequential loss, limitation of liability and time limits for claims. All this is speculative; many organisations are adopting a wait-and-see attitude.

Limitation of damages clauses. A number of small traders (including travel agents) felt very uneasy about the possibility of having to meet very large claims and accordingly Lord Hailsham introduced a new clause which is now section 11(4). It reads:

> Where by reference to a contract term or notice a person seeks to restrict liability to a specified sum of money, and the question arises (under this or any other Act) whether the term or notice satisfies the requirement of reasonableness, regard shall be had in particular . . . to
> > (a) the resources which he could expect to be available to him for the purpose of meeting the liability should it arise, and
> > (b) how far is was open to him to cover himself by insurance.

This provision, if it is ever litigated, is bound to cause problems. Do the "resources" of a sole trader or partner include his private assets? How far afield does he have to search to find insurance? What happens if the premium would destroy or seriously reduce the commercial viability of the transaction? The defendant will presumably have to plead these matters; if he fails to do so the plaintiff can ask for further and better particulars.

Reasonableness and fundamental breach. It will be recalled that where the innocent party treats the contract as discharged by reason of fundamental breach, or if he is compelled to do so

---

[63] *Post*, p. 121.

because the breach renders further performance impossible, the exemption clause cannot be relied upon by the contract breaker.[64] In certain circumstances this rule is reversed by section 9 of the 1977 Act. Section 9 applies if:

    (i) the clause on its true construction covers the breach, and
    (ii) the clause is subject to the reasonableness test, and
    (iii) the clause passes that test.

If these conditions are satisfied the clause will apply to the breach even though the contract has come to an end, or even though the innocent party has elected to treat the contract as discharged.[65] Conversely, the affirmation of the contract by the innocent party does not oust the reasonableness test if that test would otherwise apply.[66]

3. OTHER CONTROLS

Although the Unfair Contract Terms Act 1977 is by far the most important example of statutory control of exemption clauses there are many other statutory controls. One of these, section 3 of the Misrepresentation Act 1967—has already been mentioned. There are also a number of other Acts relating to the carriage of passengers by public service vehicle, rail and air (see particularly the Carriage by Air Act 1961). Other examples include the Occupiers Liability Act 1967, the Defective Premises Act 1972 and the Solicitor's Act 1974. For the summary of the statutory controls readers are referred to Chitty on Contracts, Vol. I, pp. 387–390.

---

[64] *Harbutt's Plasticine* case, *ante*, p. 104.
[65] s. 9(1).
[66] s. 9(2).

CHAPTER 9

"HOW DO I ENFORCE MY RIGHTS"

IN the previous chapters we have considered the consumer's rights and remedies and attempts to exclude them or to cut them down. We come now to the all important question—how can the rights be enforced? The lawyer tends to think immediately of court proceedings but in this branch of the law the courts should only be used as a last resort—if only because the cost of proceedings may exceed the amount in dispute.

Scheme of this chapter

A short introduction will be followed by an examination of some codes of practice—one of the most important developments in the consumer field in recent years. This will be followed by a section dealing with the London and Manchester Small Claims Courts. The final section deals with county court proceedings and arbitration.

1. HOW TO START

The obvious first step is to contact the supplier. If the client himself does not receive satisfaction he might call in to see his solicitor, Citizen's Advice Bureau, Consumer Advice Centre or the Consumer Protection Department of the local authority. A letter sent to the head office, or to the managing director, might produce results. Alternatively, a member of the staff of the Consumer Protection Department might visit the shop to see what the shop has to say. These departments are anxious to adopt a neutral role—to play the part of conciliator rather than advocate. They do, of course, compile lists of complaints and forward them from time to time to the Office of Fair Trading.

If the shopkeeper himself is not co-operative the next step might be to contact his trade association. This is especially relevant if the trader has subscribed to a code of practice recommended by the trade association. This is considered below.

Mention must also be made of the national press, the local press, radio and television. Many of these bodies have someone dealing with consumer matters and if they are satisfied that the consumer has had a raw deal they will print or publish a story about it. Needless to say they will take great care to get their facts right because damages for defamation can be very high.

Finally most of the nationalised industries have Consumers Consultative Committees which deal with consumer complaints. A short summary appears in Appendix 3.[1]

2. CODES OF PRACTICE

(A) *Introduction*

One method of improving standards of business practice across the board is to introduce legislation (with criminal sanctions) on such matters as trade descriptions, weights and measures and safety.[2] A second method is to use subordinate legislation under Part II of the Fair Trading Act 1973 to correct particular abuses.[3] A third method is to leave it to the different sectors of commerce to put their own houses in order by the introduction of voluntary codes of practice by the various trade associations. The development of voluntary codes can be regarded as the most significant contribution which the Fair Trading Act 1973 has made to the protection of individual consumers and accordingly it may be useful to examine this topic in some detail.

Section 124(3) of the Fair Trading Act places a duty upon the Director to encourage associations "to prepare, and to disseminate to their members, codes of practice for guidance in safeguarding and promoting the interests of consumers." To date 17 codes have been negotiated with the O.F.T. including cars, electrical appliances, travel agents, shoes, laundries and cleaners, mail order trading and furniture. The names and addresses of the sponsoring trade associations are given in Appendix 2.[4]

[1] *Post*, p. 356.
[2] See *post*, p. 153 *et seq.*
[3] *Post*, p. 216 *et seq.*
[4] *Post*, p. 350.

Operative from	Code
Oct. 1974	AMDEA (Association of Manufacturers of Domestic Electrical Appliances: Principles for Domestic Electrical Appliance Servicing.
Jan. 1975	ABTA (Association of British Travel Agents): Codes of Conduct.
March 1975	Electricity Boards in England and Wales: Domestic Electrical Appliance Servicing.
May 1975	SMTA (Scottish Motor Trade Association): Used Car Code.
Feb. 1976	MAA (Motor Agents Association): SMTA (Scottish Motor Trade Association): SMMT (Society of Motor Manufacturers & Traders): Code of Practice for the Motor Industry.
Nov. 1975	VBRA (Vehicle Builders and Repairers Association): Code of Practice for Vehicle Body Repair (Motor Car and Caravan Sector).
Dec. 1975	Scottish Electricity Boards: Domestic Electrical Appliance Servicing.
Feb. 1976	NASRF (National Association of Shoe Repair Factories): St. Crispin's Boot Trades Association Ltd: Code of Practice for Shoe Repairs.
April 1976	ABLC (Association of British Launderers & Cleaners Ltd.): Code of Practice for Domestic Laundry and Cleaning Services.
Aug. 1976	FDF (Footwear Distributors Federation): Code of Practice for Footwear.
Sept. 1976	RETRA (Radio, Electrical and Television Retailers' Association (RETRA) Ltd.): Code of Practice for the Selling and Servicing of Electrical and Electronic Appliances).
July 1977	MOPA (Mail Order Publishers Authority): Code of Practice.
Aug. 1978	Furniture Industry Code of Practice.
Nov. 1978	Mail Order Traders' Association: Catalogue Mail Order Code of Practice.
Mar. 1979	N.A.F.D. (National Association of Funeral Directors): Code of Practice on Funerals.
April 1979	Photographic Industry Code of Practice.
June 1979	Post Office Codes: Postal and Telecommunication Services.

Advantages?

Whether voluntary codes are to be preferred to legislation is a matter of debate. The advantage from the point of view of industry is that traders are allowed to police themselves, but this in turn is disadvantageous to the consumer. It is clear from the results of monitoring exercises undertaken by the O.F.T. in relation to cars, shoes, laundries and holidays that predictably not every member of a trade association honours its code and more surprisingly not every trade association checks to ensure that its members follow the code. For example, in monitoring the A.B.T.A. Code after its first three years of operation from January 1975 it was discovered that ten members continued to publish brochures with conditions contrary to the code: the Association took action only after this was drawn to their attention by the O.F.T. A related point is the sanctions available to associations against members who break the codes. These range from expulsion or a fine to no sanction at all except the "club" threat of social ostracism by their peers.

Another serious disadvantage of relying on voluntary methods is that, even if all members of an association comply with their obligations, the rogues in the trade may well not be members. This is particularly true of the motor trade. The Director must then turn to other weapons in his armoury, *e.g.* seeking an assurance under Part III of the Fair Trading Act 1973[5] or refusing a credit brokerage licence under the Consumer Credit Act 1974.

However some advantages can be cited. Legislation would necessarily be of a general nature and inappropriate for setting precise standards for a particular industry, for example, pre-delivery inspections of cars or service calls within 3 days for electrical appliances. Secondly, businessmen are more likely to comply with their own optional rules than with statutory obligations imposed against their will. Thirdly, codes can be improved by re-negotiation; for example, the A.B.T.A. Code was amended after a year to include surcharges and overbooking, both common causes of complaint. Lastly, the opportunity for conciliation and arbitration affords a cheap and quick mode of resolving disputes instead of taking action in the courts.[5a]

[5] *Post,* p. 230.
[5a] For an assessment of trade arbitrations see "Simple Justice," a report published by the National Consumer Council in September 1979, especially pp. 71–82.

Conciliation

All the codes provide conciliation procedures, but only some provide arbitration as a last resort. Generally conciliation procedures conform to the same pattern (suggested in Part 1 of this chapter). A dissatisfied customer should first bring his complaint to the attention of the manager, partner, proprietor or director of the business. If the complaint is not resolved, then it may be appropriate to seek the help of a trading standards officer, Consumer Advice Centre or Citizens' Advice Bureau. If the complaint relates to new goods, the customer may agree to the manufacturer being brought in. Where the dispute is still not settled and the trader is a member of a trade association, the customer should ask the association to conciliate. No charge is made for this service. However, it should be remembered that the association may appear to the consumer, rightly or wrongly, to lack impartiality and to be prejudiced in favour of its own member. If only for this reason an opportunity to put the matter before a truly independent arbitrator is valuable where conciliation fails.

Arbitration

Where a code provides for arbitration, the customer is required to pay a fee ranging from £5–£10, often refundable where the claim is upheld: this is the limit of his liability where the arbitration is on the basis of "documents only." Clearly this does not cover the full cost of the arbitration, the balance being borne by the association. The arbitrator will be appointed by the Institute of Arbitrators. Normally the arbitration will be "documents only." The expense of attended oral arbitrations is so great that they are discouraged both by the associations and by the Director[6]; for the purpose of writing arbitration procedures into the codes is to provide an inexpensive and quick adjudication of the dispute.

Publicity

It is not enough to introduce legislation and codes of practice to bolster the consumer in his perpetual confrontation with the business world. Such rights are useless unless he knows of them and can exercise them. To ensure that as far as possible the consumer is made aware of his rights the Director is empowered by section 124(1) to arrange for the publication "of such infor-

[6] See, for example, the A.B.T.A. travel agents code, pp. 140 and 344.

mation and advice as it may appear to him to be expedient to give to consumers" insofar as the matters fall within his duties under section 2(1).[7]

From its inception the O.F.T. has enthusiastically exercised this power. Numerous pamphlets and posters are available free of charge to inform the consumer and trader of their respective rights and obligations in respect of goods or services. Some attempt to persuade the consumer to consider his position before entering into a contract ("STOP AND THINK"); others advise him of his position after the event when things may have gone wrong ("How to put things right"). Retailers are brought up to date on the changes in the law relating to the sale of goods by "A Retailer's Guide." Some publications are aimed at particular age groups: "GET SMART: YOUR COMPLETE GUIDE TO SHOPPING WITHOUT TEARS" is written in the style of a comic with cartoons for the benefit of teenagers.

A series of pamphlets has been issued to provide information about the codes of practice:

Buying by post
Cars
Electrical Goods
Launderers and Dry Cleaners
Package Holidays Abroad
Furniture
Shoes

It is difficult to say whether the effect of recent consumer legislation and the codes has been to improve the quality of goods and services. The following table, taken from the Director's Annual Report for 1977, Appendix 1, shows that complaints notified to the O.F.T. in 1977 increased by 26 per cent over 1976.[7a] Probably this rise is at least partly due to the fact that consumers are better informed of their rights as a result of the publicity campaigns waged by the O.F.T. and the news media and thus more ready to complain.

---

[7] cf. the Consumer Credit Act 1974, s. 4, which imposes a *duty* on the Director to disseminate information and advice about the operation of the Act and the credit facilities available to the public.
[7a] The 1978 Annual Report (H.C. Paper No. 79, Session 1978/9) shows a decrease of 3 per cent, an encouraging trend.

Consumer complaints analysed by type of goods, servicing, or service

Goods	No. of complaints		Complaints per £M spent	
	1976–77	1975–76	1976–77	1975–76
Radio, television and electronic reproduction equipment ..	24,583	24,826	28·2	33·3
Refrigerators, deep freezers, washing machines, vacuum cleaners	18,382	17,884	61·7	70·1
Other household appliances ..	34,116	26,133	45·4	40·6
Fresh food	12,015	12,019	1·5	1·8
Manufactured food and drink	31,647	25,388	2·2	2·1
Footwear	29,400	22,835	29·7	24·8
Clothing	48,188	41,795	9·1	8·8
Textiles	9,721	6,303	14·0	10·6
Furniture	42,460	32,142	46·0	39·4
Floor coverings	15,509	14,765	20·0	21·6
Toilet requisites, soaps, detergents, etc	2,991	2,709	6·2	5·6
Toys, games, sports goods, etc	8,137	6,860	3·9	3·9
Solid fuel	2,878	2,632	5·8	6·0
Liquid fuels	9,517	7,227	3·4	2·9
Motor vehicles	57,544	44,438	22·4	20·9
Motor vehicle accessories ..	16,446	9,925	27·6	19·5
Watches, clocks and jewellery	18,959	12,385	35·8	27·4
Other consumer goods ..	62,986	44,855	8·9	7·3
Non-consumer goods ..	4,097	2,980	—	—
Servicing of goods				
Washing machines, re- frigerators and cleaners	6,453	6,429	57·1	61·2
Motor vehicles	14,408	9,576	15·1	10·7
Footwear	958	788	16·0	14·1
Radio and TV	5,875	5,741	87·7	92·6
Other repairs and servicing ..	9,541	7,463	64·5	54·1
Cleaning	8,498	7,121	45·7	40·9
Services				
Land, including houses ..	2,674	1,739	1·1	0·7
Construction	16,415	12,011	7·7	6·0
Public utilities	15,735	13,776	5·3	5·0
Transport	1,293	1,438	0·5	0·7
Entertainment and accommodation	5,688	5,068	1·4	1·4
Holidays	7,434	6,538	2·7	2·8
Professional services	12,917	9,565	6·8	5·9
Consumer credit	5,943	4,062	—	—
Special offers	2,133	1,562	—	—
General services	25,086	19,525	7·7	6·5
Total	590,627	470,503		

Note: The expenditure figures used in calculating the ratio have been taken from *National Income and Expenditure, Family Expenditure Survey,* and IPC *Marketing Manual of the United Kingdon 1977.* These have been modified where necessary by the index of retail sales taken from the *Monthly Digest of Statistics.*

B. *Particular Codes*

Cars

There are three codes:

Code of Practice for the Motor Industry.[8]

V.B.R.A. Code of Practice for Vehicle Body Repair.

S.M.T.A. Used Car Code.

The O.F.T. leaflet "Cars" explains the codes.

The Motor Industry

This code was drawn up by the M.A.A., S.M.T.A., and S.M.M.T. It governs the conduct of manufacturers, importers, distributors and retail dealers. It covers the supply of new and used cars, petrol, parts and accessories and servicing and repair. Its main provisions are set out below.

(i) New cars. Dealers should carry out the pre-delivery inspection required by the manufacturer and make available a copy of the P.D.I. check list. Order forms must make clear the total price payable to put the car on the road and their conditions must be fair and reasonable.

(ii) Manufacturers' warranties. The dealer should draw the terms of the warranty to the attention of the consumer. It must state that it does not adversely affect the consumer's remedies against the seller.[9] Transfer to subsequent owners should be allowed. The consumer may take the car to any franchised dealer for rectification work. An extension of the warranty period may be given when the car has been off the road for an extended period or if faults worked upon during the warranty period recur later.

(iii) Used cars. Dealers are reminded of their obligations under the Sale of Goods Act 1893, *e.g.*, merchantable quality. Guarantees should not purport to take away the consumer's rights and should state that they are in addition to his statutory rights. Copies of information provided by previous owners about the car's history should be passed on, *e.g.*, service records. Advice is given about odometers and the form of disclaimer to be used. This topic is also of great practical importance under the Trade Descriptions

---

[8] *Post,* p. 309. It is currently being revised.

[9] This is now a statutory requirement under The Consumer Transactions (Restrictions on Statements) Order 1976: see p. 221.

Act 1978.[10] The code also provides that all descriptions "shall be honest and truthful." This highlights the weakness of the codes; dishonest traders, against whom the public most need protection, are generally not members of the relevant trade associations and accordingly are not subject to the provisions of the codes.

(iv) Servicing. A distinction is drawn between quotations and estimates. A firm quotation should be given for a major repair. Where estimates are given, it should be made clear that they are only estimates. In either case the VAT position must be clarified. If a charge is to be made for the estimate, for example, to cover dismantling, the consumer should be notified in advance. No attempt should be made to exclude liability for loss or damage to cars or contents which must be adequately protected and insured. Repairs must be guaranteed for a specific mileage or period.

(v) Discounts. These should be based on fair comparisons, *i.e.* the dealer's previous price or manufacturer's recommended price.[11] "Worth," "value" and "up to" claims are frowned upon.

(vi) Complaints. The following procedure is laid down:
  (a) First refer the complaint to the dealer, addressing it to a senior executive, director, partner or proprietor.
  (b) If it relates to a new car warranty and the dealer does not resolve the matter, contact the manufacturer direct.
  (c) If no satisfactory solution is reached, write to the relevant trade association provided the dealer is a member:
          new car warranty claim—S.M.M.T.
          dealer in Scotland—S.M.T.A.
          dealer in the rest of the U.K.—M.A.A.

Although the code imposes no time limits, the M.A.A. have prescribed their own limit by requiring complaints to be made in writing within three months of the complaint arising. This time limit is given the appearance of propriety by being mentioned by the O.F.T. in their pamphlet "Cars." It is arguable that the operation of this bar is itself in breach of the code. In any case, three months is too short a period, bearing in mind the weeks of discussion and correspondence which may elapse before the con-

---

[10] *Post,* p. 165.
[11] Presumably this will need amendment as the O.F.T. recommendations on "Bargain Offers" have now been implemented: see p. 229.

sumer loses patience with the dealer and considers alternative steps. The problem is not academic: the M.A.A. Annual Report 1977 reveals that 244 complaints were rejected because they were "out of time limits."

(d) The trade association will try to effect a settlement between the consumer and its member.

(e) If conciliation fails, the association will arrange for arbitration. A fee of £7.50 plus V.A.T. is payable by the consumer, which may be returned if the claim is successful. A single arbitrator is appointed by the Institute of Arbitrators. The arbitration will normally be "documents only"—the cost of oral arbitration is prohibitive and none has so far been conducted under the code. A written award is made which is enforceable in the courts.

(f) Consumers must be advised that they may sue in the courts instead of choosing arbitration. However, as arbitration is cheap and reasonably quick, it is preferable in the usual, run of the mill case involving comparatively small sums.

(vii) Monitoring. The trade associations are required to analyse all complaints about the code or other matters referred to them for conciliation or arbitration.

The S.M.M.T. Annual Report 1977 shows that 642 complaints were received, of which only 9 needed to go to arbitration to be resolved. The M.A.A. Annual Report 1977 reveals 4,954 complaints. Of the 3,504 cases completed by conciliation 72 per cent were met in part at least by the dealer. Exactly 50 per cent of the 170 claims referred to arbitration were successful, although not entirely in most cases. Sums of less than £50 were involved in 80 per cent of the settled complaints. These figures clearly show the value of the code's conciliation and arbitration procedures.

Body Repairs

The V.B.R.A. Code of Practice for vehicle body repair is, as its title discloses, much more limited in its scope than the Motor Industry Code. In cases where the garage is a member of both the M.A.A. and V.B.R.A., the consumer will have the benefit of both codes, where a body repair is involved.

In many respects it is similar to the Motor Industry Code. It deals with estimates and "legal, honest and truthful" advertisements. Guarantees must last for at least six months or 6,000 miles, whichever occurs first, and be transferable to later owners.

The complaints procedure follows the pattern outlined earlier. First complain to the trader, who should give ready access to senior management. Next seek the advice of a trading standards officer, C.A.B., Consumer Advice Centre, etc. Then proceed to use the V.B.R.A. Conciliation Service under which the complaint may be referred to an independent examiner appointed by the Institute of Automotive Engineer Assessors. No fee is payable for conciliation. If a member has ceased trading and cannot comply with a settlement recommended under the Conciliation Service, the association will pay up from its "Contingency Fund" established for the purpose.

As a last resort arbitration is available. The fee is £10. The arbitrator is appointed by the Institute of Arbitrators. It is normally on a "documents only" basis.

Scottish used car code

The S.M.T.A. Used Car Code is also called the Used Car Consumer Protection Plan. It applies only to those vehicles with a special symbol on the windscreen. It defines the terms of four standard warranties ranging from six months or 6,000 miles (parts and labour) to one month or 1,000 miles (parts only). It lays down a code of preparation, including a major service, to be done before the car is offered for sale. It provides a conciliation service and for a £10 fee an arbitration service. If a garage cannot comply with a settlement or award, the association will do so.

Furniture

The Voluntary Code of Practice for Furniture, explained in the O.F.T. leaflet "Furniture," is one of the most recent codes. It was prepared by the following trade associations:

Branded Furniture Society,

British Furniture Manufacturers Federated Associations,

National Association of Retail Furnishers,

National Bedding Federation Ltd.,

Scottish House Furnishers Association.

The code covers new household furniture: it does not include contract, garden or office furniture.

The theme of the code is familiar.

(i) *Advertising*

Advertising must be clear and honest: misleading price offers are prohibited.

(ii) *Prices*

Prices charged are normally to be those ruling when the goods are offered for sale: if the retailer proposes to charge the price ruling at the delivery date, he must tell the customer so.

(iii) *Delivery and deposits*

Delivery dates should be quoted in writing, when deposits are taken, except when delivery should take place within one month. If a specific delivery date is not met, any deposit will be refunded on request.

(iv) *Labels*

A labelling system is to be introduced by the end of 1979 to inform buyers of the basic construction of the furniture, the materials used and the finish, for example, solid wood, wood veneer or plastic laminate.

(v) *Conciliation and arbitration*

The usual procedure (in this and other recent codes called a "four-step" procedure) is adopted:
- (a) Contact the retailer, where "senior management must demonstrate a high degree of interest and involvement in customer problems!"
- (b) Seek help from a local consumer adviser.
- (c) Use the trade associations' conciliation service by writing to the National Association of Retail Furnishers or the Scottish House Furnishers Association. Where an independent examiner needs to be appointed to inspect the goods, a £5 charge is payable.
- (d) Finally independent arbitration is available for an undisclosed fee, normally on a "documents only" basis.

(vi) *Glossary*

The code contains a useful eight page glossary of descriptive terms for furniture and bedding, for example, antique, melamine faced, zip and link, latex foam, hair pad, glide and other terms of art.

Launderers and dry cleaners

The Code of Practice[12] for Domestic Laundry and Cleaning Services was drawn up by the Association of British Launderers and Cleaners Ltd. which represents about 80 per cent of such traders in the United Kingdom. The O.F.T. leaflet "Launderers and Dry Cleaners" explains its main provisions.

(i) *Exclusion clauses*

Members will not exclude or limit their liability for negligence. They will reprocess free of charge any article which has been processed unsatisfactorily due to their fault. Where loss or damage is caused by fire or burglary, even though the trader is not negligent, compensation will be paid unless the customer has his own insurance cover.

(ii) *Prices*

A list of prices for standard articles should be displayed.

(iii) *Delay*

Where an article has been mislaid and not returned within a reasonable time, a reduction in the charge is recommended to compensate for the customer's inconvenience.

(iv) *Conciliation*

The A.B.L.C. has a Customer Advisory Service to whom unresolved complaints should be referred in writing. If the A.B.L.C. considers that a laboratory test is necessary, this will be made free of charge; otherwise a fee is payable—the O.F.T. leaflet indicates £10–£15.

Arbitration is not available.

(v) *Monitoring*

The O.F.T. undertook an exercise in 1977 to monitor the first year of operation of the code. Its conclusion was that the code has

---

[12] *Post*, p. 330.

brought some "major benefits" to consumers. The great majority of A.B.L.C. members are generally complying with the code's provisions and their standards of trading practice are generally superior to non-members. The following figures taken from their research paper[13] clearly show that, though adherence to the code by members is far from complete, there is a marked difference between the attitudes of members and non-members.

Practice	Members	Non-Members
Disclaimer notices displayed	16%	36%
No price list displayed	28%	52%

Shoes

There are two codes:

F.D.F. Voluntary Code of Practice for Footwear.

Code of Practice for Shoe Repairs.

The O.F.T. leaflet "Shoes" outlines their provisions.

Sales

The Code of Practice for Footwear was drawn up by the Footwear Distributors Federation and sponsored by the F.D.F. and five other associations concerned with the manufacture, distribution and retailing of footwear. Although surprisingly compliance with the code is not a condition of membership of the associations, some 6,700 distributors with about 60 per cent of the retail trade and 225 manufacturers voluntarily subscribe to the code. Its more significant features are these.

(i) **Prices.** These must be V.A.T.-inclusive. Reductions must be on the retailer's previous price or the manufacturer's recommended price: other claims are prohibited, for example, "price elsewhere."[13a] Deposits are returnable within seven days of an unmet delivery date.

(ii) **Exclusions.** Notices appearing to limit customer's rights are banned, for example, "No goods exchanged."

(iii) **Fitting.** Measuring facilities should be available where children's shoes are sold.

[13] Bee Line, Special Edition Research Paper, No. 2 (November 1977): A.B.L.C. Code—First Year of Operation.
[13a] Such a provision would in any event now be illegal—see, post p. 229.

(iv) **Labels.** The materials used in the uppers and soles and the country of origin must be marked on the shoes or labels.

(v) **Complaints.** There are no conciliation or arbitration procedures. However, an independent report may be obtained for £2 from the Footwear Testing Centre. A monitoring exercise conducted by the O.F.T. on the code's first year of operation showed that the test decisions were divided exactly evenly between customers and traders.[14] However, 18 per cent of F.D.F. members subscribing to the code refused to use the testing facilities. The paper suggests that the £2 fee is too high, particularly in relation to children's shoes, and should be reduced. Although making other criticisms its main conclusion is that "the Code of Practice is being generally well-observed by members and this is resulting in significant improvements in the standards of trading practice."

Perhaps the most important question is whether adherence to the code should be obligatory on all members of the sponsoring associations as is the case with all the other codes. As it is, if a member subscribing to the code fails to comply, he can be removed from the *scheme,* not from membership. Thus if he finds the code too burdensome, he shrugs it off. What disincentive is there to such an irresponsible attitude?

Repairs

Members of the National Association of Shoe Repair Factories and St. Crispin's Boot Trades Association, more than 7,500 in total, are governed by the Code of Practice for Shoe Repairs. It applies not only to their repair services but also to their sales: in the latter case its guidance is almost identical to the F.D.F. code discussed above.

Its repairing provisions are similar to the Laundry Code explained earlier (they came into operation within two months of each other). In the case of a complaint the associations are prepared to conciliate and to obtain an independent test report, apparently free of charge, but arbitration is not available.

[14] Bee Line, Special Edition Research Paper, No. 5 (August 1978): Monitoring the Footwear Code of Practice. 36 per cent were completely justified, 36 per cent completely unjustified and 28 per cent shared 50/50.

Electrical Goods

There are four codes:

R.E.T.R.A. Code of Practice for the Selling and Servicing of Electrical and Electronic Appliances.[15]

A.M.D.E.A. Principles for Domestic Electrical Appliance Servicing.

Domestic Electrical Appliance Servicing by Electricity Boards.

Domestic Electrical Appliance Servicing by Scottish Electricity Boards.

The O.F.T. leaflet "Electrical goods" explains the codes.

In the trade such goods fall into two categories: "white goods," *i.e.* domestic appliances, such as washing machines, refrigerators, cookers and toasters; and "brown" goods such as radios, televisions and record players. All the codes cover white goods; only the R.E.T.R.A. code includes brown goods as well.

R.E.T.R.A. Selling and Servicing Code

R.E.T.R.A. is an association of retailers and represents more than 4,000 shops. The code covers both the sale of goods and their servicing and repair. The following are some of its more important provisions.

(i) **Sale of goods.** Prices should be clearly indicated. Discounts should not involve imprecise comparisons such as "worth" or "value" claims. Refunds are encouraged even where a customer has simply changed his mind and has no right to his money back. Where a retailer receives a deposit, he should indicate the delivery period and, if delivery is not made in time, offer the customer a refund (this is, of course, no more than he is obliged to do).

A guarantee of new goods must be given, covering parts and labour for a minimum period of a year. This is additional to the buyer's rights under the Sale of Goods Act 1893 and under any manufacturer's guarantee. If the retailer cannot effect a repair within fifteen working days from the date of notification of the defect, he should normally lend a similar item or, if this is impracticable, extend the guarantee period. Where a customer moves

[15] *Post,* p. 321.

F

away, the guarantee should be transferred on request to a local retailer.

(ii) **Repairs and servicing.** The retailer should accept for repair goods sold by him but not necessarily other goods (*e.g.* bought from a rival discount shop?). Customers will be told the minimum service charge when they ask for service. Estimates should be offered in the case of major repairs. The code points out that quotations when accepted constitute a contract binding upon both parties. Customers are encouraged to return faulty goods to the workshop, which should be so organised as to be able to complete 80 per cent of all repairs within five working days. Where they request a visit, this should be made within three working days; if the repair cannot be effected then, it should normally be completed within a further 15 working days. (One is tempted to ask whether the association's aim of providing prompt and efficient after sales service is fulfilled when it may take three weeks to repair such essential equipment as a washing machine or spin drier.) The retailer will guarantee repairs on products outside the normal guarantee period for three months for parts and labour.

(iii) **Life expectancy.** The code states that "most electronic equipment can be expected to last about 7 years and in certain cases this period may be longer." Presumably "electronic equipment" means brown goods. It is arguable that this provides a guide as to the meaning of "merchantable quality" in this context, *i.e.* that the retailer will be liable, if the goods prove to be beyond economic repair within that period.

No guide is given in respect of the life expectancy of domestic appliances. However, a table is included of the availability of functional parts, which at least gives an indication of the durability of the appliances in the list. "Functional parts" are electrical and mechanical parts which are essential to the continued operation and safety of the appliance.

Small appliances.	5–8 years
Cleaners, direct acting space heaters, refrigerators and freezers, spin and tumble driers and wash boilers.	8 years

| Cookers, dishwashers, washing machines. | 10 years |
| Thermal storage space heating. | 15 years |

(iv) **Conciliation.** The now familiar sequence is suggested. First complain to the retailer or service agent. Next try the C.A.B., trading standards officer or Consumer Advice Centre. Finally complain in writing to the Secretary of R.E.T.R.A. under its Conciliation Service. If he cannot resolve the dispute, it may be referred to the R.E.T.R.A. Conciliation Panel. No fee is payable. However, arbitration is not available. If conciliation is unsuccessful, the customer will have to resort to the courts.

A.M.D.E.A. Servicing Code

A.M.D.E.A. is an association of manufacturers. The code covers only white goods. Its aim is to ensure that users of domestic appliances receive the same high standard of service, whatever the source of the product and whether the service is provided directly by the manufacturer or indirectly by electricity boards, major retailers or specialised servicing organisations.

Its provisions are similar to the servicing provisions of the R.E.T.R.A. code: advice as to minimum charges; initial visit within three working days (although in this code it is an average—so presumably the association would reject a complaint that in 10 per cent of the cases the first call was made after twelve days if the other 90 per cent of the calls were made within two days); 80 per cent of workshop repairs within five days; functional parts available for the same periods as in the table above. The recommendation relating to guarantees is weak: it specifies no minimum period, although it should cover parts and labour.

It improves on the R.E.T.R.A. code in one respect, namely by offering independent arbitration, not merely conciliation. The fee is only £5. It is normally on a documents only basis. It covers only claims relating to the appliance itself and its servicing, not claims for personal injuries.

The Electricity Boards Codes

There are two similar codes, the Electricity Boards Code, which covers England and Wales, and the Scottish Electricity Boards Code. Each is concerned only with the servicing of domestic appliances; this is an odd limitation of their after-sales responsibilities in view of their sales including brown as well as white goods.

The codes have almost identical provisions to those in the A.M.D.E.A. code. The aims of all three codes are the same: (1) to offer service within an average of three working days at a reasonable cost; (2) to carry adequate stocks of spare parts and to ensure that functional parts are available throughout the reasonable life of the product; (3) to resolve complaints and to provide conciliation and simple arbitration.

The complaints procedure is as follows:

  (i) Complain to the local manager of the Board's shop.
 (ii) Next write to the manager of the Area Electricity Board.
(iii) Conciliation is the third stage. The independent Electricity Consultative Councils perform this role. There is one for each Area Board.
(iv) Finally independent arbitration may be sought for a £5 fee.

Travel Agents

The A.B.T.A. Code of Practice[16] consists of two Codes of Conduct in the same document—the Tour Operators' Code and the Retail Agents' Code. It was first introduced in January 1975, but was amended a year later to take account of criticisms by the O.F.T. with regard to surcharges and overbooking. It should be observed that it is not limited to holidays outside the United Kingdom: the title of the O.F.T. leaflet "Package holidays abroad" may give a false impression. All A.B.T.A. members (about 300 tour operators and 1,750 travel agents) are bound by the code. The first three years' operation was monitored by the O.F.T.[17]: some of the results of that exercise are mentioned below.

---

[16] *Post,* p. 340.
[17] Bee Line, Special Edition Research Paper, No. 3. (February 1978): Monitoring the A.B.T.A. Code.

Tour operators

(i) **Booking conditions.** They should not exclude liability for mis-representation by the tour operator, his employees or agents, or for breach of his contractual duties in arranging the holiday. Customers must be given at least 28 days from the end of the holiday in which to make complaints. Surcharge conditions should be given prominence. However, a number of members were still using exclusion clauses in 1978 in breach of the code.

(ii) **Cancellation.** Problems have often been caused by holidays being cancelled or rearranged by the tour operator at the last minute. Now a cancellation must not be made after the date when the balance of the price becomes due; if it occurs before that date, customers must be informed as soon as possible and offered a choice between a comparable alternative holiday and a full refund. Exceptionally it may be necessary to cancel as a result of hostilities, political unrest or force majeure: again a choice should be offered of an alternative holiday or a refund, but in this case less reasonable expenses.[18]

There are comparable provisions relating to material alterations to holiday arrangements. That is as it should be; for what is the difference to a customer with holiday booked in Acapulco between cancelling it and offering him a holiday in Rhyl? In either case the holiday in Mexico is cancelled, either specifically or by a unilateral variation.[19]

(iii) **Overbooking.** Cancellation and alteration caused by over-booking of hotels, which may be the fault of the tour operator or the hotel management, are dealt with by separate provisions of the code. Where this occurrence is beyond the control of the tour operator, the code imposes different obligations depending on whether or not he knows of the overbooking before the departure of the customer. (1) If he is aware at that stage, he must immediately inform the customer and offer an alternative holiday or full refund as above. (2) If it is discovered only on arrival, the customer must

---

[18] In the absence of such a provision in the contract, it might be frustrated. Expenses could then be awarded out of any deposit under the Law Reform (Frustrated Contracts) Act 1943, s. 2. See also s. 3 of the Unfair Contract Terms Act 1977, *ante,* p. 111.

[19] Such terms would now be open to attack, if not reasonable, under the Unfair Contract Terms Act 1977, s. 3.

be offered alternative accommodation plus "disturbance" compensation where the location or facilities are inferior.

The code proceeds on the basis that the tour operator has complied with the code by taking all reasonable steps to ensure that arrangements are not cancelled or altered, *i.e.* he can show that the overbooking is beyond his control. Presumably if he is at fault and the blame cannot be laid at the door of "some damn unreliable foreigner", the customer will be treated at least as generously.

The monitoring exercise reveals that complaints on this score have remained at about the same level.

(iv) **Surcharges.** Surcharges resulting from fluctuations in the rates of exchange have been a major cause of discontent amongst holidaymakers. The code was strengthened in 1976 to prohibit such surcharges, unless made more than thirty days before departure, and complaints fell by over 90 per cent from 1975 to 1977. However, four of the thirty major companies were still in 1978 reserving the right to impose surcharges up to the date of departure: these breaches have been referred to A.B.T.A. by the O.F.T.

(v) **Conciliation and arbitration.** A.B.T.A. will conciliate where there is a breakdown in communication or serious disagreement. The number of complaints declined from nearly 6,000 in 1975 to about 4,000 in 1976 (3.7 million holidays were taken), suggesting that standards of business had improved as a result of the code's introduction. One might have expected the volume of complaints to increase because of the publicity given to the code.

Arbitration is available for disputes not settled by conciliation. Its availability should be included as a term of the contract in booking conditions so that customers are aware of this facility, but for the first year or so this provision was ignored more often than not by A.B.T.A. members.

"Documents only" arbitration is the norm. Attended hearings are available with the disincentive of the prospect of paying unlimited costs: from the introduction of the code in January 1975 to July 1977 there were only seven hearings out of 76 completed arbitrations, the costs in one of them amounting to £1,672, hardly a cheap method of resolving disputes. Accordingly the O.F.T. recommended in their Research Paper that attended hearings be withdrawn from the scheme. Nor was arbitration speedy in the early days—tour operators were reluctant to agree to go to arbitration and six cases took about a year to resolve. However, their attitude to the scheme has now improved and consultations are in hand with a view to introducing a stricter timetable to ensure that all arbitrations are completed within four months.

It can be seen from the tables reproduced below from the O.F.T. Research Paper that out of the 76 completed arbitrations 86 per cent of the customers received an award (62 per cent of the successful applicants being awarded over £50) and 70 per cent paid no costs at all.

Arbitration Awards

Results of Arbitration	No. of Cases
Case withdrawn	1
No award	10
Awarded £1 –£50	18
Awarded £51 –£100	20
Awarded £101–£200	16
Awarded £201–£500	8
Over £500	3
TOTAL	76

Arbitration Costs Paid by Consumer

Amount	No. of Cases
Nil	53
0–£15	15
£15–£30	6
Over £30	2*
TOTAL	76

* These were attended hearings in which the consumer lost the case and paid costs of £176 and £1,692 respectively.

Retail agents

The code relating the conduct of retail agents (the High Street travel agents) covers such matters as ensuring that counter staff "carefully study all . . . brochures" to provide accurate and impartial information to customers (yet how often is the customer simply given an armful of glossy brochures and left to work out for himself which operator offers the best terms for children, off-peak holidays etc.?); passing on immediately alterations to travel arrangements; advising on insurance, visas, currency; and generally acting as intermediaries in negotiations and disputes between the tour operators and the customers. So presumably it is now unheard of for an agent, having booked a holiday and earned his commission, to wash his hands of the matter and, like a retailer of goods, to tell the customer to go direct to the tour operator/supplier in case of difficulty.

The code does not bring retail travel agents within the conciliation and arbitration procedures. This is probably nothing more than a drafting error, as in practice A.B.T.A. does deal with complaints relating to travel agents. Possibly, however, the distinction has introduced on the ground that they are merely agents of the tour operators. All contracts are made between the tour operators and the customers and all disputes about the holiday inevitably concern only the tour operator as principal. The code describes the operators as "principals" thus fortifying the above view.

Relationship between the parties

The Law Commission Second Report on Exemption Clauses[20] touches on an interesting and difficult question—the precise legal relationship between the customer and the other organisations involved in providing his holiday (the retail agent, the tour operator, the hotelier and the airline). It is suggested that generally the position is as follows. The customer makes only one contract with one legal entity—the tour operator. This is effected via the travel agent who acts on behalf of the tour operator, not the customer. As the agent is known to be acting for a named principal, he will incur no personal responsibility to the customer on the contract. The contracts for accommodation and transportation are made by the tour operator on his own account: only he is responsible to the hotelier and airline for these costs, even though the services will be supplied by them to the tour operator's customer. Clearly the tour operator is under an implied obligation to his customer to pay the necessary sums to the carrier and hotelier to enable the customer to travel to and stay at his chosen resort without additional payment; if he fails to do so, so that the carrier

[20] Law Com. No. 69, (1975) para. 126.

or hotelier refuse to provide their services to the customer unless the customer himself pays for them direct, the tour operator will have broken his contract with the customer and be liable in damages for such additional charges.

Although the travel agent is not a party to the main holiday contract, he may incur liability to the customer in other ways. If he makes untrue statements to the customer about the subject-matter of the contract, for example, hotel amenities, he may be liable (1) in tort for deceit[21] or negligence[22] or (2) breach of an implied warranty of authority if the statement is outside his actual or ostensible authority. Further he may be in breach of a collateral contract between himself and the customer—a contract collateral to the main contract between the tour operator and the customer. Such rights against the travel agent are unlikely to be needed unless the tour operator is unable to meet his responsibilities under the main contract, e.g. because he is bankrupt or in liquidation.

Disciplinary procedures

The A.B.T.A. Codes of Conduct give the association the power to investigate infringements of the codes and to impose penalties ranging from a reprimand to a fine or even termination of membership. The record fine to date is £1,500 imposed on Intasun and a further £1,500 on Intasun North for breach of the provision relating to overbooking.[23] It is encouraging to see A.B.T.A. taking its responsibilities so seriously.

The five latest Codes

Five codes per year were launched in 1975 and 1976. Then came a quiet period with only one new code (M.O.P.A.). appearing in the two years from September 1976. However, the introduction of the Furniture Code in August 1978 heralded another period of activity with five codes in the following twelve months: presumably five per year is not an O.F.T. quota but merely historical accident.

This latest quintet includes the Mail Order Traders' Association Code, which covers mail order trading via catalogues, a huge industry with 15 million regular customers. This code complements the Mail Order Publishers' Authority Code, approved by the

[21] *Ante,* p. 78.
[22] *Ante,* p. 79.
[23] See *The Times,* October 13, 1978, news item.

O.F.T. the previous year, which deals with the supply of books and records through the post, *e.g.* book clubs. Neither code is concerned with the supply of other goods in response to newspaper and magazine advertisements: some protection is given in these cases by the British Code of Advertising Practice enforced by the Advertising Standards Authority and the "Readers' Protection Scheme" administered by the Newspaper Publishers Association. All these codes are explained by the Newpaper Publishers Association. All these codes are explained in the new O.F.T. leaflet "Buying by post."

The three latest codes will be of particular interest to the reader whose colour film of his rich aunt's exorbitantly expensive funeral has been lost in the post on the way to the processing laboratory. The National Assocation of Funeral Directors, whose members arrange 80 per cent. of funerals, negotiated their code with the O.F.T. at the invitation of the Government following the Price Commission Report on Funeral Charges in 1977. The Photographic Industry Code of Practice covers a wide range: manufacturers, importers, retailers and repairers of photographic equipment and films; the film processing industry; and professional photographers. The ambit of the latest code is self-explanatory—the Post Office Codes of Practice, dealing with its postal and telecommunications services.

3. ARBITRATION—THE MANCHESTER AND WESTMINSTER SCHEMES

Cheap, Quick, Informal

Until 1971 the consumer, faced with a supplier who was not prepared to meet his proper obligations, had no choice but to abandon his complaint unless he was determined enough to launch himself upon the uncertain seas of litigation. The prospect of such action caused the consumer considerable anxiety for three principal reasons. First, it was likely to be expensive because of the level of legal fees. Secondly—and a related point—although he could save legal fees by conducting the case himself, he was put off playing the role of the litigant in person by the formality and complexity of court proceedings. Thirdly, he knew litigation to be a long-winded affair and was unhappy at having the doubtful outcome hanging over him like the sword of Damocles for years on end. Whatever the validity of these reasons—and many within the legal profession would say that they bear little resemblance to the realities of the situation—the layman saw access to his legal rights guarded by a Cerberus whose three heads were expense, delay and formality.

These disadvantages were particularly identified in the nineteen sixties and fully discussed in "Justice out of Reach," the crucial report by the Consumer Council published in 1970. The report proposed a nationwide system of small claims courts, drawing partly upon experience in North America. (It is salutary to recall that the county courts were set up in 1846 to provide the sort of forum being ardently espoused a century and a quarter later.) The nearest we have come so far to such a system incorporating the triple desiderata of cheapness, speed and informality are the voluntary small claims arbitration schemes introduced in Manchester (1971) and Westminster (1973) and the county court arbitration scheme inaugurated in 1973.[24]

The Manchester Scheme

The Manchester Arbitration Scheme for Small Claims started in 1971: it was the first of the schemes, proving the Mancunian saying "What Manchester does to-day, the world does to-morrow." For the first three years it was financed by the Nuffield Foundation. It is now completely funded by the Greater Manchester Council and actively supported by the Manchester Law Society and the local and national C.A.Bx., all of which are represented on its management committee.

Jurisdiction

Its area of operation is limited to cases having a connection with Greater Manchester County. Claims are accepted if the claimant or respondent reside, work or carry on business there; the contract was made or to be performed there; or the accident occurred there.

Generally claims are accepted if they could go to the county court, subject to a maximum of £500—it was increased from £250 in July 1978. Claims are generally in respect of a contract, for

[24] See p. 151.

example, goods bought, work done. Wrongful dismissal is covered, but not unfair dismissal nor redundancy, *i.e.* contractual not statutory employment rights. Road accident claims are accepted, but only as regards damage to property. Personal injury claims are outside the scheme. Landlord and tenant cases (other than claims for rent arrears) are taken if they can be satisfied with a money judgment.

The claimant must usually be a private person, but the "one man business" is not turned away.

Cost
£1 fee is payable by both the claimant and the respondent: this is never refunded, even where the claim is settled. Additionally the arbitrator may, but rarely does, order one or both of the parties (usually the loser) to pay up to £10 to the scheme in reimbursement of an expert's fees and expenses.

Legal representation
Unlike the county court legal representation is prohibited. This is to ensure that proceedings do not become formal or legalistic and that the claimant is not placed at a disadvantage to the respondent, usually a trader, having a solicitor to put his case. However, either party may bring a friend to assist him. (Does no one have a lawyer as a friend?)

Voluntary
The greatest drawback is that the arbitration is voluntary: the claim will proceed to arbitration only if the respondent consents (*cf.* compulsory county court arbitration). About a third of the respondent businessmen will not agree to participate, judging quite correctly that the consumer will probably not bother to pursue them to court, if they abjure the voluntary scheme. It is primarily for this reason that support continues undiminished for a comprehensive system of small claims courts to run in parallel with the county courts as part of the legal system: only when such a general scheme is introduced will the difficulties of the litigant in person disappear.

Procedure
The procedure is simple and straightforward, as it must be if it is to fulfil its aim of enabling the consumer to bring a claim himself

whether well-educated, articulate or not. The claimant completes a form whereby he offers to submit the dispute to arbitration under the scheme and undertakes to abide by the arbitrator's award. Provided that the respondent agrees, the claim will then proceed to arbitration.

Arbitrators are appointed by the President of the Manchester Law Society. In the early days they were all lawyers, but from 1974 other experts were appointed, for example, surveyors. Thus if a dispute relates to building works, it is possible to appoint an arbitrator with relevant professional expertise, to hold the arbitration on site and to decide the claim on the spot without the need for a separate site inspection by an expert: the rules of the scheme provide for reports by experts and site inspections.

The arbitration may be on a "documents only" basis, if the arbitrator and both parties prefer; otherwise a hearing will take place. As we have seen, legal representation is not allowed. The hearing is informal with everyone in ordinary dress round a table in an office. There are no rules of evidence: hearsay evidence may be admitted.

The parties sign a form that the decision shall be final; this excludes the general right of appeal on a point of law under section 1 of the Arbitration Act 1950. All awards and costs should be paid to the scheme, not to the other party, within seven days of the decision being posted. If the loser does not pay up—and this happens in less than 2 per cent of the cases—it is necessary for the successful party to issue a default summons in the county court under the Administration of Justice Act 1977, s. 17(2). This is another disadvantage of the scheme: the award cannot be enforced directly under the scheme, as it is not a judgment of a court.

The scheme in operation

The complaints come directly from the consumer and indirectly from Consumer Protection Departments, C.A.Bx., solicitors, the press, etc. They number about 3,000 per annum of which 700 or so result in claims. No figures are published showing, for example, the proportion of claims which are successful, since this is likely to colour the attitudes of businessmen and to lead them to believe that the scheme is not impartial and leans in favour of the consumer: hence a statistical break-down of "wins" and "losses" by claimants is not divulged.

Westminster (London) Scheme

The Westminster Small Claims Court followed the Manchester scheme both chronologically in 1973 and systematically. Its first funding came from the Nuffield Foundation for a three year experiment, initiated by the City of Westminster Law Society. It was then rescued from imminent demise by the provision of office facilities in the Polytechnic of Central London and a grant from the Greater London Council, when it changed its name to the London Small Claims Court. At present it is seeking support from the London Boroughs' Association.[24a]

Although broadly following the Manchester pattern, it differs in some respects. Its jurisdiction embraces all of England and Wales in theory, but in practice claimants are unlikely to bring a dispute to London for hearing unless they are within easy, and so cheap, travelling distance. Its title—"Court," not "Arbitration Scheme"—should not mislead: it fulfils exactly the same function as its northern elder brother and suffers from the same disadvantage with regard to the enforcement of awards. Claims must normally be for sums between £10 and £350. They may relate to personal injury as well as those covered by the Manchester scheme. The fee is from £5–£10.

The future

In the light of the two serious disadvantages of both schemes—the need for the respondent's co-operation and the lack of enforcement procedures—it might have been anticipated that the extension of the county court arbitration in 1973 would have made the voluntary schemes obsolete at their very inception. This has not proved to be so. This would suggest that their popularity is due to the fact that they are not part of the "official" courts system and therefore lead the consumer to expect informality and an absence of red tape. If this diagnosis is correct, the county court facility will not replace the voluntary schemes, however informal the conduct of cases by registrars may become. Again, it may be that as the arbitration procedures under the existing codes of practice become better known and as more codes are negotiated and approved by the O.F.T., the need for the Manchester and London Arbitration schemes will diminish. Yet even then not all traders in dispute will be members of trade associations and not

[24a] The end is nigh. No funds are forthcoming from the G.L.C. or L.B.A.: *The Guardian*, October 4, 1979.

all associations, as we have seen, have arbitration procedures. So for many years there will be a continuing need for the voluntary schemes. It is to be hoped that the existing funds for Manchester keep flowing and those for London are forthcoming before the infant dies of malnutrition.

4. PROCEEDINGS IN THE COUNTY COURT

If no settlement can be reached it may be necessary to take proceedings in the county court (or in the High Court if the claim exceeds £2,000). The vital question to consider is whether the cost, trouble and anxiety of litigation will, in the end, be justified.

Legal assistance

Under the Legal Aid Act 1974 the consumer may be entitled to assistance from a solicitor and counsel if he (the consumer) qualifies financially. The ceiling for assistance is raised once or twice a year to reflect changes in earnings and inflation; by section 1(1) of the Act the consumer will qualify if:

(a) his "disposable income" (as defined) does not exceed £75 per week, or

(b) he is in receipt of supplementary benefit or family income supplement, and

(c) in either case his "disposable capital" (as defined) does not exceed £600.

If his disposable income exceeds £35 per week he may have to pay a contribution towards the costs.[25]

The scope of this form of assistance is limited in two respects. First of all, by section 2(3) this form of assistance does not cover the institution or conduct of any proceedings before a court or tribunal except negotiating a settlement. Secondly, by section 3 the cost of the assistance is limited to £25 unless this limit is increased by the Area Committee in any particular case. Thus the scheme could be useful for writing letters, negotiating settlements and giving general advice on such matters as how to draw the particulars of claim. The actual conduct of the proceedings would, however, have to be conducted by the client in person unless he can obtain a legal aid certificate for proceedings or unless he is prepared to instruct the solicitor privately.

[25] See s. 4.

Legal aid

Section 6 of the 1974 Act enables legal aid to be granted for the conduct of civil proceedings where the client has a "disposable income" (as defined) not exceeding £3,600; it may, however, be refused if he has disposable capital exceeding £1,200 and it appears that he can proceed without legal aid. Once again he may have to pay a contribution if his disposable income and/or capital exceed a specified amount.[26] There is also a general power to refuse legal aid if (inter alia) it appears unreasonable that he should receive it in the particular circumstances of the case.[27]

Costs and the statutory charge

If the claim is a very small one the grant of legal aid might be refused under section 7(5) *supra* and even if it is granted it may not be very beneficial. If a person is granted legal aid for proceedings he or she will select a solicitor from a panel. The client may have to pay a contribution to the legal aid fund (see above). If the claim succeeds then:

   (a) the defendant will be ordered to pay a sum of money (for example, damages or return of price) to the plaintiff;

   (b) the defendant *may* have to pay the plaintiff's taxed costs (but see below);

   (c) the plaintiff's solicitor will be paid out of the legal aid fund.

If we pause at point (b) we must consider C.C.R. Order 47 r. 5(4) as amended by S.I 1978 No. 794. These rules provide that solicitors' costs are not generally recoverable from the other side where the amount recovered is £200 or less; the registrar can, however, allow costs in his discretion where the amount recovered exceeds £100. The object of this rule is to encourage litigants to use the county courts for small claims (and to do without a solicitor). If he were to be liable without limit to pay the legal costs of his opponent (who might be a large corporation instructing two or three highly experienced lawyers) he would almost certainly be deterred from using the county court.

Returning now to legal aid, let us assume that the plaintiff recovers damages of £150 and no costs. Let us assume that his contribution was £30 and that the legal aid fund pay his solicitor

[26] See s. 9(1).
[27] See s. 7(5).

£160 for his costs and disbursements. The legal aid fund have now made a "loss" of £130 on the case and to that extent section 9(6) gives them a first charge on any property recovered or preserved in the proceedings. So at the end of the day, the consumer has recovered £150 of which £130 goes to the legal aid fund, leaving only £20 for the consumer himself (as he has already contributed £30 he ends up £10 out of pocket!).

Arbitration

The above figures strongly point towards "do-it-yourself" claims, but clearly the litigant in person will feel out of his depth on such matters as pleading, particulars, discovery, pre-trial reviews and, above all, the hearing in open court. As already stated, a solicitor may be able to help behind the scenes under the £25 scheme. There are also two booklets to assist the litigant in person—one published by the Consumers' Association[27a] and one published by the Office of the Lord Chancellor and available from the court.[27b] Finally, there is the system of arbitration under C.C.R. Ord. 19 r. 1. A plaintiff can ask for a reference to arbitration in his particulars of claim; if the amount claimed does not exceed £200 the proceedings will be referred for arbitration by the registrar (unless an outside arbitrator is asked for).

The object of the arbitration procedure is to remove some of the terrors of litigation for the litigant in person. Accordingly, the Lord Chancellor has issued a practice direction suggesting that the terms of the order referring the case to arbitration should usually contain the following provisions:

(a) The strict rules of evidence shall not apply.
(b) With the consent of the parties the arbitrator may decide the case on the basis of the statements and documents submitted by the parties. Otherwise a hearing date will be fixed.
(c) Any hearing shall be informal and may be held in private.
(d) At the hearing the arbitrator may adopt any method of procedure which he may consider to be convenient and to afford a fair and equal opportunity to each party to present his case.
(e) If any party does not appear at the arbitration, the arbitrator

---

[27a] How to Sue in the County Court.
[27b] Small Claims in the County Court.

   may make an award on hearing any other party to the
   proceedings who may be present.
(f) With the consent of the parties and at any time before giving
   his decision and either before or after the hearing, the
   arbitrator may consult any expert or call for an expert report
   on any matter in dispute or invite an expert to attend the
   hearing as assessor.
(g) The costs of the action up to and including the entry of
   judgment shall be in the discretion of the arbitrator to be
   exercised in the same manner as the discretion of the court
   under the provisions of the County Court Rules (or as the
   case may be).

How widely is it used?

A survey on small claims arbitration was recently carried out by
the Birmingham University Institute of Judicial Administration.
This showed that between 1974 and 1977 the number of arbitrations
rose from 5,911 to 10,017. Nearly two-thirds were in respect of
goods and services, and rather surprisingly, firms were defendants
in only twenty four per cent of the cases. This clearly suggests that
the scheme is not being extensively used for its primary purpose,
i.e. encouraging litigants in person to bring their claims to the
county court.

An article in the New Law Journal[28] contrasted the figures given
in the Report with the vast number of consumer complaints reaching the Office of Fair Trading.[29] These figures clearly illustrate the
point made at the beginning of this Chapter—namely that the
county court is there to be used as a last resort.

Postscript

The National Consumer Council have recently published a
valuable report entitled "Simple Justice." This recommends (*inter
alia*) the setting up of a small claims division in the county courts.
This report should be read by anyone concerned with small claims.

---

[28] November 2, 1978, p. 1059.
[29] See also *ante,* p. 126 and a further comment in [1978] New Law Journal, p. 1131.

PART II: THE CONSUMER AND THE CRIMINAL LAW

CHAPTER 10

INTRODUCTION

In Part I we have examined the consumer's position as far as the civil law is concerned. We saw that it is not enough for him to show that he has a right of action, for example, for breach of contract or negligence. His main problem is how to enforce that right. It is evident from the figures given at the end of Chapter 9 that the proportion of complainants who are prepared to sue to enforce their rights is minute. This encourages traders to assume that they can adopt careless and sloppy practices with impunity. If they can get away with providing shoddy goods and incompetent service, traders will be enticed into lowering their standards by the prospect of increased profitability. Not only is this clearly contrary to the interests of consumers; it is equally unfair to the honest trader who endeavours to maintain high standards and at the same time to compete with the rogues operating in the same line of business.

In pursuing its two-fold aim—to protect consumers and to ensure that honest traders are able to make a living on equal terms without the need to resort to the malpractices of their dishonest competitors—Parliament has increasingly turned to the sanctions of criminal law in its search for control. This approach has the significant advantage for the consumer that the expensive and time-consuming process of disciplining the rogue is entrusted to public servants who normally in recent legislation have a duty to enforce its provisions. If the provisions of the criminal law enable the consumer to obtain full compensation,[1] it will be unnecessary for him to rely on the rights explained in Part I: they will be superfluous.

The full range of criminal controls is very extensive.[2] The following examples show some of their ambit.

(1) The Food and Drugs Act 1955 controls the quality of food. Section 2 prohibits the sale of "any food which is not of the nature, or not of the substance, or not of the quality, of the

---

[1] See Chap. 13, *post*, p. 203.
[2] See the table on p. 155.

153

food demanded by the purchaser," for example, containing maggots, mould or metal.

(2) The Weights and Measures Act 1963 (as amended by the Weights and Measures Act 1979) empowers trading standards inspectors to test weighing and measuring equipment, and also makes it an offence to deliver short weight when goods are sold by weight, number or other measurement.

(3) The Trade Descriptions Act 1968 controls business activities at large insofar as they involve descriptions of goods, services or prices. Criminal sanctions are imposed for non-compliance.[3]

(4) The Fair Trading Act 1973, Part II, enables orders to be made outlawing general trade practices which adversely affect the economic interests of consumers, for example, the use of certain exemption clauses invalidated by the Unfair Contract Terms Act 1977. A trader who contravenes one of these orders commits a criminal offence.[4]

(5) The Consumer Credit Act 1974 creates a large number of criminal offences (*e.g.* carrying on a consumer credit business without a licence).[5]

(6) The Consumer Safety Act 1978 enables regulations to be made prohibiting the supply of unsafe goods. It is an offence to fail to comply with such regulations.[6]

In Part II we propose first in Chapter 11 to look in detail at the Act with has given rise in recent years to more consumer complaints than all the other criminal legislation put together—the Trade Descriptions Act 1968.[7] We then in Chapter 12 survey the provisions of the most recent Act in the consumer area—the Consumer Safety Act 1978. Finally in Chapter 13 we consider the important question of compensation for the victims of criminal offences. How can they obtain financial redress for any loss which they may have suffered as a result of the convicted person's failure to comply with his statutory obligations under the criminal law? Two aspects are examined—orders for compensation under the Powers of Criminal Courts Act 1973 and the right to bring civil proceedings for breach of statutory duty.

[3] See Chap. 11, p. 155.
[4] See Chap. 14, p. 214.
[5] See Chap. 18, p. 255.
[6] See Chap. 12, p. 192.
[7] See the table on p. 155.

CHAPTER 11

TRADE DESCRIPTIONS

INTRODUCTION

IN the Review of the Trade Descriptions Act 1968 published in 1976 the Director General of Fair Trading stated that "by and large, the Act has achieved what its authors and Parliament intended it to do: encourage high standards of truthfulness in describing goods and services."[1] However, although the Review contains numerous recommendations to strengthen the Act, the Director emphasised that "widely as the Act had been drawn, it was never intended to be a panacea for all consumer ills" (para. 2).

Clearly it has not proved to be so, as is evidenced by the Director's Annual Report for 1977.[2] Consumer complaints notified to the Office of Fair Trading numbered well over half a million for the year ending September 30, 1977, an increase of 26 per cent on the previous 12 months.[3] The Report is unclear whether the increase was "due to a general rise in the level of consumer dissatisfaction, a greater readiness by consumers to seek aid from the enforcement and advisory bodies, or a combination of both." The analysis of consumer complaints by criminal legislation contained in the Report shows by far the largest single category to be complaints under the 1968 Act.

Consumer complaints analysed by criminal legislation

	No. of complaints	
	1976–77	1975–76
Trade Descriptions Act 1968	35,228	33,792
Weights and Measures Act 1963	11,297	10,823
Food and Drugs Acts 1955 and 1956 (Scotland)	11,224	10,696
Trade Descriptions Act 1972	1,480	1,555
Consumer Protection Acts 1961 and 1971	1,251	531
Unsolicited Goods and Services Act 1971	763	865

[1] Cmnd. 6628, para 1.
[2] H. C. Paper No. 228, Session 1977/78. Appendix 1.
[3] But see *ante*, p. 125, note 7a.

155

Mock Auctions Act 1961	92	79
Agriculture Act 1970	126	72
Public Health Acts 1936 and 1961	445	471
Advertisements (Hire-purchase) Act 1967	42	35
Trading Stamps Act 1964	114	179
Fair Trading Act 1973	202	57
Pharmacy and Poisons Act 1933	71	74
Medicines Act 1968 and 1971	26	12
Explosives Acts 1875 and 1923	53	52
Employment Agencies Act 1973	14	24
Trading Representations (Disabled Persons) Acts 1958 and 1972	49	38
Hallmarking Act 1973	386	285
Prices Act 1974	1,763	1,365
Counter Inflation Act 1973	135	139
Consumer Credit Act 1974	1,094	669
Other criminal laws	2,812	2,546

Background to the Act

As early as 1423 an Act was passed regulating the marking of silver plate. Others dealt with the marking of gold and other precious metals, cutlery and linen. The first statute to cover goods in general was the Merchandise Marks Act 1862 which was replaced in 1887 by an Act of the same name. This was added to by later statutes culminating in the Merchandise Marks Act 1953.

Apart from these statutes dealing specifically with marking, there are related Acts dealing with other aspects of the supply of goods. For example, the Food and Drugs Act 1955, s. 6, makes it an offence for a person to display a label with any such goods or publish an advertisement which:

"(a) falsely describes the food or drug or
(b) is calculated to mislead as to its nature, substance or quality."

The Weights and Measures Act 1963, consolidating earlier legislation from 1878–1936, as its name implies, is particularly concerned with the *quantity* of certain goods being sold, *e.g.* coal and petrol, and with ensuring that weighing and measuring equipment is accurate, *e.g.* petrol pumps, whereas the 1968 Act is concerned with *quality*. There is one major similarity between the two Acts, namely, that their provisions are enforced by trading standards officers (formerly known as inspectors of weights and measures) employed by local authorities but responsible at ministerial level to the Department of Trade (as to which see *ante*, p. 3). While it is true that the above legislation has the effect of protecting the consumer, most of the legislation, like that relating to patents and trade marks, was passed with the intention of protecting one trader or manufacturer against unfair competition from another who would otherwise be tempted to make business use of the goodwill attaching to a particular mark or brand-name.

The position with regard to trade descriptions generally was looked into about twenty years ago by the Committee on Consumer Protection, generally known as the Molony Committee, which published its Final Report in 1962.[4] It paid particular attention to the working of the Merchandise Marks Acts and highlighted a number of defects:

(a) Consolidation was desirable in view of the law being contained in a multiplicity of Acts.

(b) The Acts were limited in their scope since they were only relevant where a description had been "applied" to goods, *i.e.* where goods had been physically marked with labels, dies, blocks, etc. Thus oral statements and many advertisements were not covered.

(c) Whatever the merits of the Acts, they were not generally enforced. The Acts of 1891 and 1894 gave the Board of Trade and Ministry of Agriculture, Fisheries and Food respectively the power to enforce the regulations; the Local Government Act 1933 gave a similar power to local authorities and an individual could bring a private prosecution. Yet nobody was under a *duty* to enforce them. The Committee found that only about a dozen prosecutions were brought each year by the Board of Trade, though a larger number were brought by local authorities.

These defects have been largely cured by the passing of the Trade Descriptions Act 1968.

Purpose and ambit

The 1968 Act came into force on November 30, 1968. It repealed all the Merchandise Marks Acts with exception of some provisions of the 1926 Act dealing with the origin of imported goods which

---

[4] Cmnd. 1781.

continued in force for a further three years.[5] (This relief from origin marking was short lived. It was reintroduced by the Trade Descriptions Act 1972: imported goods with a reasonably visible British name or mark must bear a conspicuous indication of the country of origin.)

The beginning of the preamble to the Act sets out its essential purpose and scope:

> "An Act to replace the Merchandise Marks Act 1887 to 1953 by fresh provisions prohibiting misdescriptions of goods, services, accommodation and facilities provided in the course of trade; to prohibit false or misleading indications as to the price of goods . . ."

The preamble discloses the three main offences:

(a) applying a false trade description to goods or supplying goods with such a description[6];
(b) giving a false indication as to the price of goods[7];
(c) making a false statement as to the provisions of services, accommodation or facilities[8].

Before considering these offences in detail, two important general features of the Act need to be grasped. First, the Act operates in the criminal area only: it probably does not give any civil remedy to the misguided consumer[8a]. Secondly, it applies only to suppliers in the course of trade or business, *i.e.* not to private suppliers.[9] However, it is irrelevant whether or not the recipient of the goods or services is a private consumer or a trader: the Act protects all and sundry[10]—domestic consumers, sole traders, partnerships and corporations.

---

[5] s. 42 and Sched. 2.
[6] s. 1.
[7] s. 11.
[8] s. 14.
[8a] See *post*, p. 211. For the possibility of a compensation order see *post*, p. 205.
[9] The by-pass provision (s. 23) is an exception. See p. 185.
[10] cf. the distinction drawn between "consumer" transactions and others in the Unfair Contract Terms Act 1977, s. 12(1)(*a*) (*ante*, p. 110); and the Fair Trading Act 1973, s. 137 (2).

In the course of trade or business

As mentioned above, the Act applies to business suppliers only. Section 1[10a] includes an express limitation to persons "in the course of a trade or business" and section 14[10b] has an almost identical limitation to persons "in the course of any trade or business": apparently the two expressions have the same meaning.

Section 11[10c] contains no equivalent phrase and is capable of a wide interpretation covering private and business transactions. However in *John* v. *Matthews,*[11] where an offence was alleged to have been committed in a working man's club, the Divisional Court held that the section did not apply in the case of domestic bodies or households. Lord Parker C.J. considered it clear on the lay-out of the Act that it related only to transactions of a commercial nature and that a limitation to trade or business was implied in the section. However, to put the matter beyond doubt, the Review recommends that section 11 be re-drafted to incorporate an express limitation.[12]

Another question giving rise to some slight doubt is whether the professions fall within the scope of the Act. Unlike the Fair Trading Act 1973, s. 137, and the Consumer Credit Act 1974, s. 189, no definition of "business" is given so as to make it clear that professional practice is included. It seems probable that the professions are covered in the light of the *obiter dicta* of the Divisional Court in *R.* v. *Breeze,*[13] a case on section 14 concerning an architectural student describing himself as an architect. The point was left open because the defendant was convicted on the basis that, as he lacked the necessary professional qualification, it did not lie in his mouth to say that he was engaging in a professional activity. Here again the Review recommends a clarifying amendment.

Clearly the Act applies where the essence of the business is the supply of the goods or services in question. Yet the Act is wider. Provided the transaction occurs in the course of *a* business, it may

---

[10a] *Post,* p. 160.
[10b] *Post,* p. 178.
[10c] *Post,* p. 173.
[11] [1970] 2 Q.B. 443.
[12] Lord Diplock expressed a similar view in *Tesco* v. *Nattrass* [1972] A.C. 153 p. 193, another section 11 case.
[13] [1973] 1 W.L.R. 994.

be caught even though it does not form part of the primary activities of the business. Thus in *Havering L.B.C.* v. *Stevenson*[14]:

> The defendant ran a car hire business. When the cars were about two years old, his practice was to sell them and to use the proceeds to buy new cars. He sold a car with a false description as to the mileage. When prosecuted he argued that the sale was outside section 1, since he did not carry on the business of a car dealer. The Divisional Court was unmoved. When a car hire business as part of its normal practice buys and sells cars, the sale of a car and the related application of a trade description is an integral part of (and thus in the course of) the car hire business.

This leaves open the situation where the sale or other transaction is an isolated occurrence. It is submitted that this too would be within the scope of the Act.[15]

GOODS

Section 1(1) prohibits false trade descriptions of goods.

> Any person who, in the course of trade or business,—
>   (a) applies a false trade description to any goods; or
>   (b) supplies or offers to supply any goods to which a false trade description is applied;
> shall, subject to the provisions of this Act, be guilty of an offence.

Business suppliers

An offence is committed only by a person acting "in the course of a trade or business." The provision does not catch supplies by private persons.

Two offences

Section 1 covers two different offences; first, the application of a false trade description to goods; secondly, the supply of goods to which such a description has already been applied. Thus the first offence would be committed by a manufacturer incorrectly labelling goods, while the second offence would occur when a retailer displays or sells those same goods.

[14] [1970] 1 W.L.R. 1375.

[15] Consider the same expressions in section 14(2) and (3) of the Sale of Goods Act 1893 and the interpretation by the House of Lords of these provisions, before their amendment in 1973, in *Ashington Piggeries Ltd.* v. *Christopher Hill Ltd.* [1972] 2 A.C. 441. The comments of Lord Wilberforce at p. 494 are particularly apposite.

Applying a false trade description

A wide meaning is given by section 4 to the word "applies." It covers:

(1) markings on the goods themselves, *e.g.* labels;

(2) markings on anything in which the goods are supplied, *e.g.* packaging;

(3) markings on anything in which the goods are placed, *e.g.* display units, vending machines, point of sale material;

(4) oral statements, specifically mentioned in section 4(2).

The inclusion of oral descriptions is one of the major differences between the 1968 Act and the Merchandise Marks Acts which were limited to the physical application of descriptions to goods.[16] This extension of the law was effected against the recommendation of the Molony Committee whose reasons for the preservation of the status quo are set out in paragraph 659 of their Report.

Descriptions used by the customer in his request for goods, when it is reasonable to infer that the goods are supplied as goods corresponding to that description, are deemed to have been applied by the supplier.[17] Thus if a customer asks a men's outfitters for a cotton shirt and is supplied with a nylon shirt, the shopkeeper applies the description "cotton" to the shirt even if he says nothing and the shirt is not labelled.

In most cases the trader has quite clearly described the goods and thus applied a description to them. However, "applies" was given a much wider meaning by the Divisional Court in *Tarleton Engineering Co. Ltd.* v. *Nattrass.*[18]

> A dealer sold a car with a false odometer reading. He had not altered the odometer himself. He did not know it was false nor did he repeat the reading or vouch for it. Held, he had applied a false trade description to the car.

It is difficult to justify such a wide interpretation of any of the expressions used in section 4. It might have been preferable to bring a prosecution under section 1(1)(*b*) on the grounds that the trader had supplied the car with a false trade description.

---

[16] See *Coppen* v. *Moore (No. 1)* [1898] 2 Q.B. 300.
[17] s. 4(3). See *R.* v. *Ford Motor Co.* [1974] 1 W.L.R. 1220.
[18] [1973] 1 W.L.R. 1261.

Supplying goods with a false trade description

The second of the two offences contained in section 1 is committed when a person "supplies or offers to supply any goods to which a false trade description is applied."[19] The offence is most likely to occur where a retailer or other distributor sells goods with a description applied by a manufacturer or importer earlier in the commercial chain.

Offer to supply

To resolve the problem that, where goods are in a shop window, on a supermarket shelf or put up at an auction, no offer for sale is made in a contractual sense by the prospective supplier—there is only an invitation to treat to customers who offer to buy—section 6 provides that a person exposing goods for supply or having them in his possession for supply is deemed to offer to supply them.

Knowledge

It appears from *Cottee* v. *Douglas Seaton (Used Cars) Ltd.*[20] that a supplier does not commit this offence, if he neither applied the description to the goods himself nor knew or had means of knowing that this had been done by another. However, where a supplier knows that a description has been applied, even though he does not know that it is false, he is liable, *e.g.* selling a car with a false odometer.

The facts of the *Cottee* case were as follows:

> Dealer A patched up the bodywork of a car which he sold to dealer B. The repair was so skilfully done that B did not discover it. B sold it to C. Held, B had not committed an offence under section 1(1)(*b*) as he was unaware of the defect. Knowledge that a trade description was applied was essential. Accordingly, A was acquitted of an offence under section 23[21] which depended upon the commission of an offence by B.

In short, knowledge of the *existence* of the description is a prerequisite, but not knowledge of its *falsity*.

Meaning of trade description

Section 2(1) defines a trade description as "an indication, direct or indirect, and by whatever means given" of any of the matters

---

[19] s. 1(1)(*b*).
[20] [1972] 1 W.L.R. 1408. The "description" in this case consisted of the covering up of the defect by A.
[21] See p. 185

exhaustively listed in its ten paragraphs. Such matters include quantity and size; composition; fitness for purpose; strength or performance; testing or approval by any person; the method, place[21a], date or person by whom manufactured, processed or reconditioned; and other history including previous ownership. There are special provisions relating to animals, agriculture and food and drugs.

Examples

The following examples may assist readers; the lettering follows that in section 2(1):

(a) size of shoes, shirts, dresses or other clothing;

(b) Axminster or Wilton carpet;

(c) shirt labelled "65% polyester, 35% cotton";

(d) "Top speed 102 mph, 28 mpg"

(e) car equipped with "five-tone horn playing 'Colonel Bogey' ";

(f) "Tested by the Road Research Laboratory";

(g) tennis racket "as used by Borg"[22];

(h) 1978 Lamborghini;

(i) "Tuned by High Performance Motors Ltd,";

(j) "Only one private owner; 46,000 miles."

Review recommendations

The Review considered the suggestion of replacing the list in section 2 with a general offence of misdescribing goods or services with the object of catching the misdescription of any feature not included in the list. However, such a suggestion was rejected on the grounds that "it seems a good principle when creating criminal offences that the offence is defined as precisely as possible[23]." To block a number of loopholes some possible additions to the list in section 2(1) are canvassed, *e.g.* the standing, importance or capabilities of a distributor or wholesaler (only manufacturers are currently covered); the contents or authorship of printed or recorded matter[24].

[21a] See also the 1972 Act, ante p. 158.
[22] See also s. 3(4).
[23] para 121.
[24] paras. 123-132.

Definition orders

Difficulties can arise where a term is used which has a special meaning and is not meant as a literal description of the goods, *e.g.* "Dover Sole" not from Dover or "Bombay Duck" which is neither duck nor from Bombay. The problem was discussed in a case under the Merchandise Marks Acts, *Lemy* v. *Watson*[25], in which it was held to be a false trade description to describe brisling as "Norwegian sardines." Darling J. used as an illustration the "Holy Roman Empire"—a description of an institution which was neither holy nor Roman nor an Empire.[26]

To alleviate this problem section 7 gives the Department of Trade power to make definition orders assigning definite meanings to expressions used as part of a trade description.

Is it false?

Let us assume that (a) there is a trade description within the meaning of section 2; (b) the defendant has either applied it or supplied goods to which it has been applied within section 1(1); and (c) the defendant has done so in the course of trade or business. The next question to consider is whether the trade description is a *false* trade description. Section 3(1) states simply and clearly that "a false trade description is a trade description which is false to a material degree." These last four words were considered by the Divisional Court in *Donelly* v. *Rowlands*.[27]

> Rowlands was a Welsh dairy farmer and milk retailer. He bottled his milk in various types of bottles, some of which were embossed Express, C.W.S., Northern and Goodwins. The foil cap on every bottle was embossed with the words "Untreated milk. Produced from T.T. cows. Rowlands" and the name of his farm. A prosecution was brought by an Inspector of Milk Vessels Recovery Limited (not by a trading standards officer) under section 1(1)(*b*). The justices decided that no offence had been committed on the basis that, as the description on the foil cap was accurate, the false description on the bottle was not false "to a material degree." The Divisional Court dismissed an appeal by the prosecutor.

The court, while agreeing that it was possible to approach the problem by looking at the description as a whole on both the bottle

---

[25] [1915] 3 K.B. 731.
[26] See also *Kat* v. *Diment* [1951] 1 K.B. 34 (non-brewed vinegar).
[27] [1970] 1 W.L.R. 1600.

and the cap, took a different line. In their view the trade description was not false to any degree at all. The words on the foil cap were an accurate trade description of the milk; the words on the bottle did not refer to the milk but merely conveyed that the bottle belonged to the company whose name was embossed.[28]

Advertisements

The Act does not create a separate offence relating to advertisements incorporating a false description. However, this is not to say that manufacturers or retailers may include false descriptions in their publicity material with impunity; they run the risk of committing offences under section 1(1)(a) and (b). The importance of section 5 of the Act, which is concerned solely with advertisements, is its relation to the section 1 offences and also to section 4 which, as we have seen, defines the ways in which a trade description may be applied.

It is to be remembered that section 4(1)(c) states that a person applies a trade description to goods if he "uses the trade description in any manner likely to be taken as referring to the goods." Section 5 provides an answer when one is trying to ascertain whether an advertisement relates to those goods which are the subject matter of proceedings: it states that where a trade description is used in an advertisement in relation to any class of goods, the description should be taken as referring to all goods of the class whether or not in existence at the time of publication of the advertisement. Factors to be taken into account in deciding whether a customer would think of his goods as belonging to the relevant class are the form and content of the advertisement and the time, place, manner and frequency of its publication.

Example

A manufacturer launches a national television advertising campaign in relation to certain goods. A retailer later supplies goods of that type. The retailer commits an offence under section 1(1)(b) if the advertisement includes false information. If the goods are accompanied by point of sale material which also includes a false trade description, the retailer will in addition commit an offence under section 1(1)(a), for he will have applied the description within the meaning of section 4(1)(b) by placing such material with the goods.

---

[28] cf. *Stone* v. *Burns* [1911] 1 K.B. 927 where an offence was committed under the Merchandise Marks Acts when Bass beer was sold in another brewer's bottles with Bass labels.

It should be noted that the meaning of "advertisement" is defined in section 39, the interpretation section, as including a catalogue, circular and price list.

Disclaimers and odometers

The Review reveals that the most prevalent offence dealt with by enforcement authorities involves tampering with odometers (or milometers) to understate the true mileage[29]. Accordingly, it is proposed to look particularly at this type of offence. Further, as the cases involving disclaimers are, in the main, concerned with false odometer readings, this area will be considered at the same time.

The first question is whether a false odometer reading can in law be a false trade description. Counsel's submission that it cannot be so was described as "bold but hopeless" by Lawton L.J. in R. v. *Hammertons Cars Ltd.*[30] The Divisional Court decided that an odometer reading is an indication of the use which the car has had and is "other history, including previous ownership or use" within section 2(1)(j).

Effect of disclaimer

In the same case the Divisional Court considered the effect of a disclaimer and the related problem of the burden of proof. Does a disclaimer prevent a trade description being applied or does it prevent a trade description which has been applied from being false? The Court considered it unwise and likely to cause confusion as to the burden of proof to try to divide the evidence into that which establishes that a trade description has been applied and that which is said to be a disclaimer of that description. Lawton L.J. stated that the right question for the court at the end of the case was, "Has the prosecution proved that the defendant supplied goods to which a false trade description was applied?"[30a]

Disclaimer in time?

To be effective a disclaimer must be introduced by the trader before he "supplies" the goods, the word used in section 1(1)(b).

[29] para. 160.
[30] [1976] 1 W.L.R. 1243.
[30a] *Ibid.* p. 1246. See also *Tarleton Engineering Co. Ltd.* v. *Nattrass* [1973] 1 W.L.R. 1261.

It is tempting to apply by analogy the contractual rules relating to the incorporation of terms and to take the view that, if a disclaimer is introduced after the contract has been made, it is entirely ineffective. However, the test is not a contractual one. Clearly if the disclaimer is sufficiently brought to the attention of the customer at an early stage during the negotiations, it will be successful. Equally clearly a disclaimer after the buyer has taken possession of the goods will fail, for a disclaimer must be made before the goods are supplied. The most difficult problem occurs where the trader endeavours at the moment of delivery to disclaim responsibility by telling the buyer only then that the odometer reading is unreliable. Supply and delivery are not to be equated, as can be seen from the judgment of Lawton L.J. in *R.* v. *Hammertons Cars Ltd.*[31] Such an oral statement at the delivery stage may not be enough to displace the impression given by the odometer reading which may linger on in the buyer's mind. "The issue for the court of trial is whether when the purchaser takes possession of the goods he gets them with a false trade description applied to them."[32] So while it is possible for a trader to disclaim when making delivery, he will have great difficulty by delaying so late in persuading a court that a false trade description has not been applied.

It is to be noted that a disclaimer can be implied from a previous course of dealing or because of an understanding between the parties, at least when both of them are experienced car dealers.[33]

General tests

A number of tests have been propounded in the cases to assist in deciding whether in a particular case a disclaimer is effective. In *Norman* v. *Bennett* Lord Widgery C.J. stated that the disclaimer must be "as bold, precise and compelling as the trade description itself" and "must equal the trade description in the extent to which it is likely to get home to anyone interested in receiving the goods."[34] Lawton L.J.'s instruction to dealers who do not want prospective purchasers to take any notice of odometer readings is that "they must take positive and effective steps to ensure that the customer understands that the milometer reading is

[31] *Ibid.*
[32] *Ibid.* p. 1248, *per* Lawton L.J.
[33] *Norman* v. *Bennett* [1974] 1 W.L.R. 1229.
[34] *Ibid.* p. 1232.

G

meaningless."[35] More recently Lord Widgery C.J. returned to the problem in *Waltham Forest London Borough Council* v. *T. G. Wheatley (Central Garage) Ltd. (No. 2)*[36] when he said., "The purpose of the disclaimer is for it to sit beside, as it were, the false trade description and cancel the other out as soon as its first impression can be made on the purchaser."[37]

All these tests come to the same thing. At the moment of delivery at the latest the buyer must be fully aware that he should place no reliance at all on the odometer reading which has been effectively neutralized or cancelled by the disclaimer, be it oral or contained in a notice, agreement or other document.

Particular disclaimers

Oral. For two reasons an oral disclaimer is least likely to be effective. First, there is the evidential problem of proving what the salesman said. Secondly, a casual remark in the course of negotiations will hardly satisfy the general criteria mentioned above. In *R.* v. *Hammertons Cars Ltd.*:

> Car dealers sold two cars to a customer. The odometers showed 25,600 miles and 25,300 miles, whereas the true mileages were 53,714 miles and 34,000 respectively. At the time of delivery the buyers were given a printed document headed "SPECIFIC GUARANTEE OF USED MOTOR VEHICLE." At the bottom of the document in small print under the heading "MILEAGE AND DATE" appeared: "any estimate or opinion of the mileage . . . which the Suppliers may have given to the Customer during negotiations . . . was given according to their best information and belief. (The suppliers are not answerable for the mileage shown on the vehicle's milometer)." The salesman also gave evidence that he had clearly given the purchasers to understand that the mileage as shown on the odometer was not guaranteed but his evidence was rejected by the jury. Held, the dealers had committed an offence under section 1(1)(*b*). A casual remark in the course of oral negotiations or small print in a contractual document are unlikely to be sufficient disclaimers.

Documents. As has just been seen, disclaimers in small print will not protect the dealer. Presumably, disclaimers printed boldly in documents read by the buyer before the goods are supplied will suffice. However, here again a distinction must be drawn between the contractual rules relating to the incorporation of terms, *e.g.* exemption clauses, and the present situation. In view of the state-

---

[35] *R* v. *Hammertons Cars Ltd.* [1976] 1 W.L.R. 1243, at p. 1248.
[36] [1978] R.T.R. 333.
[37] *Ibid.* p. 339.

ment of Lord Widgery C.J. in *Norman* v. *Bennett* that the disclaimer "must be effectively brought to the notice" of the customer, it seems that the dealer will not be able to rely on the fact that the customer happened to sign the relevant document. Thus to have the desired neutralising effect the clause must be both boldly printed and brought clearly to the attention of the customer.

Notices. In a number of cases dealers have attempted to rely on disclaimers in notices on their premises. Thus in *Zawadski* v. *Sleigh*[38]:

> Dealers auctioned three cars with false odometer readings. Disclaimers as to the mileage of the cars appeared both in the auction entry forms and in notices in the auction premises. A Divisional Court held that the general notices were insufficient to be disclaimers.

Similarly, in *Waltham Forest L.B.C.* v. *T. G. Wheatley (Central Garage) Ltd.*[39] a notice in the dealer's office was held to be an insufficient disclaimer. One difficulty is that prospective buyers looking at vehicles on the forecourt or in the showroom may not enter the dealer's office and so will not have an opportunity of seeing the notice. Even so the dealer is offering to supply the goods within the meaning of section 1(1)(*b*). It may be that prominent notices placed in close proximity to the relevant goods are apt to neutralize the odometer reading. Clearly the safest method to adopt is to place the disclaimer notice next to or over the odometer so that it does "sit beside the false description." If, in addition, there is a written contract with a boldly printed clause to the same effect and both the clause and the notice are pointed out to customers, then with this belts and braces technique the dealer is unlikely to run the danger of committing an offence.

Code of Practice. The Code of Practice for the Motor Industry states[40]:

> Dealers should pass on any known facts about a previous odometer reading to a prospective customer, and if a disclaimer is used it should be in the following form: "WE DO NOT GUARANTEE THE ACCURACY OF THE RECORDED MILEAGE. TO THE BEST OF OUR KNOWLEDGE AND BELIEF, HOWEVER, THE READING IS CORRECT/INCORRECT."

---

[38] [1975] R.T.R. 113.
[39] [1978] R.T.R. 333.
[40] para. 3.10. *Post*, p. 314.

As the Code was drawn up in consultation with the O.F.T., presumably this disclaimer is thought to be both effective for the trader and fair to the consumer. It seems that trading standards officers are unlikely to prosecute a trader using a sticker in this form, although no reported case has given it judicial approval.

The practice is for the sticker to be placed over the odometer so that the reading is obscured.[40a] As it reads, it is somewhat contradictory, but dealers are apparently intended to delete one of the alternatives at the end. Even then it can be criticised on the grounds of lack of clarity and inelegance, clearly a compromise resulting from committee drafting.

Defences

Even where a prima facie offence has been committed because the disclaimer fails in its purpose, the defendant may take advantage of the defences available under section 24(1). These are discussed later.[41] The only point to be made at this stage is that in *Simmons* v. *Potter*[42] the Divisional Court held that a car dealer who had not published a disclaimer had failed to take an obvious precaution and therefore could not rely on the statutory defence. It appears then to be advantageous for dealers to use disclaimers. On the one hand they may well prevent an offence being committed in the first place. On the other hand even if they fail in that primary objective, a dealer's attempt to disclaim responsibility may itself enable him to call in aid the section 24 defence more readily.

Illustrative cases on section 1

In all the following cases a prima facie offence was committed under section 1, although in some of them the defendant was able to rely on the section 24 defence.

[40a] In *K. Jill Holdings* v. *White* [1979] R.T.R. 120 the odometer was zeroed and a disclaimer attached. No offence.

[41] See p. 181.

[42] [1975] Crim.L.R. 354.

Beckett v. *Kingston Bros (Butchers) Ltd.*[43]
Butchers sold a turkey labelled "Norfolk King Turkey." It had in fact come from Denmark. It was held to be an offence under section 1(1)(*b*).[44]

Birkenhead & District Co-operative Society Ltd. v. *Roberts*[45]:
The Co-op sold a leg of lamb described as "for roasting English." Its origin was New Zealand. It was held by the Divisional Court to be an offence under section 1(1).

British Gas Corporation v. *Lubbock*[46]:
In response to her enquiry at a corporation showroom about a Parkinson cooker, a customer was given a brochure which stated "ignition is by the hand-held battery torch supplied with the cooker." She ordered a cooker which was supplied without a torch. It was held that the brochure referred to a "package" of goods which included the torch. The description in the brochure was an indication as to "composition" under section 2(1)(*c*); alternatively, an indication of "physical characteristics not included in the preceding paragraphs" under section 2(1)(*e*). An offence was committed under section (1)(1)(*a*). (Presumably, there was also an offence under section 1(1)(*b*) as the appellants supplied the goods as well as applying the description).

Sherratt v. *Geralds The American Jewellers Ltd.*[47]:
The jewellers sold a watch described as a "diver's watch" and engraved "waterproof." The purchaser tested the watch by immersing it in a bowl of water; it filled with water and stopped. Held, an offence under section 1(1)(*b*).

Fletcher v. *Budgen*[48]:
A private seller wished to sell his car to a car dealer. The dealer said that there was no possibility of repairing the car; repairs would not make the car safe; and the only possible course of action was

[43] [1970] 1 Q.B. 606.
[44] s. 24 defence available.
[45] [1970] 1 W.L.R. 1497.
[46] [1974] 1 W.L.R. 37.
[47] (1970) 114 S.J. 147.
[48] [1974] 1 W.L.R. 1056.

for the car to be scrapped. So the car was sold to him for £2. The dealer spent £56 repairing it and then advertised it at a price of £135. It was held to be an offence under section 1(1)(*a*), the description falling within section 2(1)(*e*). The Act applied even though the description was applied by a prospective trade buyer, the reverse of the normal situation.

R. v. *Ford Motor Co.*[48a]

Fords supplied a "new" car to a dealer who resold it to a customer. It had been damaged after leaving their factory while in the hands of their forwarding agents and properly repaired at a cost of £50. Fords were charged under section 1(1)(*b*) (and also under section 23[49] because of the dealer's section 1(1)(*b*) offence). The Court of Appeal held that no offence was committed. The description "new" is not false where the damage is superficial, or limited to parts which can be simply replaced by new parts, and is perfectly repaired, so that the car is as good as new.

Leather funwear[49a]

Suppliers described goods as "exciting leather funwear." The goods supplied—bra, panties, catsuit—were made of plastic. Held, an offence under section 1. (One is tempted to ask whether an offence would have been committed had the clothing been made of leather but proved to be neither exciting nor fun to wear.)

PRICES

"Recommended price £210, our price £170"
"Normal price £78, sale price £52"
"£8 off recommended price"
"Elsewhere £50, our price £28"
"Worth £80, our price £60"

The public and consumer bodies have been considerably concerned at the difficulty in distinguishing between genuine reductions and false comparative price claims. The Molony Committee

[48a] [1974] 1 W.L.R. 1220.
[49] *Post*, p. 185.
[49a] *The Times*, June 14, 1973.

recommended[50] that the problem should be tackled by including in the definition of trade description "the former or usual price of any goods". However, the 1968 Act instead of following this approach endeavours to deal with the mischief with separate provisions contained in section 11.

Section 11 creates three offences: (a) false comparisons with a recommended price; (b) false comparisons with the trader's own previous price; (c) an indication that the price is less than that actually being charged.

It is to be remembered that, although section 11 is not expressly confined to persons acting in the course of trade or business, the Divisional Court held in *John* v. *Matthews*[51] that it relates only to transactions of a commercial nature.

Recommended prices

Section 11(1)(*a*) makes it an offence for a person offering to supply goods to give a false indication that their price is equal to or less than a recommended price. This provision needs to be read with section 11(3)(*b*) whereby the recommended price is treated as a price recommended by the manufacturer or producer generally for retail supply in that area.

The application of this provision has caused little difficulty inasmuch as it is obvious and easy to prove from manufacturers' lists whether or not an offence has been committed. However, the Act has had no beneficial effect on the practice—indeed it has probably led to its expansion—by manufacturers of setting unrealistically high recommended prices (so-called "sky prices") to enable retailers to be able to offer an apparent bargain to their customers. The practice is particularly rife in the area of furniture and electrical goods where discount houses proliferate. The Review discusses the difficulties and some solutions, including the prohibition of recommended retail prices, but in the end the Director throws up his hands in despair stating that he "can put forward no suggestion for controlling this practice within the framework of the 1968 Act".[52]

However, concurrently with the preparation of the Review, the Office of Fair Trading was considering the control of this and other

---

[50] para. 636.
[51] *Ante*, p. 159.
[52] paras. 198–200.

price problems under the Fair Trading Act 1973. Their proposals were published in 1975 in the paper entitled "Bargain Offer Claims—A Consultative Document." Although ultimately an attack was made on some forms of bargain offers by the Price Marking (Bargain Offers) Order 1979, recommended prices have not been generally prohibited.[53]

Previous prices

The second offence, created by section 11(1)(*b*), is similar to the first offence except that the false indication relates to the price at which the supplier previously offered the goods. The purpose of this provision is to attack the practice of buying in goods especially for sales pretending that those goods were previously offered at a higher price to persuade bargain hunters that a bargain is in fact being offered. The practice is not confined to sales periods but is most rife at such times.

The 28 days/6 months problem

An obvious way round for the dishonest trader would be to display his goods at the higher price for a day or even part of a day and then to reduce the price. Section 11(3)(*a*) attempts to close up this loophole by providing that (i) an indication that goods were previously offered at a higher price shall be treated as an indication that they were so offered by that trader; and (ii) unless the contrary is expressed, that they were so offered "within *the preceding six months for a continuous period of not less than 28 days.*" The italicised words are meant to ensure that the trader has offered the goods at the higher price for a reasonably long period during the comparatively recent past. However, *The House of Holland Limited* v. *Brent London Borough Council*[54] has shown that some loopholes are large enough for a coach and horses to drive through.

> The appellants published a newspaper advertisement of a sun chair bed at 45 shillings stating "All prices further reduced. Buy now." The newspaper was dated July 27, 1969. They had previously published advertisements for the same articles at the same price in newspapers in June and early July. When prosecuted they argued that no offence was established unless the prosecution proved that they had *not* offered the same goods at a higher price for a period

[53] *Post*, p. 229.
[54] [1971] 2 Q.B. 304.

of 28 days within the six month period preceding the date of the advertisements. The Divisional Court held that no offence had been committed.

The effect of this decision is to place upon the prosecution an almost impossible burden of proof in that they have to prove a negative—that no offer at a higher price was made—and to deal with the whole six months period. To counter this difficulty the Review recommends that the burden of proof be reversed, so that unless the trader is able to produce the proof to justify his claim he should be convicted of the offence.[55]

The multiple loophole

A different loophole for traders can be illustrated as follows. A trader retailing cameras has many branches throughout the country. At one isolated shop he displays a brand XQ camera priced at £85 for a period of 28 days. At the end of that period he displays the brand XQ camera in all his shops stating "Brand XQ Camera. 20% reduction. Was £85. Now £68." The retailer has committed no offence, as the Act does not require that the offer at the higher price should be made at the same premises. Accordingly, the Review recommends that section 11(3)(*a*)(i) be appropriately amended.[56]

Disclaimers

Finally, it should be noted that disclaimers are allowed, since section 11 states "unless the contrary is expressed." It is quite common to see a notice on the following lines: "Some reduced articles have not been on sale at the higher price for a continuous period of not less than 28 days in the preceding six months." Even highly reputable traders use notices of this type. However, they are open to the objection that as a result customers cannot tell which goods are being offered at a genuinely reduced price and which are not.

Overcharging

The third offence is expressed in very wide terms in section 11(2). It broadly covers situations where the customer is charged a higher price than he would have expected to pay in view of the

[55] para. 215.
[56] para. 219.

indications as to price given to him by the supplier. The section provides that an offence is committed by anyone who offers to supply goods and gives by whatever means "an indication that the goods are being offered at a price less than that at which they are in fact being offered."

Indication

The word "indication" was considered by the Divisional Court in *Doble* v. *David Greig Limited.*[57]

> Bottles of Ribena in a self-service store were priced at 5s. 9d. and bore a manufacturer's label "the deposit on this bottle is 4d refundable on return." At the check-out point was a notice reading "In the interests of hygiene we do not accept the return of any empty bottles. No deposit is charged by us at the time of purchase." Customers paid 5s. 9d. a bottle but were refused 4d. refund. This was held to be an offence under section 11(2).

The Divisional Court took the view that the word "indication" was designedly wider than some such word as "representation" and was chosen in order to protect customers. "Section 11(2) was looking at the customers and the effect on them of whatever was said, done or displayed" (Ashworth J.) and "was intended to extend over conduct or signs of many different kinds" (Melford Stevenson J.). On the facts there was an indication likely to be taken as an indication that the purchaser who paid 5s. 9d. would be given 4d. on returning the bottle. The store had argued that the counter-indication displayed at the check-out point had the effect of disabusing the customer of a false impression which he might have obtained at the shelves. The court decided that the offence was committed when the Ribena was placed on the stack with the false indication. These was no locus poenitentiae. The court left open the question whether a disclaimer notice immediately above the relevant goods might have been effective.

Offer to supply

"Offering to supply", which is also used in section 11(1), does not mean that an offer in the contractual sense has been made. Indeed by section 11(3)(*d*) a person advertising goods as available for supply is to be taken as offering to supply them. Thus in *North Western Gas Board* v. *Aspden*[58] a display of gas fires in a showroom

[57] [1972] 1 W.L.R. 703.
[58] [1970] Crim.L.R. 301.

window, though only an invitation to treat, was held to be within the meaning of the expression.

The contention that the words presuppose an offer to sell for cash was rejected by the Divisional Court in *Reed Brothers Cycles (Leyton) Ltd.* v. *Waltham Forest London Borough Council:*[59]

> A motor cycle with a list price of £580 was advertised at the special price of £540. A buyer was refused the reduction because part of the price was to be discharged by trading-in a second-hand motor cycle. It was held that an offence was committed under section 11(2). However, the court said that the advertisement could have limited the reduction to cash sales, in which case the prospective purchaser would not have received a false impression.

The Tesco case

Probably the best known case on this provision is *Tesco* v. *Nattrass*[60] although its main significance turns on the discussion by the House of Lords of the defence in section 24(1).

> Soap powder was advertised in a supermarket "Radiant 1 shilling off giant size 2/11d." This was intended to apply only to "flash packs" which were marked "1 shilling off recommended price." As the supermarket had run out of these packs ordinary packs were on display. A customer was charged the full price of 3/11d for one of these. An offence would have been committed, were it not for the defence available under section 24.

Other comparisons

Apart from the constraints imposed by the three offences discussed above, the trader is free to make whatever comparisons he thinks fit as far as the 1968 Act is concerned. Thus he may compare his prices with those generally charged by other suppliers, *e.g.* "Price elsewhere £50, our price £45." Similarly, he may compare his price with that of a particular supplier, *e.g.* "X's price £40— our price £34." Lastly, he may indulge in the increasingly common practice of comparing the worth or value of his goods to other goods, *e.g.* "Value £200—our price £120."

However, it is important to observe that "price elsewhere" and "worth" claims have now been banned by the Price Marking (Bargain Offer) Order 1979.[60a]

---

[59] [1978] R.T.R. 397.
[60] [1972] A.C. 153. See also p. 182.
[60a] *Post*, p. 230. The second of the three examples is still permissible, *i.e.* comparison with the price charged by an *identified* person.

Review recommendations

The Review recommends that secion 11(1) be amended to cover comparisons with "any other price."[61] It further recommends that the ambit of the Act be extended beyond goods to cover the cost of rental transactions including hire-purchase; property, particularly new houses where builders claim reductions in house prices as an inducement to buyers; and also services as there is some doubt whether section 14 covers the price of services.[62]

Services

An area not covered by the Merchandise Marks Acts nor by the Molony report is services. Section 14(1) makes it an offence for any person in the course of any trade or business knowingly or recklessly to make a false statement with regard to certain specified matters, namely:

(a) the provision of any services, accommodation or facilities;
(b) their nature;
(c) the time at which, manner in which or persons by whom they are provided;
(d) the examination, approval or evaluation of them by any person;
(e) the location or amenities of any accommodation.

Like sections 1 and 11 the Act applies only to the provision of services in the course of trade or business. As has been seen it is likely that this expression includes services rendered by members of the professions.[63] Again like sections 1 and 11, this section includes oral as well as written statements.

However, although a statement made after the supply of goods has been completed is not an offence under section 1,[64] section 14 has a wider application as is shown by *Breed* v. *Cluett*.[65]

A builder built a bungalow, sold it and afterwards falsely stated that it was covered by a N.H.B.R.C. 10 years guarantee. The Divisional Court held that

---

[61] paras. 221–228.
[62] paras. 230; 233; 234.
[63] *R.* v. *Breeze* [1973] 1 W.L.R. 994. *Ante*, p. 159.
[64] *Hall* v. *Wickens Motors (Gloucester) Ltd.* [1972] 1 W.L.R. 1418.
[65] [1970] 2 Q.B. 459.

such a statement could be a statement as to the provision of services within section 14.

The distinction between this case and the later section 1 decision in *Hall's* case[66] is that the provision of services may involve continuing obligations and, had there been an N.H.B.R.C. guarantee, the builder could have been called upon to provide services during the guarantee period.

Knowingly or recklessly

Another distinction between this offence and the other offences is that section 14 is not an offence of strict liability. Section 14 requires that the person making the false statement knows it to be so or makes it recklessly. A reckless statement is defined by section 14(2)(*b*) as "a statement made regardless of whether it is true or false . . . whether or not the person making it had reasons for believing that it might be false." This definition bears a close resemblance to the tort of deceit as defined by the House of Lords in *Derry* v. *Peek*.[67] Indeed Lord Parker C.J. in *Sunair Holidays Limited* v. *Dodd*[68] stated obiter that the Act imported the common law definition of "reckless."

> Travel agents in their brochure described accommodation offered at a hotel as "all twin-bedded rooms with private bath, shower, w.c. and terrace." They had a contract with the hotel to provide such accommodation. Two couples booked holidays with them on this basis, but on arrival were given rooms without terraces. It was held by the Divisional Court that no offence had been committed. At the time the statement was made the accommodation existed and the statement was perfectly true. Nothing which happened afterwards could alter the accuracy of the description when it was made. Further, the definition of reckless does not include negligence.

However, a different view was taken by the Divisional Court in *M.F.I. Warehouses* v. *Nattrass*[69]:

> A mail order company advertised goods "on 14 days free approval" and "carriage free." These offers were intended to cover only some of the goods in the advertisement but appeared to relate to all of them. The company's conviction for recklessly making false statements as to the provision of facilities was upheld on appeal. The court considered that the chairman of the company

[66] *Ante*, p. 178, note 64.
[67] (1889) 14 App. Cas. 337.
[68] [1970] 1 W.L.R. 1037.
[69] [1973] 1 W.L.R. 307.

had given insufficient care to his perusal of the advertisement so that the company had been reckless as to its contents.

While this case to an extent throws doubt on the dictum of Lord Parker and appears to give a wider meaning to the word "recklessly," the main point of *Sunair Holidays Limited* v. *Dodd* still stands. No offence is committed merely because the trader fails to provide services which accord with the description. Provided the services or accommodation existed when the statement was made and provided that he then had an intention of providing them,[70] the statement is not false and no offence occurs.

It is important to distinguish the two related points. First one asks the question, "Is the statement false?" If the answer is "No," as in *Sunair Holidays Limited* v. *Dodd,* then one need not proceed further: there is no offence. If the answer is "Yes," then one goes on to ask, "Did the trader know that it was false or make it recklessly?"

Future services

A more recent decision showing that promises about the provision of services in the future are not caught by section 14 is *Beckett* v. *Cohen*[71];

> The defendant agreed to build a garage like the neighbours' within 10 days but did not do so. The Divisional Court held that section 14 did not apply to statements unrelated to existing facts which amounted to a promise as to the future, because these could not be true or false when made. (The court was prepared to accept for the purpose of the case that building a garage was within section 14.)

This interpretation of the section erodes very substantially the protection afforded to consumers. Even so, as has been seen, if accommodation is advertised which at the time of publication of the holiday brochure does not exist, then an offence can be committed. This is well illustrated by *R.* v. *Clarksons Holidays Ltd.*[72] where the brochures stated that Clarksons' hotels were chosen for their cleanliness, good food and efficiency of service, and included a picture of a large modern hotel with a swimming pool; this turned out to be an artist's impression as the hotel, which was still in the

[70] "The state of a man's mind is as much a fact as the state of his digestion": per Bowen L. J. in *Edgington* v. *Fitzmaurice* (1884) 29 Ch.D. 459, p. 483.
[71] [1972] 1 W.L.R. 1593.
[72] [1972] Crim.L.R. 653.

course of construction, was not finished by the time the holiday-makers arrived and was never intended to be ready by then.

Similarly in *British Airways Board* v. *Taylor*[72a] the appellants would have been liable for a statement as to the future, had the statement been made by the Board and not by their predecessors B.O.A.C. The facts were as follows.

> The case arose out of the common airline practice of "overbooking" to take account of passengers who fail to take up reservations; occasionally this results in passengers being transferred to another flight. Here a passenger received a letter confirming his reservation but in the event no seat was available on the flight. The House of Lords held that the statement in the letter was false, as at that time B.O.A.C. fully intended to off-load passengers, if too many arrived for the flight.

Review recommendations

Amongst the many recommendations made by the Review with regard to section 14 is one designed to close this gap by the creation of a new offence, namely that of supplying any services, accommodation or facilities to which a false description has been applied.[73] The court would then be able to consider whether the services provided measured up to the promises relating to their future provision. The other major extension suggested is that the section should be extended to cover land, so that descriptions of houses for sale should fall withing the Act.[74]

DEFENCES

As has been seen, liability for offences under sections 1 and 11 is strict, whereas the offence under section 14 is committed only if the trader knows the statement to be false or makes it recklessly. However, certain defences are available. Section 24(1) applies to all offences. Section 24(3) assists only in the case of a prosecution under section 1(1)(b). Section 25 is confined to the publication of advertisements.

[72a] [1975] 1 W.L.R. 1197.
[73] para. 106.
[74] para. 90.

The general defence

The defence contained in section 24(1) may be split into five defences. The defendant must prove that the commission of the offence was due to any one of the following causes[74a]:

(a) a mistake;
(b) reliance on information supplied to him;
(c) the act or default of another person;
(d) an accident;
(e) some other cause beyond his control.

Additionally, he must prove that "he took all reasonable precautions and exercised all due diligence to avoid the commission of such an offence by himself or any person under his control."[75]

Mistake

As far as mistake is concerned this is available only where the mistake is of the defendant himself; it cannot be used where someone else's mistake is involved (*e.g.* an employer pleading the mistake of an employee).[76]

Act or default

The defence most frequently relied upon is that the offence was due to the "act or default of another person," for example, an odometer run back by a previous owner. Where an employer is charged, he may rely on the default of an employee. When the Act first came into force, there were those who thought that the defence could be used only where the employee was in a junior position but it appeared to have been quickly settled that even where the "person" was a branch manager, the defence was still available.[77]

However, when the employer is a company, it is necessary to distinguish between those employees who are the alter ego of the company, when their defaults are the company's defaults, and those employees who are not thus identified with the company which can then claim that the defaults are those of another person. The difficulty was fully discussed by the House of Lords in *Tesco Supermarkets* v. *Nattrass*[78]. Their Lordships held that where the

---

[74a] s. 24(1)(*a*).
[75] s. 24(1)(*b*).
[76] *Birkenhead & District Co-operative Society Ltd.* v. *Roberts* [1970] 1 W.L.R. 1497.
[77] *Beckett* v. *Kingston Bros. (Butchers), ante,* p. 171.
[78] [1972] A.C. 153. The facts are given on p. 177.

person charged is a limited company, the only persons who can be identified with the controlling mind and will of the company are the board of directors, the managing director and any other superior officer to whom the board has delegated full discretion to act independently from the board. Thus, though a general manager may be the company's alter ego, the supermarket manager was not. Accordingly, since the offence was caused by his failure to ensure that sufficient flash-packs were available, Tesco were able to rely on his default.

To establish this defence it is not enough for the defendant to produce the list of staff who might have been at fault; he must at least try to identify the actual person responsible by carefully investigating the circumstances to discover how the offences occurred.[79]

To rely on this defence section 24(2) requires the defendant at least seven clear days before the hearing to serve on the prosecutor a written notice giving such information as he has to identify the other person.[80] The reason for this provision is to enable the prosecution to consider whether to proceed directly against the other person either for one of the main offences or under the by-pass provision in section 23.[81]

Due diligence

It is not enough for the defendant to prove one of the five defences in section 24(1)(a). He must also show that he took all reasonable precautions and exercised all due diligence. These factors have generally been considered by the courts in relation to the default defence, particularly with regard to its application in the areas of vicarious liability and odometers.

Vicarious liability

Where an employer is charged with an offence because of the conduct of an employee and endeavours to rid himself of this vicarious liability by showing that the offence was due to the act or default of the employee, broadly the employer will be acquitted if he can show that he is personally blameless. Obviously, when this defence is used somebody is to blame. The question is whether

---

[79] *McGuire* v. *Sittingbourne Co-operative Society Ltd.*, [1976] Crim.L.R. 268.
[80] See *Birkenhead & District Co-operative Society Ltd.* v. *Roberts, ante*, p. 171.
[81] See p. 185.

the offence occurred in spite of the precautions and diligence of the employer. In the *Tesco* case the House of Lords rejected the argument that the employer has to show that he and all the persons to whom he has delegated responsibility are blameless: the company was held to have satisfied the requirements of section 24(1)(*b*) by having a chain of command with a careful system of control and supervision, even though one of the cogs in this machine, the supermarket manager, had failed to carry out his responsibilities properly.

Odometers

The second group of cases relates to false odometer readings. Sometimes a car dealer honestly—not all car dealers are rogues—supplies a vehicle with an odometer which unknown to him has been tampered with by an earlier owner. Assuming that he can prove that the offence was due to reliance on information supplied, or the default of another person, the question arises whether he can also prove that he took precautions and was diligent. This normally involves checking with the person from whom he bought the vehicle and, if he has the log book, with previous owners to verify the mileage.[82] However, in *Naish* v. *Gore*[83] the Divisional Court said that is was impossible to lay down as a general principle that a dealer selling second-hand cars must have the log book and check with previous owners. In that case the defence was available to a dealer who bought from somebody with whom he had been doing business for years and re-sold the car before receiving the log book from his seller. Nevertheless, Lord Widgery C.J. warned that justices "should be very quick and alert to consider whether there are further proper precautions which might have been taken."

Suppliers' defence

In *Naish* v. *Gore*[84] the dealer also relied on the defence in section 24(3). This is confined to the offence of supplying goods with a false trade description under section 1(1)(*b*). The defence is that the defendant did not know, and could not with reasonable dili-

[82] *Richmond on Thames L.B.C.* v. *Motor Sales (Hounslow) Ltd.* [1971] R.T.R. 116.
[83] [1971] 3 All E.R. 737.
[84] The Divisional Court left open the question whether the defendant can also rely on s. 24(3), where the real defence is under s. 24(1).

gence have ascertained, that the goods did not conform to the
description or that the description had been applied to them. The
comments made above with regard to diligence and section 24(1)
appear to be relevant here also.[85]

The by-pass provision

Although the so-called "by-pass provision" in section 23 is not
a defence, it is appropriate to deal with it at this point in view of
its close interaction with the defence under section 24(1). Section
23 states, "Where the commission by any person of an offence
under this Act is due to the act or default of some other person
that other person shall be guilty of the offence." Thus where A
commits an offence, but the real culprit is B, B may be prosecuted
for the offence committed by A. It is irrelevant whether or not
proceedings have been taken against A. The corollary is that if no
offence is committed by A, B cannot be prosecuted under section
23.[86]

Example

> B a car dealer runs an odometer back. He sells the car to another dealer A.
> A sells the car to a customer. On the assumption that A has committed an
> offence under section 1(1)(*b*), B can be prosecuted under section 23 because
> A's offence is due to the act or default of B.

In this example it can be seen that the prosecution need not resort
to section 23 in order to charge B; for B has committed an offence
under section 1(1)(*a*) by applying a false trade description. The
example is not unrealistic. Quite frequently local authorities have
taken themselves into unnecessarily deep water by using the by-
pass provision instead of prosecuting directly for one of the main
offences.[87] However, section 23 is not entirely superfluous. It can
result in an offence being committed by a private person who
cannot otherwise be charged, because he is not acting "in the
course of a trade or business." Thus even if B were a private seller,
he could be charged under section 23.

[85] See *Richmond on Thames L.B.C.* v. *Motor Sales (Hounslow) Ltd.*, *ante*, p. 184.
[86] *Cottee* v. *Douglas Seaton (Used Cars) Ltd.* [1972] 1 W.L.R. 1408.
[87] *Ibid.* The facts appear on p. 162.

Interaction with default defence

Earlier, the interaction between section 23 and section 24(1) was mentioned. In the example if A is charged under section 1(1)(*b*) he may plead the section 24(1) defence, *i.e.* that the offence was due to the act or default of another person, namely B. This creates an apparently unbreakable circle. B is liable under section 23 only if A has committed an offence. So if A when prosecuted under section 1 successfully relies on section 24 due to B's default, B when prosecuted under section 23 can apparently argue that he has committed no offence in the absence of an offence by A. It would seem perverse that the real culprit B should escape with impunity merely because his guilt provides the innocent A with a defence.

This iniquitous circle was broken by the robust interpretation given to section 23 by the Divisional Court in *Coupe* v. *Guyett*.[88]

The court held that where A's sole defence is the section 24 defence, A can be regarded as having "committed" the offence for the purposes of section 23, *i.e.* for the purposes of a prosecution against B. Thus B (the real culprit) can be convicted under section 23 even though A is acquitted as a result of the section 24 defence. If, however, A has some other defence (*e.g.* absence of *mens rea* in a section 14 case) the prosecution will *not* be able to charge B under section 23, although they might well be able to charge him under one of the principal charging sections.

Review recommendation

We have already seen that the by-pass provision can result in a successful prosecution against a private person. The Review recommends that, while the possibility of such proceedings should be retained, it should be possible only where the private individual has deliberately falsified a trade description. Accordingly, their recommendation is that section 23 be amended so that the prosecution must show *mens rea* on the part of the individual in any case, be it section 1, 11 or 14.[89]

Advertisements

Section 25 affords a special defence in the case of advertisements. In any proceedings for an offence relating to the publication of an

[88] [1973] 1 W.L.R. 669.
[89] para. 38.

advertisement the defendant is free from liability if he can prove that (a) the advertisement was received and published in the course of a business involving such publication and (b) he did not and had no reason to know that the publication would amount to an offence under the Act. The defence protects not only the publishers themselves, *e.g.* of newspapers and magazines, but also those who arrange for the publication of advertisements, *e.g.* advertising agencies.

ENFORCEMENT

One of the major defects of the Merchandise Marks Acts was the absence of anybody with a duty to enforce their provisions. The Molony Committee when considering who would be most suitable to police any replacing legislation considered a number of solutions, including enforcement centrally by the Board of Trade, but finally came down strongly in favour of enforcement at local level. Section 26(1) clearly places the obligation of prosecution on trading standards officers in the following unequivocal terms: "It shall be the duty of every local weights and measures authority to enforce within their area the provisions of this Act." There are 92 such authorities. The Secretary of State for Prices and Consumer Protection may require them to report to him and, if a complaint is received that any authority is not properly discharging its duties, he may insititute a local enquiry whose report must be published.[90]

To assist the inspectors in carrying out their duties the Act gives them the power to check compliance with the Act by purchasing goods or securing the provision of services, accommodation or facilities.[91] One can picture the more zealous inspectors as a matter of duty reluctantly sunning themselves on the beaches of Acupulco in order to check that the amenities and location of hotels in travel brochures are not falsely described.

Section 28 of the Act enables them to enter premises to make spot checks and, if reasonable cause for suspicion of an offence exists, to require production of the books and documents of the business.

[90] s. 26.
[91] s. 27.

Before instituting proceedings the local authority must give notice to the Department of Trade. Such liaison helps to prevent numerous prosecutions in different areas for the same offence, for example, for goods or services advertised and supplied nationally. However, multiple prosecutions do sometimes occur.[92]

A prosecution must be brought within three years of the commission of an offence or one year from its discovery, whichever is the earlier.[93]

Finally, it should be observed that, although generally prosecutions are brought by local authorities, it is open to a member of the public to bring a private prosecution for an offence.

PENALTIES

The only sanctions under the Act for its contravention are of a criminal nature—fines or imprisonment. The Act affords the aggrieved consumer no separate civil remedy at all. Yet clearly the threat of criminal proceedings brought at public expense is a much greater deterrent to the dishonest trader than the possibility of a civil action by a private individual at his own expense.

If proceedings are brought summarily, a fine not exceeding £1,000[93a] may be imposed. If the defendant is convicted on indictment, not only may the fine be unlimited but imprisonment of up to two years may be imposed—indeed both penalties may be meted out.[94] In a number of reported cases defendants have been fined substantial sums of £1,000 or more.[95] Occasionally prison sentences are imposed but the Divisional Court stated in *R.* v. *Haesler*[96] that imprisonment is normally reserved for cases involving dishonesty. Generally, heavy fines and prison sentences seem to be a privilege of car dealers, as can be seen from the following table from the 1977 Annual Report of the Director General of Fair Trading.[97]

---

[92] *e.g.* the travel brochures in *R.* v. *Thompson Holidays Ltd.*, *post*, p. 190.
[93] s. 19(1). But see also s. 19(2) and s. 19(4).
[93a] Increased from £400 by Criminal Law Act 1977, s. 28(2) and (7).
[94] s. 18.
[95] See *R.* v. *Hammertons Cars Ltd.* [1976] 1 W.L.R. 1243.
[96] [1973] Crim. L.R. 586.
[97] *Ante*, p. 155.

Convictions and fines under the Trade Descriptions Act 1968

	No. of convictions			Total fines		
	1975	1976	1977	1975 £	1976 £	1977 £
Section 1: Misdescription						
Motor vehicles and accessories	504	473	613	61,863†	95,505*	128,719‡*§
Food and drink	75	51	61	5,815	3,230	7,120
Soap, detergents and toilet requisites	8	2	2	640	175	375
Solid and liquid fuels	29	34	20	2,190	3,000	2,410
Clothing and textiles	43	34	44	5,005	2,645	5,620†
Others	185	196	206	17,661	23,354	26,885
Total	844	790	946	93,174	127,909	171,129

Section 11: False Price Claims						
Motor vehicles and accessories	12	24	10	2,265	1,835	1,620
Food and drink	141	133	158	9,975	10,487	16,909
Soap, detergents and toilet requisites	177	174	121	16,350	15,407	12,873
Solid and liquid fuels	12	19	33	1,495	1,230	3,060
Clothing and textiles	11	11	11	990	825	985
Others	62	62	82	4,625	4,937	5,556
Total	415	422	415	35,700	34,721	41,003

Section 14: False statements about Services, Accommodation and Facilities						
Accommodation, holiday and travel	13	11	11	1,390	950	1,750
Repairs and servicing	60	69	61	5,397	7,956	7,415
Others	54	36	49	5,348	4,475	8,815
Total	127	116	121	12,135	13,381	17,980

†Included one 1 month imprisonment—suspended sentence.
‡Included two 1 month imprisonment—suspended sentences.
*Included one 6 month imprisonment—suspended sentence.
§Included one 12 month imprisonment—suspended sentence.

As was mentioned above, multiple prosecutions may be brought in different areas in respect of the same false trade description. In *R. v. Thompson Holidays Ltd.*[98]

> Tour operators published a brochure containing a false statement. They were convicted in one area for an offence under section 14. When prosecuted by a different local authority in respect of the same false statement the defendants pleaded *autrefois convict* in respect of the previous conviction.[98a] The Court of Appeal held that every time someone read one of the brochures a false statement was made, for it was made when communicated to the reader. Accordingly, a new offence was committed on each occasion and the plea was unsuccessful. Theoretically millions of prosecutions could be brought in respect of the single error in the printed brochures.

The advantage of multiple prosecutions from the point of view of the consumer is that, if he wishes to seek compensation under the Powers of Criminal Courts Acts 1973, he will require the defendant to be convicted. Thus different consumers seeking compensation in different areas would each look for separate convictions. This is discussed more fully later.[99]

CIVIL REMEDIES

We have seen that the Act is essentially one which creates criminal offences to protect consumers, but gives no right to bring a civil action. Consumers are left to pursue their civil remedies in the ordinary way, for example, for breach of contract or misrepresentation where appropriate. It may be unnecessary to make the obvious point that not every set of facts giving rise to an offence under the Act will necessarily result in a civil remedy being available either in contract or in tort.

A separate but related question is whether, assuming there to be a contractual right available to the consumer, the contract is vitiated or the right of action lost because of the statutory contravention. As far as the supply of goods is concerned this question is answered by section 35, which states, "A contract for the supply of any goods shall not be void or unenforceable by reason only of

---

[98] [1974] Q.B. 592.
[98a] This is a rule that a defendant cannot be charged more than once for the same offence.
[99] See p. 205.

a contravention of any provision of this Act." Clearly when the contract involves the supply of goods whether by way of sale, hire-purchase, rental or in any other way, the rights of both the supplier and the consumer are unaffected. Strangely section 35 is not wide enough to cover contracts for the supply of services (the Review recommends in para. 256 that section 35 should be amended to cover such contracts). However, it seems unlikely that such contracts are invalidated by the commission of an offence under the Act. Probably this is an example of what is usually described as "incidental illegality," *i.e.* illegality which has no effect on the contract. In any case the consumer's rights would not be affected, as he would not be *in pari delicto* with the guilty supplier.

As regards civil remedies the consumer is slightly worse off as a result of the 1968 Act. The Act repealed section 17 of the Merchandise Marks Act 1887, whereby a seller was deemed to warrant the accuracy of any trade description. However, this warranty was very seldom used.

Finally, two points need to be made with regard to civil remedies and compensation for the consumer. First, a conviction under the Act may be used as evidence in a later civil action by virtue of the Civil Evidence Act 1968. Secondly, compensation may be claimed under the Powers of Criminal Courts Act 1973 as a consequence of the conviction (*post*, p. 204).

CHAPTER 12

CONSUMER SAFETY

INTRODUCTION

WE have seen in earlier chapters that some consumer protection legislation is concerned as much with shoddy goods as with unsafe goods; no distinction is drawn. This is true of both civil and criminal statutes, *e.g.* the Sale of Goods Act 1893 and the Trade Descriptions Act 1968.

However, in many statutes a different approach is adopted where death or personal injury are concerned: provisions are likely to be more stringent or restrictive than in cases where only financial or economic loss results. Thus, under the Unfair Contract Terms Act 1977, section 2, a clause excluding liability for negligence is void in the case of death or personal injury, but valid if reasonable in the case of other loss or damage, *i.e.* damage to property.[1] Similarly the recent proposals to make producers strictly liable for defects in their products are confined to death and personal injury.[2] In other "consumer" areas the same emphasis is placed on ensuring that the individual receives compensation for death or injury, if not for damage to property. For example, the Road Traffic Acts since 1930 have limited the requirement of compulsory insurance for third-party risks to liability in respect of death or bodily injury.[3] Likewise the Health and Safety at Work Act 1974, section 6, restricts its control with regard to articles for use at work to ensuring that they are safe and without risk to health and safety when properly used.

There is no doubt that concern for safety at home should be as serious as concern for safety on the roads or in the work place. The Foreword to "Consumer Safety. A Consultative Document"[4] provides ample evidence.

---

[1] *Ante,* p. 109.
[2] *Ante,* p. 68.
[3] 1972 Act s. 145.
[4] Cmnd. 6398, 1976

About 7,000 people in Great Britain die each year from accidents in the home, over a tenth of them from fires. This is comparable to the number killed on the roads. In addition over 100,000 receive hospital in-patient treatment for home accident injuries. No central statistics are kept for those not admitted to hospital, but it is estimated that in England and Wales 650,000 receive out-patient care in hospitals and 500,000 attend their general practitioner for treatment.

Apart from the toll of human suffering which these figures represent, there are substantial economic costs, both direct—through damage to property, as in the case of the 50,000 or so fires in the home each year—and indirect—eg the cost of medical treatment and hours lost from work.

Home accidents occur at all ages: research has indicated that 30 per cent of victims treated in hospital are children under five, 16 per cent are aged 5 to 14, and 41 per cent aged 15 to 64. Over 65's are involved in some 13 per cent of such accidents, though this age group accounts for two-thirds of all the deaths so caused.

This Consultative Document is concerned with ways of reducing the cost and suffering caused by home accidents. It considers how information, publicity and education on causes of home accidents and means of avoiding them can be improved; and in particular it discusses how the law can best ensure that goods which reach consumers are as safe to use as the public may reasonably expect.

As the last paragraph states, the Green Paper paid particular attention to the ways in which the law could be improved with a view to ensuring that goods used by the consumer are safe. At that time this branch of the law was regulated by the Consumer Protection Acts 1961 and 1971. Several of the proposals contained in the paper for improving the legal protective framework were incorporated in the Consumer Safety Act 1978, most of which came into force on November 1, 1978.

CONSUMER PROTECTION ACT 1961

When the 1978 Act is fully in force, the 1961 and 1971 Acts will be repealed and the regulations made under the 1961 Act replaced by regulations made under the 1978 Act. This is likely to take a few years: meanwhile the following regulations remain in force.

Title	S.I. No.
Stands for Carry-cots (Safety)	1966 No. 1610
Nightdresses (Safety)	1967 No. 839
Electrical Appliances (Colour Code)	1969 No. 310
Electrical Appliances (Colour Code) (Amendment)	1970 No. 811
Electrical Appliances (Colour Code) (Amendment)	1977 No. 931
Electric Blankets (Safety)	1971 No. 1961
Cooking Utensils (Safety)	1972 No. 1957
Heating Appliances (Fireguards)	1973 No. 2106
Pencils and Graphic Instruments (Safety)	1974 No. 226
Toys (Safety)	1974 No. 1367
Glazed Ceramic Ware (Safety)	1975 No. 1241
Electrical Equipment (Safety)	1975 No. 1366
Electrical Equipment (Safety) (Amendments)	1976 No. 1208
Children's Clothing (Hood Cords)	1976 No. 2
Vitreous Enamel-Ware (Safety)	1976 No. 454
Oil Heaters (Safety)	1977 No. 167
Aerosol Dispensers (EEC Requirements)	1977 No. 1977
Packaging and Labelling of Dangerous Substances	1978 No. 209
Babies Dummies (Safety)	1978 No. 836
Cosmetic Products	1978 No. 1354
Perambulators and Pushchairs (Safety)	1978 No. 1372

As the 1961–71 Acts are obsolescent, we shall draw attention only to the salient features. Enforcement is in the hands of local weights and measures authorities. Previously they had no duty to enforce, merely a discretionary power: now they have the same duty to enforce regulations made under the 1961 Act as they have in respect of those made under the 1978 Act.[5] Section 2(1) makes it an offence to sell or have in possession for sale goods not complying with the regulations: the penalties for contravention imposed by section 3(2) are increased by the 1978 Act, section 10(3), to a maximum fine of £1,000 and three months' imprisonment. Finally, a civil action for breach of statutory duty is available

[5] 1978 Act, s. 10(4).

for breach of any of the statutory obligations[5a]: this important, but unusual, consumer remedy is discussed in the next chapter.

CONSUMER SAFETY ACT 1978

The Green Paper on "Consumer Safety," quoted above, identified a number of defects in the scope and operation of the 1961–71 Acts. John Fraser who at that time was the Minister of State for Prices and Consumer Protection, indicated the main direction in which reform would move in a speech at a London Conference on Product Safety and Liability in the autumn of 1977.

> "I am concerned to ensure that the new legislation will tackle other problems not covered by the 1961 Act. We are looking at ways to prevent inherently dangerous goods reaching the market; or where goods presenting a serious risk to health or safety have reached the market, to prohibit their sale or supply.
> Also, where such hazardous products have been sold or supplied to consumers, to ensure that they are warned of the risk. In the case of those goods or substances which are so dangerous that no regulations could protect consumers from the risks inherent in their use, power will be sought to prohibit them outright, by regulations, after full consultations with any interests likely to be affected."

The Act was introduced as a Private Member's Bill with all-party support, received the Royal Assent on July 20, 1978 and was mainly brought into force on November 1, 1978.[6] It is essentially an enabling Act like the 1961 Act. The most important changes effected by the Act are these.

(1) It gives any Secretary of State much more flexible powers to make regulations to ensure that goods are safe and to prohibit the supply of unsafe goods.[7]

(2) It enables quick action to be taken to ban the supply of dangerous goods by the use of "prohibition orders" and "prohibition notices."[8]

(3) It provides power by the service of a "notice to warn" to require manufacturers and distributors of goods, which are

---

[5a] s. 3(1).
[6] See S.I. 1978 No. 1445.
[7] s. 1.
[8] s. 3(1).

found to be dangerous only after they have been sold, to publish notices warning the public of the danger.[9]

(4) It imposes an enforcement duty on local authorities.[10]

Key definitions

Some key words need to be considered before looking at the detailed provisions of the Act: they appear in section 9.

Safe

The Act is concerned essentially with safe and unsafe goods.

> "'Safe' means such as to prevent or adequately to reduce any risk of death or any risk of personal injury from the goods in question or from circumstances in which the goods might be used or kept . . . ."

It is enough to refer to the list of regulations made under the 1961 Act[11] to find examples of unsafe goods: unstable carry-cot stands or prams; anorak hoods causing strangulation; explosive oil heaters or aerosol cans; dummies which choke; toys with sharp edges or spikes or loose dolls eyes; blankets providing heat *and* electrocution.

Electrical appliances provide frequent examples: recently the public were warned of three widely-distributed items with faulty insulation and live surfaces—vacuum cleaners, electric razors and illuminated, gold novelty gondolas (presumably even people with such appalling taste should not reap the penalty of death). Interestingly, although motor vehicles are exceptionally dangerous, they are not as yet included in any regulations under the Act: the reason is that the Motor Vehicles (Construction and Use) Regulations have so far provided adequate control.

The last dozen words of the definition deserve particular comment. Previously it had not been possible to make regulations relating to the effectiveness of safety equipment, *e.g.* life jackets, buoyancy rafts, fire extinguishers; for the risk arises not from the product itself but from the fact that, when circumstances occur in which the equipment is "used", it is found at that late, critical stage to be unsuitable and thus to expose the user to risk. The significance of the word "kept" can be seen in relation to labelling

[9] *Ibid.*
[10] s. 5(1).
[11] *Ante*, p. 194.

requirements on goods which create a hazard if not safely stored, *e.g.* sodium chloride.

There are special provisions for goods containing radioactive substances.

Goods

Certain goods are excluded insofar as they are governed by other legislation—food, animal feed, fertilizers, medicines and drugs.

Supply

A supply is caught only if made "in the course of carrying on a business (whether or not a business of dealing in the goods in question) and either as principal or agent"[12]. So the business supply is covered; the private supply is not. (This is markedly similar to the ambit of the Trade Descriptions Act 1968 and of section 14(2) and (3) of the Sale of Goods Act 1893.)

What types of transaction are "supplies"? The definition provides a detailed answer.

(i) Sale.

(ii) Hire or loan.

(iii) Hire-purchase.

Section 9(3) provides that in the case of hire, hire-purchase, credit sale or conditional sale agreements, "the supplier" is not the provider of the credit but "the further person" who is enabled to provide the goods by virtue of such financial facility.

Example

D wishes to acquire on credit terms a car owned by a dealer S. S sells the car to a finance house C. C lets the goods on hire-purchase to D. S is "the supplier" under the 1978 Act. (To use Consumer Credit Act jargon, the credit-broker S (not the creditor C) is the supplier[13]).

(iv) Work and materials.

(v) Exchange, *e.g.* for trading stamps.

(vi) Gift, *e.g.* a prize.

There are some limited exceptions, including goods supplied as scrap or to a business for repair or reconditioning.

[12] s. 9(1).
[13] See p. 284.

Safety regulations

The safety regulations made pursuant to section 1 are the equivalent of the regulations made under the 1961 Act. The regulation-making power is given "for the purpose of securing that goods are safe or that appropriate information is provided and inappropriate information is not provided in respect of goods."[14] The contents of safety regulations are exhaustively prescribed by section 1(2). They include provisions relating to:

   (i) composition or contents, design, construction, finish or packing;

  (ii) standards to be approved, *e.g.* British Standards Institution (BSI), so that goods meeting the approved standard necessarily comply with the regulations;

 (iii) testing or inspection, *e.g.* manufacturers' quality control procedures to prevent faulty batches of aerosol cans from reaching the market;

 (iv) warnings or instructions or other information on goods, *e.g.* warning symbols, first-aid instructions, lists of ingredients in cosmetics; or prohibiting the giving of "inappropriate information," *e.g.* misleading marks or insignia.

It seems likely that the first regulations under the 1978 Act will be made in the latter half of 1979 to require upholstered furniture to be resistant to matches and cigarettes: foam fillings are a serious fire hazard.

The regulations may also prohibit the supply of goods or components which are unsafe or do not satisfy the requirements of the regulations. Thus a permanent ban may be imposed on dangerous products which the Secretary of State considers to be inherently unsafe irrespective of design or construction.

Extensive consultation is required by section 1(4) before the making of regulations. Further, draft regulations must be approved by a resolution of each House of Parliament.[15] As a period of six months or more is usually spent in this way, it had proved impossible under the 1961 Act to act swiftly when dangerous goods were being marketed. There is now power to deal with such urgent situations by the use of prohibition orders and notices.

[14] s. 1(1).
[15] s. 7(7).

Prohibition orders and notices

The difference between a prohibition order and a prohibition notice is this: a prohibition order is a *general* ban on all traders, whereas a prohibition notice is a *particular* ban operating only against the person on whom it is served.

In either case the prohibition immediately prevents the manufacturer, importer, wholesaler or retailer from continuing to supply unsafe goods or components. Both of these powers are designed to deal with emergencies, particularly where the traders involved are uncooperative—normally producers and sellers are anxious to withdraw unsafe products as quickly as possible, if only because of their possible liability in negligence or contract to the consumer and intermediate parties.

The procedures for orders and notices are set out in Schedule 1, Parts I and II respectively. In both cases there is provision for advance notices to be given (28 and 14 days respectively) so that representations may be made, but this may be dispensed with in extreme emergencies "if the risk of danger . . . is such that the order must be made without delay."[16] A prohibition order lasts for 12 months at the most: it is in effect a temporary regulation which may be replaced by permanent safety regulations by the end of that period.[17] A prohibition notice is of indefinite duration.

The first action of any kind taken under the Act was the making of a prohibition order within a month of its coming into force.[18] The order related to "Tris"-treated fabrics. "Tris" was a chemical used in the U.S.A. to make children's nightwear flame-resistant. However, it was found to have carcinogenic properties. Its use was banned in this way as an emergency procedure, because a shipment had arrived from France, where its sale, but not its re-export, was banned[18a].

Notice to warn

Prohibitions orders and notices are appropriate where goods are still in the hands of the suppliers. What can be done if the goods

[16] paras. 5 and 14.
[17] para. 3.
[18] The Nightwear (Safety) Order 1978, S.I. 1978 No. 1728.
[18a] The Balloon-Making Compounds (Safety) Order 1979, S.I. 1979 No. 44 was the second order. It banned the supply of balloon-making substances containing Benzene, *e.g.* "Blobo Plastic Bubbaloons" from Taiwan; for the vapour may cause leukaemia.

H

have already reached the public and are in daily use? Prior to the Act the most that the Department of Trade could do was to ask manufacturers to publish a warning or itself to issue a press notice. Responsible manufacturers and importers readily do so. The motor industry is a good example, where as soon as any apparent defect reveals itself as a danger, *e.g.* brakes, the producer gives it widespread publicity and advises owners to take in their vehicles to be checked. (The 1978 Act does not contain a power to *order* the recall of goods.)

It is possible for a notice to warn to be served on any trader requiring him to publish a specified warning about unsafe goods at his own expense. Part III of Schedule 1 prescribes the procedure, which is similar to that for prohibition notices, but without an emergency procedure.

Offences and penalties

Offences against the safety regulations are contained in section 2. It is an offence to supply goods where the regulations themselves prohibit it; to fail to carry out prescribed tests or procedures, or to deal with goods not satisfying such matters; or to provide prohibited information.[19]

Further offences are created by section 3(3) for contravening a prohibition order or notice or a notice to warn.

In addition prosecutions may be brought under "by-pass provisions" similar to section 23 of the Trade Descriptions Act[20] where the commission of an offence is "due to the act or default of some other person."[21]

The penalty for any of these offences is the same—on summary conviction a maximum fine of £1,000 and up to three months' imprisonment.[22]

Defences

The familiar defence is available "that the accused took all reasonable steps and exercised all due diligence to avoid committing the offence", with the same duty to notify the prosecutor of

[19] s. 2(2)(*a*) and (*b*) and s. 2(3).
[20] *Ante*, p. 185.
[21] ss. 2(5) and 3(5).
[22] s. 2(4) and s. 3(3).

the identity of any one else who is being blamed.[23] The comparable trade descriptions provisions are discussed elsewhere.[24]

Enforcement

We have already commented on the fact that the 1961 Act merely gave a discretionary power to trading standards inspectors. Section 5(1) makes it their duty to enforce the provisions creating the offences explained above. Whether with the depleted resources available to them local authorities are managing to cope with their ever-increasing responsibilities—the Consumer Credit Act 1974 is also their problem—is a matter of doubt. Nevertheless this duty is one which they must do their best to fulfil unless and until the Secretary of State exercises the power given to him by section 5(2) to transfer the duty elsewhere. Schedule 2 gives the authorities the usual related powers of purchase, entry and seizure, testing, etc.

Civil Remedy

In the following chapter breach of statutory duty is examined. The Acts of 1961 and 1978 stand alone among the criminal statutes concerned with consumer protection in expressly affording the victim a civil remedy. Section 6(1) offers the remedy and section 6(2) prevents it being snatched away by invalidating any exclusion clause. Further, any contractual rights of the victim remain untouched.[25]

Example

> Retailers purchase 1,000 green anodised metal garden gnomes. The gnomes' pointed hats pose a risk of personal injury to anyone tripping over or sitting on them. The Secretary of State makes a prohibition order in respect of them. The retailers thereafter sell one to Alfred, who stumbles and falls on top of it while carrying it home and suffers personal injuries. What civil remedies has Alfred?

Whether or not an action would succeed in contract on the grounds that the goods were not of merchantable quality within s. 14(2) of the 1893 Act, Alfred will have a claim for breach of

[23] ss. 2(6), 3(4) and 3(5).
[24] *Ante,* p. 182.
[25] s. 6(4).

statutory duty. (If the retailers are convicted of an offence under section 3(3), Alfred can seek compensation under the Powers of Criminal Courts Act 1973: see the next Chapter.)

Transitional

The Act is now fully in force except those provisions of section 10, and the related Schedule 3, which in due course will repeal the 1961–71 Acts.

CHAPTER 13

CRIME AND COMPENSATION

INTRODUCTION

Examples

(A) Jane buys a used car described as "Immaculate. A really nice little bus." It is clapped out and incapable of self-propulsion. The car dealer repudiates his liability with a couple of Anglo-Saxon monosyllables.

(B) James reads a holiday brochure. The tour operator confirms that the hotel facilities are exactly as described, whereupon James books a holiday. When he reaches his destination, he discovers that the hotel bears little resemblance except in name to that shown in the brochure. The tour operator refuses to give compensation.

A commonly held view of the consumer protection lobby is that it is a waste of effort for Parliament and the courts to amend and improve upon the long-standing rights of consumers, *e.g.* under the Sale of Goods Act 1893, and to launch new assaults across a broad front on attempts to rob the consumer of those rights, *e.g.* under the Unfair Contract Terms Act 1977. Thus in both the above examples the consumers clearly have a right of action for breach of contract, but of what benefit are their rights unless machinery exists to enable them to be enforced without difficulty? The immediate need is for reform to be concentrated upon the enforcement of existing rights rather than the creation of new ones.

We discussed in Chapter 9 enforcement under the civil law. We saw that frequently the consumer has no alternative to suing the recalcitrant trader in the county court; for there is often no trade association able or prepared to bring about a settlement of the complaint by conciliation or to discipline the trader for falling below the standards set out in a code of practice; nor will such a businessman be willing to submit the dispute to arbitration under one of the voluntary schemes. In such circumstances there are clearly considerable advantages to the consumer if he can reap some benefit from the fact that the trader has committed a criminal offence in addition to having broken one of his civil obligations. However, it should be borne in mind that criminal offences are not created for the purpose of providing consumers with compensation, as is pointed out in the Review of the Trade Descriptions Act 1968, para. 281:

> "We believe that compensation is primarily a matter for the civil law, and that an award of compensation under the Powers of the Criminal Courts Act should be regarded as a windfall rather than a right which itself justified prosecution under the Act."

It is proposed in this chapter to deal with two aspects of recovery arising out of the criminal law. First, we shall look at the power of the courts on conviction to award compensation under the Powers of Criminal Courts Act 1973. Secondly, we shall briefly consider the circumstances in which it is possible to sue for breach of statutory duty.

POWERS OF CRIMINAL COURTS ACT 1973

The recommendations of the 1970 Widgery Report with regard to the remedies available under the criminal law for compensating victims of crime were broadly carried into effect by the Criminal Justice Act 1972. The particular provision which now concerns us was replaced by section 35(1) of the Powers of Criminal Courts Act 1973.

In essence it enables the court to order a convicted person to pay compensation for any damage resulting from the offence. The section states:

> "A court by or before which a person is convicted of an offence, in addition to dealing with him in any other way, may, on application or otherwise, make an order (in this Act referred to as "a compensation order") requiring him to pay compensation for any personal injury, loss or damage resulting from that offence or any other offence which is taken into consideration by the court in determining sentence."

This discretionary power is available whenever there has been a conviction in any court, including a magistrates' court. It is

especially valuable in cases brought under the Trade Descriptions
Act 1968, where the loss may be too small to justify the cost of
civil litigation.

Maximum

The amount of compensation where the conviction is on indictment in the Crown Court is unlimited. In the magistrates' court
it is limited to £1,000 (the original £400 limit was increased by the
Criminal Law Act 1977, s. 60). This limit relates to each offence
of which the accused is convicted; so if a supplier is convicted of
four offences, the order may reach £4,000.

Special care must be taken when the accused asks for other
offences to be taken into consideration for which he has not been
prosecuted. No additional sums may be awarded in respect of such
t.i.c. offences.[1]

Example

A tour operator publishes a brochure containing false statements in contravention of section 14 of the Trade Descriptions Act 1968. Forty people from
different parts of England book holidays in reliance on the brochure. The tour
operator, when prosecuted in one area, asks for the 39 other offences to be
taken into consideration. The magistrates' order for the 40 offences cannot
exceed £1,000 in total.

From the point of view of the victims in this example it would
be preferable for separate charges to be brought in each area, so
that altogether the orders would have a ceiling of £40,000.[2]

Type of loss

The compensation may relate to "any personal injury, loss or
damage." Thus claims for breach of contract (as in Examples A
and B[2a]) or for negligence are covered. Further, the Act is wide
enough for an order to be made in respect of loss for which no
civil remedy is available: in such a case in the absence of a successful
prosecution the victim would be remediless.

This is most important in the case of misleading advertising,
where usually the advertisement will not be a term of the contract

[1] See H. Street, "Compensation Orders and the Trade Descriptions Act". 1974
Crim. L.R. 345.
[2] Multiple prosecutions are discussed in the chapter on Trade Descriptions: see
p. 190.
[2a] Ante, p. 203.

nor a misrepresentation but mere puff. However, it may result in the commission of a criminal offence, *e.g.* under the Trade Descriptions Act, when compensation for the consumer's loss can be ordered.

Let us consider the second example given at the beginning of this chapter. There the statements about the hotel facilities are terms of the contract in view of the express confirmation prior to booking.[3] In the absence of that confirmation it would be difficult, but not impossible,[4] for James to show that the wording in the brochure was by itself a term or misrepresentation; nevertheless if a conviction were obtained under the Trade Descriptions Act, compensation could be claimed.

There are two exceptions where an order cannot be made[4a]: (a) for loss suffered by dependents in consequence of the victim's death; (b) for injury, loss or damage due to an accident arising out of the presence of a motor vehicle on a road unless resulting from a Theft Act offence.

Assessment

As the assessment of compensation will commonly be made by lay magistrates, it is inappropriate for the power to be exercised in complicated cases, *e.g.* where the principles of remoteness of damage need to be understood and applied. An order will be made only in straightforward cases. Lawton L.J. explained the court's approach in *R.* v. *Thompson Holidays Ltd.*[5]

"Parliament, we are sure, never intended to introduce into the criminal law the concepts of causation which apply to the assessment of damages under the law of contract or tort . . . [The court] must do what it can to make a just order on such

---

[3] See *Jackson* v. *Horizon Holidays Ltd.* [1975] 1 W.L.R. 1468 (C.A.). A four week family holiday in Ceylon proved to be a disaster, with very distasteful food apparently cooked in coconut oil, and only a shower and no bath. The holiday price was £1,200. Damages of £1,100 were awarded for breach of contract.

[4] *Jarvis* v. *Swan Tours* [1973] 1 Q.B. 233 (C.A.) is another heart-rending case. The plaintiff, on a fortnight's holiday in the Swiss Alps, spent an entire week surrounded by foreigners who could not speak English! As a further insult instead of Swiss cakes he was served crisps and desiccated nut rolls. (As their Lordships pointed out during the trial, "You don't have to go to Switzerland to get those": Stephenson L.J. "You can get them at Crewe": Edmund Davies L.J.—*The Times*, October 19th, 1972.) Damages of £125 were awarded, double the cost of the holiday.

[4a] s. 35(3).

[5] [1974] Q.B.592, at p. 599.

information as it has. Whenever the making of an order for compensation is appropriate the court must ask itself whether loss or damage can fairly be said to have resulted to anyone from the offence for which the accused has been convicted."[6]

The defendants were convicted under section 14 of the Trade Descriptions Act 1968 for making a false statement in their brochure that a hotel had a night club and swimming and paddling pools. Compensation of £50 was awarded to the complainant.

A separate point to bear in mind is that the victim must show that the defendant is liable for the amount claimed. In *R*. v. *Vivian*[7] the Court of Appeal quashed an order in respect of damage to a car alleged to have been done by a thief in a collision, as there was no proof that he was responsible for all the damage: further, the appellant claimed that the sole estimate given for the repairs was excessive. Talbot J. said[8] that the view of the court was that "no order for compensation should be made unless the sum claimed by way of compensation is either agreed or has been proved." This appears to leave a large loophole for defendants and certainly makes it necessary for victims to be less perfunctory in preparing claims, *e.g.* by obtaining more than one estimate.

Situations where it would be appropriate to make an order include misdescribed goods, *e.g.* clocked cars or the goods in Example A above,[8a] where the reduction in value or cost of repair can be easily proved; holiday cases where part of the cost can be refunded to take account of inconvenience and loss of enjoyment (Example B); or misleading prices where the complainant pays more than expected and seeks compensation for the extra sum paid.

In determining whether to make an order and, if so, for what amount, the court must take into account the defendant's means[9] and generally limits the award to a sum which he can manage to pay over two or three years. Thus in *R*. v. *McIntosh*[10] the Court

---

[6] See also *R* v. *Daly* [1974] 1 All E.R. 290; *R* v. *Kneeshaw* [1974] 1 All E.R. 896: the machinery is intended "for clear and simple cases" (*per* Lord Widgery C.J.).
[7] [1979] 1 All E.R. 48.
[8] *Ibid.* p. 50.
[8a] *Ante,* p. 203.
[9] s. 35(4).
[10] [1973] Crim. L.R. 378.

of Appeal revoked a £90 order against a burglar on the grounds that he had no means and would find it hard to obtain employment on his release from prison because of his wooden leg—surprisingly not an impediment to the nefarious activities of this Long John McSilver in a trade where one would expect agility to be a *sine qua non.*

The power is being widely used. Five hundred and seventeen orders were made in England and Wales in respect of trade descriptions offences in the two and a quarter years from January 1973 with an average award of £77. Over 80 per cent of the compensation related to motor vehicles and accessories.[11]

How to apply

No procedure is laid down for making the application for compensation. Generally it is enough for the victim to forewarn the clerk or prosecutor before the trial commences, so that the application may be brought to the notice of the court after conviction and the victim then heard. Alternatively the court may act of its initiative without an application.

An order is enforceable in the same ways as a fine[12]. Thus the court may impose a term of imprisonment in default.

Interrelation with civil rights

Generally the trial of the criminal charge will be held some time before any civil proceedings reach that stage. In the subsequent civil proceedings two points must be borne in mind. First, the conviction may be used in evidence.[13] Secondly, when awarding damages the court must take into account sums paid under the order.[14]

If exceptionally the civil proceedings have already come to an end, whether by judgment or settlement, no order can be made even though the victim can still show loss. In *Hammerton Cars Ltd.* v. *London Borough of Redbridge:*[15]

[11] O.F.T Consultative Document "A Review of the Trade Descriptions Act." See also [1976] Crim. L.R. 422 for Crown Court statistics.
[12] Administration of Justice Act 1970, s. 41.
[13] Civil Evidence Act 1968, s. 11.
[14] 1973 Act, s. 38(2).
[15] [1974] 2 All E.R. 216.

The complainant bought a car described as "in perfect condition." It was not. He settled an action against the sellers on the basis that he paid his own legal costs of £170 and expert's fee of £25. When the sellers were convicted under the Trade Descriptions Act he was awarded £195 compensation by the justices. The dealer successfully appealed against the order to the Divisional Court.

Lord Widgery C.J., doubting whether in any case the section would cover such legal costs, said:

"It seems to me to be abundantly clear that if the victim brings civil proceedings, and those civil proceedings are brought to an end, then they should be regarded as quite independent of the criminal proceedings and no compensation order should be made in respect of liabilities which arose, or might have arisen, in the civil proceedings."

BREACH OF STATUTORY DUTY

As has been seen earlier, frequently a consumer who has suffered loss will have a remedy flowing directly or indirectly from the civil or criminal law. As far as the civil law is concerned, the remedy may be for breach of contract, *e.g.* against a supplier of goods or services who has not fulfilled obligations imposed upon him by statute or the common law, or in the tort of negligence, *e.g.* against a manufacturer. Alternatively or additionally, where the supplier's activities involve a criminal offence resulting in a successful prosecution, the consumer may seek compensation under the Powers of Criminal Courts Act.

However, a hiatus exists where the supplier has not broken a contract with the consumer, maybe because they are not in a contractual relationship; nor has he been negligent; nor has the consumer recovered compensation, even though the supplier has committed a criminal offence, *e.g.* because no prosecution was brought or, even if it was and a conviction obtained, the justices would not make an order, as perhaps it was too complicated a case. (If, of course, the supplier is not guilty of any offence, the consumer has reached the end of the road.) In such circumstances the consumer's last resort is to try to show that the supplier is liable in tort for breach of statutory duty.

If it were possible for such an action to be brought in every case where a supplier has failed to comply with his statutory duties, the consumer's position would be much more straightforward. In the absence of an award of compensation under the 1973 Act, he would be able to institute civil proceedings on this basis without concerning himself with the questions of privity of contract with the supplier or proof of negligence.

The type of consumer who would most clearly gain is the member of a family injured by defective goods bought by another family member.[16] However, the courts when construing statutes have been reluctant to imply into them civil rights for the victim. The rationale seems to be that the legislation is for the protection of the public generally and is not intended to afford a civil remedy to individual members of the public. The reasoning is unconvincing. To draw an analogy from the contractual principles of offer and acceptance, where an offer is made to the world at large, contracts are formed only with those individuals who accept the offer; similarly where a duty is imposed on suppliers for the benefit of the public at large, it should be possible for those particular members of the public who suffer loss as a result of a breach of that duty to come forward and claim damages in a civil action founded upon that statutory duty.

Yet generally the courts are content to leave consumers to their separate civil rights. Thus in *Square* v. *Model Farm Dairies (Bournemouth) Ltd.*[17], where the plaintiff alleged that contaminated milk sold in breach of the food and drugs legislation had made his family ill with typhoid fever, the Court of Appeal rejected his claim because he had a remedy under the Sale of Goods Act 1893. A comparable case is *Buckley* v. *La Réserve*[18] where an action failed against a restaurant which in contravention of the Food and Drugs Act 1955 sold food unfit for human consumption (the food was snails: legal symmetry would have been attained had the contamination resulted from ginger beer). It is important to note that here the plaintiff's civil rights would not have given him a remedy, unless he could prove negligence, as he was taken to

---

[16] Such a victim's position will be greatly improved if and when the proposals are implemented for strict liability of producers. See p. 68.

[17] [1939] 2 K.B. 365.

[18] [1959] Crim. L.R. 451.

the restaurant as a guest, *i.e.* no privity of contract: nevertheless the court adopted the same stance as in the *Square* case.

Two cases involving defective cars also illustrate the courts' unhelpful attitude to consumers. In *Phillips* v. *Brittania Hygienic Laundry Co.*[19] the plaintiff failed to recover for injuries resulting from the defendants' breach of duties imposed by the antecedents to the present Motor Vehicles (Construction and Use) Regulations. Similarly a seller was not liable to a victim injured by a vehicle which the seller delivered in such a condition that its use on the road was unlawful, although he thereby committed an offence under what is now section 60(1) of the Road Traffic Act 1972.[20]

The courts' restrictive interpretation leads to this principle in the consumer field: an action for breach of statutory duty has a chance of success only if the statute *expressly* states that a breach of the duty is actionable, *e.g.* the Consumer Safety Act 1978, s 6(1)[21]:

> "Any obligation imposed on a person by safety regulations or a prohibition order or a prohibition notice is a duty owed by him to any other person who may be affected by a failure to perform the obligation, and a breach of that duty is actionable."

Where a statute states the opposite, the position is equally clear, *e.g.* the Safety of Sports Grounds Act 1975, section 13. Where a statute is silent on the point, the presumption is that it gives no civil remedy. Such a presumption is strengthened where the statute expressly preserves other civil remedies, following the reasoning in *Square* v. *Model Farm Dairies (Bournemouth) Ltd.*[22]; for then Parliament is implicitly leaving the public to their general civil rights.

It is on these grounds that we take the view that no action will lie for breach of statutory duty arising out of the Trade Descriptions Act 1968, section 35[23] of which saves civil rights by stating, "A contract for the supply of goods shall not be void or unenforceable by reason only of a contravention of any provision of the Act." That view is fortified by observing that the 1968 Act does not

[19] [1923] 2 K.B. 832.
[20] *Badham* v. *Lambs Ltd.* [1946] K.B. 45.
[21] See p. 201.
[22] *Ante*, p. 210.
[23] See also p. 190.

include any provision equivalent to section 17 of the repealed Merchandise Marks Act 1887 whereby a seller was deemed to warrant the accuracy of any trade description. The omission is deliberate and contrary to the recommendation in the Final Report of the Committee on Consumer Protection (Cmnd. 1781) that the provision should remain and "contracting-out" be prohibited. We think it fitting to end with a plea that further consideration be given by the courts and Parliamentary reformers to the view expressed in para 459 of the Report.

> "We cannot avoid the conclusion that Section 17 reflects a sound principle, namely that persons trading in goods to which false trade descriptions have been applied should be liable, not merely under the criminal law, but also to meet any civil claim in favour of a purchaser arising from the same circumstances."

PART III: ADMINISTRATIVE CONTROL

The civil and criminal sanctions discussed earlier in this book do a great deal to protect the consumer, but by themselves they are not enough. In particular:

1. Industry is never static for long and the enterprising trader is likely to come up with new business practices. Some of these, while within the law, may be harmful to consumers and swift action may be needed to curtail them.

2. There may be a number of dishonest or inefficient traders who may make large profits, *e.g.* by the delivery of shoddy goods or by practices which infringe the Trade Descriptions Act 1968. They may not be deterred by the occasional fine or award of compensation. What the consumer really needs is a system whereby such traders can be restrained from trading altogether unless and until they mend their ways.

3. The standards set by the law are minimum standards and the consumer can benefit if traders can be persuaded to undertake additional voluntary obligations.

4. Neither the civil nor the criminal law achieve one of the most important aims of consumer protection—making the consumer aware of his rights.

It is at this point that we meet the third weapon of consumer protection—administrative control. This involves a public body charged with the task of keeping the consumer scene under permanent review. The principal weapons of administrative control are to be found in the Fair Trading Act 1973 and the Consumer Credit Act 1974. The former (which also deals with monopolies, mergers and restrictive practices) is examined below and the Consumer Credit Act will be dealt with in Chapters 15–23.

CHAPTER 14

FAIR TRADING ACT 1973[1]

INTRODUCTION

UNLIKE the Consumer Credit Act 1974, which was substantially based upon the recommendations of the Crowther Committee's Report on Consumer Credit, the Fair Trading Act 1973 appeared out of the blue with no warning or consultation in the form of Green or White Papers.

Most of the Act does not break new ground inasmuch as broadly it consolidates, with some changes and improvements, the pre-existing law relating to competition, *i.e.* monopolies, mergers and restrictive practices. However, it contains five innovations. First, it creates the post of Director General of Fair Trading (Part I). Secondly, it gives to the Director powers to initiate subordinate legislation to protect the consumer by banning undesirable trade practices as and when they appear (Part II). Thirdly, it enables the Director to bring into line individual rogue traders who regularly flout their legal obligations (Part III). Fourthly, the Director is under a duty to encourage trade associations to prepare, and to disseminate to their members, voluntary codes of practice (s. 124(3)). Finally, the Director can arrange for publication of information and advice to consumers (s. 124(1)). The last two topics have already been considered in Chapter 9[1] and accordingly this chapter will examine the other novel features of the Act mentioned above.

It is true that the Act gives to the consumer no right of action or opportunity to claim compensation, but he can lodge a complaint with the Office of Fair Trading directly or via a trading standards officer or C.A.B. This gives the consumer two benefits: the satisfaction of knowing that his complaint has added to the information kept by the O.F.T. and may have helped to identify and ultimately to outlaw an undesirable trade practice within Part II; and the exhilaration of hoping that a note of his grievance on the file of the particular trader may tip the balance and provide the evidence to show that the trader is persistent in his improper activities and should be brought to book under Part III. (One should not under-

---

[1] *Ante,* pp. 121–125.

estimate the importance to the consumer of a chance to vent his feelings to a public official in the expectation, sometimes vain, that some action will ensue whether or not he is able to recover financial redress. This may be the real significance of the Ombudsmen in other areas).

The Director General

The Director is appointed by the Secretary of State for Trade for a term of office not exceeding five years (section 1). The first Director was Sir John Methven, a solicitor with a local government and industrial background, who at the end of his term joined the C.B.I. as its Director—in a way a gamekeeper turned poacher if one thinks of the consumer as fair game needing protection. His successor is Mr. Gordon Borrie, a barrister, formerly a member of the Consumer Protection Advisory Committee and Professor of Law at Birmingham University.[1a]

The Director has two general functions relating to consumer protection, which are set out in section 2(1). These duties must be carried out "so far as appears to him to be practicable from time to time." One is active, the other passive. His active rôle is to keep under review the carrying on of commercial activities which relate to the supply of goods or services to consumers and to collect information with respect to such activities and the persons by whom they are carried on. He is to do this with a view to becoming aware of and ascertaining the circumstances relating to practices which may adversely affect the economic interests of consumers— only the economic interests, nothing else. His other rôle, his passive function, is to receive and collate evidence becoming available to him with respect to such activities. The purpose of this is to build up dossiers of evidence on practices which may adversely affect consumer interests but in this case the interests may be not only economic but also interests with respect to health, safety or other matters. An example given in the debates on the Act was unsafe child "safety" harnesses. So unless economic interests are affected, the Director is obliged to do nothing except to wait to see what information comes in to him.

[1a] For a resume of his functions by the Director himself, see the transcript of a lecture to the Bar Association for Commerce, Finance and Industry (1977) 74 L.S. Gaz, 70.

In addition the Director must assist the Secretary of State when required to do so and he can make recommendations to him (s. 2(3)).

The Office of Fair Trading

The O.F.T. is not specifically created by or mentioned in the Act. Section 1(5) enables the Director to appoint such staff as he thinks fit—there are over 300 now. The O.F.T. is the Director and his staff in aggregate. It is a Government department but not all of the staff are civil servants. Its address is Field House, Breams Buildings, London, EC4A 1PR.

Perhaps it might be useful at this point to mention one matter which the O.F.T. does *not* do; *it does not deal with individual complaints* (although it will keep a record of the complaint which may become relevant in a future investigation).

The Consumer Protection Advisory Committee

The C.P.A.C., established under section 3, has between 10 and 15 members appointed by the Secretary of State. It has merely an advisory role. It cannot take any initiative by making proposals for action and exists to consider references to it under section 14 and, if the references are coupled with proposals under section 17, to consider the proposals too. The controlling and directing power lies with the Secretary of State. This is clear from section 12, which states that the Secretary of State may give general directions indicating considerations to which the Director should have particular regard in determining the order of priority in which matters are to be brought under review under section 2, whether to make a reference to the Committee under Part II, etc.

ADVERSE CONSUMER TRADE PRACTICES

The essential differences between Parts II and III is that Part II is concerned with undesirable *practices*, whereas Part III is concerned with undesirable *traders*. Thus under Part II it is possible for a statutory order to be made banning certain undesirable trade practices, whereas under Part III the attack is not upon a general practice but upon an individual trader who persistently acts in a way which is unfair to consumers.

The point of Part II is to refer consumer trade practices to the

C.P.A.C. so that the C.P.A.C may consider whether they adversely affect the economic interests of consumers and then report. More importantly it is possible to couple with that reference proposals for action, so that the C.P.A.C. when reporting may give its view on those proposals.

Consumer trade practice

There is no complete freedom of choice as to what practices may be referred; the term "consumer trade practice" is exhaustively defined in section 13, *i.e.* any practice carried on in connection with the supply of goods or services to consumers and which relates to one of the six matters specified in paragraphs (a) to (f) of the section:

(a) the terms or conditions of supply, *e.g.* the continued use of void exemption clauses, VAT-exclusive prices;

(b) the manner in which those terms are communicated, *e.g.* the size of print;

(c) promotion, *e.g.* advertisements, labels, double pricing of goods ("3p off recommended price");

(d) methods of salesmanship, *e.g.* doorstep selling, traders masquerading as private sellers in small ads;

(e) packaging, *e.g.* large containers only half filled but accurately marked with the amount of their contents;

(f) methods of demanding or securing payment, *e.g.* requiring a deposit when an order for goods is placed.

The procedure

A reference under section 14 can be made by the Director or any Minister. The C.P.A.C. considers "whether a consumer trade practice specified in the reference adversely affects the economic interest of consumers" and reports back. Unless the reference falls within section 17 and includes proposals, that is the end of the matter. This is sometimes called a study reference because it does not result in action by anybody, only study. As yet none has been made.

There are some exclusions from section 14. No reference may be made in respect of certain professions, *e.g.* legal, medical, dental, where it appears that a monopoly situation exists[2] nor,

---

[2] s. 15 and Schedule 4.

without Ministerial consent, in respect of the supply of certain goods or services, *e.g.* gas, electricity, rail, post.[3]

The real punch in Part II lies in section 17, which provides that references by the Director—by no one else—may include proposals for action by the Secretary of State. The scope of section 17 is narrower than section 14 in that, although the reference must again relate to a consumer trade practice as defined in section 13, the practice must also fall within one of the four paragraphs of section 17(2). It is necessary for the Director to consider that the practice has or is likely to have the effect of:

(a) misleading consumers as to, or withholding from them adequate information as to, or an adequate record of, their rights and obligations under relevant consumer transactions; or

(b) otherwise misleading or confusing consumers with respect to any matter in connection with relevant consumer transactions; or

(c) subjecting consumers to undue pressure to enter into relevant consumer transactions; or

(d) causing the terms or conditions, on or subject to which consumers enter into relevant consumer transactions, to be so adverse to them as to be inequitable.

The common flavour of these four recipes is of misleading or confusing consumers or pressurising them to enter into unfair transactions. Schedule 6 to the Act gives half a dozen illustrations, but not exhaustively, of matters falling within the scope of section 17 proposals. The third one is "prohibition of the inclusion in specified consumer transactions of terms or conditions purporting to exclude or limit the liability of a party to such a transaction in respect of specified matters"; this proved to be the substance of the first order under Part II.[3a]

The sequence of a section 17 reference is as follows. The reference is made by the Director who may—but there is no obligation—include proposals for recommending to the Secretary of State that he exercise his powers under the Act. The reference must be published in the London, Edinburgh and Belfast Gazettes and no doubt any interested party will submit evidence to the Committee. The C.P.A.C. considers the reference and proposals

[3] s. 16 and Schedule 5.
[3a] *Post,* p. 220.

and reports within three months, unless that period is extended by the Secretary of State.[4] In fact all four of the reports to date have taken six months or more to be published. In its report the C.P.A.C. states whether the practice is adverse, and if so, for which of the reasons mentioned in section 17. Where the practice is adverse, it must also state whether it agrees with the Director's proposals as they stand, would agree with them if they were modified in a manner specified in the report, or disagrees with them and does not desire to suggest any modification.[5] Unless the C.P.A.C. disagrees with the proposals, the Secretary of State may make an order by statutory instrument giving effect to the proposals as set out in the reference or as modified by the C.P.A.C. in its report.[6] This order will not be effective until it has been approved by a resolution of each House of Parliament.

Penalties and enforcement

Orders under section 22 are enforced by criminal sanctions only. There is a marked similarity between Part II of this Act and the Trade Descriptions Act 1968 as regards penalties, defences and enforcement.[7] Accordingly, it is not proposed to discuss such provisions in detail in this chapter: readers are referred to Chapter 11.[7a]

Briefly, the maximum penalties for contravention of a prohibition are a £1000 fine on summary conviction; an unlimited fine or two years' imprisonment or both if convicted on indictment.[8] Proceedings may be taken against any director, manager, secretary or other similar officer of a company, where an offence by the company was committed with his consent or connivance or is attributable to his neglect.[9]

Section 25 provides the same five defences, *e.g.* mistake, act or default of another person, etc. Again the defendant must prove the two factors of reasonable precautions and due diligence. There is also a "by-pass provision" in section 24.

Enforcement is once more by local weights and measures author-

---

[4] s. 20.
[5] s. 21.
[6] s. 22.
[7] See *ante*, pp. 181–188.
[7a] *Ante*, p. 155.
[8] s. 23.
[9] s. 132.

ities[10] whose officers have powers to make test purchases[11] and to enter premises to inspect and to seize goods and documents.[12]

The Act provides no special civil remedy but does not vitiate any such remedy which may otherwise be available, *e.g.* for breach of contract.[13]

Speedy procedure?

The intention and expectation was that it would be possible to identify new abuses at an early stage, to recommend and quickly to put into effect prohibitive measures and thus to squash the practice before it mushroomed. Indeed, in April 1974 the Director stated, when announcing the first reference to the C.P.A.C., that he hoped that in six months a statutory order would be made: it actually appeared two and a half years later. Both Directors have expressed disappointment with the slow working of Part II. There are many reasons. Sometimes the C.P.A.C. is unable to agree a report within the three months period (first and fourth references); on other occasions (second and third references) publication of the reports is delayed by the Government while it clarifies its own intentions. Further delays occur when the report passes from the O.F.T. to the Department of Trade for implementation. In part at least the cause is a shortage of draftsmen, who, in the consumer protection area alone, are concurrently trying to cope with the complexities of the regulations to be made under the Consumer Credit Act 1974 which have fallen years behind the original programme. It may be significant that, in relation to bargain offers, the Director chose to sidestep the C.P.A.C. completely by using his power to present the Secretary of State with a recommendation for action.[13a]

However, although the Part II procedure is time-consuming there can be little doubt that it is quicker than waiting for Parliamentary time to legislate on each particular matter. One comparison will suffice. In 1966 a Working Party was established to assist the Law Commission in its consideration of exclusion clauses relating to negligence and contracts for the supply of services. This

[10] s. 27
[11] s. 28.
[12] s. 29.
[13] s. 26.
[13a] s. 2(3), *ante*, p. 216.

resulted, after the intervening publication of a Working Paper and Report, in the Unfair Contract Terms Act 1977. Perhaps that places in perspective the two and half years from reference to Order in the case of the first reference, to which we now turn.

Orders made under Part II

(a) *Restrictions on statements*
   "No refunds"
   "Money will not be refunded. Credit notes only"
   "Sale goods may not be returned"

The first reference to the C.P.A.C. in April 1974 was described in the Director's Dossier 17/1 as "The Purported Exclusion of Inalienable Rights of Consumers and Failure to Explain their Existence." The reference, the report and the Order embraced the supply of goods by way of sale, hire-purchase and trading stamps.

It covers three practices. The first is the continuing use of void exemption clauses. It will be remembered that the Supply of Goods (Implied Terms) Act 1973, section 4, amended section 55 of the Sale of Goods Act 1893 so as to invalidate exemption clauses in consumer sales.[14] However, such clauses, though void, were not illegal. So the practice continued of exhibiting shop notices like the above examples which purport to take away the buyer's right of rejection and money back for breach of condition. Similarly, there was nothing to prevent a car dealer or other seller from incorporating an exclusion clause in his printed sales agreement with the intention and result that a customer reading the agreement would mistakenly think that the clause was valid and effective and that therefore he had no remedy for defects. Terms of sale printed in price lists and catalogues could be similarly misleading.

The second practice is concerned with written statements furnished by suppliers of goods which purport to set out the rights and obligations of the parties but fail to advise consumers of their inalienable rights, *e.g.* under sections 13–15 of the Sale of Goods Act 1893. Thus a car dealer might give a three months guarantee on a second-hand car, covering parts but not labour, without revealing to the buyer that, irrespective of the guarantee, the buyer has the benefit of the implied conditions under the 1893 Act.

[14] Section 55, subsections (3) to (11), were repealed by the Unfair Contract Terms Act 1977. The relevant provisions are now sections 6 and 12 of the 1977 Act. See Chap. 8, *ante,* p. 112.

The third practice is similar to the second practice except that the written statements relate to the consumer's rights against *third parties* such as manufacturers. Thus, a shopkeeper may pass on to his customer a manufacturer's guarantee giving the impression that the customer's rights for defects lie only against the manufacturer under the terms of the guarantee without explaining the buyer's statutory rights against the shopkeeper qua seller.[14a] The Dossier identifies the problem as follows:

> "There is apparently a wide spread belief among consumers that manufacturers are primarily responsible to them *in law* for defects in manufactured goods, (particularly goods which are packed by the manufacturer, so that a retailer may be unaware of the defect); and this belief is often fostered by shop staff, who are naturally eager to preserve the retailer's reputation when faulty goods are identified or returned, by attributing responsibility to the manufacturer. Thus in a situation where goods fail to correspond to their description or are unfit for the purpose made known to the seller, or are of unmerchantable quality or fail to correspond with the sample—or where goods are deficient on more than one of these counts—this aspect of the practice undermines the consumer's proper understanding of his legal position."

The C.P.A.C. published its Report[15] in December 1974. It found that all three practices fell within section 13(a) and adversely affected the economic interests of consumers by having the effects specified in section 17(2), namely of misleading consumers as to their rights under relevant consumer transactions or otherwise confusing them as to the terms of the transaction. They agreed with the Director's proposals subject to certain modifications narrowing their scope. Those modified proposals were put into effect by the Consumer Transactions (Restriction on Statements) Order 1976,[16] made on November 1st, 1976.

The order came into operation in three stages. On December 1, 1976 it became an offence to display at any place where consumer transactions are effected, *e.g.* a shop or car showroom, a notice

[14a] See Chap. 6, *ante,* p. 68.
[15] H.C. 6 Session 1974/75.
[16] S.I. 1976 No. 1813, as amended by S.I. 1978 No. 127 in consequence of the repeal by the 1977 Act of s. 55(3) to (11) of the 1893 Act: no substantive changes result.

containing a term invalidated by what is now section 6 of the Unfair Contract Terms Act 1977 (Article 3(*a*)). On November 1, 1977 a ban was imposed on the following items insofar as they relate to consumer transactions and include similar void terms—advertisements, including catalogues and circulars; goods or their containers; and documents (Article 3(*b*), (*c*) & (*d*)). Thus Article 3 has dealt with the first practice mentioned in the reference.

The second practice was outlawed by Article 4 on November 1, 1978. It makes it an offence to supply goods, their container or a document to a consumer with a statement about his rights against the supplier with regard to defects, fitness for purpose or correspondence with description unless there is, in close proximity to that statement, another clear and conspicious statement to the effect that the statutory rights of the consumer are not affected. Like Article 3 this applies only where the goods or documents are supplied in a transaction where there is a contractual relationship between the supplier and the consumer.

The third practice was prohibited by Article 5 which also came into operation on November 1, 1978. The prohibition is similar to that in Article 4, *i.e.* an obligation on the supplier to draw the consumer's attention to his statutory rights where the goods, their packaging or a document contain statements setting out the obligations accepted by the supplier. The difference between the two is that Article 5 applies where, although there is no direct consumer transaction between the business supplier and the consumer, the supplier intended or might reasonably have expected his goods to become the subject of a subsequent consumer transaction. Thus the provision applies to a manufacturer's guarantee where the manufacturer realises that the goods will reach a consumer indirectly via a retailer. There is one transitional provision to help suppliers: no contravention occurs where the goods etc. ceased to be in their possession before the Order came into operation.

One practice which is still legal and unaffected by the Order is that of displaying notices stating "Goods may not be *exchanged.*" The reason is simply that there is in law no right to claim a replacement however defective goods may be—the remedies for breach are the right to reject and to claim damages. Such a term is not, therefore, invalidated by the 1977 Act and so falls outside the Order. It is true that notices of this sort are likely to mislead the public in so far as the man in the street is unlikely to see the distinction between refunds and exchanges and may well think that a notice denying one implicitly denies the other. Indeed the Director proposed that such statements should fall within the Order but this was one of the points on which the C.P.A.C. modified his proposals. Their view was that the Order should be limited to void terms.

A few prosecutions have already been successfully brought including one against a ladies fashion shop for displaying a notice reading "We willingly exchange goods but regret that money cannot be refunded"; the last four words were the offending ones.

Since the reference to the C.P.A.C. was made the wider statutory attack on exemption clauses made by the Unfair Contract Terms Act 1977 has invalidated further contractual terms and notices, *e.g.* certain exemption clauses in contracts for the supply of goods by way of hire or in work and materials contracts and also clauses and notices excluding liability for death or personal injury resulting from negligence.[16a] Statements relating to such matters, though void, are not illegal as they are not within the ambit of the 1976 Order. They can still be seen in such places as car parks and cloakrooms either in notices on the wall or in the tickets issued, or coach operators' tickets. If these practices are to be prohibited under Part II then a separate reference will have to be made to the C.P.A.C. However, it may be that section 2 of the Act, discussed below,[16b] will be used instead.

(b) Mail order transactions

"Send c.w.o."

"Payment with order POST FREE"

"Send now only £1 per pair including postage"

The second reference made in May 1974 related to "Prepayment in Mail Order Transaction and in Shops."[17] It concerns the practice whereby suppliers require prepayments in full, or a deposit, when goods are ordered, without specifying a delivery period or specifying a delivery date which is not met. Such problems are most frequent in mail order businesses where a wide range of goods is available either direct from the manufacturers or from the postal bargain trade, *e.g.* records, binoculars, beds, greenhouses, garages Difficulties are more likely to arise when ordering from traders

[16a] See Chap. 8 *ante*, p. 105 *et seq.*
[16b] *Post*, p. 229.
[17] Dossier 17/2.

advertising in newspapers, magazines and colour supplements, than from the established catalogue firms whose business is conducted mainly on credit. However, the practice is not confined to mail order business. Frequently shops ordering goods which are not held in stock require deposits when taking orders, *e.g.* for furniture. Of course the civil remedy available to the buyer if goods are not delivered within the specified time or, if none, within a reasonable time is to treat the contract as repudiated and to demand his money back, but if he is not repaid he must resort to civil proceedings.[17a]

The Director's proposals were that mail order catalogues and advertisements should state a delivery period by prescribed wording, *e.g.* "Despatch within . . . days of order or refund"; if the trader did not supply the goods on time, he would have to send a refund to the customer within seven days of receiving a request. Similar proposals were made with regard to shop transactions where the prepayment was £10 or more. The C.P.A.C. in their Report[18] supported the Director's proposals relating to mail order business. However, the Secretary of State was unwilling to make traders criminally liable for failing to return money in time and put into effect only one comparatively minor proposal. This is contained in The Mail Order Transactions (Information) Order 1976[19] which came into operation on January 1, 1977. It merely requires the name and address of the business to be given where an advertisement, circular or catalogue (other than an advertisement by radio, television or film) invites orders for goods by post where payment is to be made before the goods are despatched. The effect of the damp squib has been minimal. The Director's Report for 1977 reveals that complaints from consumers who have paid in advance continue at a high level. In consequence the O.F.T. is pursuing the possibility of further statutory action to deal with the problem, particularly in relation to non-mail order transactions.

(c) Business advertisements

> ELECTRIC FIRE, £4.95. 2-bar coal effect, new.—Tel. Whitehaven 0000
> GOLF CLUBS, half set, new, £23.50.—Tel. Whitehaven 0000

[17a] See *ante*, p. 65.
[18] H.C. 285 Session 1975/76.
[19] S.I. 1976 No. 1812.

SPANISH STYLE GUITAR, full size. Brand new, £7.95.— Tel. Whitehaven 0000

These are three of 10 advertisements placed by one trader in one newspaper on one day. It is not obvious to a reader when seeing them scattered amongst the other small ads that he will be dealing with a trader. There are three obvious disadvantages to a consumer who deals with a trader masquerading as a private person. First, if the goods prove to be defective, the buyer will be advised that, as the seller was not selling in the course of a business, the implied conditions of merchantable quality and fitness for purpose do not apply. Secondly, if he discovers that any of the descriptions used are false, a trading standards officer will be reluctant to take action as the Trade Descriptions Act 1968 catches only descriptions applied in the course of a trade or business. Lastly, because he thinks that he is dealing with a private seller he is likely to be less suspicious and may think that he is getting a better bargain than if he were dealing with a trader.

The Director's third reference to the C.P.A.C. in March 1975 covered this consumer trade practice describing it as "Seeking to Sell Goods Without Revealing that they are being Sold in the Course of a Business."[20] The C.P.A.C. Report "Disguised Business Sales" was published in May 1976.[21] It showed the practice to be particularly widespread in relation to second-hand cars, furniture and electrical appliances.

The Director's proposals were approved by the C.P.A.C. and put into effect by The Business Advertisements (Disclosure) Order 1977 which came into operation on January 1, 1978.[22] The Order requires business sellers of goods to make it clear in their advertisements directed at consumers that they are traders. The fact may be made apparent by "the contents of the advertisement, its format or size, the place or manner of its publication or otherwise."[23] This can be achieved in a number of ways: by using an obvious business name or company name; by placing an advertisement of a business size or format; or by adding the word "dealer," "trader" or "trade" at the end of the advertisement.

[20] Dossier 17/3.
[21] H.C. 355 Session 1975/76.
[22] S.I. 1977 No. 1918.
[23] Article 2(1).

The effect of the Order can be observed by perusing the small ad columns of any newspaper where the last method will be seen to be common practice.

There are two exemptions—sales by auction or tender; and agricultural produce or game produced or taken by the seller himself.

Reference on VAT-exclusive prices

"£15.24 VAT extra"
"Recommended retail price £58.50 excluding VAT"

Since the introduction of VAT consumers frequently have been asked to pay more than they anticipated for goods or services. Sometimes, *e.g.* in do-it-yourself shops or builders' merchants, goods on display are priced but when the consumer reaches the cash desk VAT is added although the price shown appeared to be VAT-inclusive.[24] On other occasions as in the above examples an indication is given that VAT is payable in addition to the specified price but neither the amount nor rate of VAT is mentioned. These practices were referred to the C.P.A.C. in January 1977 and six months later they published their report "VAT-Exclusive Prices. A Report on Practices relating to Advertising, Displaying or otherwise Quoting VAT-Exclusive Prices or Charges."[25]

The Director identified two practices which he considered should be banned. The first, illustrated by the first of the above examples, is the practice of advertising, displaying or quoting to consumers as the price for goods or services an amount which excludes a sum to be added on account of VAT. The second practice, illustrated by the second of the examples, is that of advertising recommended retail prices which take no account of the VAT amount which the retailer is likely to add when selling to a consumer. The C.P.A.C. in its report concluded that the first practice, but not the second, adversely affected the economic interests of consumers and went on to consider the Director's proposals only in respect of the first practice. The main economic detriment to the consumer is the extra amount which he will have to pay even though sometimes,

---

[24] In relation to goods this may result in an offence under section 11(2) of the Trade Descriptions Act 1968. Successful prosecutions have been brought. See p.175.
[25] H.C. 416 Session 1976/77.

as a matter of contract law, he may only be liable for the lower amount. In some cases it will be too late to withdraw from the transaction, *e.g.* when he has eaten a meal in a restaurant or has had his car serviced and wishes to drive it away. In other cases where withdrawal is possible he may be too embarrassed to argue about the price at the cash desk or unwilling to go to the bother of starting his search again in other shops.

Broadly, the C.P.A.C. agreed with the Director's proposal that only VAT-inclusive charges should be shown. However, they recommended a modification whereby there would be no prohibition on showing a VAT-exclusive price provided the amount (not rate) of VAT is shown as prominently adjacent to the VAT-exclusive price. Thus in the first example no offence would be committed if the price was quoted either as "£17.52" or "£15.24 plus £2.28 VAT." The C.P.A.C. could not accept that a criminal offence should arise merely because the last two figures had not been added together. They also suggested some modifications with regard to estimates for building work; supplies to schools; and long-term contracts and long-life catalogues, *e.g.* television hire or reservation of hotel or accommodation where the rate of VAT might change between the issue of the catalogue and the making of the contract or between the making of the contract and the date of supply.

As yet not order has been made. Even so the practice has already disappeared in many areas of business, *e.g.* men's wear and restaurants. Indeed this is one of the problems of the C.P.A.C. when looking at a practice. The very fact that the trade knows that the practice is about to be or has been referred to the C.P.A.C. means that it disappears in many quarters. By the time the C.P.A.C. look for evidence of the practice there may be much less than there was when the Director identified it and referred it to the Committee. Then when the Secretary of State considers the C.P.A.C report, the practice may have virtually died with the result that it may seem unnecessary to introduce secondary legislation to kill a corpse. Thus the consumer can benefit in a very real sense by the very fact that the legislation exists. We shall meet a similar point when we consider the licensing system under the Consumer Credit Act.[25a]

[25a] See *post*, p. 255.

Bargain offers

"Worth £10. Yours for £8.50"
"At least £7.85 elsewhere, only £4.75"
"Save up to half price"
"R.R.P. £460, save £115, our price £345"
"At least 3p off recommended price"

We have already seen that section 11 of the Trade Descriptions Act 1968 is not wide enough to catch all claims of alleged price reductions.[26] Bargain offers are of many types. The above examples illustrate five common types:

"worth and value" claims;
"price elsewhere" claims;
"up to" or range reduction claims;
retailer's reduction from manufacturer's recommended price;
manufacturer's reduction from his own recommended price,
  e.g. flash packs.

For some years the O.F.T. has been examining bargain offer claims and their effects on consumers. The Director's original intention was to refer the matter to the C.P.A.C. under Part II. However, it appeared that it might be difficult to provide evidence that the practice adversely affects the economic interests of consumers. Comparatively few complaints are made about bargain offers either because consumers do not realise that they have been misled or because they are chary of revealing that they have been duped and that the marvellous bargain which they obtained was not so after all. It is no doubt relevant that the C.P.A.C. were unconvinced on this very economic detriment point in relation to the second practice included in the Director's VAT-inclusive proposals discussed above.

Accordingly, early in 1978 the Director made his first recommendations to the Secretary of State under section 2(3) of the Act. This provision enables the Director to by-pass the C.P.A.C. and to make recommendations "as to any action which in the opinion of the Director it would be expedient for the Secretary of State or any other Minister to take in relation to any of the matters in respect of which the Director has any such duties," e.g. his duties

---

[26] See p. 177.

under section 2(1). The apparent disadvantage of this procedure is that, if the Secretary of State agrees with the recommendations, he will normally have to incorporate them in primary legislation: he has no general power to legislate by secondary legislation similar to that under Part II of the Act. The "bargain offers" reference was unusual in that the Secretary of State did have a regulation-making power (under the Prices Act 1974) and he has recently exercised that power (The Price Marking (Bargain Offers) Order 1979 S.I. 1979 No. 364, as amended by S.I. 1979 No. 633). The provisions are complex and what follows is merely a broad summary of their general effect.

The effect of the Order is to prohibit "worth", "price elsewhere" and "up to" claims (the first three of the five examples given above). However, a trader may still validly make comparison with his own previous or future prices (*e.g.* introductory offers) or with prices charged by another *identified* person. With regard to the much-discussed question of "reduction from recommended price" (the fourth and fifth examples set out above) the Director recommended an outright ban but the Order is more limited. The ban only applies to goods or services which are specified in the Schedule to the Order and at the present time only beds are listed in the Schedule. Nevertheless this list may be extended, when consultations are completed, so as to include carpets, furniture, electrical and electronic goods.[26a] Accordingly the days of "sky prices" may be numbered.

The Order came into force on July 2, 1979 (with transitional provisions relating to such matters as pre-packed goods and catalogues).

PERSISTENTLY UNFAIR TRADERS

I, Robert James Pickersgill, of Import House, Northallerton Road, Croft on Tees, Nr. Darlington trading as Solaire Electric, hereby give to the Director General of Fair Trading written assurances sought by him pursuant to section 34(1) of the Fair Trading Act 1973:

"That I will use all reasonable precautions and exercise all due diligence to avoid continuing the following courses of conduct or any similar course of conduct in the course of my business, namely—

(1) Committing offences under section 1 of the Trade Descriptions Act 1968 by applying false trade descriptions to goods or by supplying or offering to supply goods to which a false trade description is applied.

[26a] See now S.I. 1979, No. 1124.

(2) Committing offences under section 11(2) of the Trade Descriptions Act 1968 by giving indications likely to be taken as indications that goods offered by me are being offered at a price less than that at which they are in fact being offered.

(3) Committing breaches of contract with consumers by supplying goods:
  (a) which do not correspond with any description by which they are sold as required by subsection (1) of the amended section 13 of the Sale of Goods Act 1893, or
  (b) which are not fit for a particular purpose for which they are being bought as required by subsection (3) of the amended section 14 of that Act.

(4) Failing to return to consumers money to which they are legally entitled, that has been received from them in the course of mail order transactions."

For the purpose of these assurances the word "goods" means lamps intended to emit ultra violet rays and/or to emit infra red rays and any accessory supplied or offered for supply with such a lamp.

This is the historic first assurance given in October 1974 to the Director under Part III of 1973 Act. The increasing use of this power to curtail the activities of rogue traders is evidenced by the numbers of assurances obtained—36 in all in 1974–76, 40 in 1977 and 62 in 1978. Used car dealers, home improvement firms, electrical goods and mail order businesses figure most prominently, but the club membership also includes a wide range of other commercial activities, *e.g.* a correspondence school for free-lance writers, a chain of 74 restaurants, and a door-to-door salesman of goods said to be made by the blind.

The first assurance is typical insofar as it covers three improper practices which frequently result in assurances being sought, viz. Trade Descriptions Act offences, breaches of the Sale of Goods Act implied conditions and non-delivery of goods paid for in advance.

Section 34(1) requires the Director to try to obtain an assurance where a person has persisted in a course of conduct which is both:
(a) detrimental to the interests of consumers in the U.K., whether those interests are economic or in respect of health, safety or other matters,[27] and
(b) unfair to consumers.

Business

The section applies only to a person carrying on a business where the conduct occurs in the course of that business. "Business"

---

[27] These criteria are similar to those laid down in section 2(1)(*b*). See p. 215.

I

includes a professional practice and any undertaking which supplies goods or services otherwise than free of charge.[28] Thus private sellers are not caught, whereas charitable institutions are.[29] A firm of solicitors could be asked for an assurance if frequent, justified complaints were made about their negligent conduct of clients' matters.

Persistent

Part III is aimed at the trader who is a rogue in the sense that he repeatedly breaks his civil or criminal obligations and thumbs his nose at dissatisfied customers and trading standards officers alike. Only if he has persisted in such a course of conduct may the Director take action. Evidence is built up from many sources: direct complaints from consumers; complaints passed on by trading standards departments, C.A.Bx., consumer advice centres, etc.; convictions and civil judgments notified by the courts. The Director must have regard to all such complaints and information in determining the question of persistence.[30]

No criteria are laid down by the Act. Clearly what may amount to persistent conduct in the case of a small trader with one outlet may not be sufficient in the case of a retail chain with dozens of branches: the number of breaches must be weighed against the overall turnover and number of outlets of the business. It seems likely that successful prosecutions and civil actions carry more weight than complaints, however justified, and that a small trader with a half dozen or so judgments and a score of complaints against him may well find himself being required to give assurance. The message for the consumer is clear: if he fails to have a complaint properly dealt with by a trader, complain to the trading standards department and thus add weight to the trader's file—indeed, the suggestion that this is about to happen may accelerate a compromise.

---

[28] s. 137(2).
[29] cf. the definition in the Unfair Contract Terms Act 1977, s.14, *ante*, p. 107.
[30] s. 34(4).

Unfair

Conduct is not to be regarded as unfair unless it is one of the two types specified in the Act: there is no general concept of unfairness to which to resort. First, it may be contravention of an enactment imposing duties, prohibitions or restrictions enforceable by *criminal* proceedings.[31] It seems that some traders are still prepared to flout the provisions of the Trade Descriptions Act or the Food and Drugs Act on the basis that if they are prosecuted, the fines imposed are outweighed by the profitability of their unfair trading. Another example is offences under Part II Orders.

Secondly, the unfair conduct may consist of breaches of contract or other wrongs enforceable by civil proceedings.[32] For example, a trader may be content to sell defective goods confident in the knowledge that very few buyers are likely to go to the trouble and expense of suing him for the few pounds required to repair the goods; even if he is sued, his profits from this form of trading may far exceed the occasional damages awarded against him. In addition to such breaches of section 14(2) and (3) of the Sale of Goods Act 1893, other common courses of conduct are the supply of goods not corresponding with their description in accordance with section 13 of the 1893 Act; the failure to carry out contracts for work and materials in a proper and workmanlike manner; the failure to deliver goods; and the failure to return money for goods or services not supplied.

It is important to notice that there is no need to show that the trader has in fact been prosecuted or sued, as section 34 states that it does not matter whether or not the person has been convicted or the subject of civil proceedings.

Court proceedings

The Director's first step is to "use his best endeavours" to obtain a satisfactory written assurance from the trader that he will discontinue the course of conduct and will not carry on any similar course of conduct.[33] If the trader gives the assurance, it is given wide publicity and included in the Director's Annual Report. If the trader abides by his assurance the matter rests there.

[31] s. 34(2).
[32] s. 34(3).
[33] s. 34(1).

If the trader fails to observe his assurance or refuses to give one, the Director may bring proceedings against him before the Restrictive Practices Court.[34] Alternatively, the county court (or sheriff court in Scotland) has jurisdiction except in the case of a company with share capital exceeding £10,000 or except where a question of general application is involved.[35] The court may accept an undertaking or, if it considers that the respondent is likely to continue as before in the absence of an order, may make an order to restrain the continuation of the malpractice.[36] The trader is then faced with the prospect of a fine or imprisonment for contempt of court if he does not comply with the order or undertaking. Thus the end of the road for a trader who fails to honour his civil responsibilities can be imprisonment—this is the ultimate sword of Damocles to deter him under Part III.

As yet is has rarely been necessary for the Director to have recourse to court proceedings. He regards them as the last resort. Three orders were made in 1977 against traders who had broken assurances—one in an English county court, one in a Welsh county court and one in a Scots sheriff court.

In 1978 legal proceedings were instituted against three businesses for refusal to give assurances. In one case the assurances were obtained at the door of the court; in another an undertaking was given by a trader whose place in the history of consumer protection is so far unchallenged with a record 800 complaints about him notified to the O.F.T. Lastly, in the first case to come before the Restrictive Practices Court, *Director General of Fair Trading* v. *Smiths Bakeries (Westfield) Ltd.*,[37] undertakings were accepted from the company and its director as accessory who had refused to give assurances following 46 convictions under the Food and Drugs Act 1955 over a period of three years.

Accessories
An obvious loop-hole would be for a rogue trader to trade as a company and, when cornered into giving an assurance on behalf of X Ltd., to set up in business with a different identity as Z Ltd. Sections 38 and 39 make this device ineffective by giving the

[34] s. 35.
[35] s. 41.
[36] s. 37.
[37] *The Times*, May 11, 1978.

Director power to seek an assurance, order or undertaking from an "accessory" who has consented to or connived at the company's conduct. An accessory is defined as a director, manager, secretary or other similar officer, or someone with a controlling interest in that he can determine the way in which one-half of the votes can be cast at a general meeting.[38] Thus the above trader, who doubtless will be an accessory of X Ltd., can be required to give a personal assurance which will limit his activities when he puts X Ltd. into liquidation and starts up in the guise of Z Ltd.

There are also provisions enabling the court to make an order binding members of a group of "interconnected bodies corporate", *i.e.* broadly a holding company and its subsidiaries.[39]

[38] s. 38(2) and (7).
[39] s. 40 and 137(5).

PART IV: SPECIAL PROTECTION IN CREDIT TRANSACTIONS

CHAPTER 15

THE BACKGROUND TO CONSUMER CREDIT

1. INTRODUCTION

THERE has been a dramatic increase in consumer credit in the present century—both in this country and in other Western industrialised countries. By far the greatest area is house purchase but there are many others including furniture, electrical appliances, clothing, vehicles, holidays and home repairs and improvements. The scale of consumer credit can be seen from figures published in the Crowther Report on Consumer Credit. In the year 1966 the amount of medium and long-term credit extended totalled £3,692,000,000, (house purchase credit accounted for approximately 45 per cent. of this figure). At the end of the year the total outstanding was £9,684,000,000, of which some 80 per cent. was attributable to houses and flats.

The Crowther Committee clearly realised that

> "The use of consumer credit . . . enables individuals to enjoy the services of consumer durable goods sooner than they otherwise would and in a period of inflation offers them a real prospect of acquiring them more cheaply. Consumers in general are able to obtain a more satisfying "basket" of goods and services with the same income. Thus consumer credit may be said to enhance consumer satisfaction. Furthermore, some individuals, who lack the self-discipline to save up for the purchase of a durable consumer good but are nevertheless unlikely to break their contract with a creditor, are able to buy a durable consumer good which might otherwise never be theirs."[1]

One need only add that this reason applies, *a fortiori*, to house purchase.

The situation described above has its corresponding dangers and these are two-fold. First, borrowers may be tempted to overstretch their resources—either through bad economic planning or because they do not appreciate the full extent of their obligations. Secondly, some lenders might be tempted to "cash in" on the attractions of consumer credit by inducing borrowers (some of whom may already

[1] Cmnd. 4596, p. 118.

be under severe financial stress) to sign agreements which are one-sided and impose unduly onerous obligations.

Until the passing of the Consumer Credit Act 1974 the law developed in a fragmentary and piecemeal fashion—following rather than leading, checking abuses *after* they had come to light rather than laying down ground rules in advance. Thus:

(1) The Bills of Sale Acts 1878–1882 were passed to deal with *(inter alia)* mortgages of personal property where the borrower retained possession.

(2) The Moneylenders Acts 1900–1927 were passed to regulate the activities of certain moneylenders (but not, *e.g.* banks).

(3) The Pawnbrokers Acts 1872–1900 regulated the activities of pawnbrokers.

(4) The Hire-Purchase Act 1965 regulated hire-purchase agreements where the hire-purchase price did not exceed £2,000 and where the hirer was not a body corporate. (This limit was recently increased to £5,000—S.I. 1978 No. 461).

The unsatisfactory nature of this fragmentary approach can be seen by looking at moneylending. If the lender happened to be a bank, the Moneylenders Acts did not apply at all, even though the borrower may have been an inexperienced private individual and even though the contract may have been a harsh one on the particular facts. On the other hand, if the lender was within the provisions of the Act the full rigours of the Act were applied, even though the borrower was a large public company well able to look after itself. Again, as new forms of credit developed (*e.g.* credit cards) the absence of any regulatory machinery meant that there was virtually no effective control at all. All this will change as a result of the Consumer Credit Act 1974. When this Act is fully in force it will be the most comprehensive and sophisticated Act of its kind in the Western world.

The Act is designed to sweep away the piecemeal controls listed above and to replace them with a single code governing all forms of lending. The only pieces of legislation which will remain unrepealed are the Bills of Sale Acts 1878–1872—the reason being that the Consumer Credit Act does not regulate mortgages of personal property. A suggestion made by the Crowther Committee that the Government should introduce a Lending and Security Act has not so far been implemented.

2. Consumer Credit Act 1974—Ten Preliminary Points

The scope and effect of the Consumer Credit Act will be examined in detail in the next eight Chapters. In the remainder of this Chapter it is proposed to deal with ten preliminary matters.

(1) The Act contains no definition of the word "consumer." We have already seen that under the Unfair Contract Terms Act 1977 the term "consumer" means a "private consumer" as opposed to a business consumer, and the Fair Trading Act 1973 adopts a similar approach. *The Consumer Credit Act 1974 is not limited in this way.* In the two major types of agreement—consumer credit and consumer hire—the Act provides control where the debtor or hirer is an "individual" but the definition of this term is not what one might expect. By section 189

> "individual" includes a partnership or other unincorporated body of persons not consisting entirely of bodies corporate."

So then, the unincorporated trader is protected just as much as the private individual. Conversely, the Act regulates (at least in part) agreements where the creditor or owner is *not* acting in the course of a business.[2]

(2) The Act received the Royal Assent on July 31, 1974, but it is taking a very long time to bring it into force. Even when it is fully in force it will often be necessary to discover the extent to which a particular provision is retrospective, having regard to the general principle that, on matters of substantive law, a statute is presumed to be non-retrospective. The answer will often be found in Schedule 3 read with the appropriate commencement order. Thus, if we turn to Schedule 3, para 12(1), read with the second commencement order, we find that:

> Section 56 applies to negotiations in relation to an actual or prospective regulated agreement where the negotiations begin after May 16, 1977.

On the other hand, para 42, read with the same commencement order, tells us that:

> Sections 137–140 (extortionate credit bargains) come into operation on May 16, 1977, and apply to agreements and transactions whenever made.

It follows that the legislation repealed by the Act will remain important for several years.

---

[2] See *post*, p. 246.

(3) Section 189 adopts the very helpful practice of drawing together all the definitions which appear throughout the Act. Section 189(1) contains no less than 117 definitions. Some are defined in the section itself (*e.g.* the term "individual"[3]). In other cases section 189 refers to the section where the definition is to be found, *e.g.*

"exempt agreement" means an agreement specified in or under section 16.

It is vitally important to refer constantly to section 189 because words are often used in unexpected ways. Thus, for example, the definition of the word "surety" is wide enough to include the principal debtor (unless the context otherwise requires).

(4) Another helpful innovation (not so far copied by the draftsman of the annual Finance Act) is Schedule 2 which contains 24 worked examples showing the use of the new terminology. Section 188(3), however, provides that:

In the case of conflict between Schedule 2 and any other provision of this Act that other provision shall prevail.

A learned writer has expressed doubts as to the accuracy of example 21 which relates to cheque cards.[4]

(5) Although the Act is a long one a very large part of the detail will be contained in regulations. They cover (or will cover) such matters as the total charge for credit, regulated and exempt agreements, advertising, documentation and rebates for early settlements.

(6) The control provided by the Act is twofold:
   (a) Control of business activity—notably through the licencing system administered by the Director General of Fair Trading.[5]
   (b) Control of individual agreements.

(7) The Act provides various civil and criminal sanctions, as well as the administrative sanctions in sections 29 and 32 (non-renewal, suspension and revocation of a licence). The criminal sanctions are usefully collected together in Schedule 1. Section 170(1) provides that:

[3] *Ante,* p. 238.
[4] See Dobson [1977] J.B.L. at p. 126.
[5] See Chap. 18, *post,* p. 255.

> A breach of any requirement made (otherwise than by any court) by or under this Act shall incur no civil or criminal sanction as being such a breach except to the extent (if any) expressly provided for under this Act.

Thus section 48 makes it an offence to canvass certain types of agreement (*e.g.* personal loans) off trade premises. If a person borrows money in a case where the lender has contravened section 48 he cannot avoid liability under that contract by pleading that it is illegal. Nor could he bring an action for breach of statutory duty. Such claims or defences are shut out by section 170(1). Presumably the criminal court would still be able to award compensation under section 35 of the Powers of Criminal Courts Act 1973.[5a]

(8) As one might expect, the statutory rights enjoyed by the debtor, the hirer, a surety or a relative[6] cannot in any way be cut down or fettered by the agreement.[7]

(9) One of the features of the Act is that certain steps can only be taken if the court or the Director General makes an order to that effect. An example of the former is the enforcement of an agreement which has not been properly executed.[8] An example of the latter is the enforcement of an agreement made by a creditor or owner while he was unlicensed. In either case section 173(3) provides that consent of the debtor or hirer "given at that time" shall be as effective as an order. The words "given at that time" presumably refer to the time of enforcement so that a provision for consent in the contract would not be effective. Clearly the court would examine the facts very carefully to ensure that there was a true consent.

(10) It may be useful to end this Chapter by setting out a few important definitions which will be met from time to time in the next six Chapters.

(a) *Hire-purchase agreement*

This is defined as an agreement under which goods are bailed in return for periodical payments by the bailee and the property in the goods will pass to the bailee if the terms of the agreement are complied with and one or more of the following occur:

[5a] *Ante*, p. 204.
[6] As to which see *post*, p. 241.
[7] See s. 173(1) and (2).
[8] *Post*, p. 290.

  (i) the exercise of an option to purchase by the bailee or
 (ii) the doing of any other specified act by any party to the
      agreement or
(iii) the happening of any other specified event.

(b) *Conditional sale agreement*

This is an agreement for the sale of goods or land under which
the purchase price or part of it is payable by instalments and the
property in the goods or land is to remain in the seller (notwith-
standing that the buyer is to be in possession of the goods or land)
until such conditions as to the payment of instalments or likewise
as may be specified in the agreement are fulfilled. If, however,
there is a straight sale of goods on credit terms the property will
usually pass to the buyer immediately (Sale of Goods Act 1893,
s. 18, rule 1[8a]) and the agreement would be a credit sale agreement,
not a conditional sale agreement.

(c) *Relative*

Relative means husband, wife, brother, sister, uncle, aunt,
nephew, niece, lineal ancestor or lineal descendant. Relationship
by marriage is also included and the reference to "husband or
wife" includes a former or a reputed spouse.

(d) *Associate*

The associate of an individual means (i) a relative and (ii) a partner,
or the relative of a partner, of that individual.

(e) *"Restricted-use" and "unrestricted-use"*

These terms are defined in section 11 and are largely self-explanatory. If the debtor can physically use the credit in any way he
wishes the agreement will be an "unrestricted-use" agreement,
even though certain uses would constitute a breach of contract.
Thus a loan paid by the lender to the borrower would be an
unrestricted-use agreement. On the other hand, a hire-purchase
agreement, or sale on deferred terms, or a loan where the money
went straight from the lender to a third party (*e.g.* the supplier of
goods or services) would be a restricted-use agreement. We shall
meet the distinction at several points in the following chapters.

[8a] *Ante,* p. 60.

CHAPTER 16

WHAT AGREEMENTS ARE CAUGHT BY THE ACT?

IN this Chapter and in chapters 17–23 a reference to "the Act" is a reference to the Consumer Credit Act 1974 (unless otherwise stated) and a reference to a section is to that section in the Act.

We have already seen that the scope of the Act is very wide. In this Chapter it is proposed to work through the very intricate provisions of the Act and regulations to find out the precise extent of control. The scheme of this Chapter is as follows:

1. Regulated agreements
2. Partially regulated agreements
3. Exempt agreements
4. Linked transactions

1. REGULATED AGREEMENTS

In order to find out whether an agreement is regulated, it is necessary to proceed in two stages:

(1) Does the agreement come within the definition of "consumer credit agreement" in section 8 or "consumer hire agreement" in section 15? If the answer is no, the agreement will not be a regulated agreement.

(2) If the answer to (1) above is yes, then by sections 8(3) and 15(2) any such agreement *is* a regulated agreement unless it is an exempt agreement. The concept of "exempt agreement," which depends on section 16 and regulations is dealt with later in this chapter.[1]

(1) Consumer credit agreement

Let us start by summarising the many types of agreement which can come within this term. They include:

(a) Hire-Purchase
(b) Conditional Sale

[1] *Post,* p. 247.

(c) Credit Sale
(d) Personal Loan
(e) Overdraft
(f) Loan secured by land mortgage
(g) Credit card
(h) Pledges, and
(i) Budget accounts in shops.

Section 8(2) defines a consumer credit agreement as an agreement whereby one person (the creditor) provides an individual (the debtor) with credit not exceeding £5,000. Four points are worthy of note:

(i) There must be an "agreement." Thus where a sale is for cash and on delivery of the goods the buyer asks for time to pay, the granting of "credit" would not amount to an "agreement" unless it was under seal or supported by consideration.

(ii) The creditor can be an individual, a partnership or a body corporate, but the debtor must be an "individual."[2]

(iii) The Act draws a sharp distinction between the "credit" and the "total charge for credit." The term "credit" includes a cash loan and any form of financial accommodation[3] and clearly refers to the loan etc. itself. The term "total charge for credit" refers to interest and other charges.[4] Section 9(4) provides that:

> An item entering into the total charge for credit shall not be treated as credit even though time is allowed for payment.

(iv) As an illustration of the above principles section 9(3) defines the "credit" in a hire-purchase agreement as the total price of the goods less (a) the deposit (if any) and (b) the total charge for credit.

Thus, to take an example (Schedule 2, example 10) C agrees to let goods on hire-purchase to D (an individual). The total price is £7,500; this includes a down payment of £1,000 and a total charge for credit of £1,500. When these two items are deducted from the price (£7,500–£2,500) one is left with credit of £5,000. This is, therefore, a consumer credit agreement within section 8(2). The provisions may be contrasted with the provisions of the Hire-Purchase Act 1965. Under that Act protection is limited to

---

[2] See *ante,* p. 238.
[3] s. 9(3).
[4] See *post,* p. 249.

cases where the hire-purchase *price* does not exceed £5,000. Under the 1974 Act the *price* may be far higher; what matters is the amount of the *credit*.

Fixed and running-account credit

The term "consumer credit agreement" is subdivided into "fixed-sum credit" and "running-account credit"—the distinction is important in deciding whether an agreement is regulated or exempt[5] and for certain other purposes. Section 10(1)(*a*) tells us that:

> running-account credit is a facility under a personal credit agreement whereby the debtor is enabled to receive from time to time (whether in his own person or by another person) from the creditor or a third party cash, goods and services (or any of them) to an amount of value such that, taking into account payments made by or to the credit of the debtor, the credit limit (if any) is not at any time exceeded.

Perhaps the two most common examples are bank overdrafts and budget accounts in shops. It would clearly be possible to take the agreement outside the definition of "consumer credit agreement"[6] by fixing a credit limit in excess of £5,000 or by fixing no credit limit at all. Section 10(3) is designed to block attempts to oust the Act in this way. It provides, in effect, that a running-account will still qualify as a consumer credit agreement if:

(i) the debtor cannot draw more than £5,000 at any one time or

(ii) a term unfavourable to the debtor (*e.g.* raising of the rate of interest) will become operative if the debit balance rises above a specified amount (being an amount of £5,000 or less) or

(iii) at the time of the agreement it is unlikely that the debit balance will rise above £5,000. An example of this provision (Schedule 2, example 7) is where X agrees to provide Y with short-term finance to enable Y to acquire trading stock from time to time; at the time of the contract Y has trading stock worth £1,000 and it is therefore unlikely that he will require credit in excess of £5,000.

---

[5] See *post*, p. 247.
[6] *Ante*, p. 243.

Debtor-creditor-supplier (D-C-S) agreements and debtor-creditor (D-C) agreements

These terms are defined in sections 12 and 13 and it is necessary to mention them at this point because a knowledge of them is vital when considering the all important question of whether the agreement is *regulated* or *exempt*.[7] The distinction between D-C-S and D-C turns on the relationship between the supplier of the credit and the supplier of the land, goods or services. The effect of sections 12 and 13 can be summarised as follows:

(i) If the supplier of the credit and the supplier of the goods etc. are the same person then it is D-C-S. Examples would include hire-purchase, credit sale and sale of land where the vendor agrees to leave the price outstanding.

(ii) If the supplier of credit and the supplier of the goods etc. work together under "arrangements" then again it is D-C-S. Thus, a credit card company has "arrangements" with its approved suppliers and a finance company might have "arrangements" with a car dealer whereby they would provide loans to finance sales made by him to customers. In both these cases the credit contract would be a D-C-S agreement.

(iii) If there are no such arrangements the agreement is a D-C agreement. Thus if a customer borrows £1,000 from his bank to pay for central heating or for a holiday or to finance his business this would be a D-C agreement.

(iv) If an agreement is made to refinance an existing indebtedness, whether to the creditor or any other person, then again it is D-C.

As already stated the distinction is critical on the "regulated or exempt" point—we shall see that under a D-C-S agreement the critical factor is the number of instalments, whereas under a D-C agreement the critical factor is the annual percentage rate of charge for credit. The distinction is also important for other purposes, including joint responsibility of supplier and creditor in cancellation cases[8] and under section 75.[9]

---

[7] *Post,* p. 247.
[8] *Post,* p. 273.
[9] *Post,* p. 281.

(2) **Consumer Hire Agreements**

The second type of agreement to which the Act applies is the consumer hire agreement. Clearly, this type of agreement is far less important than the consumer credit agreement but it is worth remembering that it covers not only the domestic hiring of, *e.g.* a television set but also the commercial hiring of, *e.g.* equipment. Section 15 makes it clear that there are six elements:

    (a) a bailment of goods

    (b) by one person (the owner)

    (c) to an individual (the hirer), provided that

    (d) it is not hire-purchase, and

    (e) it is capable of lasting for more than three months and

    (f) it does not require the hirer to make payments in excess of £5,000.

Only the last point calls for comment. In deciding on how much the hirer is *required* to pay one must look at his minimum contractual liability, having regard to any contractual right to terminate. Thus, if a three year hiring (with no break clause) required the hirer to pay a rental of £2,000 per annum, this would bring the total to £6,000 and it would *not* be a consumer hire agreement (see Schedule 2, example 20). The position would be different if, for example, the hirer had a right to terminate, without further payment, at the end of the second year.

2. Partially Regulated Agreements

As already stated, the all important distinction is between *regulated* and *exempt* agreements. Before considering the nature of exempt agreements it might be useful to mention two types of agreement which are regulated in part only.

(1) **Non-commercial agreements**

By section 189 a non-commercial agreement is an agreement not made by the creditor or owner in the course of a business carried on by him. It is important to notice the words "*a* business." If, for example, a manufacturer made loans to his employees to enable them to buy season tickets or houses, the loans *would* be made in the course of *a* business (even though it was not a consumer credit or consumer hire business) and accordingly it would not be "non-commercial." If, however, the agreement is non-commercial then a number of specific provisions do not apply. The most important area is formalities and cancellation.[10]

(2) Small agreements

A small agreement is defined in section 17 as either;

(a) a regulated consumer credit agreement for credit not exceeding £30, other than a hire-purchase or conditional sale agreement,[11] or

(b) a regulated consumer hire agreement which does not require the hirer to make payments exceeding £30.

There is a further condition, namely that the agreement is unsecured or secured by a guarantee or indemnity only. Not surprisingly, section 17(3) blocks attempts to split up a transaction into a series of small agreements (at one time encyclopaedia salesmen were notorious for this) by providing that in such a case each small agreement shall be treated as a regulated non-small agreement.

Some small agreements are exempt from most of the provisions relating to formalities and cancellation.[12]

3. EXEMPT AGREEMENTS

Having decided that an agreement is a consumer credit or consumer hire agreement, we must now decide whether it is taken out of control by one of the exemptions. These are to be found in section 16 and in regulations (S.I. 1977 No. 326). The first four of them relate to land.

(1) A debtor-creditor-supplier agreement is exempt if (a) the creditor is a building society, local authority or a body named in the regulations and (b) the agreement finances (i) the purchase of land, or (ii) the provision of dwellings on any land and is secured by a mortgage of *that* land.[13]

(2) A debtor-creditor agreement is exempt if (a) the lender is a building society or local authority and (b) the agreement is

[10] See s. 74(1)(*a*) and ss. 77–79.
[11] See *post*, pp. 240–241.
[12] See *post*, pp. 263 and 268.
[13] s. 16(2)(*a*).

secured by a mortgage of land. It will be apparent that in this case the purpose of the loan is immaterial.[14]

(3) A debtor-creditor agreement is exempt if (a) the lender is a body named in the regulations and (b) the agreement is secured by a mortgage of land and (c) the agreement is to finance the purchase of land, the provision of dwellings or business premises on land and certain ancillary purposes.[15]

The bodies named in the regulations include a large number of insurance companies, friendly societies and charities. Also included are certain public bodies (*e.g.* electricity boards, development corporations), but there the exemption only applies to a more limited class of purpose which is set out opposite to their names in Part II of the Schedule to the regulations.

(4) Even if an agreement to finance the purchase of land is not exempt under (1)–(3) above (*e.g.* because the lender is not one of the specified bodies) a further exemption is to be found in regulation 3(1)(*b*) which exempts a debtor-creditor-supplier agreement to finance the purchase of land if the number of payments to be made by the debtor does not exceed four.

(5) A debtor-creditor-supplier agreement is exempt under regulation 3(1)(*a*)(i) if (a) it is not hire-purchase or conditional sale and (b) it is for fixed-sum credit and (c) the number of payments to be made by the debtor *in respect of the credit* does not exceed four. This exempts *(inter alia)* normal trade credit and the weekly milk and newspaper account.

(6) A debtor-creditor-supplier agreement is exempt under regulation 3(1)(*a*)(ii) if (a) it is not hire-purchase or conditional sale and (b) it is for running-account credit and (c) the whole of the credit for a period is repayable by a single payment. This will exempt many budget accounts in shops and certain credit card agreements, *e.g.* American Express and Diners' Club.

(7) The final exemption is to be found in regulation 3(1)(*c*) and relates to debtor-creditor agreements in respect of which the rate of the total charge for credit does not exceed the higher of (a) 13 per cent. or (b) 1 per cent. above the last Bank of England minimum lending rate in force 28 days before the making of the agreement. Thus, for example, a loan by an employer to an

[14] reg. 2.
[15] *Ibid.*

employee would be exempt if the interest etc. does not exceed the statutory ceiling. The meaning of "total charge for credit" will be considered below, but one matter can be disposed of at this point. What about a term in the agreement whereby the debtor's liability fluctuates according to a specified formula (*e.g.* the retail price index or changes in Bank of England minimum lending rate)? Here again it is necessary to distinguish sharply between *credit* and *the total charge for credit*. If the credit can fluctuate then exemption under regulation 3(1)(*c*) is destroyed. On the other hand the fluctuation of the annual rate of credit is permissible and this will not destroy the exemption—provided that *at the date of the agreement* the rate did not exceed the statutory ceiling set out above.

> Thus if the agreement provided for interest to be paid at "1 per cent above Bank of England minimum lending rate for the time being" the agreement will be exempt if at the date of the agreement the minimum lending rate was the same as, or less than, the last rate prevailing 28 days before the making of the agreement. An increase in the rate after the date of the agreement will not destroy the exemption.[16]

The total charge for credit

We have already met this term on several occasions and it is now necessary to examine it more closely. It is vitally important for at least three reasons:

(a) Any sum forming part of the total charge for credit does not form part of the credit[17] and must, therefore, be ignored in deciding whether or not the credit exceeds £5,000.

(b) Under regulation 3(1)(*c*)[18] a debtor-creditor agreement is exempt if the annual percentage rate of charge does not exceed the statutory amount.

(c) One of the cardinal principles of the Act is to give the debtor information on various matters and one such matter is the "true cost of borrowing."[19] In the United States this is known as "truth in lending." One of the objects of the legislation is to give the debtor an opportunity of "shopping around" and comparing the cost of credit offered by different lenders. It is certainly debatable whether many debtors are likely to take advantage of this facility

[16] See *post,* p. 251.
[17] s. 9(3) *ante,* p. 243.
[18] *Supra.*
[19] See s. 20.

and it could well be that the effect of this requirement could be counter-productive, in that the extra cost involved will doubtless increase the cost of borrowing and may put the credit beyond the reach of some prospective borrowers.

The total charge for credit is dealt with in the Consumer Credit (Total Charge for Credit) Regulations 1977. The object of these regulations is three-fold, namely (a) to specify what items are to be included (b) to specify what items are to be excluded, and (c) to require the charge to be calculated as an annual percentage rate.

Items included

Regulation 4 provides that there shall be included (a) the total of the interest payments and (b) other charges at any time payable under the transaction by or on behalf of the debtor or a relative of his, whether to the creditor or to any other person. This would clearly cover the general costs incurred in setting up the agreement—survey fees, legal fees, stamp duty are obvious examples.

Items excluded

The generality of regulation 4 is cut down by regulation 5. Among items excluded are the following: (a) sums payable on default (b) sums which would be payable in any event even if it was a cash transaction (*e.g.* VAT), (c) sums paid under a maintenance or insurance contract where the debtor had a free choice in the matter and could have made substantially the same arrangements elsewhere. On the other hand, an insurance premium *will* be included if the policy monies are to be used to repay the credit.

Annual percentage rate

To enable comparisons to be made regulation 7 requires the total charge to be stated as an annual percentage rate reflecting (a) annual compounding and (b) the continuing repayment of credit. If a prospective borrower is told by a finance house that the rate of interest is twelve per cent this is seriously misleading, because it does not acknowledge that the outstanding capital is reducing all the time.

As part of the policy of providing an annual percentage rate, regulation 8 provides a formula for converting a period rate (*e.g.* 10 per cent. per 6 months) into an annual rate. Conversely, regulation 9 provides a formula whereby the annual rate can be extracted where the whole indebtedness (credit and total charge) is repayable in a single lump sum.

This leaves the question—how can the annual rate be calculated in the case of a land mortgage or hire-purchase agreement where capital and interest are being repaid over several years? The calculation can be a nightmare but fortunately the Government has produced Consumer Credit Tables in 15 volumes. These will produce the annual percentage rate, provided that the instalments and the repayment periods are equal. Thus, for example, the tables cannot be used if the final hire-purchase instalment is larger than the others because it contains a small extra amount (*e.g.* £1) for the option to purchase.

If the tables cannot be used, the annual rate must be calculated (by trial and error) in accordance with regulation 10. This provides (in effect) that the annual rate is the rate at which the present value of all future repayments equals the amount of the credit.

The above explanation presupposes that all the items are constant and known at the date of the agreement. In practice this may not be so and the regulations recognise this by making certain assumptions. For example, a provision giving the creditor the right to increase the charges (very common in mortgage contracts) must be disregarded.[20] Similarly, there may be a clause for the index linking of the total charge for credit; here again it is to be assumed that changes will not occur (regulation 14). If, however, the amount of a particular item is unknown at the date of the agreement and is not covered by the assumptions, then it seems that the exemption for low cost credit[21] cannot be claimed. This could arise where, for example, the creditor's insurance company require the debtor to pay for the installation of a burglar alarm and the cost of this is not known at the date of the agreement.

4. LINKED TRANSACTIONS

Having examined the crucial distinction between regulated and exempt agreements, it is necessary to end this chapter by a brief

[20] reg. 2(1)(*c*).
[21] See *ante*, p. 248.

mention of linked transactions, *i.e.* transactions which are linked to an actual or prospective regulated agreement. The term "linked transaction" is important for a variety of reasons, including withdrawal, cancellation, early settlement and extortionate credit bargains. It is clear from section 19 that an agreement for security will not be a linked agreement but, subject to this, the following are included:

(1) A transaction entered into in compliance with a term of the principal agreement *e.g.* "the debtor shall insure his life with XYZ insurance company and shall enter into a maintenance contract with Eezikleen Ltd."

(2) A transaction to be financed by a debtor-creditor-supplier agreement; thus where the supplier of a car and the supplier of the credit have "arrangements," the sale of the car is "linked" to the loan contract, so that cancellation of the latter will also cancel the former.[22]

(3) The transaction was entered into by the debtor or hirer or a relative at the suggestion of the creditor, or owner, or an associate of his[23] or a person negotiating the principal agreement. Thus a dealer might say to a prospective borrower "you would have a better chance of getting a loan from the finance company if you took out a life policy."

A linked transaction is ineffective until the principal agreement has been made.[24]

[22] s. 69(1), *post,* p. 272.
[23] *Ante,* p. 241.
[24] s. 19(3).

CHAPTER 17

HOW MUCH OF THE ACT IS IN FORCE?

THE next six chapters have been written on the basis that the Consumer Credit Act is fully in force; unfortunately this is far from being the case. The present position, as at October 1, 1979, is set out below and must be borne in mind when reading the following chapters.

(1) Control of business activities

The licensing and canvassing provisions discussed in Chapter 18 are fully in force. The advertising provisions are not yet in force but regulations are expected in the coming months.

(2) Formalities

The various formal requirements discussed in Chapter 19 are not yet in force and it is likely to be some considerable time before the documentation regulations are published. In the meantime it will be necessary in many cases to refer to other Acts which lay down detailed formal requirements. The two most important examples are the Moneylenders Acts 1900–1927 and the Hire-Purchase Act 1965 (and regulations made under that Act).

(3) Withdrawal, termination, cancellation

These provisions, discussed in chapter 20, are not yet in force. If the agreement falls within the Hire-Purchase Act 1965 (and this includes certain conditional sale and credit sale agreements as well as hire-purchase) there may be a right of cancellation or termination under the provisions of that Act.

(4) Misrepresentation and Breach of Contract

The provisions discussed in Chapter 21 are in force.

(5) Credit tokens

The provisions discussed in Chapter 22 are not yet in force and there is no statutory control over this increasingly important form of credit.

253

(6) Enforcement orders, early settlement, rebates, restrictions or repossession, judicial control and extortionate credit bargains

Most of the provisions discussed in Chapter 23 are not yet in force. The only exception is sections 137–140 which deal with extortionate credit bargains; as we have seen, these provisions were brought in on May 16, 1977 and apply to all agreements whenever made.

If the agreement falls within the Hire-Purchase Act 1965 there are a number of provisions imposing restrictions on repossession but there is no statutory right to complete payments ahead of time and no statutory right to a rebate on early settlement.

Chapter 18

CONTROL OF BUSINESS ACTIVITIES

We have already seen that the Consumer Credit Act controls business activities as well as individual agreements. It is clear that business control is of very great benefit to the consumer. It should help to ensure that the other party to the transaction is a reputable trader and that he (the consumer) is not pressurised into a transaction by misleading advertising or other undesirable business practice. In this chapter it is proposed to consider this aspect of consumer protection under three main headings, namely:

1. Licensing
2. Advertising
3. Canvassing

1. Licensing

The licensing system set out in sections 22–24 and 147–150 can be described as the lynchpin of the whole Act. For the first time a centrally administered licensing system will enable the entire credit industry to be kept under close scrutiny. There is little doubt that the threat of the refusal or revocation of a licence (*i.e.* loss of livelihood) is by far the strongest sanction provided by the Act. It is a perfect example of the administrative control mentioned earlier in this book.[1]

Who needs a licence?

The Act lists seven types of business for which a licence is required, namely:

(a) consumer credit;
(b) consumer hire;
(c) credit brokerage;
(d) debt-counselling;
(e) debt-adjusting;
(f) debt-collecting;
(g) credit reference agency.

[1] *Ante*, p. 213.

A number of problems arise. The first one is "what is a business?" The Act merely tells us that it includes a profession or trade; presumably cases from other branches of the law (*e.g.* income tax) can offer some guidance. The key factors include (i) the frequency of the transactions (ii) the manner of operation and (iii) profit motive. The word "frequency" leads on naturally to section 189(2) which provides that:

> a person is not to be treated as carrying on a particular type of business merely because *occasionally* he enters into transactions belonging to a business of that type [italics supplied].

There will clearly be borderline cases. Thus section 189 defines "consumer credit business" by reference to the crucial phrase "regulated agreement" which was considered in Chap. 16. It provides that:

> "consumer credit business" means any business so far as it comprises or relates to the provision of credit under regulated consumer credit agreements.

Let us take an example. Suppose that John sells television sets. Most of his customers pay cash but from time to time he sells a set on credit. Such a sale will be a debtor-creditor-supplier agreement and will be regulated, unless the credit is repayable by four or fewer instalments. Whether John needs a licence will depend on whether the credit sales take place more than "occasionally." If they only took place at very long intervals, and if they formed a very small part of John's turnover, then no licence would be required.

Even if there is a business a licence will only be required if the trader makes *regulated* agreements. Thus, if he only makes exempt agreements, or if the credit always exceeds £5,000, or if the debtors are all companies, no licence will be required.

The above remarks also apply, mutatis mutandis, to a consumer hire business, but when we turn to the five other types of business defined in section 145 (the Act uses the term "ancillary credit business") we find that there is one significant difference—the concept of "regulated agreement" is not critical. Thus, for example, an estate agent who introduces clients to a building society will require a licence as a credit broker, even though his clients make (a) agreements which are not consumer credit agreements at all (because the credit exceeds £5,000) or (b) agreements which are exempt under section 16.[1a]

A local authority does not require a licence[2] even though the agreements which it makes may be regulated by the Act.

Nature and duration of licences

A licence is personal and non-assignable[3] and normally lasts for 10 years.[4]

The criteria and the wide powers of the Director

The onus is on the applicant to prove to the Director that he is a fit person to engage in activities covered by the licence.[5] In considering the application the Director must consider any circumstances appearing to him to be relevant.[6] The section then sets out a non-exhaustive list of relevant matters including offences involving dishonesty or violence, contravention of the Act or certain other legislation, sex and race discrimination and undesirable business practices. In all these cases the section refers not merely to the trader himself but also to his employees, agents and associates (past or present). It is important to appreciate that the conduct in question need not involve any breach of the law (*e.g.* certain types of high-pressure salesmanship). As an alternative to refusing a licence the Director-General may limit the licence to certain specified activities.[7]

If the Director-General is "minded to refuse" an application he must invite the applicant to make written representations and to give notice, if he thinks fit, that he wishes to make representations orally. Appeal against refusal lies to the Secretary of State who delegates his powers to certain appointed persons.[8] Further appeal lies to the High Court on a point of law. The above procedure is also followed in cases involving variation, suspension and revocation.[9] It will be seen that these provisions provide a potent

[1a] *Ante,* p. 247.
[2] See s. 21.
[3] See s. 22(2).
[4] See S.I. 1979. No. 796.
[5] s. 25(1)(*a*).
[6] s. 25(2).
[7] See s. 23(2).
[8] See s. 41 and S.I. 1976 No. 837.
[9] See ss. 31–33.

weapon for the consumer. If a licensed trader is guilty of breaches of the Sale of Goods Act, or of the Trade Descriptions Act, or continues to exhibit void exemption clauses, these matters may come to the attention of the Director-General via trading standards inspectors or via the courts.[10] Even a letter from an individual consumer will be relevant in building up evidence against the trader and such evidence can, in appropriate cases, lead to refusal, suspension or revocation of the licence. The very existence of these provisions can have a salutary effect; thus they may induce the trader to alter his business practices before he applies for a licence.

Contracts by or through unlicensed traders

An unlicensed trader who engages in any activity for which a licence is required commits an offence for which the maximum fine on summary conviction is £1,000. If he is convicted on indictment the maximum penalty is two years imprisonment or a fine or both.[11] It may well be, however, that the most effective sanction is the non-enforceability of agreements. Thus by section 40 a regulated agreement made by an unlicensed trader is only enforceable if the Director-General makes a validating order. The Director-General must consider (inter alia) the extent to which debtors and hirers have been prejudiced, the degree of culpability and whether or not he would have granted a licence to the trader if he had applied for it. He can limit the order to specific agreements and he can impose conditions.

These sanctions are a powerful deterrent against unlicensed trading. Section 149 goes one step further; it places the creditor or owner under a duty to ensure that the credit-brokers with whom they do business are themselves licensed.

The creditor or owner has a strong incentive to check on this; the section provides that a regulated agreement made by a debtor or hirer who, for the purpose of making that agreement, was introduced to the creditor or owner by an unlicensed credit-broker is only enforceable against the debtor or hirer if the Director-General makes a validating order. Thus a finance company might be unable to enforce a hire-purchase agreement if the debtor was introduced to them by an unlicensed dealer.

[10] See s. 166.
[11] See Schedule 1.

Section 148 contains a similar "unenforceability" provision where an agreement is made for the services of an unlicensed person carrying on an ancillary credit business. Such a person can only enforce the agreement if the Director-General makes a validating order. The wording of the section is not entirely clear. If we take the case of an estate agent whose business includes that of being a "credit-broker," does the unenforceability apply solely to an introduction fee payable to him by the borrower, or does it mean that he cannot sue the vendor for his commission? On principle the former view should prevail—the sanctions imposed by the Act should be confined to his activities *qua* credit-broker and the words "agreement for the services of a person carrying on an ancillary credit business" should be construed accordingly.

In considering these provisions it must be borne in mind that consent by the debtor or hirer is as effective as a validating order.[12]

2. ADVERTISEMENTS

We have already seen that the very nature of credit carries the danger that the consumer may overcommit himself. The likelihood of this is greatly increased if the creditor is allowed to exhibit a misleading advertisement with words like "five years to pay" in bold type and a very high interest charge tucked away in the small print. Accordingly, sections 43–47 contain provisions which enable advertising regulations to be made, with criminal liability for infringement.

Scope of advertising regulations

The advertising provisions are wider than most of the other provisions of the Act because they are not confined to the making of regulated agreements. Whether these provisions apply or not depends on two factors, namely (a) the nature of the advertiser's business and (b) the wording of the advertisement.

(a) *The advertiser's business*

By section 43(2) the advertiser must carry on:
  (i) a consumer credit business, or

---

[12] s. 173(3) *ante*, p. 240.

(ii) a consumer hire business, or

(iii) a business in the course of which he provides credit to individuals secured on land, or

(iv) a business which comprises or relates to agreements which are unregulated solely because they are governed by a foreign system of law.

(b) *The wording of the advertisement*

If an advertisement published under (a) above indicates that the advertiser is willing to provide credit the Act will apply unless it indicates that (i) the credit must exceed £5,000 and that no security is required, or that the only security is to consist of property other than land or (ii) the credit is available only to bodies corporate.

An advertisement published under (a) above advertising the hiring of goods will not be regulated if it indicates that the advertiser is not willing to enter into a consumer hire agreement.

The power to make regulations

The Act itself merely provides the broadest possible framework and leaves the detail (which will be very complex) to be filled in by regulations. The regulations must ensure that:

> having regard to its subject-matter and the amount of detail included in it, an advertisement conveys a fair and reasonably comprehensive indication of the nature of the credit or hire facilities offered by the advertiser and their true cost to persons using them.[12a]

It is likely that the regulations will make a distinction between "simple," "intermediate" and "full" advertisements. A simple advertisement will contain nothing more than the advertiser's name and occupation: in these limited circumstances the regulations will not apply. In contrast a full advertisement will have to contain very detailed information, *e.g.* the cash price, the rate of the total charge for credit, the frequency and number of repayments.

Restricted-use agreements

It will be recalled that the essence of a restricted-use agreement is that the debtor never gets his hands on the credit.[13] In this type of case a prospective borrower can only assess the true cost of

[12a] s. 44(1).
[13] *Ante*, p. 241.

credit if he knows what the cost would be if he were to buy the land, goods or services for cash. Accordingly, section 45 provides that an offence is committed if (a) the advertisement indicates that a person is willing to provide restricted-use credit and (b) the supplier of the goods or services does not hold himself out as prepared to sell the goods, or provide the services, for cash.

Criminal liability

There is criminal liability under section 45[14] or under section 46 if the advertisement conveys information which in a material respect is false or misleading. Section 47 extends liability to certain other persons, *e.g.* an advertising agency and the "publisher" of the advertisement. The term "publisher" is not defined but it would certainly include the newspaper in which it appeared and the ITV or local radio company responsible for the programme which carried it. The publisher has a defence if he received the advertisements in the course of a business and did not know, and had no reason to suspect, that its publication would be an offence. Needless to say, the ever-present administrative sanction (the threat of licence revocation) must always be borne in mind.

3. CANVASSING

Section 49 follows the precedent set by the Moneylenders Acts by prohibiting the canvassing of debtor-creditor agreements, *e.g.* personal loans, off trade premises.

When is an offence committed?

The canvasser must be an individual and he must solicit the debtor into the making of a regulated agreement by making oral representations to the debtor, or to any other individual, during a visit by the canvasser to non-trade premises. The visit must have been for the purpose of making such oral representations, so that a crime is not committed if one individual makes representations to another individual while they are both guests at a party. On the other hand, a social visit can be caught if the underlying intention was to make representations leading to the debtor-creditor agreement.

[14] See above.

Previous request

No offence is committed if the visit was in response to a request made on a previous occasion, provided that the request was in writing signed by or on behalf of the person making it.[15] Presumably the person making the request need not be the debtor.

Trade premises

For *this* purpose the term trade premises is defined[16] as any premises where a business is carried on (whether on a permanent or temporary basis) by (a) the creditor or owner, or (b) the supplier, or (c) the canvasser's employer, or (d) the debtor.

Overdrafts

The Director-General may exempt the soliciting of an agreement enabling the debtor to overdraw on specified types of current account, provided that the debtor already keeps an account with the creditor. This could be relevant where a bank manager invites his customer, ostensibly for a meal or a game of golf, but in reality to offer him overdraft facilities.

---

[15] s. 48(1)(*b*) and 49(2).
[16] *cf.* cancellation, *post*, p. 270.

CHAPTER 19

"I CAN'T REMEMBER WHAT I SIGNED."

IN the previous chapter we examined vitally important provisions relating to the control of business activities.

We now turn to the other main form of control—the regulation of individual agreements. The law is to be found in Parts V–IX of the Act and much of it is modelled on the previous hire-purchase legislation. This chapter is concerned with formalities and copies.[1] The object of the legislation is to make sure that the debtor or hirer is made aware of his obligations and that he can obtain further information if, for example, he has failed to keep a record of his payments. Once again a large amount of the detail will be contained in regulations.

The sanctions for non-compliance are potentially severe. If the creditor or owner fails to comply with the various formalities, the agreement is said to be "improperly executed." By section 65 the creditor or owner cannot enforce such an agreement against the debtor or hirer unless (a) the court makes an enforcement order[1a] or (b) the debtor or hirer consents to enforcement (s. 173(3)).[1b] What happens if the creditor or owner, in defiance of section 65, enforces the agreement by retaking the goods? If the repossession amounts to the tort of trespass or conversion, the creditor or owner will be liable for this. If, however, the repossession is only unlawful because it contravenes section 65, it seems that any civil or criminal sanctions are shut out by section 170(1).[1c] That leaves merely the administrative sanction of taking action which can put the licence of the creditor or owner in jeopardy.

Pre-contractual information

As part of the policy outlined above, section 55 enables regulations to be made whereby specified information must be disclosed to the prospective debtor or hirer before a regulated agreement

[1] ss. 58–65 and 77–80.
[1a] *Post*, p. 290.
[1b] *Ante*, p. 240.
[1c] *Ante*, p. 240.

K

is made. It is likely that this will include the "true" cost of borrowing.

Special pre-contract formalities in land mortgage cases

We have already seen that many land mortgage cases are outside the main control provisions because (i) the credit exceeds £5,000 or (ii) the agreements are exempted under section 16 or by regulations.[2] If, however, the agreement is a regulated agreement (*e.g.* a loan not exceeding £5,000 granted by a non-exempt lender) section 58 lays down a special pre-contractual period of reflection and isolation; the reason for this is that the post-contractual cancellation provisions do not apply to any agreement secured on land.[3] In two cases, however, the special reflection rules do not apply, namely (a) a restricted-use agreement to finance the purchase of the mortgaged land and (b) an agreement for a bridging loan in connection with the purchase of the mortgaged land or other land. In these two cases the debtor will have neither reflection rights nor cancellation rights.

Let us suppose that John, a moneylender, is prepared to lend George £4,000 on the security of George's house. The reflection and isolation rules can be summarised as follows:

(1) At least seven days before sending the unexecuted agreement for signature, John must give to George a copy of the agreement (and of any document referred to therein) containing a notice in the prescribed form indicating George's right to withdraw from the transaction.[4]

(2) When seven days have elapsed, John can post the agreement for signature unless he has received a notice of withdrawal.[5]

(3) John must not approach George in any way during the "consideration period" except at George's specific request. The consideration period begins when the "reflection copy" is sent[6] and ends seven days after the sending of the agreement for signature[7] or, if earlier, its return by George duly signed.

The above also apply to a regulated consumer hire agreement secured by land mortgage.

[2] See *ante*, p. 247.
[3] s. 67 *post*, p.270.
[4] s. 58(1) and 61(2).
[5] s. 61(2) and (4).
[6] See (1) above.
[7] See (2) above.

Formalities of the agreement itself

Section 60 enables regulations to be made to ensure that the debtor or hirer is made aware of his rights and duties, the amount and rate of the total charge for credit and the protection and remedies available to him under the Act. Thus it is likely that the debtor under a consumer credit agreement must be made aware of *(inter alia)* his right of termination,[8] his right to a rebate on early settlement[9] and the restriction on the creditor's right to repossess protected goods.[10] The regulations will also deal with such matters as legibility, size (and perhaps even the colour) of print, the prominence to be given to particular parts of the agreement, and the place where the debtor or hirer must sign.

The Act itself lays down three broad requirements in section 61, namely that:

(a) a document in the prescribed form containing all the prescribed terms and conforming to regulations under section 60[11] is signed in the prescribed manner both by the debtor or hirer and by or on behalf of the creditor or owner, and

(b) the document embodies all the terms of the agreement, other than implied terms, and

(c) the document is, when presented or sent to the debtor or hirer, in such a state that all its terms are readily legible.

The wording of para (a) makes it clear that the debtor or hirer must sign *personally*. It also seems clear that a signature on a blank form, with the details filled in later, would not be sufficient.[12]

Copies

Sections 62–63 contain copy provisions which are similar, but not identical, to the provisions in the Hire-Purchase Act 1965. The basic rule is that the debtor or hirer is always entitled to at least one copy of the agreement; in many cases he is entitled to two copies. The critical factor is the nature of the document which is signed by the debtor or hirer, *i.e.* was it a *contract* or merely on *offer*?

[8] *Post,* p. 276.
[9] *Post,* p. 292.
[10] *Post,* p. 295.
[11] *Supra.*
[12] Consider *Eastern Distributors* v. *Goldring* [1957] Q.B. 600 a decision on a slightly different provision in the Hire-Purchase Act 1938.

(a) *Signature of agreement*

If the creditor or owner presents the document personally to the debtor or hirer and, if on the occasion of his signature it becomes an executed agreement, the creditor or owner must give the debtor or hirer a copy of the executed agreement there and then.[13] Likewise, if an unexecuted agreement is sent to the debtor or hirer for signature a copy must be sent at the same time, but if the effect of his signature is to convert the document into an executed agreement no further copy is required.[14]

(b) *Signature of offer*

In most cases the document which is signed by the debtor or hirer is merely an offer which has be be sent to the creditor or owner for acceptance. In such a case the effect of sections 62 and 63 is to give the debtor or hirer the right to two copies. The first copy is a copy of the unexecuted agreement and this will show whether or not the document was complete when he signed it. If the agreement is presented to the debtor or hirer personally, the first copy must be handed to him as soon as he has signed.[15] If the agreement is sent for signature, the first copy must be sent at the same time.[16] In either case the second copy (a copy of the executed agreement) must be delivered or sent within seven days of the making of the agreement.[17]

Other documents

The duty to supply a copy includes a duty to supply a copy of every other document referred to in the agreement. Presumably this would not require the creditor or owner to supply a copy of the Consumer Credit Act merely because the agreement referred to it. It is to be hoped that the regulations will put the matter beyond doubt.

Cancellation cases

Special provisions apply in cancellation cases.[18]

[13] s. 63(1).
[14] s. 63(2)(*b*).
[15] s. 62(1).
[16] s. 62(2).
[17] s. 63(2).
[18] *Post,* p. 271.

Additional information on request

The copy provisions are supplemented by sections 77–79 which, as already stated, are designed to assist the debtor or hirer who has failed to keep a record of his payments (alternatively, he may have mislaid either or both of the copies referred to above). In each of these cases the debtor or hirer must make a written request and send the sum of 15 pence. To ensure that the creditor or owner is not put to unreasonable trouble, the sections require him to send to the debtor or hirer, within the prescribed period, a copy of the executed agreement and a signed statement containing certain particulars (e.g. as to sums paid, due and payable) "according to the information to which it is practicable for him to refer." Further, to prevent the creditor or owner from being inundated with such requests, the information need not be given at all if the request was made within one month of a previous request having been complied with.

Sanctions for non-compliance

In the case of sections 77–79 the sanctions are two-fold. Thus (a) while the default continues the creditor or owner cannot enforce the agreement and (b) if the default continues for one month he commits an offence.

Additional information without request

In the case of a running-account credit agreement, other than a small agreement[19], the creditor must send to the debtor a periodic statement at least once every twelve months.[20]

Information as to the whereabouts of the goods

So far all the provisions have required information to be given by the creditor or owner, but section 80 is concerned with the reverse situation. It provides that where a regulated agreement requires the debtor or hirer to keep goods in his possession or control, he must within seven working days after receiving a written request from the creditor or owner tell the creditor or owner where the goods are. If the information is not given within 21 days of receiving the request the debtor or hirer commits an offence.

[19] *Ante,* p. 247.
[20] s. 78(4).

CHAPTER 20

"CAN I GET OUT OF THE AGREEMENT?"

WE have seen that a debtor or hirer may over-commit himself
(perhaps aided by an over-enthusiastic salesman). In this chapter
we shall consider his right of withdrawal from a regulated agreement and the financial consequences of his doing so. The subject
will be considered under four headings, namely:

1. Withdrawal
2. Rescission and Repudiation
3. Cancellation
4. Termination

1. WITHDRAWAL

On general contractual principles a prospective debtor or hirer can
withdraw from the transaction at any time before his offer has
been accepted. In the case of a regulated agreement his position
is strengthened by section 59(1) which provides that an agreement
is void if it binds a person to enter, as prospective debtor or hirer,
into a prospective regulated agreement. This provision may, however, be cut down by regulations.[1]

Section 57, which deals with withdrawal, provides that no special
form of wording is required[2] and the notice of withdrawal can be
written or oral. Two important points should be noted:

(1) The list of persons to whom notice of withdrawal can be
given is surprisingly wide. It includes not only the credit-broker
or supplier but also "any person who, in the course of a business
carried on by him, acts on behalf of the debtor or hirer in any
negotiations for the agreement."[3] Thus if, for example, the prospective debtor had instructed a solicitor to negotiate on his behalf
a notice given by him to that solicitor would be sufficient. Such a

---

[1] s. 59(2).
[2] s. 57(2).
[3] s. 57(3).

deemed agent is under a deemed contractual duty to transmit the notice to his deemed principal (the creditor or owner) forthwith.[4]

(2) Withdrawal has the same effect as cancellation. Thus (a) the prospective debtor or hirer can recover all payments made by him to the creditor or owner (*e.g.* a pre-contract deposit, or a payment made for a survey of the house); (b) the withdrawal will also terminate any linked transaction[4a] and sums paid under it become repayable; (c) under a three party D-C-S agreement[5] the creditor and the supplier are jointly liable to repay the sums paid by the debtor; and (d) the prospective debtor or hirer will have a lien over the goods until sums repayable to him have been repaid.[6]

2. RESCISSION AND REPUDIATION

On general contractual principles a debtor or hirer may have a right to rescind an agreement for misrepresentation or to treat it as repudiated by a breach by the creditor or owner. One example of this is considered in the next Chapter. The deemed agency provisions referred to above also apply to rescission.[7] The principal distinction between rescission and accepting a repudiation is that the former is retrospective and the innocent party is treated as if the agreement had never been made. In the latter cases obligations arising before the acceptance of repudiation remain enforceable, although they can usually be reduced or extinguished by a claim for damages.

3. CANCELLATION

The cancellation provisions in sections 67–73 are modelled on those in the Hire-Purchase Act 1965, although there are significant differences between them. The object of the legislation is clear enough—to give the debtor or hirer a chance for second thoughts

---

[4] s. 175.
[4a] For the meaning of this term see *ante*, p. 251.
[5] *Ante,* p. 245.
[6] The consequences of cancellation are considered in more detail on pp. 272–275.
[7] See s. 102.

(*i.e.* a "cooling-off period"). in a case where he may have been pressurised by a doorstep salesman into signing an agreement. The matter can be considered under the following headings:

(1) What agreements are cancellable?
(2) The copy provisions
(3) The time for cancellation
(4) How is cancellation effected?
(5) Effect of cancellation
(6) Duty to return goods
(7) The part-exchange allowance

(1) **What agreements are cancellable?**

A regulated consumer credit or hire agreement is cancellable if two conditions are satisfied, namely that (a) oral representations were made by or on behalf of the negotiator in the presence of the debtor or hirer and (b) the unexecuted agreement was not signed by the debtor or hirer at premises where a business was carried on by (i) the creditor or owner, or (ii) any party to a linked transaction (other than the debtor or hirer or a relative of his) or (iii) the negotiator in any antecedent negotiations.

Let us suppose that John, a trader, goes to a car dealer to buy a new car. The transaction is financed by a loan from a finance company who require John to take out a life policy with an insurance company. The car dealer (the negotiator) makes oral representations in John's presence. If John signs the agreement at the office of the dealer, finance company or insurance company, he will have no right of cancellation. On the other hand, if he signs at his own home, or at his own business premises, then cancellation is available. Thus, the definition of business premises does *not* include the business premises of the debtor or hirer.[8] The place where the representations were made is immaterial. They must, however, have been made in the *presence* of the debtor or hirer. Representations made on the telephone would not give cancellation rights. If no oral representations were made at all (*e.g.* a mail-order purchase) there is no right of cancellation.

In the case of land transactions the concept of post-contractual cancellation can result in considerable administrative problems. Accordingly, the cancellation provisions do not apply to (a) an

---

[8] Contrast the canvassing rules, *ante,* p. 262.

agreement secured on land, nor (b) a restricted-use agreement to finance the purchase of land, nor (c) a bridging loan in connection with the purchase of land. It will be recalled that in case (a) above the prospective debtor or hirer will have a pre-contractual period of reflection and isolation.[9]

Two other types of agreement are not cancellable. They are (a) a non-commercial agreement[9a] and (b) a small debtor-creditor-supplier agreement for restricted-use credit.[9b]

> Let us suppose that a doorstep salesman induces Mrs. Smith to buy a children's encyclopaedia at a price of £25 payable by five instalments of £5. Nothing is said about the passing of property. (i) This is a "small" agreement;[9c] (ii) since the supplier of the goods and the supplier of the credit is the same person it is "debtor-creditor-supplier;" (iii) since Mrs. Smith cannot get her hands on the credit it is "restricted-use;" (iv) therefore no cancellation is possible.

(2) The copy provisions

The basic rules in sections 62 and 63[10] are modified in three respects by section 64. Thus:

(a) each copy must contain a notice in the prescribed form indicating the right of cancellation, how and when it is exercisable and the name and address of a person to whom notice of cancellation may be given[11];

(b) in cases where a second copy is required it must be sent *by post*[12] (s. 63(3));

(c) in cases where a second copy is not required a notice, containing the information mentioned in (a) above, must be posted to the debtor or hirer within seven days of the making of the agreement.[13]

We shall see that the usual "unenforceability" sanction can be particularly severe in these cases.[14]

[9] *Ante*, p. 264.
[9a] *Ante*, p. 246.
[9b] s. 74(2).
[9c] *Ante*, p. 247.
[10] *Ante*, p. 265.
[11] s. 64(1)(*a*).
[12] s. 63(3).
[13] s. 64(1)(*b*).
[14] See *post*, p. 291.

(3) The time for cancellation

The cancellation period starts when the debtor or hirer signs the unexecuted agreement and ends five days after the debtor or hirer *receives* the statutory second copy or notice.[15] Thus, if the second copy is received on a Friday the cancellation period runs out at midnight on the following Wednesday. If the second copy is delayed in the post the cancellation period will, to that extent, be prolonged since the period only starts to melt away when the debtor or hirer *receives* the second copy. What happens if the second copy is not received at all and the creditor or owner then sends a further copy? Alternatively, what happens if the second copy or notice is sent off more than seven days after the making of the agreement? The wording of the Act is ambiguous. If the third copy or the late copy could be regarded as given "under" section 63 then it would start the five day period running. On the other hand it could be argued that a notice is only given "under" section 63 if it is posted within seven days; if this is correct then the effect of delay or non-receipt would be that the right of cancellation would remain permanently available. This seems so absurd that the court is likely to prefer the former view.

(4) How is cancellation effected?

By section 69 the agreement can be cancelled if the debtor or hirer serves a notice of cancellation on (a) the creditor or owner or (b) the person specified in the copy or notice or (c) the agent of the creditor or owner (including his deemed agent).[16] No special form of wording is required but it is clear from the definition of "notice"[17] that it must be in writing. If it is posted it takes effect as from the date of posting, and the mere fact that it is not received by the creditor or owner is immaterial (this is in marked contrast to the second copy or notice which only triggers off the cancellation period when it is received).

(5) Effect of cancellation

Subject to two exceptions the general effect of cancellation is to treat the agreement, and any linked transaction,[18] as if it had

[15] s. 68.
[16] See *ante*, p. 268.
[17] s. 189.
[18] *Ante*, p. 252.

never been made.[19] Thus the debtor or hirer can recover his payments and is discharged from liability to make further payments. In the case of a three-party D-C-S agreement[20] for restricted-use credit the creditor and supplier are jointly and severally liable to repay sums paid by the debtor or a relative. The debtor, hirer or relative has a lien over the goods until repayable sums are repaid to him. Thus, if Albert paid a £200 deposit to buy a £2,000 car and the remaining £1,800 was paid by a creditor who had "arrangements" with the seller, the effect of a cancellation of the loan agreement would be that (a) the sale contract, as a linked transaction, would also be cancelled (b) the seller would be under an obligation to repay the £1,800 to the creditor[21] and (c) the seller and creditor would be jointly and severally liable to repay the £200 to Albert.

The first exception is in section 70(2) and deals with a debtor-creditor-supplier agreement for restricted-use credit to finance (a) the doing of work or supply of goods to meet an emergency or (b) the supply of goods which have become incorporated in any land or thing before service of the notice of cancellation. Since the debtor is unable to return the goods it would clearly be wrong to allow him to avoid payment simply by serving a notice of cancellation. Accordingly, in this type of case the cancellation will wipe out the credit part of the agreement but the debtor will remain liable to pay the cash price for the goods or work.

The second exception is to be found in section 71 and it deals with a case where the credit has already been advanced by the creditor before the expiry of the cancellation period. Here the strict application of the cancellation provisions would cause hardship. On the one hand, since the agreement is treated as never having been made, the creditor might be able to bring an action to recover money lent. On the other hand the debtor might try to avoid all liability in reliance on section 70(1)(b) which provides that any sum payable by the debtor or his relative shall cease to be payable. To deal with these problems section 71 starts by providing that cancellation of a regulated consumer credit agree-

---

[19] s. 64(4).
[20] *Ante,* p. 245.
[21] s. 70(1)(c).

ment (other than a debtor-creditor-supplier agreement for restricted-use credit) shall not destroy the obligation to repay the credit and interest. The words in brackets are inserted because, as we have seen, this type of transaction does not raise the type of problem at which section 71 is aimed—the supplier merely repays the credit to the creditor. The section then goes on to provide a complex formula. First of all it provides that if the whole or part of the credit is repaid within one month of cancellation, or not later than the first instalment repayment date, no interest is chargeable on the amount repaid. It then goes on to deal with a credit which is repayable by instalments where any part of the credit is still outstanding after the first repayment date. In such a case the creditor must serve a notice recalculating the instalments over a period starting when this notice is served and ending with the final contractual repayment date. This shortening of the repayment period will often mean larger instalments.[22]

(6) Duty to return goods

Let us remind ourselves at this point of the distinction between debtor-creditor-supplier agreements and debtor-creditor agreements

(a) Where the debtor under a debtor-creditor agreement uses the credit to buy goods, the sale contract is *not* a linked transaction and is not affected by cancellation of the credit agreement.

(b) In the case of a debtor-creditor-supplier agreement the supply of the goods is either an integral part of the credit agreement itself (*e.g.* hire-purchase) or it is a linked transaction under section 19 which is cancelled along with the credit agreement. In either case the debtor will have to restore the goods to the other party under the rules set out below.

Section 72 deals with a case where a debtor-creditor-supplier agreement for restricted use credit, a consumer hire agreement, or a linked transaction (to which the debtor, hirer or a relative is a party) is cancelled after the debtor, hirer or relative has obtained possession. In such a case the possessor is under a duty to restore the goods to the person from whom he got them and in the

---

[22] For examples see Goode, *Consumer Credit Legislation*, Main Vol. pp. 98–99.

meantime to retain possession and to take reasonable care. The duty to restore the goods is merely a duty to redeliver them at his own premises on receiving a written request from the other party. The duty is also discharged if the possessor delivers the goods (whether at his own premises or elsewhere) to any person to whom a notice of cancellation could have been sent other than the "deemed agent."[23] Alternatively, he can send the goods to such a person, but in this case he must take reasonable care to see that they are received by the other party and are not damaged in transit. The duty to take reasonable care comes to an end twenty-one days from cancellation unless within that time the possessor has received a written request for redelivery and has unreasonably failed to comply with it.

There is, however, a sting in the tail. The duty to restore does not apply to emergency or incorporation cases where, as we have seen, the debtor remains liable to pay the price.[24] Nor does it apply to perishable goods, nor to goods which by their nature are consumed by use and were so consumed before cancellation—a classic case of having one's cake and not having to pay for it!

Any breach of section 72 is actionable as a breach of statutory duty.

(7) The part-exchange allowance

Section 73 deals with a case where, as part of a cancelled agreement, the negotiator agreed to take goods in part exchange and those goods have been delivered to him. The effect of section 73(2) is to give the debtor or hirer a right to recover the part-exchange allowance from the negotiator unless within 10 days of cancellation the goods were returned to the debtor or hirer in substantially the same condition. If the negotiator was the supplier in a three-party debtor-creditor-supplier agreement the negotiator and the creditor are jointly and severally liable to repay the allowance and the lien of the debtor or hirer[25] extends to cover the return of the goods (during the 10 day period) or the part exchange allowance.

---

[23] See *ante*, p. 272.
[24] s. 69(2)(*b*) *ante*, p. 273.
[25] *Ante*, p. 273.

4. Termination

If there is no right of withdrawal, rescission or cancellation the final possibility (apart from any contractual right of termination) is a right of termination under sections 99–101. These are limited in scope; sections 99–100 only apply to regulated hire-purchase and conditional sale agreements while section 101 relates to regulated consumer hire agreements. In either case the statutory rights cannot be cut down by agreement; on the other hand if the agreement is *more* favourable to the debtor or hirer he can take advantage of it.

(1) Hire-purchase and conditional sale

The provisions of sections 99–100 are very closely modelled on the corresponding provisions in the Hire-Purchase Act 1965, although modifications have had to be made because the 1974 Act extends to land as well as goods. The right to terminate a hire-purchase or conditional sale agreement is available at any time before the last instalment falls due and it can be exercised by giving notice to any person who is entitled or authorised to receive payments. However, there are two cases in which the right to terminate is not available. The first is where, under a conditional sale agreement relating to land, title has passed to the buyer. The second is where, under a conditional sale of goods, the property has become vested in the buyer and has then been transferred to a third person, *e.g.* a sub-buyer.

Termination only operates for the future, so that sums which have accrued due remain payable.[26] The effect of termination may well be to leave the creditor with heavily depreciated goods. In order to provide some measure of compensation section 100(1) requires the debtor to pay such further sum (if any) as will bring the total payments up to one-half of the total price. If, however, in any action the court is satisfied that a smaller sum is adequate to cover the creditor's loss the court may order such smaller sum to be paid. This could clearly be relevant if, for example, a hirer bought a car with a hire-purchase price of £3,000 and then wished to terminate the agreement after only a few week's use. He would presumably tender a sum falling far short of one-half, leaving it

---

[26] s. 99(2).

to the creditor to take court proceedings. The court has no discretion with regard to sums which have already accrued due.

The debtor may also have to pay damages if he is in breach of an obligation to take reasonable care of the goods[27] and he must allow the creditor to retake them.[28]

If the creditor agrees to carry out any installation and if the cost of the installation forms part of the total purchase price it is clearly reasonable that he should be paid for this in full. Accordingly, the reference to one-half is a reference to the installation charge in full and one half of the balance.[29]

Example

A television set is let out on hire-purchase at a price of £300, including a £30 installation charge. The debtor pays a £50 deposit and one instalment of £10 is outstanding. He now wishes to terminate the agreement. He must first of all pay the £10. Then (unless otherwise ordered) he must bring his payments up to one-half of the total price:

$$\text{one half} = £30 + \frac{270}{2} \quad = \quad £165$$

$$\text{less sums paid and due} \quad = \quad 60$$

$$\text{further sum payable}[30] \quad = \quad £105$$

(2) Consumer hire

Section 101 gives the hirer a limited, non-excludable right to terminate the agreement, but the earliest termination date is 18 months after the making of the agreement (unless the contract provides for an earlier termination date).[31] Once again termination only operates for the future and sums which have accrued due are not affected. The hirer must give a termination notice equal to the shortest payment interval, or three months, whichever is less. Thus, if rentals are payable monthly, the hirer can end the agreement by giving one month's notice at the end of month 17.

---

[27] s. 100(4).
[28] s. 100(5).
[29] s. 100(2).
[30] s. 100(1).
[31] s. 101(3).

The exercise of a right of termination can often cause financial problems to the owner, especially where the owner leases out commercial equipment. Accordingly, section 101(7) provides that in three cases the statutory right of termination is not available at all. These are:

(a) where the total payments (disregarding sums payable on breach) exceed £300 in any one year;

(b) where goods are let out for the hirer's business and were selected by the hirer and acquired by the owner, at the hirer's request, from a third party;

(c) any agreement where the hirer requires the goods to re-let them in the course of a business.

Apart from these special cases the Director General has a general power to exclude the operation of section 101 from agreements made by a particular trader.[31a]

The section does not mention damages for failure to take reasonable care but on principle the hirer owes a duty of reasonable care as a bailee at common law and will be liable to pay damages for breach of that duty.

[31a] See s. 101(8).

CHAPTER 21

"THE GOODS ARE DEFECTIVE"

In Part I of this book we considered the terms implied by sections 12–14 of the Sale of Goods Act 1893, and we also dealt briefly with hire-purchase and hiring agreements. In this Chapter we shall consider these problems again in the context of credit transactions. The basic point can be made very briefly at the outset—the differences between cash and credit transactions are very slight. It is proposed to consider this topic under five headings and for convenience the term "connected lender" will be used in preference to "creditor with whom the supplier had arrangements." The five headings are:

1. Cash Sale—unconnected lender
2. Cash Sale—connected lender
3. Credit Sale and conditional sale
4. Hire-Purchase
5. Hire

1. Cash Sale—Unconnected Lender

Let us suppose that Robert borrows money from his bank and uses it to buy a car. The loan is a debtor-creditor agreement and, as we have seen, the purchase of the car is not a linked transaction. As between seller and buyer, the position is governed by the Sale of Goods Act 1893, as amended, and this has been fully discussed in Chapters 3 and 4. Alternatively, if the seller was guilty of misrepresentation Robert may be entitled to rescind the contract or to claim damages.[1] As between Robert and his bank the bank are not affected by any breach of contract on the part of the seller. It follows that Robert will have to continue to repay the loan and his sole remedy is against the seller. His sole right as against the

---

[1] *Ante,* p. 77.

bank is to wait for a notice of default[2] and then apply to the court for a time order.[3]

2. CASH SALE—CONNECTED LENDER

Let us now suppose that the seller introduces Robert to a finance company with whom the seller has arrangements. The finance company make a loan to Robert to finance the sale. This is a three-party debtor-creditor-supplier agreement. As between Robert and the seller, the position is exactly the same as in the previous example. As regards the position between Robert and the finance company there are two overlapping provisions of considerable practical importance which may enable Robert to hold the finance company responsible for the seller's default.

The first provision is section 56 of the Consumer Credit Act which applies *(inter alia)* to antecedent negotiations with the debtor conducted by the supplier in relation to a transaction financed by a debtor-creditor-supplier agreement.[4] The key provision is section 56(2) which reads as follows:

> Negotiations with the debtor . . . shall be deemed to be conducted by the negotiator in the capacity of agent of the creditor as well as in his actual capacity.

In other words, if the seller made a misrepresentation (*e.g.* as to credit terms or the quality of the goods), he will have made it as agent for the finance company. Thus Robert could bring proceedings against the finance company, or he could merely discontinue his payments, wait to be sued and then counterclaim. It remains to add that section 56(3) makes void a clause (a) purporting to make the negotiator the agent of the dealer or (b) relieving a person from liability for acts or omissions of any person acting as, or on behalf of, a negotiator. This raises a problem in relation to a clause in a contract between creditor and debtor excluding liability for all misrepresentations, including those made by the dealer. Would such a clause automatically be void under section 56(3) or would it still be subject to the reasonableness test under

---

[2] *Post,* p. 293.
[3] *Post,* p. 293.
[4] s. 56(1)(c).

section 3 of the Misrepresentation Act 1967.[5] It is felt that a carefully drafted clause should be given the latter construction—it would seem strange thắt the creditor should be in a worse position merely because the misrepresentation was made by the dealer rather than by the creditor himself or by some other agent.

The second provision affecting three-party debtor-creditor-supplier agreements is section 75. In this situation it is provided that:

> (1) if the debtor . . . has . . . any claim against the supplier in respect of a misrepresentation or breach of contract, he shall have a like claim against the creditor, who, with the supplier, shall accordingly be jointly and severally liable to the debtor.

Subsection (3) lays down two limitations.

> Subsection (1) does not apply to a claim
>
> (a) under a non-commercial agreement, or
> (b) so far as the claim relates to any single item to which the supplier has attached a cash price not exceeding £30 or more than £10,000.

As already stated there is substantial overlap between sections 56 and 75. If the "negotiator" makes a misrepresentation, the buyer/borrower will have a claim against the creditor under either section. In one respect section 56 is wider, because the limitations in section 75(3)[6] do not apply. The real importance of section 75(1) lies in the words "or breach of contract." It means that the creditor will be liable not merely for the misrepresentation or for breach of express terms but also for breach of the implied terms under the Sale of Goods Act 1893. This seems reasonable enough; the finance company who finance the transaction by letting the goods out on hire-purchase have been responsible for the quality of the goods ever since 1938. The effect of section 75 is to place them in basically the same position if they choose to finance the transaction by means of a loan. From the debtor's point of view the effect of section 75 can be very favourable. In an extreme case he might have a claim against a solvent finance company whereas a person buying with his own money, or with money borrowed from an unconnected lender, might only have had a claim against an insolvent seller.

---

[5] As redrafted by s. 8 of the Unfair Contract Terms Act 1977, *ante,* p. 116.
[6] See above.

In the example above[7] we took the case of a car buyer, dealer and connected lender. Another situation where section 75 is highly relevant is in relation to buyer, credit card company and approved supplier. If goods bought with a credit card prove to be defective and cause enormous damage (*e.g.* death or personal injury) the buyer (or his personal representatives) will have a claim against the credit card company for the full amount of the damage. In this connection a dispute has arisen on the effect of the transitional provisions of the Act. Under the third commencement order section 75 applies to regulated agreements *made* after July 1, 1977. The problem area is where a card was issued before that date and is used after that date. One view is that the credit card is merely a standing offer, or a "unilateral contract" and that no regulated agreement is made until the card is used. On this view the date of issue of the card is irrelevant and section 75 applies to any use of the card after July 1, 1977 (assuming that such use constitutes a regulated agreement).[8] The second view, put forward by the credit card companies but rejected by the O.F.T., is that the initial credit card agreement constitutes one single regulated agreement; on this view an agreement made before July 1, 1977 would be outside section 75 even though it was renewed after that date. The O.F.T. put forward the third view (with which the authors respectfully agree) that each renewal of the card is a new regulated agreement[9]; on this view the companies are subject to section 75 if the renewal took place on or after July 1, 1977. The position is not free from doubt[10] but the credit card companies have agreed, under pressure from the O.F.T. to accept liability of *up to the amount of the credit,* where the card was renewed on or after July 1, 1977. In many cases, however, the claim will go beyond this and in the authors' view, the consumer should succeed in bringing his claim within section 75.

As between creditor and supplier the creditor is entitled to join the supplier as a party to the proceedings and to claim an indemnity from him.[11]

---

[7] See p. 279.
[8] See Goode, *Consumer Credit Legislation,* Supplement, p. 0/2.
[9] See also ss. 14(3) and 64(2) which support the view that the credit token is issued in pursuance of an agreement.
[10] See (1978) 128 N.L.J. 448, 541, 593
[11] s. 75(2) and (5).

3. CREDIT SALE AND CONDITIONAL SALE

A dealer may sell goods and allow the customer to pay by instalments. If nothing is said about the passing of property it will pass as soon as the contract is made[12] and the sale will be a credit sale. If, however, the passing of property is postponed it will be a conditional sale.[13] In either case the obligations of the seller with regard to the goods are to be found in the Sale of Goods Act 1893 (as amended). In one minor respect there has been a drafting amendment in what is now Schedule 4 to the Consumer Credit Act 1974. It will be recalled that under the implied condition of fitness the buyer must make known the particular purpose for which he requires the goods. To whom must that notification be made? In a cash sale the purpose must be made known to the seller, but where the price or part of the price is payable by instalments the effect of para. 3 of Schedule 4 is that the buyer can make his purpose known

   (a) to the seller, or
   (b) where the purchase price or part of it is payable by instalments and the goods were previously sold by a credit-broker to the seller, to that credit-broker.

Thus, if we vary the previous example the dealer might sell the goods to a finance company who would re-sell on credit to the buyer. In such a case the buyer will have been conducting his negotiations with the dealer and it is sufficient if he makes his purpose known to the dealer.

There are just two further points. First, the amended provisions of the Sale of Goods Act apply even though the agreement is outside the Consumer Credit Act (*e.g.* because it is a debtor-creditor-supplier agreement with four or fewer instalments). Secondly, a trader who buys goods on credit for his trade will not be "dealing as consumer" and therefore an exemption clause which satisfies the reasonableness test will be binding on him.

4. HIRE-PURCHASE

In the case of a hire-purchase agreement (whether or not it is regulated by the Consumer Credit Act) the implied obligations

---

[12] *Ante,* p. 241.
[13] *Ante,* p. 241.

with regard to the goods are contained in sections 8–11 of the Supply of Goods (Implied Terms) Act 1973. These provisions have been redrafted so as to bring the terminology into line with that in the Consumer Credit Act and the re-drafted version is set out in Schedule 4 to the Consumer Credit Act. The terms are virtually identical to those for the sale of goods and they include notification of purpose to a credit-broker.[14] Section 12, which dealt with exemption clauses, has itself been largely repealed and replaced by the Unfair Contract Terms Act 1977.[15]

In practice, the dealer will frequently sell the goods to the finance company, who will then let the goods out on hire-purchase. If the hire-purchase agreement is a regulated agreement the dealer will be a "credit-broker" or "negotiator" and section 56[16] will apply. In other words, any representations made by the dealer are treated as made as agent for the finance company as well as in his personal capacity. Thus, the debtor has two concurrent remedies; he can bring a claim against the finance company who are bound by the dealer's representations. He can also bring a claim against the dealer, either in negligence[17] or on the basis of a collateral contract.[18]

5. HIRE

The terms implied at common law have already been considered[19] and the law is not affected in any way by the Consumer Credit Act.

---

[14] See above.
[15] *Ante*, p. 113.
[16] *Ante*, p. 280.
[17] *Hedley Byrne & Co. Ltd.* v. *Heller and Partners Ltd. ante*, p. 32.
[18] *Andrews* v. *Hopkinson* [1957] 1 Q.B. 229.
[19] *Ante*, p. 55. See also Law Commission Report No. 95.

CHAPTER 22

"I HAVE LOST MY CREDIT CARD"

THE credit token, and especially the credit card, is of growing importance as a form of consumer credit and the 1974 Act brings them within the ambit of control.

The Act contains a number of provisions relating to "credit tokens" and "credit token agreements" and these provisions will be considered in this Chapter.

What is a credit token?

The term is defined in section 14(1) as a card, check, voucher, coupon, stamp, form, booklet or other document or thing given to an individual by a person carrying on a consumer credit business who undertakes

(a) that on production of it (whether or not some other action is also required) he will supply cash, goods and services (or any of them) on credit, or

(b) that where, on the production of it to a third party (whether or not any other action is also required), the third party supplies cash, goods and services (or any of them), he will pay the third party for them (whether or not deducting any discount or commission) in return for payment to him by the individual.

Thus the term clearly includes credit cards and trading checks used in a form of credit known as "check trading." It does *not* include a cheque card, because the bank issuing a cheque card merely promise to honour cheques. Nor does it cover trading stamps nor free gift vouchers (*e.g.* on the back of a cereal packet), because the customer will not receive goods *on credit.*

Unsolicited credit tokens

The mass-mailing of Access cards provoked widespread criticism and now section 51 makes it an offence to give a person a credit token if he has not asked for it. The request must be in writing and signed by the person making it, unless (a) the credit token agreement is a small debtor-creditor-supplier agreement or (b) the card is renewed.

What is a credit token agreement?

By section 14(2) (read with section 189) it is a regulated consumer credit agreement for the provision of credit in connection with the use of a credit token. Thus the term will not apply to an agreement (a) where the credit exceeds £5,000 nor (b) where the debtor is a body corporate nor (c) where the agreement is exempt. It will be recalled that agreements involving the use of Diner's Club or American Express cards are exempt agreements, because they are debtor-creditor-supplier agreements for running-account credit and the indebtedness over a period has to be discharged by a single payment.[1]

Modification of formalities

The formalities required for a regulated agreement were considered in Chapter 19. They are modified in two minor respects in the case of a credit token agreement. The first relates to the sending of the second copy; by section 63(4) it need not be given within seven days following the making of the agreement if it is given before or at the time when the credit token is given to the debtor. The second relates to the notice setting out cancellation rights; by section 64(2) it need not be posted within seven days following the making of the agreement if it is posted to the debtor before the credit token is given to him, or if it is sent by post with the credit token.

Additional copies

Where, under a credit token agreement, the creditor issues a new token to the debtor he must at the same time give the debtor a copy of the executed agreement (if any) and of any document referred to in it. Failure to do so has the usual consequences, *i.e.* the creditor cannot enforce the agreement while the default continues and, if it continues for one month, he commits an offence.[2] The section does not apply to a small agreement.[3]

Liability of debtor

We come now to the problem which is likely to be the most troublesome one in practice—the extent of the debtor's liability

---

[1] *Ante,* p. 248.
[2] s. 85.
[3] *Ibid.*

if the token is used by someone else without the debtor's authority. This matter is primarily governed by sections 66 and 84. By section 66 the debtor under a credit token agreement is not liable for use made of the token by another person unless (a) the debtor had previously accepted the token or (b) its use constituted an acceptance by him. The debtor accepts a credit token when he or a person authorised by him to use it under the terms of the agreement:

(a) signs it, or
(b) signs a receipt for it, or
(c) uses it.

If the token has been accepted under section 66 we can turn to section 84 to consider the debtor's liability for its misuse by someone else. The provisions of this section can be summarised as follows:

(a) The underlying principle is that the debtor should give notice of the loss or misuse as soon as possible. Accordingly, the credit token agreement must contain, in the prescribed manner, particulars of the name, address and telephone number of a person to whom notice of loss etc can be given. If the agreement does not contain this information the debtor will not be liable for misuse at all.[4]

(b) The debtor is not liable for any loss arising after the creditor has been given written or oral notice that the token has been lost or stolen or is otherwise liable to misuse.[5] The notice takes effect when received, but if it is given orally the agreement may provide that it is not effective unless confirmed in writing within seven days.[6]

(c) Subject to (a) and (b) above, the debtor's liability depends on the person by whom the token was misused. If it was misused by a person who acquired possession of the token with the debtor's consent he is liable *without limit*[7]. In other cases (*e.g.* loss or theft) his liability is limited to £30, or the credit limit if lower, for misuse in a period beginning when the token ceased to be in the possession of an authorised

[4] s. 84(4).
[5] s. 84(3).
[6] s. 84(5).
[7] s. 84(2).

person and ending when the token is once again in the possession of an authorised person.[8]

Thus the moral is clear: the onus is on the debtor to notify the loss to the creditor without delay.

Cancellation

If the debtor cancels a credit token agreement he can only recover a sum paid for the token, and he will only cease to be liable for such a sum, if the token has been returned to the creditor or surrendered to a supplier.[9]

---

[8] s. 84(1).
[9] s. 70(5).

CHAPTER 23

"I CAN'T AFFORD TO PAY"

IN practice there are two main areas where a debtor is likely to
seek legal advice. The first is where he is dissatisfied with the
goods. This has been considered in Part I of this book and in
Chapter 21. The second is where, for one reason or another, he
finds himself in difficulties with his payments. The legal adviser
can approach the problem by asking a number of preliminary
questions:

(1) Is there a contract at all?

If, for example, the document signed by the debtor was merely
an offer, revocation is possible before it has been accepted.[1]

(2) Is the contract voidable for misrepresentation?

If so, it can be rescinded, and money recovered, if it is not too
late.[2]

(3) Has the debtor a claim for breach of contract against the creditor?

If so, he may be able to treat the contract as repudiated, or he
may have a claim for damages which he can set against the
instalments.[3]

(4) Is the agreement cancellable?

If so, the debtor may be able to serve a notice of cancellation
under provisions which have already been discussed.[4]

(5) Was the agreement "improperly executed?"

We have seen that if the creditor fails to comply with the statutory
formalities as to pre-contract disclosure, contents, signature and
copies (and pre-contractual reflection in certain land mortgage

---

[1] See also s. 57, *ante,* p. 268.
[2] See *ante,* pp. 79 and 279.
[3] *Ante,* p. 82.
[4] *Ante,* p. 269.

cases) the agreement can only be enforced against the debtor or hirer on an order of the court[5] or with the consent of the debtor or hirer given at the time.[6]

One of the features of the legislation is the very wide power given to the court to rewrite the agreement or to postpone its enforcement. If the creditor or owner brings proceedings for an enforcement order the court must consider the degree of culpability for the defect and the prejudice (if any) which it has caused to any person.[7] The court can then do any of the following things:

(a) it may make an enforcement order;
(b) it may make a "time order" under section 129[8];
(c) it may modify the agreement as set out below and then make an enforcement order relating to the agreement as modified; or
(d) it may dismiss the application—but only if it considers it just to do so having regard to the matters mentioned above.[9] There are, however, three cases where an enforcement order *cannot* be made and these are considered below.

Power to modify agreement
Section 127(2) provides that:

> If it appears to the court just to do so, it may in an enforcement order reduce or discharge any sum payable by the debtor or hirer or any surety, so as to compensate him for prejudice suffered as a result of the contravention in question.

We must also consider sections 135 and 136 which are not confined to proceedings for an enforcement order but apply to any order made by the court in relation to a regulated agreement. By section 135(1) an order may include a provision:

(a) making the operation of any term of the order conditional on the doing of specified acts by any party to the proceedings;
(b) suspending the operation of any terms of the order until such time as the court subsequently directs or until the occurrence of a specified act or omission (*e.g.* default).

[5] s. 65.
[6] s. 173(3).
[7] s. 127(1).
[8] *Post*, p. 293.
[9] s. 127(1).

These very wide powers cannot be used to suspend an order requiring a person to deliver up goods unless the court is satisfied that they are in that person's possession or control.[10] In the case of a consumer hire agreement the section cannot be used to extend the period for which the hirer is entitled to possession.[11]

We must also mention certain special powers available to the court in the case of hire-purchase and conditional sale agreements. These are considered later.[12]

Finally, the court has a general power under section 136 to amend any agreement or security in consequence of a term of the order.

It is likely in practice that these wide powers will only be exercised if the court feels that the debtor or hirer has been prejudiced by the failure to comply with the formalities. If the breach is only a technical one (*e.g.* the second copy sent a few days late) the court is likely to waive the breach entirely.

Three special cases

There are however three cases where the court has *no* power to make an enforcement order at all. In these cases the fortunate debtor or hirer can retain possession and cannot be sued for any instalments or other payments. These three cases are dealt with in sections 127(3) and (4) and can be summarised as follows:

    (a) If the agreement was not signed as required by section 61(1)(*a*) no enforcement order can be made unless some other document, containing all the prescribed terms, was signed by the debtor or hirer (whether or not in the prescribed manner).

    (b) In a cancellation case the court cannot make an enforcement order if sections 62 or 63 (copy provisions) are not complied with, and if the creditor or owner did not give a copy of the executed agreement (and of any other document referred to in it) to the debtor or hirer before the commencement of the proceedings.

    (c) The court cannot make an enforcement order in a cancellation case if the provisions of section 64(1) were not complied with. It will be recalled that section 64(1) deals with

[10] s. 135(2).
[11] s. 135(3).
[12] *Post,* p. 297.

the duty to include cancellation information in the copies, and also in certain cases, requires a notice to be posted to the debtor or hirer within seven days of the making of the agreement.

In the case of contravention the debtor or hirer may sometimes have a double right—the agreement cannot be enforced against him and (if the defect relates to the second copy or notice) it may well be that the right of cancellation remains open.

There is one final question—what happens if the creditor or owner purports to terminate the agreement and repossesses the goods? If it involves entry on premises without the consent of the debtor or hirer there may be liability for breach of statutory duty.[12a] Apart from this there may be very little that the debtor or hirer can do about it, because of the "no sanctions" rule in section 170.[12b] The section does not however prevent the grant of an injunction[13] and it is just possible that a mandatory injunction could require the goods to be returned to the debtor or hirer. Apart from this, the only sanction is the ever-present administrative sanction of reporting the matter to the Director General of Fair Trading.

(6) Can the debtor terminate the agreement?

This has already been considered.[14]

(7) Can the debtor pay off early and obtain a rebate?

The debtor may be able to find another source of credit which is less expensive to him. In the case of hire-purchase the debtor may be better advised to settle early, become the owner of the goods and re-sell them. Section 94 gives him a non-excludable right to complete the agreement ahead of time on service of a notice on the creditor and on payment of all sums due, less any statutory rebate of the charge for credit. The regulations setting out the calculation of the rebate have not yet been made.

In calculating the total charge for credit the critical factor is the time during which the creditor will be kept out of his money. Accordingly, it is clearly reasonable to allow for a rebate where the debtor pays off early, because the creditor will be able to earn

---

[12a] s. 92(3) *post*, p. 295.
[12b] *Ante*, p. 263.
[13] s. 170(3).
[14] *Ante*, p. 276.

fresh interest on the repaid amount. Section 95 enables regulations to be made for the calculation of this rebate, which will apply in any case of early settlement—whether by reason of re-financing, breach or for any other reason. How then is the rebate to be calculated? It is likely that the regulations will reflect two principles:

    (a) the total charge for credit should be spread actuarially over the repayment period and the debtor should get a rebate corresponding to the proportion of the total charge for credit which would have accrued after the settlement date;

    (b) a completely even spread would be unfair to the creditor because certain expenses are incurred right at the beginning of the transaction. Accordingly, the settlement date will be notionally deferred for a few months so that these expenses can be reflected in the reduced rebate.

If a debtor is contemplating making an early settlement he can ask the creditor, in writing, to give him a statement containing the settlement figure.[15] If the creditor fails to comply the usual consequences will follow.[16]

(8) If the debtor or hirer is unable to withdraw, rescind, cancel, terminate or settle early, and if all the formalities have been complied with, the next possibility is to apply for a "time order"

Apart from section 127[17] the debtor or hirer can apply for a time order (a) after he has been served with a notice of default or (b) where the owner or hirer brings proceedings to enforce a regulated agreement or any security or to recover possession of any goods or land to which a regulated agreement relates.[17a]

Notice of default

The agreement may provide that, on default by the debtor or hirer, the creditor or owner shall become entitled to take certain action, *e.g.* to terminate the agreement, or to demand early payment of any sum, or to recover possession of any goods or land, or to enforce any security, or to treat any right conferred on the debtor or hirer (*e.g.* an option to purchase in the case of a hire-purchase agreement) as terminated, restricted or deferred. The effect of section 87 is that such a provision will not be enforceable

[15] s. 97.
[16] See *ante*, p. 267.
[17] *Ante*, p. 290.
[17a] s. 129.

unless the creditor or owner first serves on the debtor or hirer a
notice of default in the prescribed form. The notice must contain
the following information:

(i) it must specify the breach;

(ii) if the breach is capable of remedy (*e.g.* default in payment)
the notice must indicate what action has to be taken to
remedy it and the date before which it must be done;

(iii) if the breach is incapable of remedy (*e.g.* causing permanent
damage to the goods) what compensation (if any) is required
and the date before which it is to be paid; and

(iv) the consequences of non-compliance.

The date in (b) and (c) above must be not earlier than seven days
after the service of the notice of default. Presumably, if the notice
is posted on February 1 it can specify February 8 as the date before
which the act must be done.

Effect of notice

If, before the specified date the debtor or hirer takes the steps,
specified in the notice, the default is treated as never having taken
place.[18] Alternatively, as already stated, the debtor or hirer can
apply under section 129 for a "time order." Such an order may
contain either or both of the following provisions:

(a) a provision that any sum owed by the debtor or hirer or any
surety shall be payable at such times as the court, having
regard to the means of the debtor or hirer and any surety,
considers reasonable;

(b) a provision that a breach by the debtor or hirer (other than
the non-payment of money) shall be remedied within such
period as the court may specify.

Effect of repossession

The Act does not specify what remedies are available if the
creditor or owner repossesses the goods or land without a default
notice. The section provides that the creditor or owner is not
entitled to repossess etc. without serving a notice of default. It may
well be, therefore, that non-compliance could be actionable as
trespass to goods or conversion or there might be a breach of the
implied warranty for quiet possession. There may also be liability

---

[18] s. 89.

for breach of statutory duty if there is unauthorized entry on premises[18a] and the "snatch-back" of protected goods[18b] will lead to the severe sanctions set out in section 91[18c].

(9) Additional protection in hire-purchase and conditional sale cases

The notice of default provisions are backed up by four other provisions aimed at what is known as "snatch-back"—the repossession of goods or land without an order of the court.

(a) In the case of a regulated hire-purchase or conditional sale agreement the creditor or owner cannot enter any premises to repossess the goods without an order of the court.[19] Clearly, a contractual provision conferring such a right would be void[20] but a consent at the time of entry would be effective.[21]

(b) If the debtor is in breach under a conditional sale agreement relating to land the creditor cannot recover possession of the land from the debtor, nor from any person claiming under him, without an order of the court.[22] The point relating to the debtor's consent will be equally relevant here.

In both (a) and (b) above section 92(3) does provide a sanction—any entry in contravention of either of these provisions is actionable as a breach of statutory duty.

(c) *Protected goods*

In the case of hire-purchase and conditional sale it is clearly inequitable that the debtor, having paid a substantial part of the price, should have the goods snatched away (with no credit for his payments) merely because he gets into arrears. Accordingly, section 90 gives him protection if (a) he is in breach and (b) he has not terminated the agreement and (c) he has paid or tendered to the creditor one-third or more of the total price and (d) the property in the goods remains in the creditor. In such a case the goods are called "protected goods." The creditor cannot recover

[18a] *Infra.*
[18b] *Infra.*
[18c] *Post,* p. 296.
[19] s. 92(1).
[20] s. 173(1).
[21] s. 173(3).
[22] s. 92(2).

L

possession of the goods from the debtor without an order of the court. These provisions are modelled upon the provisions in the Hire-Purchase Act 1965 and both Acts impose serious sanctions for contravention. By section 91 if goods are recovered by the creditor in contravention of section 90 the agreement, if not already terminated, will terminate, the debtor is released from all further liability and he can recover from the creditor all sums paid by him under the agreement. A number of points arise under this very important provision:

(i) Where the agreement requires the creditor to carry out any installation work, and if the cost of this work forms part of the total price, then the fraction of one-third is calculated by taking the installation charge in full and adding one-third of the balance.[23] Thus, if the price of £300 includes an installation charge of £30 the fraction of ⅓ will be:

$$£30 + \frac{270}{3} = £120$$

(ii) A dealer might be tempted to avoid the "protected goods" provisions in one of two ways. First of all there might be an agreement for a television set with a price of £150, of which £60 has been paid. If the customer then comes in for a £300 music centre the dealer might say "let us cancel the original agreement and make a new one for both items (£450) with a credit for sums already paid (£60)." Secondly, if the original agreement (with payments exceeding one-third) related to a tape recorder and a camera, he might suggest the the tape recorder should be treated as fully paid up and that a new agreement should be made relating solely to the camera. In either case the debtor starts inside section 90 and ends up outside it—because he has not paid one-third under the new agreement. To prevent such avoidance the effect of section 90(3) is to bring the new agreement within the section, even though one-third has not been paid.

(iii) Repossession of the goods from the debtor without a court order kills the agreement. Thus, on the one hand, the debtor cannot claim the return of the goods[24] while on the other hand the

[23] s. 90(2). Similar to s. 100(2), *ante*, p. 277.
[24] *Carr* v. *Broderick & Co. Ltd.* [1942] 2 K.B. 275.

creditor cannot breathe any fresh life into the agreement by returning the goods to the debtor.[25]

(iv) Section 90 only prohibits recovery of possession "from
the debtor." Thus, if the creditor seizes the goods which the debtor
has abandoned the section is not infringed.[26] A similar principle
would apply where the creditor seizes the goods from a third party
to whom the debtor has purported to sell them.[27]

(v) A consent by the debtor given at the time is as effective
as an order of the court[28] but the court is likely to examine the
facts closely to make sure that there was a true and free consent.[28a]

(d) *Additional powers of the court*

In any proceedings for an enforcement order, or for a time
order, or in proceedings by the creditor to recover possession, the
court may (in addition to its other powers) make (i) a return order
or (ii) a transfer order.[29] A return order, as the name implies,
requires the debtor to return the goods to the creditor. A transfer
order is, in effect, a "split" order, in that it orders the debtor to
return *some* of the goods to the creditor and it vests in the debtor
the creditor's title in the remainder. This is subject to a ceiling set
out in section 133(3) viz. that the maximum transferable to the
debtor is found by deducting from the sum paid one-third of the
unpaid balance. Thus, if the debtor had paid £80 out of a total
price of £200, the court can vest in the debtor goods to the value
of:

$$£80 - \left[\frac{200 - 80}{3}\right] = £40$$

In practice, the court frequently makes a return order and then
exercises its powers under section 135 to suspend the operation of
the order on condition that the debtor pays the balance by instalments fixed by the court.

[25] *Capital Finance Co. Ltd.* v. *Bray* [1964] 1 W.L.R. 323.
[26] *Bentinck Ltd.* v. *Cromwell Engineering Co. Ltd.* [1971] 1 Q.B. 324.
[27] Consider *Eastern Distributors* v. *Goldring* [1957] 2 Q.B. 600.
[28] s. 173(3).
[28a] The matter could be raised if the debtor took proceedings alleging a breach of
section 90 and denying his consent to the repossession.
[29] s. 133.

L*

(10) **Additional protection in consumer hire cases**

A number of provisions which are relevant to consumer hire have already been considered earlier in this Chapter. They include section 65 (improperly executed agreements), section 87 (notice of default), section 92 (no entry on premises without court order) and section 129 (time orders). In addition section 132 provides that where the owner recovers possession otherwise than by action the hirer may apply to the court for an order (a) extinguishing any further liability to make payments in whole or in part or (b) requiring the owner to repay sums paid by the hirer in whole or in part. The court can also include such a provision when it makes an order for delivery to the owner. Such a power could be exercised where, for example, the hirer has paid a year's rental in advance and then finds it necessary to terminate the hiring after only a few weeks.

It will be recalled that the general power to make a "suspended" order under section 135 cannot extend the period for which the hirer is entitled to possession.[30]

(11) **Appropriation of payments**

A debtor or hirer may have two or more separate regulated agreements with the same creditor or owner. If he finds himself unable to pay a sum to cover all the sums due, he can send in a smaller amount and section 81 allows him, on making the payment, to appropriate it to one or more of the agreements in such proportions as he thinks fit. If he fails to appropriate at the time of payment then section 81(2) may come into play. It provides that where one or more of the agreements is a hire-purchase, conditional sale, consumer hire or secured agreement, the payment shall be appropriated in the proportion which the sums *due* bear to each other.

Example

£20 is due under a hire-purchase agreement relating to a dishwasher and £10 is due under a hire agreement relating to a television set. The debtor/hirer sends in a cheque for £12. If he fails to appropriate at the time of payment £8 will go towards the dishwasher and £4 towards the television set.

[30] *Ante,* p. 290.

Finally, if the debtor fails to appropriate in a case to which section 81(2) does *not* apply (*e.g.* if he has two debtor-creditor agreements with the same creditor) the general law will apply and the creditor will have the right of appropriation.

EXTORTIONATE CREDIT BARGAINS

The final weapon available to a debtor who finds himself unable to pay is to claim that the agreement is extortionate. The law is to be found in sections 137–140 of the Act.

Scope

These provisions are wider than most of the rest of the Act because they apply to a "credit bargain." This is defined as (a) an agreement whereby a creditor provides an individual (the debtor) with credit of *any amount,* plus (b) any other transactions which must be taken into account in computing the total charge for credit (*e.g.* a linked transaction). Thus these provisions will apply even though the limit exceeds £5,000 and even though the agreement is an "exempt agreement." The only feature common to the whole Act is that the debtor must not be a body corporate.

Is it retrospective?

The powers are exercisable as regards all agreements "whenever made."[31] Clearly these words are wide enough to cover agreements made before the commencement date viz. May 16, 1977. They are even wide enough to cover agreements which have been completed by payment, but the court may be reluctant to reopen, such agreements after long delay.

What bargains are extortionate?

Section 138 provides that a bargain is extortionate if it requires the debtor or a relative of his to make payments which are grossly exorbitant or otherwise grossly contravenes ordinary principles of fair dealing. The section then sets out a non-exhaustive list of relevant factors which include:

---

[31] Schedule 3, para. 42.

(a) prevailing interest rates at the time when the bargain was made;

(b) factors affecting the debtor such as age, health, business capacity and the extent to which he was under financial pressure;

(c) factors affecting the creditor, such as his relationship with the debtor and the degree of risk undertaken by him;

(d) the extent to which a linked transaction was reasonably required for the protection of the debtor or the creditor.

How and when can the matter be raised?

The debtor or a surety can take proceedings to have the bargain re-opened;[32] in the case of a regulated agreement such proceedings must be brought in the county court.[33] Alternatively, the debtor or surety can raise the matter (a) in any proceedings to which the debtor and creditor are parties, being proceedings to enforce the agreement or any security or any linked transaction, or (b) in other proceedings where the amount paid or payable under the credit agreement is relevant. This could include bankruptcy proceedings, or proceedings where the debtor's wife brings a claim for financial provision, or where the registrar investigates the means of the debtor as a preliminary to the enforcement of a judgment against him. Section 171(7) provides that if the debtor or surety alleges that the bargain is extortionate the onus is on the creditor to prove that it is not. It is likely, however, that the court will require some evidence from the debtor or surety before putting the creditor to proof.

Powers of the court

The court has wide powers to (a) direct accounts to be taken (b) set aside obligations imposed on the debtor or a surety (c) order sums to be repaid to the debtor or a surety (d) order property given as security to be returned and (e) re-write the terms of the agreement of any security instrument.[34]

[32] s. 139(1).
[33] s. 139(5).
[34] s. 139(2).

Conclusion

A great deal will depend on how the courts will exercise these sweeping new powers and how they will interpret the factors listed in section 138. What about the debtor who is old, ill, inexperienced and under great financial pressure from many sources? On the one hand the creditor must not take an unfair advantage of such a person, and if he does so the courts may well treat the bargain as extortionate. On the other hand, the risk undertaken by the creditor in this type of case is unusually high and may well justify an interest rate which reflects this added risk.

CHAPTER 24

THE EEC DIMENSION

ON January 1, 1973 the United Kingdom became a member of the European Economic Community and any book on consumer law would be incomplete without some mention of the very considerable activity of the EEC Commission in the consumer protection field in the past few years. The matters discussed in the next few pages do not, at present, give new rights and remedies to the consumer but they indicate how things might develop in the years ahead.

The Treaty of Rome

To set the scene let us consider four Articles of the Treaty of Rome which set up the EEC in 1957.

Article 2, which corresponds to the "main objects" clause of a company memorandum, provides that:

> The Community shall have as its task, by establishing a common market . . . to promote throughout the Community harmonious development of economic activities, a continuous and balanced expansion, an increase in stability, an accelerated raising of the standard of living and close relations between the States belonging to it.

This then is the central aim—the treatment of the Member States as one single market, with an unrestricted flow of goods and a system to ensure that competition is not distorted. Article 3(*h*) specifies as one of the activities of the Community:

> the approximation of the laws of Member States to the extent required for the proper functioning of the common market.

Article 3(*h*) leads us on directly to Article 100 on which the recent flurry of activity has been based. It reads:

> The Council shall, acting unanimously on a proposal from the Commission, issue directives for the approximation of such provisions laid down by law, regulation or administrative

action in Member States as directly affect the establishment or functioning of the common market.

The Assembly and the Economic and Social Committee shall be consulted in the case of directives whose implementation would, in one or more Member States, involve the amendment of legislation.

The twenty-second Report of the House of Lords Select Committee on the EEC has criticised the Commission for giving a very wide interpretation to its powers under Article 100. The Law Reform Committee of the Council of The Law Society have made a similar criticism. They make the valid point that a new Act may throw up unforeseen difficulties, so that an amendment is urgently required; if the amendment has to be dealt with at Community level the task of getting "running repairs" quickly is made vastly more difficult.

The final Article to consider here is Article 189 which provides that:

A directive shall be binding, as to the result to be achieved, upon each Member State to which it is addressed, but shall leave to the national authorities the choice of form and methods.

The 1975 programme

In April 1975 the Commission drew up an ambitious programme of measures for consumer protection and information. This programme has no binding force but it gives an indication of the Commission's thinking. No doubt the preparation of the programme was partly inspired by the desire to improve the image of the EEC amongst its 260 million consumers. Under this programme it has submitted draft directives to the Council on a number of important topics. These draft directives are then discussed by the Ministers of the Member States who make up the Council of Ministers and who may eventually decide by unanimous vote to adopt the directive. It is therefore vitally important for English lawyers to study the draft directives at the formative stage, decide how far they are appropriate to trading conditions in this country, and make representations to the UK representatives. A further draft programme was published in June 1979.

Four draft directives

In the remainder of this chapter it is proposed to consider briefly the draft directives relating to:
(a) advertising
(b) doorstep contracts
(c) consumer credit
(d) product liability

(a) *Advertising*

In February 1978 the Commission presented to the Council a Draft Directive on misleading and unfair advertising. The question of whether the laws on this topic need to be approximated is certainly open to debate, but the preamble to the draft directive expresses the Commission's view that:

> the laws against misleading and unfair advertising now in force in the Member States differ widely; whereas since advertising reaches to a large extent beyond the frontiers of individual Member States, it has a direct effect on the establishment and the functioning of the common market.

The Commission's proposals. The draft directive (as amended) is concerned with misleading and unfair advertising.

(a) The term "advertisement" is widely defined as "the making of a representation in any form in the course of a trade, business or profession for the purpose of promoting the supply of goods or services." Rather surprisingly the term "goods" includes immoveable property.[1]

(b) An advertisement is *misleading* if it is entirely or partially false or if it is presented in a manner which is likely to mislead.[2] This is broadly similar to the position in English law under the Trade Descriptions Act 1968.

(c) The concept of an *unfair* advertisement is an unfamiliar concept in English law and it is questionable how far some of the matters are suitable for legal regulation. Among the matters listed in Article 2 are advertisements which
(i) abuses or unjustifiably arouses sentiments of fear or promotes discrimination on grounds of sex, race or religion

[1] See Art 2.
[2] Arts 2 and 3.

(ii) casts discredit on another person by reference to his nationality, origin, private life or good name; or

(iii) abuses the trust, credulity or lack of experience of a consumer . . . or is likely to influence a consumer or the public in general in any other improper manner.

The substance of the draft directive is to be found in Article 5. This starts by requiring Member States to adopt adequate and effective laws against misleading and unfair advertising. This is followed by a requirement that such laws must provide persons affected by misleading or unfair advertising, as well as "associations with a legitimate interest in the matter," with quick, effective and inexpensive facilities for initiating appropriate legal proceedings or bringing the matter before an administrative authority with adequate powers.[2a] A proposal that a person affected by the offending advertisement should be able to obtain an immediate injunction to ban further publication was rejected by the House of Commons in December 1978. The reference to "associations with a legitimate interest" could open the way to a form of "class action"—a concept familiar in the United States but unknown in the United Kingdom. It can be strongly argued that such fundamental procedural changes should not be introduced as a sidewind to an advertising directive.

It is clear that much work remains to be done.

(b) Doorstep contracts

Introduction It will be recalled that under a consumer credit agreement the debtor will have a right of cancellation if (a) oral representations were made in his presence and (b) he signed the agreement at a place other than business premises—(as defined).[3] Under English law there is no corresponding right of cancellation in the case of a cash transaction—even though the need for a cooling-off period may well be equally strong. In January 1977 the EEC produced a draft directive "to protect the consumer in respect of contracts which have been negotiated away from business premises."

Scope of draft directive. The approach adopted in the Draft Directive is surprising; it applies to contracts—cash or credit—

[2a] The Advertising Standards Authority would appear to be the appropriate authority.

[3] See *ante,* p. 238.

where "negotiations have been initiated [by the trader] away from business premises." This is in marked contrast to the Consumer Credit Act 1974 and, indeed, to the draft directive on consumer credit[4] where the critical factor is the place where the debtor signed. Thus

(i) negotiations begin in the shop, but the customer signs at home. The draft directive does not apply.

(ii) the customer is rung up at home and signs at the shop. It seems that the draft directive does apply.

The draft directive does *not* cover *(inter alia)* contracts which have been negotiated solely in writing and contracts relating to immoveable property or any rights thereto. There is a further exclusion for small transactions

Proposals of the Commission. The broad outline of the proposals are similar to those in Part V of the Consumer Credit Act 1974.

Thus:

(i) the contract must be in writing;

(ii) the customer must sign personally;

(iii) the contract must contain specified information;

(iv) a copy must be given or sent to the customer as soon as he has signed the agreement;

(v) the customer must have a seven-day cancellation period.

Criticism. This draft directive differs in several respects from the consumer credit directive which is mentioned below. It would clearly be most unsatisfactory to have two directives with conflicting rules both applying to credit transactions. Accordingly the doorstep directive will not apply to any agreement covered by the consumer credit directive.

(c) *Consumer credit*

This draft directive, submitted by the Commission to the Council, deals in very general terms with a number of matters which are already dealt with, for the most part, in the Consumer Credit Act 1974. Article 18 allows Member States to "introduce or retain more stringent provisions to protect consumers." The term "consumer" is defined as "a natural person not acting predominantly in a commercial or professional capacity." This definition is narrower than the definition in the Consumer Credit Act, which, as

---

[4] *Post,* p. 307.

already stated,[5] protects the business debtor just as much as the private debtor.

Apart from the definition of "consumer" there are a number of other differences and these include the following:

(i) Under the draft directive the list of excluded transactions is wider. Thus, for example, all transactions secured on land are excluded.

(ii) Leasing agreements (*i.e.* contracts of hire) are excluded.

(iii) Section 48 of the Consumer Credit Act prohibits the canvassing of debtor-creditor agreements "off trade premises." In contrast, Article 4 of the draft directive seems to impose a total ban on the unsolicited canvassing of loans.

(iv) A credit agreement which is not in writing is to be "invalid."[6] Under the Consumer Credit Act it is merely unenforceable by the creditor or owner.

(v) Under Article 5 of the draft directive the creditor must display his charges at his business premises. This is one of those areas where continental and United Kingdom practice differ widely. On the continent it is common for a lender to have a fixed rate of charge, whereas in the United Kingdom the lenders operate a very large number of different charges having regard to such matters as the status of the debtor and whether or not security is provided.

(vi) A right of cancellation is available under Article 9 "where a consumer enters into a credit agreement away from the business premises of the supplier or creditor, or a person acting on their behalf." There is no need to show that oral representations were made in the presence of the debtor.

Conclusion. It is unlikely that this directive, if adopted by the Council, will lead to radical alterations to English law. The provisions of Article 18 which have already been mentioned[7] and Article 2 (which allows different Member States to adopt different financial limits for agreements regulated by the directive) suggest that many differences will remain. It seems, therefore, that the Commission is taking a broad view of its powers and responsibilities and is working towards a certain level of consumer protection

[5] *Ante,* p. 238.
[6] Art. 7.
[7] *Ante,* p. 306.

M

throughout the Community without aiming for complete harmonisation.

(d) *Product liability*

We saw in Chapter 6 that the subject of product liability was an international one which was under consideration by no less than four bodies—the Law Commission, The Royal Commission chaired by Lord Pearson, the Council of Europe and the EEC. The Pearson Commission reported last and they were undoubtedly influenced by the fact that both of the European bodies had proposed a system of strict liability.

In the following summary of EEC proposals we shall indicate the points at which they diverge from those of the Law Commission.

(1) The producer of a product is to be strictly liable for damage caused by a defect in the article.

(2) The term "producer" includes (a) the producer of the finished article (b) the producer of any material or component (c) the person who represents himself as the producer (*e.g.* a supermarket putting its brand mark on to an article) and (d) any person who imports an article into the United Kingdom. The Law Commission would clearly (and reasonably) confine liability to articles produced in the course of a business, whereas the EEC draft directive does not spell this out.

(3) The producer shall not be liable if he proves that the article was not defective when he put it into circulation.

(4) The principles of strict liability shall apply to (a) pecuniary loss resulting from death or personal injury and (b) damage to property in certain cases. The Law Commission proposals disagree on these points. On the one hand, they propose that damages for death or personal injury should include non-material loss (*e.g.* for pain and suffering). On the other hand, they are equally emphatic that strict liability should not apply to damage to property—partly because the consumer may well have some form of property insurance.

(5) The producer's liability is to be limited (a) as regards individual claims to 15,000 European Accounts Units, (or 50,000 EAUs for immoveables) and (b) globally to 25 million EAUs. The Law Commission dissent strongly from both of these proposals. The practical problems posed by the global limit would clearly be enormous.

(6) There is to be a basic limitation period of three years, but the producer's liability shall finally cease ten years after he first put the product into circulation.

(7) Injury caused by nuclear accidents are excluded.

(8) Liability under the draft directive cannot be excluded or restricted (under the Unfair Contract Terms Act 1977 it is still possible to exclude or restrict tort liability, insofar as such liability goes beyond negligence).

Conclusion

The subject of product liability is a sensitive and controversial one and the debate is still raging. It is an area where the potential scope of liability is enormous and where complete insurance cover is often unobtainable. Producers of natural products, chemicals and pharmaceuticals may well feel that they should be given special treatment. Strict liability could inhibit the development of new products (with their inevitable risks) and could therefore work against the public interest. Nevertheless, no less than four major inquiries (two in the United Kingdom and two in Europe) have come down in favour of strict liability. Like so many other legal problems it is all a question of balance and the prevailing view is that if a product causes injury the loss should fall on the producer rather than the consumer. It seems likely, therefore, that the principle of strict liability will be incorporated into English law within the next few years.

Postscript

Negotiations are still in progress but it now seems likely that the régime of strict liability proposed by the Commission, will after all, include damages for pain and suffering.

APPENDIX 1

FOUR SELECTED CODES OF PRACTICE

(A) CODE OF PRACTICE FOR THE MOTOR INDUSTRY*

Introduction

This Code of Practice has been drawn up by the Society of Motor Manufacturers and Traders (SMMT), the Motor Agents Association (MAA), and the Scottish Motor Trade Association (SMTA) in consultation with the Director General of Fair Trading, to govern the conduct of manufacturers and retailers in relation to the supply of new and used cars, petrol, parts and accessories† and car servicing and repair, and embodies principles which have been observed by the majority of the industry for many years. It will, moreover, be brought up to date from time to time as the occasion demands.

The principles set out are not intended to interpret, qualify or supplement the law of the land, and are not intended to be applied to non-consumer sales.

The associations concerned regard it as a duty laid on their members that they will accept the Code in its entirety. A consumer who feels dissatisfied with the treatment he has received from a member will be able to submit his grievance to the conciliation and advisory service operated by the relevant association.

It should not be overlooked that the consumer also has his part to play. It is only by co-operating fully with those who make, sell and service cars that the consumer can get the maximum benefit from his purchase. In particular, by maintaining his car in accord-

---

* Published with the permission of: The Motor Agents Association, in association with the Society of Motor Manufacturers and Traders and the Scottish Motor Trade Association.
† A separate Code of Practice in relation to car tyres is being prepared by the British Rubber Manufacturers Association in consultation with the Director General of Fair Trading.

ance with the manufacturer's instructions and giving as much information as possible to anyone servicing it, he can ensure he gets the best possible use out of his car, and his troubles reduced to a minimum.

Throughout the Code:

The term MANUFACTURER	is taken to include concessionaire or importer.
The term DEALER	is taken to include retail dealer or distributor or supplier of goods or services.

1 New Car Sales

1.1 Manufacturers relying on dealers to carry out a standard Pre-Delivery Inspection shall provide dealers with a standard check list for the particular model of car, and a copy of this PDI check list should be made available to the consumer.

1.2 The dealer should ensure that the car is delivered in a clean condition and that any PDI check required by the manufacturer has been properly carried out. Each car must conform fully to all legislation affecting its construction, use and maintenance. This paragraph does not affect any legal responsibilities which may be placed on manufacturers and users to ensure this.

1.3 The benefit and limitations of any treatment over and above that already provided by the manufacturer which is recommended by the dealer in order to inhibit the growth of rust or other corrosion should be explained to the consumer.

1.4 Order forms are intended to help both parties to the contract by spelling out the terms and conditions on which business is being done. Such terms and conditions must be fair and reasonable and set out clearly, together with a statement of the circumstances under which the order can be cancelled.

1.5 All documents must be clearly legible.

1.6 Order forms must contain details of all charges additional to the car price so that the consumer may understand clearly the total price he has to pay to put the car on the road.

1.7 Manufacturers and dealers should ensure that the manufacturer's handbook relating to the model of car being sold is available to the consumer at the time of sale of the car and for a reasonable length of time thereafter.

1.8 The terms of the manufacturers' warranties should be drawn to the attention of the consumer, and any relevant document published by the manufacturer must be handed over to him.

2 Car Manufacturers' Warranties
(or Guarantees hereafter called Warranties)

2.1 A manufacturer's warranty is a simple and straightforward way for the consumer to have faults of manufacture appearing within certain times (or before the car has done a certain mileage) put right at little or no cost to the consumer without the necessity of his pursuing legal rights against the seller.

2.2 The warranty must not adversely affect the consumer's remedies against the seller under the Sale of Goods Acts and must include a statement making this clear to the consumer.

2.3 The warranty must include a statement advising the consumer that it is in addition to any other remedies he may have under the contract of sale.

2.4 The warranty will not extend to cover defects arising from a failure by the consumer to have the car serviced in accordance with the manufacturer's recommendations.

2.5 The terms of the warranty must be easily understandable particularly in relation to any items specifically included in or excluded from its provisions. Manufacturers and dealers should also give advice to consumers as to who is responsible and what to do if they have a problem regarding parts and accessories not covered by the manufacturer's warranty.

2.6 The manufacturer should permit the transfer of the unexpired portion of any warranty to a second or subsequent owner.

2.7 The manufacturer should make clear that rectification work may be done under warranty by one of his franchised dealers who was not the selling dealer.

2.8 Manufacturers will operate fair and equitable policies to permit the extension of warranty in the event of a car being off the road for an extended period for rectification of warranty faults, or of the repetition outside warranty of a fault which had previously been the subject of rectification work during the warranty period.

2.9 There is no automatic right to a loan car or contribution towards hiring charges in circumstances where a consumer's own car is off the road for repair under warranty. Whether there is any such right will depend on the normal legal rules relating to damages.

2.10 Manufacturers must give clear advice to their dealers as to the circumstances in which a loan car or contribution towards hiring charges should be provided. Such guidance should take full account of the legal position and should be made available to consumers on request.

2.11 Where a loan car is made available, this will merely be as reasonable alternative transport rather than an exact replacement for the car which is off the road.

3 Used Car Sales

3.1 Used cars sold to consumers must conform to legislation affecting the construction and use of cars and should, where appropriate, be accompanied by a current Department of the Environment Test Certificate.

3.2 Dealers must bear in mind that sales of used cars are subject to the Sale of Goods Act 1893 and the Supply of Goods (Implied Terms) Act 1973, and attention is specifically drawn to the conditions of merchantable quality and fitness for purpose contained in these Acts.

3.3 If a dealer sells a used car subject to a printed guarantee or warranty, that guarantee or warranty should not purport to take away or diminish any rights which the consumer would otherwise enjoy in law. The warranty document should also include a statement advising the consumer that the warranty is in addition to his statutory or common law rights.

3.4 If a printed guarantee or warranty is not used, then any specific promises which the dealer is willing to make in relation to the used car should be set out in writing.

3.5 Used cars should be subject to a pre-sales inspection in accordance with a predetermined schedule, a copy of which should be available to the consumer.

3.6 All descriptions, whether used in advertisements or in negotiations regarding the sale of used cars should be honest and truthful. Terms which are likely to be misunderstood by the consumer and which are not capable of exact definition should be avoided.

3.7   Copies of relevant written information provided by previous own-ers regarding the history of cars should be passed on to the con-sumer. This may include service records, repair invoices, inspection reports, handbooks and copy of warranty, as applicable.

3.8   Reasonable steps should be taken to verify the recorded mileage of a used car.

3.9   Unless the seller is satisfied that the quoted mileage of a used car is accurate, such mileage should not be quoted in advertisements, discussions or negotiations or in any documents related to the supply of the used car.

3.10 Dealers should pass on any known facts about a previous odometer reading to a prospective customer, and if a disclaimer is used it should be in the following form:
      "WE DO NOT GUARANTEE THE ACCURACY OF THE RECORDED MILEAGE. TO THE BEST OF OUR KNOWL-EDGE AND BELIEF, HOWEVER, THE READING IS CORRECT/INCORRECT."

3.11 Under the Sale of Goods Acts, if the buyer examines the goods before the contract is made there is no condition of merchantable quality as regards defects which that examination ought to reveal. Dealers should therefore provide all reasonable facilities to enable prospective customers or their nominees to carry out an exami-nation of the car prior to sale, in order that any defects which ought to be revealed at the time of sale are made known to both parties.

4 Replacement Parts, Accessories and Petrol

4.1   Dealers must bear in mind that in sales of goods to consumers they are responsible under the Sale of Goods Acts that the goods shall be of merchantable quality and fit for the purpose for which they are required. Statements in apparent conflict with this prin-ciple must be avoided.

4.2   Whenever goods are offered for sale a clear indication of cash price must be available to the consumer.

4.3   Terms must not be used in advertisements if they are likely to be misunderstood by the consumer or if they are not capable of exact definition.

4.4   With offers of promotions or trading stamps, any restrictions which are attached to sales other than cash sales must be clearly stated.

4.5   A dealer must not display any notices or make any statement which might mislead a consumer about his legal rights in relation to the purchase of faulty goods.

4.6   Discounts offered will be based on fair comparisons. Such discounts should be based either on the dealer's own previous price or manufacturers' recommended prices. Misleading price offers relating for example to "worth", "value", "up to £x off" should not be used.

5 Repairs and Servicing
(excluding work carried out under a manufacturer's warranty)

5.1   Manufacturers accept a responsibility for ensuring the reasonable availability of spare parts throughout the distribution chain.

5.2   Spare parts should be readily available from the time that a new car is offered for sale. Manufacturers should indicate the minimum period for which functional and non-functional parts will remain available after production of a specific model has ceased.

5.3   Wherever possible a firm quotation for the cost of major repairs should be offered. However, where this is not possible, it should be made clear to the consumer that an estimate is being made. An estimate or quotation must indicate whether it is inclusive of VAT and, where applicable, the rate at which it is chargeable. If required, estimates will be in writing. Any dismantling costs which are necessary to arrive at such estimates should be notified to the consumer in advance on the clear understanding whether or not dismantling costs are to be charged on an estimate which is refused. If, during the progress of any work, it appears that the estimate will be exceeded by a significant amount, then the consumer should be notified and asked for permission to continue with the work. Provision of a quotation should be treated with care, and it should be realised by both parties that the acceptance of a quotation constitutes the basis of a contract.

5.4   Parts replaced during service or repair will be made available for a reasonable period for return to the consumer unless a warranty claim is involved or unless the parts have to be submitted to the supplier because replacement parts are being supplied on an exchange basis. Dealers are advised to identify by means of notices the periods for which they are prepared to keep displaced parts available to consumers.

5.5 Invoices should be clearly written or typed and give full details of the work carried out and material used. The amount and rate of VAT should be clearly indicated. Dates and recorded mileages should always be noted where applicable.

5.6 Dealers should exercise adequate care in protecting consumer's cars and possessions while they are in their custody, and should not seek by disclaimers to avoid their legal liability for damage or loss. Dealers should carry adequate insurance to cover such legal liability.

5.7 Repairs must be guaranteed against failure due to workmanship for a specific mileage or time period. Dealers are advised to ensure that they are adequately insured against consequential loss claims arising from any such failure.

5.8 A dealer's rules as to the method of payment he will require on completion of the work should always be notified to the consumer before the work is accepted.

5.9 When it is necessary to sub-contractors work, the dealer will agree to be responsible for the quality of the subcontractors' work. Any estimate given to the consumer must include the sub-contracted work and in the event of any increase in charge for the work, the principles in para 5.3 must apply.

5.10 While a dealer's contractual responsibility is limited to the exact terms of the consumer's instructions or, for standard services, the schedule prepared by the manufacturer or other body or person, he should make it a general rule to advise the consumer of any defects which may become apparent while the work is being carried out.

6 Advertising

6.1 All advertising by manufacturers and dealers must comply with the codes and standards set by the Advertising Standards Authority and the Independent Broadcasting Authority, and with the requirements of the Trade Descriptions Act. In particular, references to credit facilities must conform to the appropriate legal requirements current at the time.

6.2 Advertisements must not contain any references to guarantees or warranties which would take away or diminish any rights of a consumer, nor should they be worded as to be understood by the consumer as doing so.

6.3 Advertisements must not contain the words "guarantee" or "warranty" unless the full terms of such undertakings, as well as the remedial action open to a consumer, are either clearly set out in the advertisement or are available to the consumer in writing at the point of sale or with the product.

6.4 Claims and descriptions in advertisements should not be misleading. In particular, any comparison with other models of different manufacturers should be based on a similar set of criteria and should not be presented in such a way as to confuse or mislead the consumer.

6.5 If advertisements quote fuel consumption figures for a particular model of car, the test method used to obtain these figures should be stated (the figures should be derived from internationally agreed test procedures when these have been established). Where any comparative claims for fuel consumption are made with models of the same or different manufacture, figures for the other model(s) and the test procedures used should be given.

6.6 In principle, a price quoted should be a price at which the consumer can buy the goods. Manufacturers and dealers should therefore quote prices for new cars, whether in advertisements or in showrooms, inclusive of the price of any extras known to be fitted to the car together with the appropriate VAT (quoting the rate applicable) and Car Tax. If the price excludes delivery charges, number plates, or seat belts such exclusions must be clearly specified.

6.7 Advertisements for used cars must quote prices inclusive of VAT and they should state that the prices are inclusive.

6.8 In the description of used cars, terms likely to be misunderstood by the consumer or which are not capable of exact definition should be avoided. For example, if the word "reconditioned" is used, the nature of the reconditioning must be carefully explained.

6.9 In the description of a used car, any year must be either:
   (a) the year of first use, or
   (b) the year of first registration, or
   (c) the last year that the car complied with the manufacturer's specification of a model sold as new during that calendar year
   whichever is the earliest.

6.10 In statements regarding the previous ownership of a car, ownership by a manufacturer, dealer or finance house does not have to be included unless the car was used by them in the course of their business, or for any private or pleasure purpose.

6.11 Where an advertisement quotes the price of one model in any model range but depicts another, the actual price of that other model should also be shown.

6.12 Where a manufacturer advertises a rust-proofing process, information about the process and its limitations should be made freely available.

6.13 Discounts offered will be based on fair comparisons. Such discounts should be based on the dealer's own previous price or manufacturers' recommended prices. Misleading price offers relating for example to "worth", "value", "up to £x off" should not be used.

7 Handling Complaints

7.1 Manufacturers and dealers must ensure as appropriate that effective and immediate action is taken with a view to achieving a just settlement of a complaint. To this end, there will be, from the point of view of the consumer, an easily identifiable and accessible arrangement for the reception and handling of complaints. In addition, manufacturers must give every assistance to their dealers in handling complaints under warranty, or those in which the manufacturer is otherwise involved.

7.2 When complaints are raised through a third party (*e.g.* the Automobile Association, the Royal Automobile Club, a trading standards officer or a citizen's advice bureau), willing guidance must be given to that body and every attempt should be made to re-establish direct communication with the complaining consumer and to reach a satisfactory settlement with him.

7.3 In the event of there being an inability to reach agreement, manufacturers and dealers must make it clear to a consumer that he has a right to refer the complaint to the appropriate trade association.

7.4 Manufacturers and dealers will give every assistance to the association concerned while it is investigating a complaint. The SMMT, the MAA and the SMTA will establish liaison as necessary.

7.5 Where conciliation has failed to resolve a dispute, the SMMT, the MAA and the SMTA have agreed to co-operate in the operation of low cost arbitration arrangements which will be organised by the Institute of Arbitrators. Details of the arbitration arrangements are set out in Appendix 1. Consumers must always be advised that they have the option of taking a claim to the Courts.

7.6   The award of the arbitrator is enforceable in law on all parties.

8 Monitoring

8.1   As subscribers to the Code of Practice, retailers should ensure that the symbols of their appropriate association(s) are clearly displayed for the information of consumers as indicating adherence to the industry's Code of Practice.

8.2   All manufacturers and dealers should maintain an analysis of justified complaints relating to any of the provisions of the Code of Practice, and should take action based on this information to improve their service to the consumer.

8.3   The SMMT, the MAA and the SMTA will analyse all complaints about the Code or matters referred to the association for conciliation or arbitration. The results of such analyses will be published in the Annual Report of the relevant association.

Appendix 1: Complaints and Arbitration

1   A consumer who has a complaint about the quality of the goods or service to his motor car should in the first place refer it to the dealer concerned.

2   The complaint should be addressed to a senior executive, a director, a partner or the proprietor. Some dealers will have an executive specially appointed to deal with complaints.

3   If the complaint relates to warranty on a new car and the dealer is unable to resolve the matter, the consumer should take his complaint direct to the manufacturer concerned.

4   If attempts to reach a satisfactory solution fail, the consumer has a right to refer his complaint in writing to one of the trade associations who subscribe to the Code of Practice for the Motor Industry, if the dealer concerned is a member of that association.

(a) if the complaint refers to a manufacturer's warranty or lies against a dealer who is a member, the address is:
The Legal Department,
Society of Motor Manufacturers & Traders Ltd,
Forbes House, Halkin Street, London SW1X 7DS.

(b) if the complaint lies against a dealer situated in any part of the United Kingdom except Scotland, the address is:
The Investigation and Advisory Service,
Motor Agents Association Ltd.
201 Great Portland Street, London W1 6AB.

(c) if the complaint lies against a dealer situated in Scotland, the address is:
Customer Complaints Service,
Scottish Motor Trade Association,
3 Palmerston Place, Edinburgh EH12 5AQ.

5   The appropriate trade association (SMMT, MAA or SMTA) will use its best endeavours to try to resolve the complaint.

6   If the trade association fails to reach a satisfactory solution, its member will agree to go to arbitration except in those cases where the trade association is of the opinion that it would be unreasonable for the member to be required to do so.

7   Parties to arbitration will be asked to pay the registration fee laid down by the Institute of Arbitrators. When, later the arbitrator makes his award, he will consider whether the registration fee should be returned to the successful party.

8   The parties will also be asked to sign an application for arbitration which will be sent, together with the registration fee, to:
The Institute of Arbitrators,
75 Cannon Street, London EC4N 5BH.

9   In order to keep costs as low as possible, the arbitration will normally rely on documents. In these cases, none of the parties to the dispute may be present, nor may they be represented by any other person.

10   The trade association will submit to the Institute of Arbitrators all the documentary evidence in their possession that they consider relevant to the case. The Insititute of Arbitrators will advise the parties to the dispute of the written evidence they have available on which to base their judgement, and invite the parties to submit any further evidence which they consider relevant.

11   The President of the Institute of Arbitrators will appoint a single arbitrator and will make all the necessary arrangements for the arbitration to be conducted as speedily as possible.

12   In suitable cases, the Arbitrator has the right to conduct an oral arbitration, and the parties may then attend to present their evi-

dence. Legal representation may only be employed if the Arbitrator so directs.

13   The Arbitrator will have the power to direct any party to provide to him and to the other party(ies) any additional document or information he considers to be relevant to the matter under dispute.

14   The award of the Arbitrator will be published in writing to the parties to the dispute and to the relevant association.

15   The award of the Arbitrator is enforceable in the Courts by any party.

(B)   R.E.T.R.A.

CODE OF PRACTICE FOR THE SELLING AND SERVICING OF
ELECTRICAL AND ELECTRONIC APPLIANCES*

1 Pricing

1.1   All goods to be sold will have a clear indication of the cash price
      at which they are offered for sale.
1.2   The retailer will at all times do everything possible to ensure that
      any customer who may have been charged too high a price arising
      from an error in his shop will have any excess charge refunded.

2 Discounts

2.1   Where a discount is offered the retailer will ensure that it is clearly
      understood and easily verified by the customer. Imprecise com-
      parisons with claims of "worth", "value" and "price elsewhere"
      are not to be used.
2.2   The retailer shall at no time attempt to confuse or mislead the
      customer or falsely describe any of the goods he offers for sale.

3 Refunds

3.1   Although the retailer is under no obligation (subject to the pro-
      visions of the Hire-purchase Acts and the Consumer Credit Act)
      to refund payments when a customer has changed his mind or
      simply does not like the goods, retailers may in these circumstances
      give a full cash refund at their discretion.
3.2   The retailer shall advise customers at the time of sale of any special
      conditions that he wishes to apply to the sale of goods or the use
      of credit cards or credit tokens and to the exchange or return of
      goods sold. Where possible, a notice should be displayed to this
      effect.

* Published with the permission of: The Radio, Electrical and Television Retailers
Association (R.E.T.R.A.) Ltd., R.E.T.R.A. House, 57–61 Newington Causeway,
London SE1 6BE.

322

4 Deposits

4.1 Any retailer who accepts an advance payment or deposit for goods shall indicate the period during which the delivery of the goods will be made to the customer. If delivery is not made to the customer within this period then the retailer shall offer the customer the option of a refund.

4.2 Failure by the customer to perform his contractual obligation to pay the balance of the purchase price may give the retailer the legal right to retain some or all of the deposit to compensate for his loss.

5 The sale

5.1 The retailer will give the customer as much information as possible about the goods and this will normally include such items as:

Correct method of unpacking
Correct pre-usage checks
Correct method of installation
Correct usage
Details of additional guarantees and service
Indication of the correct mains plug fuse value

The retailer will provide the manufacturer's handbook or instructions wherever possible.

5.2 The retailer will make clear at the point of sale the exact terms of the contract for the goods including any additional costs for delivery, installation and commissioning of the goods.

5.3 When work is not carried out by the retailer or by his appointed agent the retailer will advise his customers of the limitation of his responsibility for loss or damage resulting from such matters as faulty installation.

5.4 The retailer should provide customers with documentary evidence of proof of purchase and the date. Customers are to be advised to keep such documentary evidence and if possible to produce it when asking for service or making any complaint about the goods.

5.5 The retailer will ensure that the goods he stocks are manufactured to the relevant safety standards. When an item is found to be electrically or mechanically dangerous the retailer will, wherever possible, take steps to contact customers so that the merchandise can be modified or exchanged.

6 Retailer's guarantee

6.1   Without detracting from the customer's legal rights including those under the Sale of Goods Act 1893 as amended by the Supply of Goods (Implied Terms) Act 1973, the retailer shall guarantee new goods for both parts and labour for a period of not less than twelve months from the date of purchase and this shall apply even if the manufacturer's guarantee is for a shorter period.

The retailer's guarantee given under 6.1 does not apply in the following respects:

(a) Damage or faults caused by customer misuse, negligence or failure to adhere to the manufacturer's or retailer's instructions.

(b) Certain goods and replaceable parts that may have a limited life span (e.g. low cost transistor radios, styli, fuses, lamps, drive belts and batteries).

6.2   The terms of any guarantee given will be clearly set out at the time of sale.

6.3   If during the guarantee period the retailer is unable to effect a repair within fifteen working days from date of notification of defect, he will by the expiration of such period, endeavour to lend the same or a similar item to the customer. This obligation does not necessarily apply where the retailer is not the service agent. If the retailer finds that it is impracticable to lend such an item, he shall always extend the period of the original guarantee by the period of time during which the customer was without the use of the item.

6.4   Where a customer moves outside the retailer's normal service area, the retailer may not be in a position to implement effectively all guarantees and services normally offered. Where possible, however, the retailer will transfer any servicing or guarantee arrangements to a local retailer in the customer's new area if the customer so requests. R.E.T.R.A. operate a National Rental and Service Transfer Scheme that may be used for this purpose.

7 Advertising

The retailer's advertisements shall be clear and honest and in accordance with any statutory requirements and the British Code of Advertising Practice and in particular the attention of the retailer is drawn to the unacceptable practice of "switch selling" set out in Section 4 thereof.

8 Repairs and servicing

8.1 The retailer will make clear the exact terms of the contract for any repairs or servicing work to be carried out. Invoices should be clearly presented showing details of the work carried out, the materials used and VAT charged.

8.2 The retailer will accept for repair or service goods that he has sold but may not be able to accept for repair or service goods purchased from other sources (but see 6.4 above). The retailer will encourage customers to return faulty goods to his workshop where practicable. If the customer requests a visit to his home, the retailer shall ask the customer to provide as much of the following information as possible in order to identify these goods, expedite the repair and minimise costs:
   (i) make of appliance
   (ii) model number
   (iii) serial number
   (iv) description of fault
   (v) name of purchaser
   (vi) address where the equipment is located (indicating any special difficulties)
   (vii) a suitable time for the engineer to call, giving working day alternatives am/pm
   (viii) whether it is an in-guarantee fault, out of guarantee fault or service call for maintenance.

8.3 The retailer will provide service and spares to the best of his ability but where he is unable to provide such a service he will give the information listed in 9.2.

8.4 Where goods are handed in or collected for repair or service, the retailer shall provide the customer with a receipt where requested.

8.5 Many retailers offer a same day service. However, when a customer requests a service visit (and the retailer supplies the service) under normal conditions the initial call will be offered to be made within three working days after receiving the request.

8.6 When a request for service is received from the customer, the retailer shall advise the customer of any minimum service charge which is to be made. At the same time the customer shall be informed of payment arrangements for any service call, inspection or repair.

8.7   Should the fault fail to be repaired either in the workshop or *in situ,* the engineer or retailer will report the suspected fault to the customer and the reasons why a repair has not been effected. Reference should be made to one or more of the following categories:

(i) lack of spare parts
(ii) the equipment requires major repair
(iii) unable to trace defect
(iv) several other important defects are apparent
(v) appliance unsafe (mechanical, electrical, electronic or physical)
(vi) appliance unrepairable
(vii) appliance not worth repairing (age or hazardous)

The provisions of section 6 of this Code apply in the case of in-guarantee repairs on goods referred to therein.

8.8   Retailers will, upon request, advise customers of their own conditions for the servicing and repair of products. Field service repairs which cannot be completed at the time of the first visit should be completed normally within fifteen working days from the date of the first visit. In the case of workshop repairs, manpower and facilities should be calculated to achieve completion of 80 per cent of all repairs within five working days from the date of receipt of the product in the workshop. Completion of repairs will be dependent upon availability of spares, normal working conditions and the maintenance of electricity supply and transmissions.

If the retailer finds there will be an undue delay in performing the repair, he will notify his customer of this giving the reason for the delay.

9   Where the retailer is not the service agent

9.1   Some manufacturers allow only their service engineers to perform in-guarantee work. Where this situation arises although the retailer fully accepts his responsibility under the law, he is not in a position to provide service.

9.2   The retailer undertakes where in-guarantee service is required to provide the customer with the name, address and telephone number of the manufacturer or service agent.

In appropriate circumstances the retailer will accept the goods brought in by the customer for return to the manufacturer or service agent for service.

9.3 The retailer also undertakes, where the manufacturer fails to provide an adequate service to his customer to use his best endeavours to procure such a service for his customer and if necessary to enlist the assistance of the R.E.T.R.A. Conciliation Service.

10 Delayed, cancelled or abortive calls

10.1 Where the retailer has agreed to an appointment which has to be cancelled through circumstances beyond the normal running of the retailer's business, he will endeavour to advise the customer, where practicable, of any change in call times.

10.2 Retailers shall advise customers of the inconvenience and expense that can be caused by the customer's failure to cancel or re-arrange appointments.

11 Guarantee of repairs on products outside normal guarantee period

A specific repair performed by the retailer will be guaranteed both in parts supplied and fitted and workmanship for a minimum period of three months. This guarantee shall not detract from the legal rights of the customer.

12 Estimates

If requested, the retailer shall offer to provide customers with estimates of the cost of all major repairs. The customer shall be advised in advance whether or not the estimate is free and that circumstances may require its variation. The customer shall be advised that if the equipment is beyond economic repair, or if he is unable to accept the estimate, the retailer may not be able to return the goods in the condition in which they were originally received. Where a quotation for repair work is provided, as distinct from an estimate, it should be realised by both parties that the acceptance of a quotation constitutes a contract embodying the terms of the quotation.

13 Life expectancy

13.1 The economic life expectancy of any product is difficult to determine as some products which have been cheap and basic in manufacture, may in some instances far outlive the normal expected life of such a product.

13.2 Functional parts are electrical and mechanical parts which are essential to the continued operation and safety of the appliance. To assist customers in determining whether or not a product is repairable the following table on the availability of functional parts after the date on which the production of the appliance ceases, has been prepared by the Association of Manufacturers of Domestic Electrical Appliances.

Small appliances	5–8 years
Cleaners, direct acting space heaters, refrigerators and freezers, spin and tumble driers and wash boilers	8 years
Cookers, dishwashers, washing machines	10 years
Thermal storage space heating	15 years

13.3 It is important for retailers to advise that the availability of spares quoted for any particular group of appliances does not make all appliances repairable or economic to be repaired.

14 Life expectancy—electronic equipment

Most electronic equipment can be expected to last about 7 years and in certain cases this period may be longer. Customers should be advised, however, that non-functional parts may not be available for this length of time.

15 Spare parts

15.1 Retailers will make every effort to keep a comprehensive stock of commonly used parts. With the increasing complexity of modern goods and a vast overall range of spares, the retailer, unless exceptional circumstances prevail, will be unable to stock all spares.

15.2 Spares other than these will therefore be drawn from the retailer's suppliers and the retailer will use his best endeavours to ensure a swift delivery.

15.3 Non-functional parts may only be available by special order from the manufacturer and the retailer may request payment with order for replacements on goods out of guarantee.

15.4 Retailers should ensure that products they sell can be serviced during their normal life expectancy. Where they cannot ascertain this they should advise the customer accordingly.

16 Conciliation services

16.1 There is no doubt that the vast majority of sales and or service calls are performed satisfactorily. Situations will arise, however, when either the customer or the retailer feels he has been unfairly treated by either the other party or by the supplier.

16.2 Customers with a complaint should always be encouraged to return to the retailer or service agent. The retailer or service agent should examine the matter speedily and sympathetically and must take decisive action if justification is established.

16.3 Disputes are usually local matters and customers who are dissatisfied with the retailer can be referred to the local Trading Standards Officer, Consumer Advice Centre or Citizens' Advice Bureau. Each customer or retailer, however, shall also have the right to apply for assistance, in writing, to the Secretary of the Association assisted if necessary by the R.E.T.R.A. Customer Conciliation Panel.

16.4 The objective of the R.E.T.R.A. Conciliation Service is to provide prompt and informal conciliation where the retailer and the customer cannot resolve their dispute.

16.5 The customer should indicate the nature of the complaint in writing in the first instance, to the Secretary of R.E.T.R.A.

16.6 If the Secretary is unable to resolve the complaint it may be referred to the R.E.T.R.A. Conciliation Panel. The Panel consists of:

  (i) an independent chairman
  (ii) a Trading Standards Officer
  (iii) a Consumer representative
  (iv) a member of the R.E.T.R.A. Council
  (v) a representative of such manufacturers' association as is appropriate.

The Panel will be able to ask R.E.T.R.A. to obtain as much information as is necessary to assist it in its task. The retailer or the customer may, if required, attend the meeting of the Panel but in the majority of cases the Panel should be able to reach its decision on the basis of documentary evidence.

16.7 The retailer and the customer will be advised of the Panel's decision and any award or action recommended by the Panel will be honoured by the member of R.E.T.R.A. within 15 days, provided that the customer also fully accepts the recommendations of the Panel.

16.8 The Secretary of R.E.T.R.A. will prepare an annual report on the disputes referred to the Panel. Copies of the report will be submitted to the R.E.T.R.A. Council and to the Office of Fair Trading.

17 Use of courts

The customer can of course at any stage pursue his normal legal rights and seek redress from the County Courts in England and Wales or the Sheriff Court in Scotland. The simple arbitration procedure now available in the County Courts in England and Wales may be suitable for settling the dispute if the customer is not satisfied with the award or action recommended by the R.E.T.R.A. Conciliation Panel. R.E.T.R.A. will advise him of the availability of the courts to resolve the complaint.

18 Monitoring

The Association will monitor the compliance of its members with the Code of Practice and discuss with a member any persistent breach of any provisions. Each year details of cases dealt with will be made available to the Office of Fair Trading.

(C) CODE OF PRACTICE FOR DOMESTIC LAUNDRY AND CLEANING
SERVICES*

Code of Practice Statement

*As a member of the Association of British Launderers and Cleaners
Limited we undertake not to restrict our liability under the general
law and shall so far as is reasonably practicable:*

1. Handle all clothes, linens, furnishings and other items accepted
   by us for processing with proper and due care and attention.
2. Investigate any complaint promptly and, if requested, re-process, free of charge, any article which is unsatisfactory due to
   fault on our part.
3. Pay fair compensation for loss or damage due to negligence on
   our part.
4. Train our staff to be competent, courteous and helpful at all
   times.
5. Keep our shops, vans, containers and premises clean and tidy.
6. Maintain the highest possible standard of quality and service
   consistent with the price charged.
7. Display in shop premises a list of prices for standard articles.
8. Have all orders ready or delivered at the time stated, unless
   prevented by exceptional circumstances.

*The ABLC's customer advisory service is available to help resolve
any disputes which arise between members of the association and
customers. The association's address is: Lancaster Gate House, 319
Pinner Road, Harrow, Middlesex HA1 4HX.*
Telephone No. 01-863 7755

* Published with the permission of: The Association of British Launderers and
Cleaners Ltd., Lancaster Gate House, 319 Pinner Road, Harrow, Middlesex HA1
4HX.

General Principles of the Code

General

1 The Code of Practice applies to all services, including repairing and dyeing, normally provided by domestic laundry and/or drycleaning Members to customers who are private individuals, but does not apply to services provided by launderettes and coin operated drycleaning establishments.

2 The Code of Practice Statement is set out in full on the previous page. The principles that underlie the series of undertakings contained in the Statement can best be explained by considering each undertaking individually in the following way:

Preamble

★As a member of the Association of British Launderers and Cleaners Limited we undertake not to restrict our liability under the general law.

3 The significance of the Preamble is that it sets the tone for the whole Code of Practice. By virtue of these words, ABLC Members undertake not to contract out of liability imposed on them by the law of the land. The Code of Practice Statement then sets out the series of undertakings with which ABLC Members will, so far as is reasonably practicable, comply.

Liability at Common Law

4 At Common Law, if a launderer or cleaner loses or destroys a customer's article through his negligence or that of his employees he is liable for the market value of the article at the time it is lost or destroyed i.e. allowing for depreciation but reflecting to some extent the cost of replacement at current costs. If the article is only damaged and is capable of adequate repair the launderer/cleaner is only liable for the cost of that repair save that if this exceeds the market value of the article at that time, the launderer/cleaner is only liable for the latter.

5 The liability of the launderer/cleaner is a liability for negligence, that is to say for a breach of duty or obligation, whether imposed by the Common Law or by an express or implied term in a contract, to take reasonable care or exercise reasonable skill in relation to

the articles left with him. In considering negligence it must be remembered that the launderer/cleaner holds himself out as possessing specialised knowledge and might be held to be negligent if he uses an unsuitable process or fails to realise that a particular article would be damaged, at any rate where such a risk would be generally recognised by others in the Industry.

6   It must be emphasised that because the launderer's/cleaner's liability is based on negligence, any damage which cannot be attributed to negligence cannot be the responsibility of the launderer/cleaner. Among the possible causes of damage for which neither the Common Law nor common sense expects the launderer/cleaner to be responsible (unless, and to the extent that, the launderer/cleaner adds to the damage by his negligence) are:

faulty manufacture (e.g. fugitive colours, relaxation of stretch imparted during manufacture, inadequate seaming, incorrect care labelling, etc.), (See para 11)

prior misuse by the customer (e.g. drying of razor blades on towels, excessive use of bleach, spillage of acids or other corrosive liquids on fabrics etc.),

normal but unrecognised wear (e.g. weakening of curtains by exposure to light).

Paragraph one

★*Handle all clothes, linens, furnishings and other items accepted by us for processing with proper and due care and attention.*

7   This undertaking reflects the basic philosophy underlying the service provided by ABLC Members, and is self explanatory.

Paragraph two

★*Investigate any complaint promptly and, if requested, re-process, free of charge, any article which is unsatisfactory due to fault on our part.*

8   Any complaint should first be made to the launderer/cleaner concerned who will do all he can to resolve the complaint in a mutually acceptable fashion. If a mutually acceptable conclusion cannot be reached however, the complaint may be referred by the customer or by the launderer/cleaner to the Association's Customer Advisory Service (see later).

9   ABLC Members accept that customer complaints should always be treated with respect. Every ABLC Member is expected to have a proper and efficient system for receiving and for promptly acknowledging and investigating customer complaints and for acting in response to justified complaints, both towards the complainant to give satisfaction and within the firm to avoid repetition. A customer should always receive an adequate and considered response to his complaint.

10   ABLC Members are encouraged to co-operate with Trading Standards Departments of local authorities, Consumer Advice Centres, Citizens' Advice Bureaux etc. to assist in resolving complaints which have been referred to those bodies by customers, although the ABLC Customer Advisory Service is always available to help in such cases.

11   ABLC Members who find examples, in any particular range of articles, of a manufacturing fault (see para 6) which prejudices successful laundering or drycleaning can refer the matter to the Association which will arrange for the matter to be taken up with the manufacturers or retailer concerned to see how such fault (which may amount to a breach of the Sale of Goods Act) can be eliminated.

12   Where it is accepted that an article may have been processed unsatisfactorily because of fault on the part of the launderer/cleaner, the ABLC Member will offer to reprocess the article, at no charge to the customer, in an attempt to obtain a satisfactory result.

Paragraph three

★*Pay fair compensation for loss or damage due to negligence on our part.*

13   ABLC Members undertake to pay **fair** compensation in the above circumstances, and what is fair is a matter which has to be determined according to the facts of each case. The launderer/cleaner is not obliged at law to replace a lost or damaged article with a new article, nor to reimburse the customer the complete cost of buying a new article. Both parties should take into account the depreciation, wear and tear which had occurred to the article prior to the loss or damage as this may affect the article's value in respect of which compensation is assessed.

Exclusion Clauses

14 Any clause which is intended to exclude, limit or restrict the launderer's/cleaner's liability at Common Law is contrary to the Code. Members of the Association will therefore not attempt to restrict either their liability for certain types of damage caused by their negligence, or the amount of fair compensation which they will pay. They may however wish to ask the customer, at the time the article is accepted, for an indication of the value which the customer places on the article; this may be done when the article is clearly of exceptional value or of unusual manufacture. (See para 19).

Owner's Risk Clauses

15 These clauses are only inconsistent with the Code if their effect may be to exclude, limit or restrict Common Law liability. There may be certain articles however, such as curtains, where the launderer/cleaner can foresee that some damage may be an inevitable consequence of the application of the laundering, drycleaning or dyeing process even though that process will be expertly applied. In such cases therefore the launderer/cleaner may ask the customer to acknowledge (in writing) his acceptance of the risk of such damage occurring. Acceptance of this risk by the customer will not relieve the launderer/cleaner from liability if he is negligent and so this procedure is in complete accordance with the Code.

Fire and Burglary

16 Naturally if a customer's article is lost or damaged by fire or burglary whilst in the launderer's/cleaner's custody, the customer will look to the launderer/cleaner for compensation. At Common Law the customer is entitled to compensation only where the fire or burglary in question was caused by the launderer's/cleaner's negligence. To eliminate this potential source of dissatisfaction and hardship, and as a positive contribution to the maintenance of good customer relations, ABLC Members undertake to pay fair compensation for loss or damage caused by fire or burglary—in cases where the article in question is not covered by the customer's

own insurance policy—even though no negligence can be attributed to the Member.

Paragraph four

> ★*Train our staff to be competent, courteous and helpful at all times.*

Paragraph five

> ★*Keep our shops, vans, containers and premises clean and tidy.*

17   These two undertakings reflect ABLC Members' determination to ensure that the image of the Industry is maintained at a high level.

Paragraph six

> ★*Maintain the highest possible standard of quality and service consistent with the price charged.*

Paragraph seven

> ★*Display in shop premises a list of prices for standard articles.*

18   ABLC Members will do all they can to ensure that customers are always made aware of the nature, extent and price of the service they are buying. Those Members who offer special services, whether relating to the time within which they are performed e.g. Express Service, Two Hour Service, Same Day Service, or to the nature of the process e.g. hand finish, re-pleating etc., will explain these terms and clearly state the circumstances in which such special services are available. Members undertake to ensure that all advertising in shop premises or elsewhere is clear and accurate, particularly relating to any special offers or discounts.

19   So far as price lists are concerned, the very wide range of different articles offered to launderers and drycleaners for processing makes it impossible to prepare a printed price list covering every type of article that might be submitted by their customers. ABLC Members therefore display a list of prices covering principal standard articles and services. Prices for other standard articles or services will be quoted on request. Where articles are of exceptional value or of an unusual nature Members reserve the right to charge a special price. (See para 14).

20   In the case of collection and delivery services prices for individual articles or services may be obtained from the van roundsman although in some cases requests for prices for unusual or exceptionally valuable articles may have to be referred to the main office.

21   It is accepted that it is in the interests of both customers and ABLC Members that any doubts and uncertainties relating to price and service are eliminated before the service is performed. As a means of achieving this, ABLC Members undertake to enter, on receipts or tickets they issue from their retail premises, the price for cleaning the article or providing the service in question. In certain cases however this will not be possible because of the very nature of the article or service:

   —where an article of exceptional value or of an unusual nature is involved and the exact price will not be known until the article is examined at the main office; in these cases arrangements can be made between the Member and the customer for the price to be advised at a later date but before the work is carried out.

   —where prices are expressed as a charge per unit of measurement e.g. repairs, where the price is often expressed per inch (or centimetre), or carpet cleaning where the unit may be square feet (or square metres); in such cases the customer will be told the charge per unit.

   —in the case of a laundry bundle (for which an itemised receipt cannot be given).

Paragraph eight

   ★*Have all orders ready or delivered at the time stated, unless prevented by exceptional circumstances.*

22   ABLC Members undertake that where they give customers an estimated date by which their order will be ready or delivered they will adhere to that date, in so far as they are able to do so. Naturally ABLC Members cannot avoid delays which arise from exceptional circumstances, such as staff sickness, industrial action, power restrictions, breakdowns etc.

23   No one anticipates that in ordinary circumstances any monetary loss will be suffered by a customer purely as a result of delay in

returning an article, and indeed in the great majority of cases no loss is suffered. Accordingly, it is the effect of the law that, unless special circumstances where delay would cause loss are brought to the attention of the launderer/cleaner when the articles are delivered to him and the position is accepted by him, damages are not normally recoverable in respect of delay in returning the articles. Nonetheless, ABLC Members are well aware that delay can cause inconvenience to customers and, therefore, in cases where an article has been mislaid by the launderer/cleaner after acceptance and not returned to the customer within a reasonable time ABLC Members are recommended to consider favourably, in the interest of good customer relations, making a reduction in the standard process charge for the article concerned.

Trade Descriptions Act

24   A trader who makes a false statement as to the nature of the service he is offering, including the time within which the service will be performed, may be guilty of an offence under the above Act if he knows, when making it, that the statement is false or if he is reckless as to whether it be true or false. It therefore follows that if at the time his statement is made the trader genuinely expects to be able to keep to it no offence is committed.

25   Should exceptional circumstances arise which oblige ABLC Members temporarily to suspend the operation of special services such as Same Day Service or Two Hour Service, the notices relating to those special services will be withdrawn or qualified for so long as the exceptional circumstances persist.

Hours of Business

26   To avoid possible misunderstandings leading to inconvenience for customers, ABLC Members display a notice in their retail premises clearly stating their normal opening and closing hours. Advance notice of arrangements over public holiday periods will also be displayed during the days immediately preceding such periods.

Uncollected Goods

27   Under Common Law the launderer or cleaner is a bailee of articles

accepted by him and he can never acquire the right to dispose of them, unless specially agreed by the launderer or cleaner and the customer at the time the contract is entered into. ABLC Members are therefore entitled within the terms of the Code prominently to display a notice to the effect, or otherwise clearly make known to the customer, that any article not collected within six months, or such other longer period as may be stated, may be disposed of by the launderer/cleaner and the proceeds applied to defray the process charge.

28 This right will be exercised only after all reasonable attempts have been made to contact the customer with a view to his collecting the articles and paying the process charge.

ABLC customer advisory service

29 The vast majority of laundering, drycleaning, dyeing, etc. is performed expeditiously and satisfactorily and the few complaints which do arise are usually settled by the Member concerned to the satisfaction of the customer.

30 However the ABLC Customer Advisory Service, which is an integral part of the ABLC's organisation, is available to provide conciliation to help resolve those relatively few disputes between Members and customers which for one reason or another cannot be resolved by the parties concerned. The Service will consider complaints referred to it by customers direct, by consumer bodies (such as Citizens' Advice Bureaux, Consumer Advice Centres, Trading Standards Departments of local authorities etc.) on behalf of customers, or by ABLC Members themselves.

Conciliation

31 The first step taken by the ABLC in each case is to make sure that the dispute has first been referred by the customer to the launderer/cleaner concerned.

32 Once this has been established, the customer is invited, if he has not already done so, to provide the ABLC in writing with details of the complaint or dispute. There is no standard application form or other unnecessary documentation to worry about.

33 The ABLC will then look at each case individually and will use

N

its good offices to try to bring the dispute to a conclusion which is satisfactory to both parties.

34 If the dispute involves technical considerations, the ABLC Customer Advisory Service may consider that a laboratory test on the article is necessary. In such a case the customer will be offered test facilities at a choice of independent establishments e.g. British Launderers Research Association, British Leather Manufacturers Research Association, Dyers and Cleaners Research Organisation, Manchester Testing House, Retail Trading Standards Association or Shirley Institute. If this offer is made no charge for the test will be made to the customer but the customer will be expected, and the ABLC Member required, to abide by the findings of the test. A copy of the test report will of course be made available to the customer.

35 Should a laboratory test not be considered necessary by the ABLC Customer Advisory Service, for reasons made clear to the customer, and should the customer wish to have a laboratory test at his own expense, the Association will make the necessary arrangements on his behalf subject to prior payment of the test fee by the customer to the Association. The amount of the test fee will be returned in whole or in part to the customer if the findings of the test substantiate his claim wholly or in part.

> A customer can of course at any stage seek redress from the Sheriff or County Court. A simple procedure for dealing with small claims is available in the County Court in England and Wales.

Monitoring of the code

36 The Association will monitor compliance of its Members with the Code of Practice and discuss with a Member any continued breach of any provision. Every year the Association will publish in its annual report a summary of the operation of the Code and any action taken in connection therewith.

(D)   A.B.T.A. CODES OF CONDUCT*

Code of Conduct Between ABTA Tour Operators and Members of the Public

1   **Minimum Standards of Brochures**
Every brochure published by or in the name of a tour operator shall contain clear, comprehensive and accurate information to enable the client to exercise an informed judgment in making his choice, including:

 (i) all information necessary to comply with the regulations for the time being of the Civil Aviation Authority and any other governmental or statutory licensing authority;
 (ii) the legal identity of the tour operator responsible for publishing the brochure containing the tour, holiday or travel arrangements offered;
 (iii) the means of travel (e.g. ship, coach, charter or other aircraft);
 (iv) the destination and/or itinerary where applicable;
 (v) the date, time and place of departure and return;
 (vi) the nature of accommodation and meal facilities offered;
 (vii) any additional facilities or special arrangements offered;
 (viii) the total price or the means of arriving at the total price, together with a clear statement of the services included therein, the date on which the price in the brochure was calculated and the conditions under which such price can be amended;
 (ix) the procedure for booking and the contractual conditions under which the booking shall be made, if any.

2   **Statutory Requirements for Brochures**
Every brochure published by or in the name of a tour operator shall observe the requirements of the Trade Descriptions Act 1968, the Misrepresentation Act 1967 and the Civil Aviation Act 1971 or any amendment or re-enactment therof.

* Published with the permission of: The Association of British Travel Agents Ltd., 55–57 Newman Street, London W1P 4AH.

3   **Publication and Sale of Brochures**
     No tour operator shall publish or consent to the publication, or
     sell or consent to the sale of, holidays from any brochure which
     does not conform with the requirements of all the relevant para-
     graphs of this Code.

4   **Booking Conditions**
     (i) Booking conditions, if any, shall define the extent of the
         responsibilities as well as the limits of the liabilities of tour
         operators towards clients and shall be so designed that they
         are easily read and understood.
     (ii) Booking conditions shall not include clauses:—
         (a) purporting to exclude responsibility for misrepresentations
             made by the tour operator, his servants or his agents;
         (b) purporting to exclude responsibility for the tour operator's
             contractual duty to exercise diligence in making arrange-
             ments for his clients or for consequential loss following
             from breach of his duty; and
         (c) stating that complaints will not be considered unless made
             within a fixed period after the end of a tour or holiday if
             such a period is of less than 28 days' duration.
     (iii) Booking conditions (and/or brochures) shall prominently
         indicate the circumstances in which and the conditions on
         which surcharges may be made to clients.
     (iv) Booking conditions shall conform with all relevant provisions
         of this Code.
     (v) Tour operators shall in practice interpret their booking con-
         ditions in accordance with the provisions of this Code.

5   **Cancellation of Tours, Holidays or other Travel Arrangements by
     Tour Operators**
     (i) A tour operator shall not cancel a tour, holiday or other travel
         arrangements after the date when payment of the balance of
         the price becomes due unless it is necessary to do so as a result
         of hostilities, political unrest or other circumstances amounting
         to force majeure, or unless the client defaults in payment of
         such balance.
     (ii) If a tour operator, for reasons other than hostilities, political
         unrest or other circumstances amounting to force majeure,
         cancels a holiday, tour or other travel arrangements on or

before the date when payment of the balance of the price becomes due, he shall inform agents and direct clients as soon as possible, and shall offer clients the choice of an alternative holiday of at least comparable standard if available, or of a prompt and full refund of all money paid.

(iii) If a tour operator has to cancel a tour, holiday or other travel arrangements as a result of hostilities, political unrest or other circumstances amounting to force majeure, he shall inform agents and direct clients without delay and shall offer clients the choice of an alternative holiday of at least comparable standard, if available, or a prompt and full refund of all money paid less reasonable expenses.

6   **Alterations to Tours, Holidays or other Travel Arrangements**
As soon as material alterations become necessary to tours, holidays or other travel arrangements for which bookings have already been made, the tour operator shall inform agents and direct clients without delay and shall give clients the choice of either accepting the alteration which must be of comparable standard or of receiving a prompt and full refund of all money paid (less reasonable expenses when the alteration is due to hostilities, political unrest or other circumstances amounting to force majeure).

7   **Overbooking of Hotels**
(i) A tour operator shall take all reasonable steps to ensure that tours, holidays or other travel arrangements are not cancelled or altered as a result of overbooking of hotels.

(ii) Where tours, holidays or other travel arrangements are cancelled or altered as a result of overbooking of hotels, a tour operator shall only be deemed to have taken all reasonable steps to prevent the cancellation if he can show that the overbooking occurred for reasons beyond his control.

(iii) If, despite sub-paragraphs (i) and (ii) above, a hotel is overbooked and a tour operator knows this before the departure of the affected clients, he shall immediately inform those clients and shall offer them the choice of an alternative holiday of at least comparable standard, if available, or a full and prompt refund of all money paid.

(iv) If, despite sub-paragraphs (i) and (ii) above, a hotel is overbooked and a tour operator does not know this before the departure of affected clients, such clients shall on arrival at their destination be offered alternative accommodation and shall also be offered reasonable compensation for "disturbance" where the location and/or facilities of the alternative accommodation can reasonably be regarded as inferior to that originally booked.

8 **Cancellation of Tours, Holidays or other Travel Arrangements by Clients**
A tour operator shall clearly state in his booking conditions the amount of the cancellation fees which the client shall be liable to incur, as well as the terms and conditions under which the client shall be liable to incur such fees.

9 **Complaints**
Complaints shall be dealt with promptly and efficiently and in the event of a dispute with a client every effort shall be made to settle the matter amicably and as quickly as possible.

10 **Conciliation**
In the event of a breakdown in communication or a serious disagreement between the tour operator and the client, ABTA is prepared to intervene to give help and impartial guidance and to offer the facilities of conciliation.

11 **Arbitration**
Tour operators shall include as a term of any contract relating to the sale of their inclusive holidays or tours a provision whereby any dispute arising out of, or in connection with, such sale which is not amicably settled, may be referred to arbitration under a special scheme devised for the travel industry by the Institute of Arbitrators by arrangement with the Association of British Travel Agents. It shall also be stated that:—

    (a) the scheme provides for a simple and inexpensive method of arbitration on documents alone with restricted liability on the client in respect of costs;

    (b) provision for a normal attended hearing is also included in the scheme but in this case the liability of the client for costs is not limited; and

    (c) details of the scheme will be supplied on request.

12 **Advertising**
All advertising by tour operators shall comply with the Codes or Regulations of recognised organisations or associations such as the Advertising Standards Authority, the Code of Advertising Practice Committee, the Independent Broadcasting Authority, the Independent Television Companies Authority, and the Association of Independent Radio Companies which regulate the standards and practices of tour operators in relation to advertising.

13 **Transactions and Correspondence**
Transactions with clients shall be treated as confidential and correspondence shall be dealt with promptly.

14 **Foreign Currency Surcharges relating to ground arrangements**
(i) A tour operator shall not make an additional charge to a client as a result of a variation in the rates of exchange relating to ground arrangements less than 30 clear days before the date of the commencement of such client's holiday, tour or other travel arrangements.
(ii) A tour operator shall not make such an additional charge to a client more than 30 days before such date unless he can show that it is necessary for him to do so for reasons beyond his control.

15 **Surcharges (Other than Foreign Currency Surcharges relating to ground arrangements)**
A tour operator shall not make an additional charge to a client as a result of increases in costs (for instance the cost of coach or aviation fuel) other than those arising from variations in the rates of exchange relating to ground arrangements unless he can show that it is necessary for him to do so for reasons beyond his control.

16 **Direct Selling by Tour Operators**
Tour operators who sell their tour, holiday or travel arrangements direct to the public shall conform so far as is applicable to the Retail Agents' Code of Conduct in respect of such sales as if they were retail agents.

17 **General**

Tour operators shall act in accordance with the aims of this Code
of Conduct and the foregoing specific provisions shall not be
deemed to be comprehensive in expressing those aims.

18 **Transitional Provision**

A tour operator shall not be deemed to have committed a breach
of sub-paragraphs (iii) or (iv) of paragraph 4 of this Code on the
grounds that the booking conditions in a Winter 1975/76 or a
Summer 1976 brochure do not conform with those sub-paragraphs
if the reason for such non-conformity is that prior to the publication
of those sub-paragraphs such brochure was printed or had reached
such an advanced stage of preparation that it could not reasonably
be altered.

Code of Conduct Between ABTA Retail Agents and Members of the Public

1 **Standard of Service**

   (i) Retail agents shall maintain a high standard in serving the
       public and shall comply with all relevant statutory
       requirements.

   (ii) Retail agents shall make every effort to ensure that accurate
        and impartial information is provided to enable their clients
        to exercise an informed judgment in making their choice of
        facilities.

   (iii) Retail agents shall make every effort to ensure that their
         clients are not sold tours, holidays and travel arrangements
         incompatible with their individual requirements.

2 **Advertising**

   (i) All advertising by retail agents shall comply with the Codes
       or Regulations of recognised organisations or associations such
       as the Advertising Standards Authority, the Code of Adver-
       tising Practice Committee, the Independent Broadcasting
       Authority, the Independent Television Companies Authority,
       and the Association of Independent Radio Companies which
       regulate the standards and practices of retail agents in relation
       to advertising.

(ii) No advertisement, document or other publication, whether in writing or otherwise, shall contain anything which is likely to mislead the public.

(iii) Any advertisement, document or other publication, whether in writing or otherwise, advertising travel arrangements shall accurately state all material information.

3 **Alteration to Travel Arrangements**

When alterations are made to travel arrangements for which bookings have already been accepted retail agents shall inform their clients immediately they are advised of the situation and act as intermediaries between their principals and clients in any subsequent negotiations.

4 **Booking Conditions**

(i) Retail agents shall draw the attention of their clients to booking and other published conditions applicable to their travel arrangements.

(ii) Retail agents shall ensure that their conditions of booking are not in conflict with this Code of Conduct.

5 **Counter Staff**

Retail agents shall ensure that their counter staff carefully study all tour, holiday and travel programmes and brochures so that they are able to impart accurate information to their clients and to sell more efficiently.

6 **Booking Forms**

Retail agents shall ensure that booking forms are completed correctly in every detail. All booking references shall be shown.

7 **Insurance Facilities**

Retail agents shall draw the attention of their clients to any insurance facilities and cover available, including insurance relating to cancellation, and shall indicate any exclusions and limitations so that their clients may seek additional cover if deemed desirable or necessary.

8 **Travel Documents**

Retail agents shall ensure that all travel and other documents received from principals are checked before delivering them to their clients and that any points requiring clarification are explained to their clients.

9   **Passports, Visa and Health Requirements**
     Retail agents shall advise clients of the necessary passport, visa and health requirements for the journey to be undertaken and shall assist them with any other ancillary services which they may request and which are not covered by the booking, e.g. currency.

10   **Disputes**
     (i) In the event of a dispute with a client, retail agents shall make every effort to reach an amicable and speedy solution.
     (ii) Retail agents shall make every reasonable effort to deal with complaints of a minor and general character with a view to avoiding recourse to principals. When complaints are of such a nature that reference to the principal is necessary, a retail agent shall use his best endeavours acting as an intermediary to bring about a satisfactory conclusion.

11   **Transactions and Correspondence**
     Transactions with clients shall be treated as confidential and correspondence shall be dealt with promptly.

12   **Retail Agents Engaged in Tour Operating**
     Retail agents operating their own inclusive tours or holidays shall conform to the Tour Operators' Code of Conduct in respect of such tours or holidays, including the provisions of that Code relating to Conciliation and Arbitration.

13   **General**
     (i) Retail agents shall familiarise themselves and their staff with all provisions of this Code of Conduct.
     (ii) Retail agents shall observe not only the letter but also the spirit of the Code and its ethics and ideals, thus giving true significance to the ABTA symbol.
     (iii) Retail agents shall act according to the aims of this Code of Conduct and the foregoing specific provisions shall not be deemed to be comprehensive in expressing those aims.

NOTES:

(i) The above provisions represent those paragraphs of the ABTA Codes of Conduct which govern the conduct between ABTA tour operators and ABTA retail agents on the one hand, and members of the public on the other. The Codes of Conduct also contain provisions relating to conduct between tour operators; between retail agents; between retail agents and tour operators; and between retail agents and other principals.

(ii) The ABTA Codes of Conduct contain provisions for the enforcement of the Codes by the Tour Operators' Council and by the Retail Agents' Council. The penalties which may be imposed in the event of a proved infringement of the Codes are a reprimand and/or a fine or termination of membership of ABTA. The Codes provide that any penalties imposed and the reasons therefor shall be published in the ABTA News.

ADDRESSES OF TRADE ASSOCIATIONS SPONSORING CODES OF PRACTICE AGREED WITH THE OFFICE OF FAIR TRADING

(1) **Cars**

The Customer Relations Adviser,
Society of Motor Manufacturers & Traders Ltd.,
Forbes House,
Halkin Street,
London SW1X 7DS.

The Investigation and Advisory Service,
Motor Agents Association Ltd.,
201 Great Portland Street,
London W1N 6AB.

Customer Complaints Service,
Scottish Motor Trade Association,
3 Palmerston Place,
Edinburgh EH12 5AQ.

The Chief Executive.
Vehicle Builders and Repairers Association,
Belmont House,
102 Finkle Lane,
Gildersome,
Leeds LS27 7TW.

(2) **Electrical goods**

Customer Conciliation Service,
Radio, Electrical & Television Retailers' Association, (R.E.T.R.A.) Ltd.,
RETRA House,
57/61 Newington Causeway,
London SE1 6BE.

Consumer Relations Department.
The Association of Manufacturers of Domestic Electrical
    Appliances,
AMDEA House,
593 Hitchin Road,
Stopsley,
Luton LU2 7UN.

(3)   **Electricity Consultative Councils**
    (In each case contact "The Secretary.")
    London Electricity Consultative Council.
    Room 157,
    4 Broad Street Place,
    Blomfield Street,
    London EC2M 7HE.

    South Eastern Electricity Consultative Council,
    1 Boyne Park,
    Tunbridge Wells,
    Kent TN4 8EL.

    Southern Electricity Consultative Council,
    8A St. Mary's Butts,
    Reading,
    Berks.

    South Western Electricity Consultative Council,
    Northernhay House,
    Northernhay Place,
    Exeter EX4 3RL.

    Eastern Electricity Consultative Council,
    16/18 Princes Street,
    Ipswich.

    East Midlands Electricity Consultative Council,
    Caythorpe Road,
    Lowdham,
    Nottingham.

Midlands Electricity Consultative Council,
Shawton House,
794 Hagley Road West,
Oldbury,
Warley,
West Midlands B68 0PI.

South Wales Electricity Consultative Council,
Caerwys House,
36 Windsor Place,
Cardiff CF1 3UF.

Merseyside and North Wales Electricity Consultative Council,
Martins Bank Buildings,
Exchange Street West,
Water Street,
Liverpool L2 3SP.

Yorkshire Electricity Consultative Council,
The Woodlands,
Wetherby Road,
Scarcroft,
Leeds LS14 3HR.

North Eastern Electricity Consultative Council,
2nd Floor,
Bamburgh House,
Market Street,
Newcastle-upon-Tyne NE1 6JD.

North Western Electricity Consultative Council,
Longridge House,
Corporation Street,
Manchester M4 3AJ.

Electricity Consultative Council for the North of Scotland
    District,
North Clyde Street Lane,
St. Andrew Square,
Edinburgh EH1 3EW.

Electricity Consultative Council for the South of Scotland
District,
North Clyde Street Lane,
St. Andrew Square,
Edinburgh EH1 3EW.

(4) **Funerals**

The National Secretary,
The National Association of Funeral Directors,
57 Doughty Street,
London WC1N 2NE.

(5) **Furniture**

The National Association of Retail Furnishers,
3 Berners Street,
London W1P 4JP.

The Scottish House Furnishers Association,
203 Pitt Street,
Glasgow G2 4DB.

(6) **Launderers and dry cleaners**

The Customer Advisory Service,
The Association of British Launderers & Cleaners Ltd.,
Lancaster Gate House,
319 Pinner Road,
Harrow,
Middlesex HA1 4HX.

(7) **Mail order**

The Director,
Mail Order Publishers' Authority,
1 New Burlington Street,
London W1X 1FD.

The Secretary,
Mail Order Traders' Association,
507 Corn Exchange Building,
Fenwick Street,
Liverpool L2 7RA.

(8) **Photographic industry**
     The British Photographic Association,
     8 St. Bride Street,
     London EC4.

     The British Photographic Importers' Association,
     8 St. Bride Street,
     London EC4.
     (representing manufacturers of film and equipment)

     The Photographic Dealers' Association,
     232–238 High Street North,
     London E12 6SB

     (representing specialist photographic retailers)

     The National Pharmaceutical Association,
     Mallinson House,
     40–42 St. Peter's Street,
     St. Albans,
     Herts AL1 3NT.

     (representing retail pharmacists)

     The Association of Photographic Laboratories,
     50 Great Russell Street,
     London WC1.

     (representing the photographic processing industry)

     The Institute of Photographic Apparatus Repair Technicians,
     228 Regents Park Road,
     Finchley,
     London N3 3HP.

     (representing the repairers)

     The Institute of Incorporated Photographers,
     Amwell End,
     Ware,
     Herts.

     (representing professional photographers)

(9) **Post Office**
Post Office Users National Council,
Waterloo Bridge House,
Waterloo Road,
London SE1 8UA.

Post Office Users Council for Northern Ireland,
Chamber of Commerce,
22 Great Victoria Street,
Belfast BT2 7PU.

Post Office Users Council for Scotland,
Alhambra House,
45 Waterloo Street,
Glasgow G2 6AT.

Post Office Users Council for Wales,
2 Park Grove,
Cardiff CF1 3BN.

(10) **Shoes**
Footwear Distributors Federation,
69 Cannon Street,
London EC4N 5AB.

The Secretary,
National Association of Shoe Repair Factories,
82 Borough High Street,
London SE1 1LL.

The Secretary,
St. Crispin's Boot Trades Association Ltd.,
St. Crispin's House,
Desborough,
Northants NNJ4 2BR.

(11) **Travel**
Association of British Travel Agents,
53/54 Newman Street,
London W1P 4AH.

APPENDIX 3

A BRIEF SUMMARY OF CONSUMER PROTECTION IN
THE NATIONALISED INDUSTRIES

(1) **Gas.**
There are a number of Regional Gas Consumers' Councils and
one of their functions is to consider complaints from individual
consumers; they operate through local committees.

(2) **Electricity**
There are 12 areas and each of them has a consultative council.
In practice the procedure for complaints is governed by the vol-
untary Code of Practice which has been explained in Chapter 9.[1]

(3) **Coal**
At the centre we have a statutory body—the Domestic Coal
Consumers' Council—which was set up under the Coal Industry
Nationalization Act 1946. In practice the consumer's main point
of contact with the industry is the local retail merchant. The
industry has undertaken an important exercise in self-policing by
setting up the Approved Coal Merchants Scheme. The members
of the scheme (in which the National Coal Board is heavily
involved) undertake to investigate promptly and sympathetically
all complaints by consumers regarding fuel or service and, where
they appear justified, to make adequate and speedy redress. The
scheme also has a number of regional panels but they only become
involved if the merchant has failed to rectify a justified complaint.

(4) **Railways**
Complaints relating to services provided (or not provided) by
British Rail are dealt with at local level by 11 Transport Users
Consultative Committees set up under the Transport Act 1962.

---

[1] *Ante*, p. 138. The addresses are given in Appendix 2.

One of the features of the procedure (both here and in other industries) is that the complaints can relate to the general quality of the service and need not be confined to breaches of the law.

(5) Air travel

In many cases the consumer will be able to invoke the Code of Practice of the Association of British Travel Agents.[2] He may also be able to make a complaint to the airline. In addition the Air Line Users Committee, set up under the Civil Aviation Act, exercises a supervisory role and considers complaints of a general nature (*e.g.* overbooking). The British Airports Authority has also set up Airport Consultative Committees at Edinburgh, Gatwick, Stanstead, Prestwick and Heathrow.

(6) The Post Office

The Post Office has recently put into operation a Code of Practice and this has been mentioned in Chapter 9.[3]

FURTHER READING

"The Citizen and the Public Agencies—Remedying Grievances", is a report published by Justice in 1976 containing much valuable information, including 28 examples of particular complaints and the solutions.

[2] *Ante*, p. 138.
[3] *Ante*, p. 144.

INDEX

CONSUMER CREDIT ACT—*cont.*
overdraft, soliciting for, 262
pre-contractual information, 264, 265
protected goods, 295–297
rebate, 292, 293
regulated agreements, 242–246
consumer credit agreement, 242–245
license required, 256
partially, 246, 247
repossession, 293–298
repudiation and, 269
rescission and, 269
restricted use agreements, 241
advertisement, 260, 261
return of goods, 293–298
return of money paid, 298
return order, 297
running amount credit, 244
settlement figure, 293
signature, 265, 266
small agreements, 247, 271
"snatch-back" of goods, 295
statements, 267, 293
termination of agreement, 276–278
repossession, by, 296, 297
"time order," 290, 293–295
"total charge for credit," 249, 250
transfer order, 297
transitional, 238
unenforceability of agreement, 258, 259, 271
unlicensed business, 258, 259
validating order, 259
variation of agreement by court, 290, 291
whereabouts of goods, debtor's duty, 267
withdrawal from agreement, 268, 269

CONSUMER PROTECTION,
bodies, 3–6
EEC in, 3. *See also* EEC.
generally, 1–3

CONSUMER SAFETY ACT,
civil remedies and, 201, 202
defences, 200, 201
enforcement, 201
excluded goods, 197
Greeen Paper, 192, 193, 195
notice to warn, 199, 200
offences under, 200
penalties, 200
prohibition orders and notices, 195, 198–200
"safe," definition and examples, 196, 197
safety regulations, 198
supplier's liability, 197
transitional, 202

CONTRA PROFERENTEM RULE, 101, 102

CONTRACT,
breach of,
pleading convictions, 191
doorstep, 305, 306
formalities, *See* CONSUMER CREDIT ACT.
fundamental breach, 102–104
machine, made with, 99, 100
negligent performance. *See* NEGLIGENCE.
negotiations, 34
obligations under, 110–112
privity of,
compensation where no, 210, 211
exemption clause, effect on, 100
merchantable quality and, 43, 44
Unfair Contract Terms Act 1977, 107
U.S.A., under fire in, 3
repudiation,
exemption clause, effect on, 104
rescission of, *See* RESCISSION.
restricted use agreement, 241
severence of, 85
statutory, 119
term of, 28
ticket, terms on, 98–100
time for performance, 65, 66
Trades Descriptions Act, effect on of breach, 190, 191
unlicensed trader, by, 258, 259. *See also* CONSUMER CREDIT ACT.
warranty included, 34, 35
work and materials, 40, 41, 113, 114
examples, 41, 54
false trade descriptions. *See* FALSE TRADE DESCRIPTIONS, Services.
motor industry's code of practice, 128–130
seller's duty, 54, 55

CONVERSION,
damages for, 25

COUNTY COURT, 149–152
arbitration in, 151, 152
costs, 150, 151
jurisdiction, 149
Fair Trading Act proceedings, 234

CREDIT,
consumer. *See* CONSUMER CREDIT ACT; CREDIT CARDS.

CREDIT CARDS, 237
acceptance of, 287
agreement, defined, 286
cancellation, 288
copies of, 286
defective goods bought with, 282

DEFINITIONS—*cont.*
"unrestricted use," 241
warranty, 35

DEPOSIT, 84, 133

DESCRIPTION,
fitness and, 39
puff, 27–29
sale by, 35–39
sale by
passing of property in, 62–65
strict compliance with, 37, 38
term of contract, 28, 34–39
trade meaning, 38

DISCLAIMERS,
See EXEMPTION CLAUSE; FALSE
TRADE DESCRIPTIONS.

DISCOUNT,
electrical industry's code of practice,
135
motor industry's code of practice, 128

EEC,
consumer protection in, 3, 303
directives, 302, 303
advertising, on, 304, 305
comsumer credit, on, 306–308
doorstep contracts, on, 305, 306
product liability, 68, 308, 309
objects of, 302, 303
Treaty of Rome, 302, 303

ELECTRICAL GOODS,
code of practice, 135–138

ELECTRICITY BOARD,
code of practice, 138

ENFORCEMENT OF RIGHTS,
See ARBITRATION; CODES OF PRAC-
TICE; COUNTY COURT; SMALL
CLAIMS COURT.

ESTIMATE, 67

ESTOPPEL,
nemo dat rule and, 10, 11

EXCLUSION CLAUSE,
See also EXEMPTION CLAUSE.
launderers, 132
shoes, 133

EXTORTIONATE CREDIT BARGAINS, 299,
300

EXEMPTION CLAUSE,
See also FALSE TRADE DESCRIPTION,
disclaimers.
"all warranties," 101
auctions, at, 111
construction of, 101–104
criticism, 96

EXEMPTION CLAUSE—*cont.*
Consumer Credit Act, 240
defective premises and, 107
deviation from contract, 102
disclaimer distinguished, 168
fundamental breach, 102–104, 118,
119
incorporation of, 97–100
indemnity in, 114
insurance, in policy of, 107
judicial control of, 97–105
examples, 95, 96
justification, 96
Fair Trading Act, 217, 224
land in contracts relating to, 107
merchantable quality, 114
misrepresentation and, 81, 98, 115,
116
notice, brought to buyers, 98–100
oral promise, inconsistent, and, 102
privity of contract and, 100
repudiation, effect of, 104
unfair Contract Terms Act 1977, 105–
119
"business liability," 106, 107
generally, 5, 106–109
guidlines, 117, 118
implied terms and, 112–114
reasonableness test, 116, 117
transitional provisions, 105
work and materials, in contract for,
113, 114

FAIR TRADING,
See OFFICE OF FAIR TRADING.
office of, 3, 4, Chap. 9 *passim. See
also* TRADE DESCRIPTIONS ACT.

FAIR TRADING ACT,
adverse consumer trade practices,
216–230
defined, 217
generally, 216, 217
referral of, 217–219, 220, 221
companies, liability of, 182, 183, 234,
235
complaints, 215, 216
Consumer Protection Advisory Committee, 216, Chap. 14 *passim.*
defences, 219
director general, 215, 216
enforcement, 219, 220
exclusion of liability, 218
exclusions from, 217, 218
offences, 219, 220
orders under, 220–230
business advertisements, 225–227
bargain offers, 229, 230

GOODS—*cont.*
rejection of, 84–90
See also acceptance, *ante*
part, 89
repossession 263, 265, 293–298
risk, who bears. *See* PROPERTY IN
GOODS.
safety of. *See* CONSUMER SAFETY ACT.
second-hand, 45, 47, 48
specific, 36, 60
title. *See* TITLE.
unsolicited, 57–59
unspecified, defined, 60
work and materials distinguished, 41

GUARANTEE,
electrical goods, of, 135, 136
generally, 69, 70
negligence, excluding liability for, 70,
114, 115
repairs, 129, 130

HIRE,
See GOODS, hired.

HIRE-PURCHASE
See also CONSUMER CREDIT ACT.
conditional sale distinguished, 241
damages for defective goods, 93. *See
also* DAMAGES.
defective goods on, 283, 284.
See also MERCHANTABLE QUALITY.
defined, 40, 41, 240, 241
description of goods, 39
implied terms, 113
right to sell, 24
safety of goods on, 197.
See also CONSUMER SAFETY ACT.
sale of goods held on, 20–22
termination of agreement, 276, 277
title of goods on, 18–20
implied terms, fitness. *See* MERCHANT-
ABLE QUALITY.
hire-supplied, in 113
merchantable quality. *See* MER-
CHANTABLE QUALITY.
private sales, 113
quality of goods, of 65
right to sell goods, 23, 24
sale of goods, in, 112
Unfair Contract Terms Act, 112–114

IMPROVEMENTS,
compensation for, 23–26

INDEMNITY,
unreasonable, 114

INJUNCTION,
right to sell, negation, 23
return of Goods, for, 292

INSURANCE,
compulsory, 192
exemption clauses in, 107

LAUNDRY. *See* CODES OF PRACTICE,

LEGAL AID AND ASSISTANCE, 149–151

LICENSE,
See CONSUMER CREDIT ACT.

LINKED TRANSACTIONS,
See CONSUMER CREDIT ACT.

MANUFACTURER,
duty of care, 31–34
electrical goods, of, code of, 137
guarantees. *See* GUARANTEE.
liability of, 68–76, 222
liability,
EEC directive, 308, 309
negligence of, *See* NEGLIGENCE.
U.S.A., liability in, 2, 3

MAIL ORDER,
property in goods on, 63, 64
code of practice, 143, 144
Fair Trading Act, 224, 225

MARKET OVERT, 13–16

MERCANTILE AGENT,
disposition by, 12, 13, 18–20

MERCHANTABLE QUALITY, 40–46
See also FITNESS FOR PURPOSE.
acts to be done before use, 50
aesthetic considerations, 46
caveat emptor, 42, 43
Consumer Safety Act and, 201, 202
definition, 45–50
electrical goods, 136, 137
examination,
after contract, 86
before contract, 51, 52
exemption clause, in, 114
"goods supplied," 45
"in the course of business," 44, 45
liability, 44, 68
minor defects, 48–50
negligence and, 44
private seller, 42, 43
privity of contract and, 42, 43
"sale" goods, 51–52
seller's liability for, 68
second-hand goods, 45, 47, 48
when merchantable, 45, 46, 50, 51,
59, 87.
See also PROPERTY IN GOODS.
work and materials, 40, 41

MISREPRESENTATION,
See also FALSE TRADE DESCRIPTION;
REPRESENTATION.

REMEDIES,
Consumer Safety Act, 201
compensation, 90–94
deposit, return of, 84
fraudulent misrepresentation, for, 78
improvements, compensation for, 24–26
misrepresentation, for,
See rescision *post.*
repairs, compensation for, 23–26, 83
repudiation, 84, 85, 269
rescision, 16, 17
Consumer Credit Act, 289–293
misrepresentation, for, 16, 17, 29–31, 78–81, 84
notice of, 17
return of money paid, 84–90
specific performance, 82, 83
Trade Descriptions Act, under, 158

REPAIRS,
compensation for, 23–26
cost of, recovery of, 76
electrical goods, 136
motor, 129, 130
right to, 83
shoes, 134

REPRESENTATION,
See also MISREPRESENTATION.
contractual warranty distinguished, 29, 30
puff distinguished, 27–29
reliance on, 31

RESCISSION,
See REMEDIES.

SAFETY,
See CONSUMER PROTECTION ACT, 1961; CONSUMER SAFETY ACT 1978.
"SALE" GOODS, 51, 52
false trade descriptions, 174, 175

SAMPLE,
sale by, 35

SALE OR RETURN,
title in goods on, 61, 62

SECOND-HAND GOODS, 45, 47, 48

SELLER,
agent for finance company, 280
business, false, 225–227
estoppel of, 10, 11
merchantable quality, liability for, 68
obligations of, 22, 23, 41
possession, in, sale by, 17, 18
private
merchantable quality, 42, 43
skill and judgement of, 53
title of, 23, 24

SERVICES,
See CONTRACT, work and materials

SPECIFIC GOODS,
destruction of, effect on contract of, 64

SMALL CLAIMS COURT, 144–149
generally, 144, 145
jurisdiction, 145, 146, 148
procedure, 146, 147

SPECIFIC PERFORMANCE, 82, 83

STATUTORY DUTY,
breach of, 209–212
Consumer Protection Act, 194, 195
Consumer Safety Act, 201, 202
entry onto premises, 292
restore goods, duty to, 275

STOLEN GOODS,
See TITLE, *nemo dat* rule.

SUB-CONTRACTOR,
contractor's liability for, 55

TERMINATION,
See CONSUMER CREDIT ACT.

TERMS OF CONTRACT,
See CONTRACT; EXEMPTION CLAUSE.

"TIME OF THE ESSENCE," 66

TITLE, 8–26.
See also PROPERTY IN GOODS.
buyer in possession, 18–20
exemption from warranty, 23, 24
fundamental term, 22–24
hire-purchase, sale of goods held on, 18–20
nemo dat rule, 9–23
estoppel and, 10, 11
exceptions, 9–22
market overt, sale in, 13–16
mercantile agent, disposition by, 12, 13, 18–20
previous sale, after, 17, 18
seller in possession, 17, 18
stolen goods, 8–26
See also nemo dat rule.
voidable, 16, 17, 19

TORT,
damages for, 94

TOUR OPERATOR,
See CODES OF PRACTICE, travel agents.

TRADE ASSOCIATIONS, 6
See also CODES OF PRACTICE.

TRADE DESCRIPTIONS ACT,
See also FALSE TRADE DESCRIPTIONS.